MAPS

1 **Bloemenmarkt** (page 187)

2 ***Sunflowers*, by Vincent van Gogh, at the Van Gogh Museum** (page 57)

3 **National Monument, in Dam Square** (page 43)

4 **NEMO, the children's hands-on science museum** (page 68)

5 **Red Light Secrets Museum of Prostitution** (page 146)

6 **Begijnhof** (page 40)

DISCOVER AMSTERDAM

The Amsterdam that most people envision is real. In this romantic, crowded city, tulips blossom between cobblestones, centuries-old houses perch alongside winding canals, and bicycle bells ring in time with carillon bells echoing from historic church steeples. At night, music pulses from trendy nightclubs, smoke wafts out the doors of coffee-shops, and the notorious Red Light District winks suggestively at passersby.

Amsterdam is where you'll find art from renowned Dutch masters and the hottest street artists only blocks apart. It's home to medieval churches and avant-garde theaters. It's a tolerant place that has historically welcomed hedonists and religious pilgrims in equal measure. Amsterdam embraces and embodies its contradictions.

In the summer, Amsterdam becomes a leafy oasis, dotted with parks and sunny terraces. Blue herons silently observe the parade of boats along the canals. Neighbors chat as they purchase bread, cheese, and produce at outdoor markets. By winter, the city retreats into itself as cold and sometimes snowy days hit. People seek shelter in the city's cozy brown bars and cafés, designed to lift even the lowest of spirits. Museum-going is practically a national pastime here, and the many options mean you could visit a different world-class museum for every bad-weather day. This is the locals' Amsterdam, where the emphasis is on appreciating life.

10 TOP EXPERIENCES

1 **Rijksmuseum:** Witness the works of Rembrandt and other Dutch masters at this world-famous art museum (page 55).

2 **Stedelijk Museum:** See Europe's best collection of abstract and modern art (page 58).

3 **Van Gogh Museum:** Take in the largest collection of Vincent van Gogh's works in the world (page 57).

4 National Holocaust Memorial: Learn about some of the 100,000 Jews who were deported from the Netherlands during the Nazi occupation (page 63).

5 Anne Frank House: You've read her diary. Now experience for yourself the annex where Anne Frank and her family hid for two years (page 51).

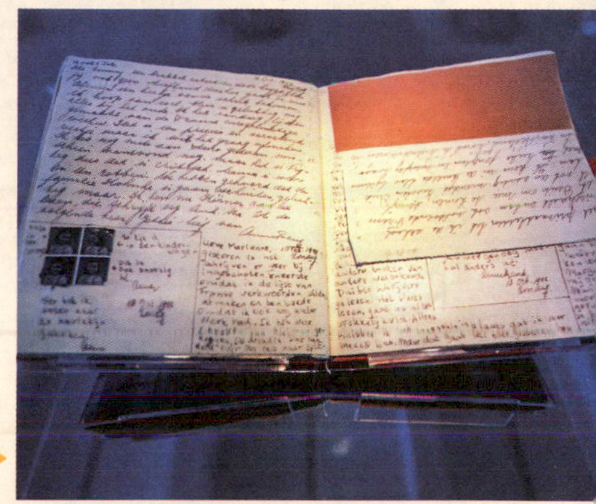

6 Cannabis Culture: Several million tourists a year visit Amsterdam's "coffeeshops"—cannabis dispensaries that double as cafés (page 114).

7 **Canals:** Whether you're on a terrace or inside a boat, it's easy to find enchantment canalside (page 169).

8 **Bicycles:** Join the majority of Amsterdam's population by exploring the city on two wheels (page 167).

9 **Brown Bars:** These cozy bar-cafés are known for their candlelit ambience, dark walls, and creaking stools. Order a *biertje* (small beer) and blend in with the locals (page 107).

10 **Outdoor Markets:** On nearly every corner of every neighborhood you'll find bustling markets selling local organic produce, books, clothing—even tulip bulbs (page 178).

EXPLORE AMSTERDAM

THE BEST OF AMSTERDAM

The biggest attraction in Amsterdam is wandering the city. This itinerary hits the city's top sights and experiences in three days. The neighborhoods covered are easy to reach on foot or by taking public transportation.

Consider staying in the Canal Belt. Though hotels are pricey, you'll be in a central location where you can easily reach the city's other neighborhoods and attractions.

>DAY 1: OLD CENTER

Start off the day by watching the city awaken at **Dam Square.** From this spot, you can admire **Nieuwe Kerk (New Church)** and the **Royal Palace (Koninklijk Paleis).** Make your way to the **Begijnhof (Beguines Courtyard),** a pretty green courtyard where peace and quiet are the order of the day. Next, hop over to the adjacent **Amsterdam Museum,** where you can spend as much time as you want learning about the city's history—or

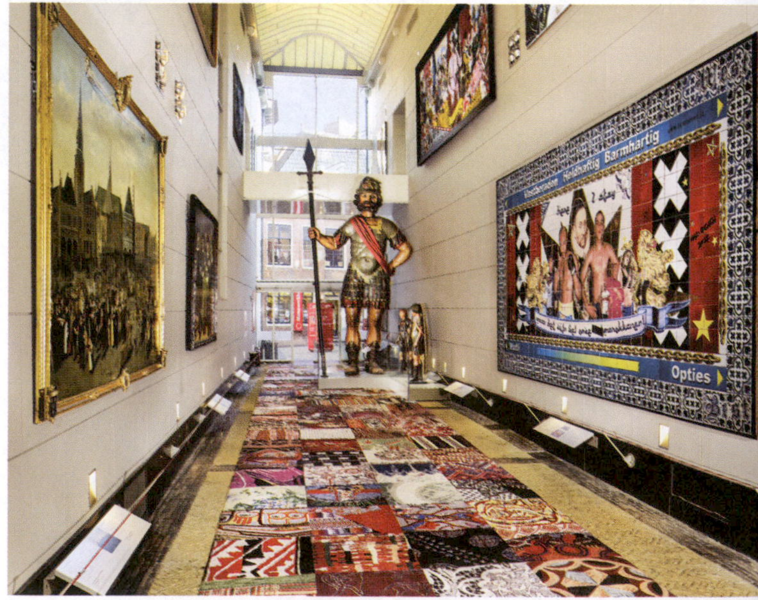

Amsterdam Museum

BEST VIEWS

BLUE BRIDGE (BLAUWBRUG)
Walk along this bridge for great views of the Stopera building and some of the city's canal houses (page 66).

EYE FILM INSTITUTE
This cultural hub boasts a café with floor-to-ceiling windows that overlook the IJ River (page 163).

LA PLACE
Nearly all of Amsterdam's Old Center can be seen from this café on the top floor of the city's public library (page 102).

MULLIGANS
The upstairs balcony of this Irish bar near Rembrandtplein offers a great view of the Amstel River (page 123).

NEMO
Even if you're not visiting this fun kids' science museum, you can still access the museum café's rooftop deck in the summer (page 68).

SKYLOUNGE
Sip on a swanky cocktail at this rooftop lounge. The view is stunning no matter the time of day (page 140).

TWENTY THIRD BAR
Head up to the 23rd floor of the Okura Hotel to take in a panoramic view of the city while sipping champagne (page 131).

just get your first glimpse at a Rembrandt painting.

Walk back toward **Amsterdam Centraal Station,** the city's transit hub. For lunch, pop inside the station for a quick bite. The Old Center's narrow streets seem to wind in circles, easily confusing visitors, so a ride along the canals with **Open Boat Tours** is a good way to orient yourself while still taking in the city's many sights.

Head to the Red Light District and grab dinner at one of the many Asian spots in Chinatown, like **Oriental City** or **New King.** Finish the day in one of several uniquely Amsterdam ways: at a brown bar, like **Lokaal 't Loosje** in Nieuwmarkt; a coffeeshop such as **Greenhouse Effect;** or a locals' bar, like the stylish **Mata Hari** in the Red Light District.

>DAY 2: MUSEUMPLEIN AND THE CANAL BELT

Start the day by picking up a pastry from Museumplein's **Arnold Cornelis,** then head straight for the neighborhood's world-class museums. Choose from the famous **Van Gogh Museum,** the **Rijksmuseum,** with its massive collection of Dutch masters, or the contemporary **Stedelijk Museum.** If you have the time and the will, it's possible to visit two of these in one morning, but trying to do all three is too much for most people.

Once you've had your fill of art, make your way west to the large and leafy **Vondelpark.** If you need a snack or refreshment, stop at **Blauwe Theehuis,** a two-story café in the middle of the park.

Now it's time to head into the **Canal Belt** and let yourself wander for a while, admiring the pretty canals, romantic bridges, and stunning canal houses. Walk through **Leidseplein,** which becomes party central in the evenings, and admire the architecture of the **Stadsschouwburg** concert hall.

From here, make your way to **Westerkerk,** the largest Protestant church in the Netherlands. Behind it is the **Homomonument,** the first monument in the world to commemorate the homosexual victims of the Third Reich. On the next block is the **Anne Frank House,** which is hard to miss with its long lines. (Advance tickets are required and issued for specific times between 9am and 3:30pm; feel free to join the queue if it's later in the day.)

If you're ready for dinner, grab a table at **Bistro Bij Ons** for Dutch soul food. Head over to the beer bar **Arendsnest** after dinner, where you can sample one (or several) of the more than 100 different Dutch beers. Or you can stay on Prinsengracht and stop at **Vyne** for a glass of wine before heading back to your hotel.

>DAY 3: DE PIJP AND PLANTAGE

Today starts in the De Pijp neighborhood, with brunch at **Little Collins.** Fuel up so that you can devote all your energy to browsing the wares at **Albert Cuypmarkt,** the city's best outdoor market.

Next, head over to the **Heineken Experience** for a self-guided tour through a former Heineken brewery. Once you're ready to move on, make your way over to the Plantage and cross the famous **Skinny Bridge (Magere Brug).**

Continue farther into the Plantage to the **National Holocaust Memorial (Hollandsche Schouwburg).** This building was taken over by Nazis and turned into a holding center for Jews. Today, it serves as a humbling tribute to the millions of Jewish victims of the Holocaust. To get a better sense of how the Dutch fought back against the Nazi occupation, head to the **Dutch Resistance Museum (Verzetsmuseum).**

Have a quick lunch at **Burgermeester** before continuing on to either the **Botanical Gardens (Hortus Botanicus)** or the **Artis Zoo.** For a refreshment, stop in at **Café Koosje,** across from the zoo.

The afternoon is the perfect time to visit the **Hermitage Amsterdam,** a satellite of the original Hermitage in St. Petersburg, Russia. Admire as many of the sumptuous exhibits as you can.

Make your way back to De Pijp for dinner. Try North African cuisine at **Mamouche** or splurge on cosmopolitan sushi at **Izakaya.** To top it all off, have a chichi cocktail at **Twenty Third Bar** on the 23rd floor of the Okura Hotel. Enjoy the panoramic nighttime view of the city before calling it a night.

With More Time

If you have another day to spend in Amsterdam, head for the waterfront along the **IJ River.**

- Rent a bike from **Star Bikes** or a boat from **Canal Motorboats** and explore the city on wheels or by water.
- Catch a jazz show at **Bimhuis** or, if you're lucky, you might be able to see a free classical concert at the distinctive-looking concert hall **Muziekgebouw aan 't IJ.**
- Have a highbrow multicourse French dinner at **Choux,** or go casual at **Frank's Smoke House,** where you can fill up on different types of smoked fish.
- Have a nightcap at **SkyLounge,** a rooftop bar offering the best views in all of Amsterdam.

AMSTERDAM WITH KIDS

Don't let Amsterdam's wild reputation keep you from bringing the kids along. The Netherlands is often said to have the happiest children and Amsterdam is no exception. Rain or shine, there are plenty of family-friendly activities here. Many museums are kid-friendly. Bike rental shops usually offer baby seats, trailers, and kid-size bikes, so your little ones can see the city just like the local tykes do.

>DAY 1: PLANTAGE AND IJ RIVER

The two top kid-centric attractions in Amsterdam are undoubtedly the science and learning center **NEMO** and the popular **Artis Zoo.** Both are packed with activities, and it would be easy to split a day between the two.

Bike over to **Bakhuys Amsterdam** in the Plantage, where you can pick up a pastry and some caffeine—you'll need it! It's just a few blocks to Artis Zoo. Check out the elephants and seals and be sure to visit the zoo's aquarium, insectarium, and even planetarium.

Saddle the bikes up again for the ride toward the IJ River. Bypass NEMO for now and head to **La Place,** a cafeteria-style café with great views of the city. Refuel yourself and the kids, then retrace your path to NEMO, which offers five floors of entertainment—and learning!—for the whole family.

Head back to the Plantage for a seafood dinner at **Een Vis Twee Vis,** then pack it in for the night.

NEMO

>DAY 2: OLD CENTER

Start your morning at **De Laatste Kruimel,** a French bakery in the Old Center. While the kids dig into muffins, the adults can savor a slice of quiche. When you're ready, it's a five-minute walk north to **Damstraat Rent-a-Bike.** Get everyone set up with their rental, then pedal around the city for a while.

Once it's time for a break from biking, make your way to **Body Worlds: The Happiness Project,** which curious minds will love. (Though the squeamish may want to stay away from the exhibition, which uses preserved human cadavers to display the nervous system and the effects of smoking and cancer.) There's a children's wing at the **Amsterdam Museum** that tells the story of Amsterdam's 17th-century orphanage.

Sample Indonesian cuisine for dinner at **Kantjil & De Tijger,** a budget-friendly restaurant on Spuistraat.

BEST PEOPLE-WATCHING

ALBERT CUYPMARKT

This is one of the best outdoor markets in the city and a magnet for people of all types. Grab a seat at one of the cafés that surround the market and watch the shoppers browse away (page 200).

CANALSIDE TERRACES

Amsterdam offers innumerable bars and restaurants with patios. Sip or snack as you watch people bike, boat, and walk by. Try the brown bar **De Doelen** (page 106).

NATIONAL MONUMENT

On the eastern side of Dam Square, the wide, circular steps that loop around this monument are perfect for sitting with a coffee and watching the bustle of the city center (page 43).

SPUI SQUARE

This quaint, leafy square offers prime people-watching, especially if you settle in at one of several cafés (page 41).

VONDELPARK

Amsterdam's most popular park is a great place to take in crowds of people chatting, listening to music, and kicking around soccer balls (page 60).

PLANNING YOUR TRIP

WHEN TO GO

The best time to come to Amsterdam is during the sunny months. **High season** starts in late April and lasts until September, with **low season** spanning October to March. **Summer** is the warmest time of year and when the city overflows with tourists. Though **spring** is a gamble weather-wise, the **tulips are in bloom** from March to May.

While **autumn** and **winter** are the off-seasons, a trip during this time can still be worth it. The holiday atmosphere kicks off in November, when **ice rinks** and **Christmas markets** begin to open. Cafés become cozier as the weather cools and the short days are softened by candlelight. Hotels are **cheaper,** museums are **less busy,** and the city feels more intimate than during the chaotic summer.

The city is well known for its **unpredictable weather** throughout the year. Amsterdam's seaside location means mild summers and winters, but humidity, rain, and wind are never too far away.

Catholics across the country come to join the **Silent Procession (Stille Omgang)** (www.stille-omgang.nl) in mid-March to commemorate the Miracle of Amsterdam. Participants walk quietly together through the Old Center from midnight to 4am. All are welcome to join.

Every year on April 27, millions of Dutch adorn themselves in shocking orange on **King's Day (Koningsdag)** and proceed to celebrate the royal family.

Amsterdam Gay Pride parade

Because the Netherlands was the first country to legalize same-sex marriage, in 2001, early August's **Amsterdam Gay Pride** (www.amsterdamgaypride.nl) is an especially popular weekend-long celebration, blanketing the city in rainbows and dance parties, kicking off with a spirited boat parade.

ENTRY REQUIREMENTS

Visitors coming from almost 60 countries—including the United States—can enter the Netherlands with just a **valid passport.** European Union citizens only need their national identity card. There is a **90-day limit** for U.S. citizens traveling in the European Union.

Always be sure that your passport is valid for at least **six months** beyond your departure date.

If Amsterdam is just one stop on your European trip, consider applying for a **visa** that will allow you to freely cross borders of the **Schengen area** (generally, the European Union, but some other countries are also included). For more information, visit the U.S. Department of State's website (http://travel.state.gov).

TRANSPORTATION

Amsterdam's **Schiphol International Airport (AMS)** is the main hub for international flights in and out of the Netherlands.

It's a 20-minute direct train ride from the airport to **Amsterdam Centraal Station,** the city's main train station. Trains leave about every 10 minutes from the airport, and travelers can buy **one-way tickets** (€3.70) at the yellow kiosks in the main airport plaza.

Amsterdam Centraal Station is the main hub for **national and international trains,** including fast trains to London, Paris, Brussels, and many German cities.

Amsterdam offers many types of public transportation. Buses, ferries, a metro system, and trams weave across the city. Most of the options available in the city center are the **above-ground trams.**

Amsterdam is a compact and **walkable** city. It's flat, with numerous **bike lanes** and **sidewalks.** Among locals, **biking** is the most popular form of transportation.

RESERVATIONS

To avoid waiting in the famously long line (1-3 hours) for the **Anne Frank House,** reserve your tickets online (for a specific time slot) up to two months in advance.

Of all the city's art museums, the **Van Gogh Museum** is the only one for which you should reserve tickets online to skip the line. When you're making your reservation, you'll select a time slot. Be sure to stick to it; if you arrive more than 30 minutes after your assigned time, your ticket will be invalid.

Hotels spike their rates in summer and are often fully booked weeks out, so making accommodations reservations should be at the top of your to-do list after buying plane tickets.

Many **restaurants** are located in the city's famously narrow canal houses. Consider making reservations for your must-eats the day

DAILY REMINDERS

- **Wednesday:** Local children get out of school by noon and are usually out and about in the city.
- **Thursday:** Shops stay open a few hours later. Many Dutch workers go out for happy hour drinks and snacks on Thursdays.
- **Friday:** The Van Gogh Museum and Stedelijk Museum are open until 10pm. The Spui Book Market is a Friday-only affair at Spui Square. Most bars, clubs, and restaurants stay open a few hours later than usual.
- **Saturday:** Bars, clubs, and restaurants stay open a few hours later. The Noordermarkt Organic Farmers Market is only open on Saturdays—as is the Noordermarkt Flea Market.
- **Sunday:** Many shops close early. Most outdoor markets are closed, except for the Artplein-Spui at Spui Square, which runs March to December.

before or just as the restaurant opens on the same day you want to eat there.

PASSES AND DISCOUNTS

The **Museumkaart** (www.museumkaart.nl; adults €60, children €33) is for museum junkies. This card allows access to over 400 museums in the Netherlands, but the best perk is that it pays for itself if you use it at the Van Gogh Museum, Stedelijk Museum, and Rijksmuseum. Basically all of the city's museums are covered, including the Hermitage, NEMO, and the Rembrandt House. It does not include entrance to the Anne Frank House. The card is only valid for one month for visitors (one year for residents). You can buy the card at any participating museum or online.

The **I Amsterdam City Card** (www.iamsterdam.com; €55-85) includes admission to the Van Gogh Museum, Stedelijk Museum, Artis Zoo, Nieuwe Kerk, and many others. The card is good for 24, 48, 72, or 96 hours and includes all public transit (except for airport transportation) in the time frame. The card does not include entrance to the Anne Frank House or the Rijksmuseum. Other pluses, like a free canal cruise and some discounts, are included as well.

The **Last Minute Ticket Shop** (www.lastminuteticketshop.nl) offers half-price day-of tickets for musicals, plays, and other performances.

GUIDED TOURS

Sandeman's New Amsterdam Tours (meeting point Dam Square, www.newamsterdamtours.com; 5 tours/day; free) are popular walking tours led by young, knowledgeable, and witty guides. Tours are a few hours long and cover many Old Center highlights and much of the city's history. The guides work off tips alone.

While there are a few specialized tours of the Red Light District, the **Prostitute Information Center's Red Light District Tour** (Enge Kerksteeg 3, tel. 020/420-7328, www.pic-amsterdam.com; 2 tours per week; €12.50) is a one-hour tour led by a former sex worker who explains the neighborhood from an insider's perspective.

Hungry Birds (www.hungrybirds.nl; tour times vary; €69) offers intimate three- to four-hour foodie tours of Amsterdam, sampling wares from cheese shops, breweries, and outdoor markets.

Amsterdam Alternative Tours (meeting point Dam Square, tel. 068/259-2148, www.freeamsterdamtours.com; 10:30am and 1:30pm daily; free) leads free walking tours that focus on Amsterdam's counterculture. See iconic street art and graffiti and get recommendations on the best coffeeshops and the most quirky bars. Tours are about three hours long and guides work on a tips-only basis.

NEIGHBORHOODS

Old Center

Map 1

The cobblestoned Old Center is a testament to Amsterdam's 900-year history of commerce. The city's oldest borough encompasses the **Red Light District** and Dam Square, the Royal Palace, and the medieval **Begijnhof,** a beautiful and secluded garden courtyard. Damrak and Rokin streets are the main drags for tourist traffic and home to many chain stores and souvenir shops.

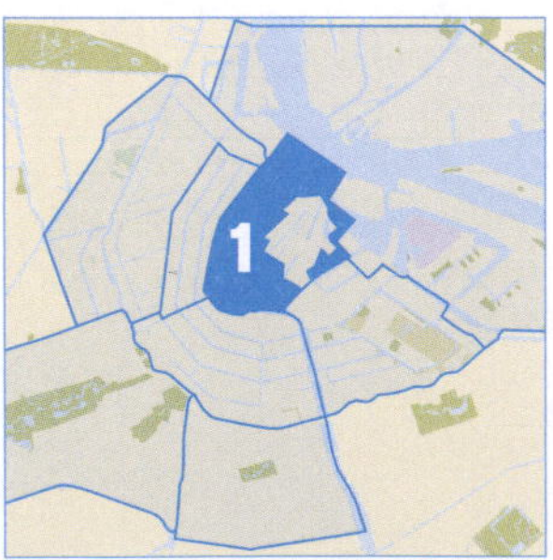

TOP SIGHTS

- Begijnhof (Beguines Courtyard) (page 40)

TOP RESTAURANTS

- The Seafood Bar (page 73)
- Cannibale Royale (page 74)

TOP NIGHTLIFE

- Café de Jaren (page 106)

TOP SPORTS AND ACTIVITIES

- We Bike Amsterdam (page 166)

TOP SHOPS

- Heinen Delfts Blauw (page 178)

TOP HOTELS

- Hotel Brouwer (page 217)

GETTING THERE AND AROUND

- Metro lines: 51, 53, 54
- Metro stations: Centraal Station, Nieuwmarkt, Waterlooplein

- Tram lines: 1, 2, 5
- Tram stops: Centraal Station, Nieuwezijds Kolk, Dam, Spui

Red Light District and Nieuwmarkt

Map 2

A curious combination of pious and sinful, the Red Light District is home to the city's oldest church, **Oude Kerk,** as well as the infamous **red light windows** and **coffeeshops.** The Red Light District can sometimes feel like Amsterdam's main attraction, running steadily on tourist curiosity and decades of ribaldry—on the part of both visitors and locals. Nearby Nieuwmarkt is home to leafy plazas.

TOP SIGHTS

- Oude Kerk (Old Church) (page 45)

TOP RESTAURANTS

- Oriental City (page 77)
- Cafe Bern (page 77)
- De Bakkerswinkel (page 78)

TOP NIGHTLIFE

- Wynand Fockink (page 112)
- Coffeeshop Bluebird (page 113)

TOP HOTELS

- Misc Eatdrinksleep (page 217)

GETTING THERE AND AROUND

- Metro lines: 51, 53, 54
- Metro stations: Nieuwmarkt, Waterlooplein
- Tram lines: 9, 14
- Tram stops: Waterlooplein

Canal Belt South **Map 3**

Amsterdam's Grachtengordel, or Canal Belt, consists of three concentric canal rings hugging the Old Center. The western half boasts museums like **Foam** and the **Museum of Bags and Purses,** housed in mansions with original frescoes, lavish decor, and stunning courtyards. Leidseplein and Rembrandtplein are the main squares for the city's **nightlife scene,** offering everything from **brown bars** to **dance clubs.** The **gallery district** at Nieuwe Spiegelstraat is saturated with art and antiques.

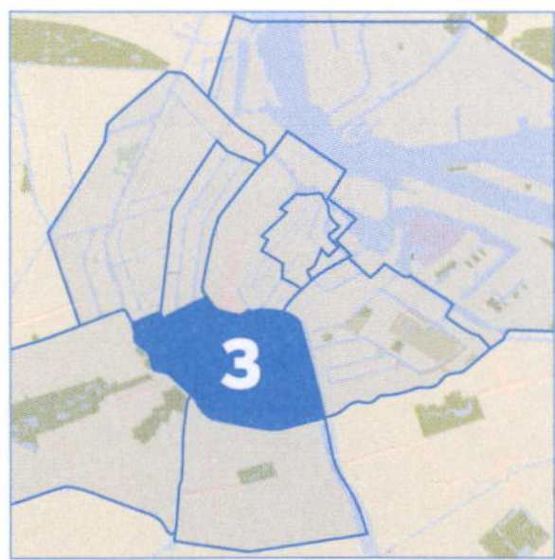

TOP RESTAURANTS

- Café de Klos (page 81)

TOP NIGHTLIFE

- Café de Spuyt (page 116)
- Paradiso (page 119)
- L&B Whiskeycafe (page 124)
- Café Montmartre (page 124)

TOP ARTS AND CULTURE

- Foam (page 147)
- Museum of Bags and Purses (Tassenmuseum Hendrikje) (page 147)
- The Public House of Art (page 149)
- Stadsschouwburg (page 151)
- Pathé Tuschinski (page 152)

TOP SHOPS

- Bloemenmarkt (Flower Market) (page 187)

TOP HOTELS

- Hotel Weber (page 219)
- Seven Bridges Hotel (page 219)

GETTING THERE AND AROUND

- Tram lines: 1, 2, 4, 5, 9, 14
- Tram stops: Koningsplein, Leidseplein (1, 2, 5); Rembrandtplein (4, 9, 14)

Canal Belt West

Map 4

This western portion of the Canal Belt, which surrounds the city center, is an ode to the Dutch Golden Age, with historic canal houses dotting the waterside and alleyways lined with fun, indie **boutiques.** The **Anne Frank House** is also here, alongside the melodious **Westerkerk,** whose famous bells chime regularly.

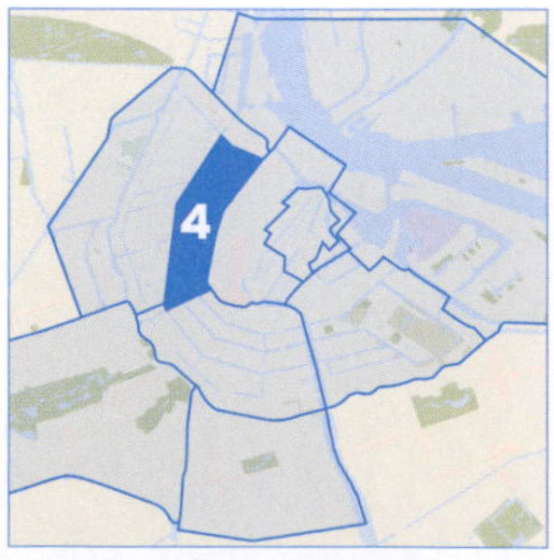

TOP SIGHTS

- Anne Frank House (page 51)
- Westerkerk (page 53)

TOP RESTAURANTS

- The Pancake Bakery (page 84)

TOP NIGHTLIFE

- Grey Area (page 125)
- Arendsnest (page 126)

TOP ARTS AND CULTURE

- Huis Marseille Museum for Photography (page 153)

TOP SPORTS AND ACTIVITIES

- Sauna Deco (page 168)

TOP SHOPS

- Denham Concept Store (page 191)
- Marlies Dekkers (page 191)
- Van Ravenstein (page 192)
- De Reypenaer (page 195)

TOP HOTELS

- The Toren (page 222)
- The Hoxton, Amsterdam (page 223)

GETTING THERE AND AROUND

- Tram lines: 13, 14, 17
- Tram stops: Westermarkt, Marnixstraat

Museumplein

Map 5

A visit to Museumplein is time well spent. Relax on the grass at **Vondelpark,** peruse the quaint and leafy squares, and browse the **modern boutiques.** The **Van Gogh Museum, Rijksmuseum,** and **Stedelijk Museum** make up the neighborhood's namesake square. Also here are **trendy live music venues** and **ethnic restaurants.**

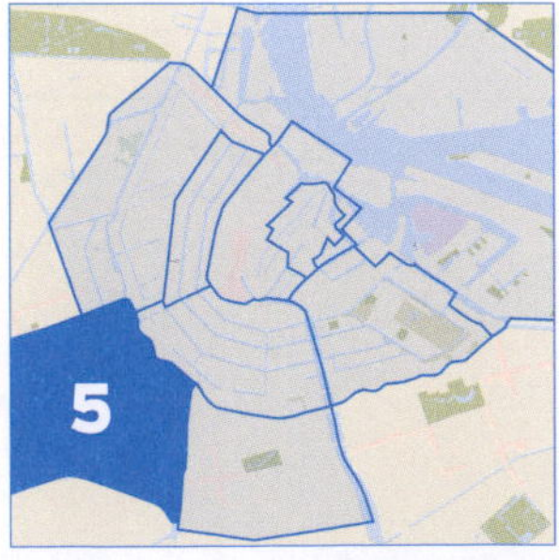

TOP SIGHTS

- Rijksmuseum (page 55)
- Van Gogh Museum (page 57)
- Stedelijk Museum (page 58)
- Vondelpark (page 60)

TOP RESTAURANTS

- Blauw (page 86)
- Lalibela (page 88)

TOP NIGHTLIFE

- OCCII (page 128)
- OT301 (page 128)

TOP ARTS AND CULTURE

- Royal Concertgebouw (page 155)

TOP SPORTS AND ACTIVITIES

- ICE Amsterdam (page 170)
- Plan B (page 170)

TOP SHOPS

- 't Schooltje (page 197)
- Shoebaloo (page 198)
- Pied a Terre (page 199)

TOP HOTELS

- Flying Pig Uptown (page 228)

GETTING THERE AND AROUND

- Tram lines: 2, 3, 5
- Tram stops: Museumplein (3, 5), Rijksmuseum (2, 5)

De Pijp

Map 6

Also known as Amsterdam's Latin Quarter, De Pijp is a modish melting pot of a neighborhood. The narrow pipe-like streets that give the borough its name host **trendy concept stores,** colorful **culinary spots,** and the city's famous outdoor **Albert Cuypmarkt.**

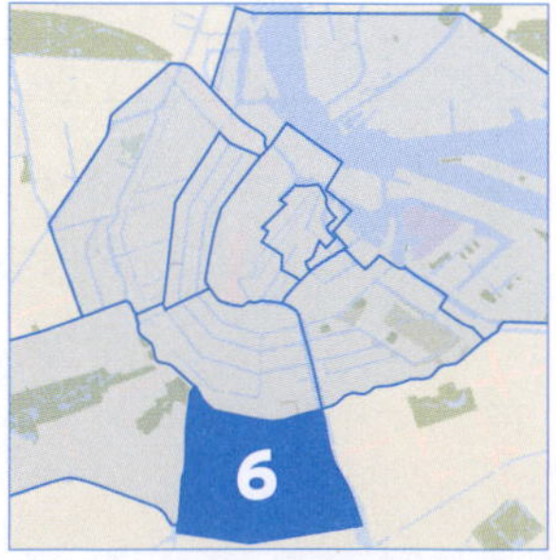

TOP RESTAURANTS

- Warung Spang Makandra (page 91)
- Izakaya (page 92)

TOP SHOPS

- Albert Cuypmarkt (page 200)
- Hutspot (page 201)
- Baskèts (page 201)

GETTING THERE AND AROUND

- Tram lines: 16
- Tram stops: Albert Cuypstraat

Jordaan

Map 7

The Jordaan is a charming borough, originally built for the city's working class centuries ago. Zigzag through the picture-perfect canal streets and the quaint residential alleys, stopping at **cozy bars,** browsing **boutique shops,** and discovering local gems like **Electric Lady Land** and **Westerpark.**

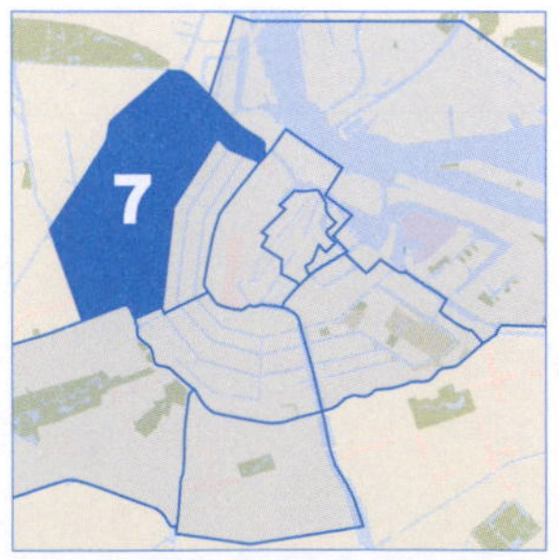

TOP RESTAURANTS

- Daalder (page 96)

TOP NIGHTLIFE

- Festina Lente (page 131)
- Waterkant (page 134)

TOP ARTS AND CULTURE

- Electric Lady Land (page 156)

TOP SPORTS AND ACTIVITIES

- Those Dam Boat Guys (page 171)

TOP HOTELS

- Frederic Rent-a-Bike (page 231)

GETTING THERE AND AROUND

- Tram lines: 3
- Tram stops: Haarlemmerplein

Plantage

Map 8

For centuries, the Plantage was a part of Amsterdam's Old Jewish Quarter. Its streets are dotted with memorials and echoes of **Jewish culture** at places like the **Dutch Resistance Museum** and the **National Holocaust Memorial.** The historic borough also features a swath of greenery thanks to several parks and gardens.

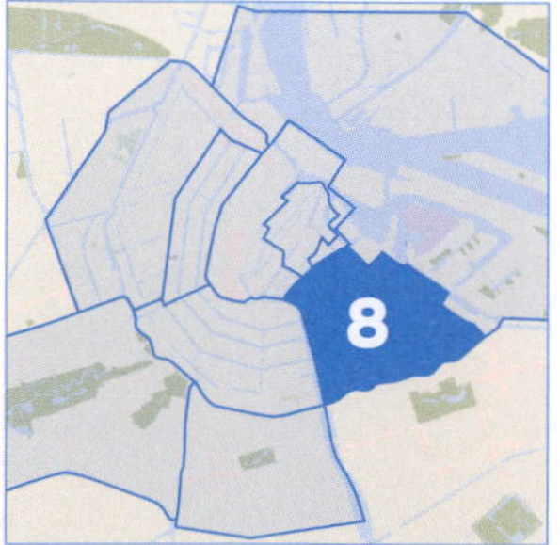

TOP SIGHTS

- National Holocaust Memorial (Hollandsche Schouwburg) (page 63)
- Dutch Resistance Museum (Verzetsmuseum) (page 63)
- Rembrandt House (Rembrandthuis) (page 64)

TOP NIGHTLIFE

- Green House (page 137)

TOP ARTS AND CULTURE

- Hermitage Amsterdam (page 158)
- Dutch National Opera & Ballet (page 159)

TOP SHOPS

- Waterlooplein Market (page 210)
- Episode (page 210)

TOP HOTELS

- InterContinental Amstel Amsterdam (page 232)
- Ecomama (page 233)

GETTING THERE AND AROUND

- Metro lines: 54
- Metro stations: Weesperplein
- Tram lines: 4, 9, 14, 16
- Tram stops: Mr. Visserplein, Artis, Weesperplein

IJ River

Map 9

Once a gritty industrial area, the city's waterfront is now an up-and-coming neighborhood, attracting a young and dynamic community and growing at a rapid pace. This area not only offers some of the best **cultural attractions** in the city, but also **waterfront views** that you can't find elsewhere in Amsterdam.

TOP SIGHTS

- NEMO (page 68)

TOP RESTAURANTS

- Gebr. Hartering (page 101)

TOP NIGHTLIFE

- Brouwerij 't IJ (page 138)
- SkyLounge (page 140)

TOP ARTS AND CULTURE

- Bimhuis (page 162)
- Muziekgebouw aan 't IJ (page 162)

TOP SPORTS AND ACTIVITIES

- Canal Motorboats (page 173)
- Star Bikes (page 173)
- De Klimmuur (page 173)

GETTING THERE AND AROUND

- Ferry lines: 902
- Ferry stations: IJplein

SIGHTS

From its colorful tulip-filled spring to the dark, atmospheric winter, Amsterdam is a year-round attraction. In good weather, it's a great place to picnic in Vondelpark, wander along its many canals, or sit on a sunny bench in Museumplein and watch the crowds go by. In the winter, bundle up and explore the world-class Van Gogh Museum or the equally impressive Rijksmuseum, then wander through historic homes and churches.

traditional wooden clogs

Amsterdam encapsulates history and modernity in one place. This impeccably preserved city is home to structures from as far back as the medieval period, like the city's oldest church, Oude Kerk, which was built in the 1200s. Lining the canals are well-maintained houses from the Dutch Golden Age, an era when the city and its merchants prospered. It also offers modern—and titillating—attractions like the Cannabis College and the Prostitute Information Center, giving visitors the chance to experience the city as it is today.

The city's neighborhoods reveal different facets of its personality. Both the Old Center and Museumplein offer just what their names suggest: The city center is paved with cobblestones, revealing its history, while Museumplein houses world-famous collections of art and artifacts in the form of the Rijksmuseum, the Van Gogh Museum, and the Stedelijk Museum. The Red Light District houses the city's most infamous elements (the red light windows) and its oldest church.

HIGHLIGHTS

- **BEST HIDDEN RESPITE:** Seek out the **Begijnhof (Beguines Courtyard)** to experience a peaceful reprieve from the frenetic city (page 40).
- **MOST IRONICALLY PLACED CHURCH:** Don't be surprised to find **Oude Kerk (Old Church),** the city's oldest church, smack-dab in the middle of the Red Light District (page 45).
- **MOST FAMOUS STORY:** See for yourself the annex at the **Anne Frank House,** where Anne and her family hid for two years (page 51).
- **BEST BELLS: Westerkerk** is most well-known for its carillon bells, which Anne Frank wrote about in her diary—the family's hiding place was just a few blocks away (page 53).
- **BEST JOURNEY THROUGH DUTCH HISTORY:** A visit to the **Rijksmuseum** means seeing relics from the Middle Ages and artwork from Rembrandt and other Dutch masters all in one place (page 55).
- **MOST ICONIC ART MUSEUM:** The **Van Gogh Museum** boasts the largest collection of the Post-Impressionist master's works in the world (page 57).
- **BEST COLLECTION OF MODERN ART:** The **Stedelijk Museum** is home to Europe's best collection of abstract art, along with many other examples of modern art (page 58).
- **MOST BEAUTIFUL PARK:** Check out the sculptures, soak up the sun, or meander around the ponds at the 100-acre **Vondelpark** (page 60).
- **MOST IMPACTFUL EXPERIENCE:** At the **National Holocaust Memorial (Hollandsche Schouwburg),** learn about some of the 100,000 Jewish people who were deported from the Netherlands during the Nazi occupation (page 63).
- **BEST INSIGHT INTO THE DUTCH RESISTANCE:** Learn about how the Netherlands staged the only known mass act of resistance against Nazi occupation at the **Dutch Resistance Museum (Verzetsmuseum)** (page 63).
- **BEST WAY TO SEE HOW A DUTCH MASTER LIVED:** Visit the **Rembrandt House (Rembrandthuis)** to get a sense of how the famous artist lived and worked (page 64).
- **BEST KID-CENTRIC ATTRACTION:** At the hands-on science center **NEMO,** kids can work their way through five floors of experiments and brain teasers (page 68).

Old Center

Map 1

✪ Begijnhof (Beguines Courtyard)

The Begijnhof is a courtyard that was once home to the Beguinage, a community of Christian women, resembling a convent. Though the women were not actually nuns, they lived and worked in the Beguinage, helping the city's sick and poor citizens. With its historic structures, gardens, and sculptures, the Begijnhof today is still a peaceful haven in the center of the city.

the Houten Huys (wooden house) in the Begijnhof

The courtyard features two churches, the oldest wooden house in the country, gardens, and private residences. The most visible building in the courtyard is the **English Reformed Church** (www.ercadam.nl, viewings 11am-3pm Mon. and Thurs., 12:30pm-3pm Tues., 1pm-5pm Fri.), originally a Catholic chapel from 1490 that became a Protestant church during the Protestant Reformation. Inside, check out the pulpit, whose engraved wood panels were created by Piet Mondrian. Vincent van Gogh frequently attended services here.

Look carefully for the **Begijnhof Kapel,** one of only two remaining clandestine Catholic chapels built in 1671. Protestant council members demanded that it not look like a church, so it sits, hidden in plain sight, across from the English Reformed church. On the walls are paintings depicting the Miracle of Amsterdam (wherein a communion wafer emerged unburnt from a fire). A room next door houses a small gift shop (12:30pm-3:30pm Mon.-Sat.) with religious and historical books, candles, and trinkets. Mass is still held here daily, and visitors are free to enter and look at the modest interior anytime. Entrance to both churches is free, but donations (a few euros) are appreciated.

Next door to the Begijnhof Kapel at No. 34 is the oldest wooden house in the Netherlands, the **Houten Huys** (wooden house). Built in 1465, the home's facade is a rustic black with white trim and an asymmetric array of windows. To the left of Houten Huys is a wall of replica gable stones (stone tiles with engraved images representing family titles and occupations).

Don't miss the grave of Sister Cornelia Arens, who died in the Begijnhof in 1654. Refusing to be buried in the English Reformed Church, the Beguine claimed she'd rather be buried in the gutter than in a Protestant church. The story goes that although she was laid to rest in the church, her coffin kept appearing in the Begijnhof's gutter until it was re-buried there. Her brick grave is on the right of the courtyard's main entrance at Gedempte Begijnensloot.

Enter through an inconspicuous archway on the west side at Spui Square or the south side at Gedempte Begijnensloot. Residents of the Begijnhof ask visitors to keep the peace and be as quiet as possible. Although the quiet courtyard is blissful, resist taking an actual break here and opt for a café on Spui instead. Photography is allowed, but without flash.

MAP 1: Begijnhof 30, tel. 020/622-1918, www.begijnhofamsterdam.nl; 9am-5pm daily; free

Spui Square

Spui (pronounced to rhyme with cow) is a quaint, leafy, cobblestone square nestled between the Begijnhof and Kalverstraat, surrounded by bookshops and cafés. Like most of old Amsterdam, Spui was nothing but water until it was filled in 1882 due to city expansions. On the west side of the square is a bronze of a young boy, called *The Little Darling*, which was donated by a cigarette company in 1960. The taboo donation made the area a gathering spot for hundreds of activists called the Provos (short for "provocative") in the 1960s. The square has since evolved into a charming hangout for locals and visitors alike and is a nice spot for a drink and people-watching. A small **book market** (www.deboekenmarktophetspui.nl, 10am-6pm Fri.) is held here every Friday and a **local art market** (www.artplein-spui.com, 10am-6pm Sun.) occurs every Sunday.

MAP 1: South end of Spuistraat

Rasphuis Gate

This white lithic gate from 1596 is all that remains of the 16th-century men's prison Rasphuis (Grind House). Rasphuis prisoners spent their time here rasping (grinding) Brazilian wood. The wood was ground into a powder, which was used as pigment for painting ships. If a prisoner refused to work, he was sent to the basement's drowning cell, where water would slowly rise to drowning levels if prisoners didn't vigorously push from a hand pump.

Above the arched gate is a sculpture of two male prisoners chained together and a woman (symbolizing Amsterdam) holding a shield decorated with the city's flag. Beneath her feet is the word "Castigato" ("punishment" in Latin), engraved in gold lettering. The phrase below it reads in Latin, "It is virtuous to punish those before whom others run in fear." A relief underneath the words depicts a wheelbarrow loaded with wood and driven by a man with a whip. His load is being pulled by lions, a bear, a wolf, and a boar.

The gate has stood while the surrounding buildings changed; it now serves as an entrance to a shopping center.

MAP 1: Heiligeweg 9

Mint Tower (Munttoren)

Jutting out between Kalverstraat shopping street, Singel Canal, and the Amstel River, the Munttoren is a historic building and landmark of contrasting architecture. The original structure was built in 1480, a large gate with two towers and a guardhouse within Amsterdam's city wall. What remains today is a 19th-century guardhouse and one of the towers. The tower's lower half is the original medieval brick, while the top half was redesigned in 1620 by architect Hendrick de Keyser. Its open spire holds a 13-bell carillon; a carillonneur plays a live performance on Saturdays between 2pm and 3pm. The guardhouse, which was used to mint coins in the 17th century (hence, the tower's name), now holds a Delftware (Delft pottery) shop.

MAP 1: Muntplein

Spinhuis Gate

The entrance to the former 16th-century women's prison known as Spinhuis (Spin House) sits quietly on a hidden alley. This was where law-breaking women were sent to endure long days spinning wool and sewing textiles. The stone relief above the wooden door depicts two female prisoners being whipped by the prison's mother superior. Below it is a phrase in Latin, written by the 17th-century Dutch poet Cornelis Hooft, that reads, "Do not be surprised, be good and avenge me no harm. Punishment is my hand but my soul is sweet." Above the relief is Amsterdam's coat of arms.

Continual restorations have retained the blue and gold paint on the gate since it was built in 1649. The building has been a part of the University of Amsterdam since 1990.

MAP 1: Oudezijds Achterburgwal 185

Berlage Stock Exchange (Beurs van Berlage)

The imposing, historic Beurs van Berlage stands on Damrak street, a bulky, red brick building built in 1903. Its open, high-ceilinged interior holds mostly offices and the main floor is used for a variety of trade fairs and autumn's annual Bok Bier Festival. The building is closed to the public, though guided tours are scheduled once a month for stock market diehards (dates vary). For those not quite that curious, the **B van B Grand Café** (10am-6pm Mon.-Sat., 11am-6pm Sun.), on the south side, offers a glimpse inside Beurs van Berlage. The original entrance to the stock exchange basement safe deposits is still visible, as are paintings by Dutch-Indonesian impressionist painter Jan Toorop. The oldest stock market in the world started in Amsterdam by the Dutch East India Company in the 17th century just a block away at Dam Square.

MAP 1: Damrak 243, tel. 020/530-4141, www.beursvanberlage.nl; 8:30am-5:30pm Mon.-Fri.; guided tour €14.50

Dam Square

Dam Square is the heart of central Amsterdam. If you miss it, you really haven't experienced the city center. This bustling spot was built atop the first dam of the Amstel River, which gave the city the name Amstelledam in 1270. The Royal Palace, Nieuwe Kerk, De Bijenkorf department store, NH Grand Hotel Krasnapolsky, Madame Tussauds, and a dozen souvenir shops make up the square's perimeter. The Red Light District begins just beyond the northeast corner. Both of the largest pedestrian shopping streets in the country, Kalverstraat and Nieuwendijk, start at Dam Square.

Dam Square has seen a lot of action in its time. In the 14th century, it was the setting of a deadly battle between town officials and religious fanatics, where men had their hearts cut out and thrown in their faces. Two days after the end of World War II was announced, on May 7, 1945, intoxicated Nazis opened fire with machine guns here, killing 22 people and wounding 120 others. Nowadays the square is much calmer. People come here to watch street performers and attend the occasional beach volleyball tournament or carnival.

MAP 1: Bordered by Damstraat and Warmoesstraat

National Monument

On the east side of Dam Square stands the towering National Monument, a 70-foot-tall obelisk made of travertine and concrete, erected in May 1956 in memory of the end of Nazi occupation in the Netherlands. On the front, a relief of four men in chains represents the suffering caused by the war. Above them, the statue of a woman and child stands for victory and peace. To either side of the monument stand sculptures of men with dogs, symbolizing resistance. Two lion statues, a few meters in front of the monument, represent the Netherlands. The wall behind holds 12 urns with soil from World War II execution grounds (and one with soil from Indonesia to commemorate injustice when the island was a Dutch colony). The monument is on a concentric ring of steps, which is a popular meeting point and hangout space. Every year on May 4, the king places a peace wreath beneath the monument and holds a two-minute moment of silence to commemorate those who perished in World War II.

MAP 1: Dam Square

Royal Palace (Koninklijk Paleis)

The grand Koninklijk Paleis was originally built in 1648 as the largest city hall in Europe before becoming a palace for King Louis Napoleon (Louis I), and later the Dutch royal family. The palace, the largest building on Dam Square, is made of German sandstone, stretching over 240,000 square feet and three stories, with classical columns and a cupola dome with the proportions of Da Vinci's *Vitruvian Man*. The architect was Jacob van Campen, who stormed off the project due to disputes with a governing council and died before seeing its completion. Today, the palace serves as a temporary home when the royal family visits the capital.

Inside, visitors can explore the palace's main floor with impressive rooms, halls, furnishings, and statues. The audio guide (free) is handy when roaming the dozen or so rooms. The most remarkable room in the building, the **Citizen's Hall,** has a 100-foot ceiling and is covered in a brilliant white marble. Two maps engraved on the floor showcase Amsterdam as the center of the 17th-century trade world. A sculpture of Atlas holding the world stands in a nook high on a wall above the doorway. Other white sandstone and marble sculptures, friezes, and stone reliefs, crafted by Belgian artist Artus Quellinus, depict biblical, mythological, and historic figures.

Most rooms look as they did during the 19th century when King Louis I ruled. Some rooms are open to walk through, while others have just enough space cordoned off to lean in for a peek. The most famous room is the **Proclamation Gallery,** a balconied chamber from where the Dutch royals greet their subjects.

MAP 1: Dam Square, tel. 020/522-6161, www.paleisamsterdam.nl; 11am-5pm daily July Aug.; noon-5pm Tues.-Sun. Sept.-June; €10 adults, free under 18

Nieuwe Kerk (New Church)

Nestled close to the Royal Palace is the large and dramatic Nieuwe Kerk, with tall spires, vertical windows, and high lancet arches. This 17th-century church functions as a venue for royal weddings, ceremonies, and large art exhibitions, such as the annual World

Press Photo exhibition. While no religious services happen here anymore, the church is open daily to visitors.

The building's foundation dates back to 1385. Three different fires led to extensive renovations by 1645. One of the few furnishings that survived is the wooden choir chamber with its elaborately gilded baroque screen. The church interior is surrounded by glass windows and white sandstone arches. On the west side of the church is a massive organ with over 5,000 pipes. There is also a floor-to-ceiling spiral staircase and an ornate pulpit that took 14 years to create.

Many Dutch naval heroes are buried here; the most significant is Admiral Michiel de Ruyter, who died in battle on the Mediterranean Sea in 1676. His marble tomb, on the church's east side, is the largest ever made for a naval hero in the country.

From July to September there are organ recitals noon-12:30pm daily as well as 4pm-5pm on Tuesdays.

MAP 1: Dam Square, tel. 020/626-8168, www.nieuwekerk.nl; 10am-5pm daily; admission varies by exhibition

Narrowest House

Amsterdam's character is defined by its endless narrow houses, the pinnacle of which is the building at Singel 7, which looks more like a filled gap between two other houses. The house with the narrowest front has a whitewashed facade that can barely fit a door and window, measuring about three feet wide. This is actually the back entrance to a larger house. This is a private residence, so admire from a distance.

MAP 1: Singel 7

Amsterdam Centraal Station

Centraal Station is the largest international railway station in the country and the main entrance point to the city. It's the hub for city and regional buses, city trams, the metro, and ferry boats traveling across the IJ River to Amsterdam Noord Station. Large and impressive, the station's red brick facade stretches 1,000 feet across, with an ornate iron roof, two square towers, and the Amsterdam coat of arms as its golden centerpiece. On the west side of the building is a three-story bicycle parking garage.

Centraal Station was built in 1889 on an artificial island between the city and Amsterdam's main waterway, the IJ River. The building's architect was Pierre Cuypers, who also designed the Rijksmuseum. Similarities between the two structures can be seen in the neo-Gothic and Renaissance Revival details—turrets, large arched windows, and ornate trim. The three semicircular stone reliefs above the central entrance depict personifications of Europe and America on the left, Amsterdam in the center, between Greek sea gods Oceanus and Tethys, and Asia and Africa on the right.

Inside are cafés, takeout restaurants, newsstands, and shops. The interior is modern; the only remaining authentic rooms are the first class waiting rooms on the second platform, now a restaurant and café.

While the station is open 24 hours, most shops are open roughly 9am-6pm and eateries are open about 7am-midnight.

MAP 1: Stationsplein, tel. 0900/400-4040 (per minute charge), www.iamsterdam.com; 24 hours daily

Red Light District and Nieuwmarkt

Map 2

Oude Kerk (Old Church)

Built atop a crypt, with a floor made entirely of gravestones, the Oude Kerk has been in the heart of the Red Light District since the 1200s. The brick and sandstone structure looks small from the outside, even with its giant arched windows and clock tower. The broad inside has an open floor and the largest wooden vault ceiling in Europe. Rembrandt and his family attended services here—the tomb of his wife, Saskia, is a popular draw. Nowadays, the city's oldest church is home to a number of contemporary art exhibitions and new media installations. There's a once-weekly service (in Dutch) on Sundays at 11am.

Some unusual elements are the spiral "stairway to heaven" that climbs to the ceiling and the stained-glass windows, one covered with coats of arms. Of the four organs inside, the baroque wooden one is particularly detailed; the choir stalls from the 15th century have unique carvings on the seats.

Around the church, two bronze sculptures allude to the surrounding Red Light District: On the west side is the statue *Belle,* a small metal figure of a woman leaning on a windowsill, a tribute to sex workers worldwide. On the south side, between the cobblestones, is a bronze of a woman's torso with a hand on her breast, which appeared anonymously in the church

The massive Oude Kerk sits in the heart of the Red Light District.

one night; neighbors have insisted it remain in place as it's gained sentimental value.

Visitors can climb the church's clock tower for €7.50 (1pm-6pm Mon.-Sat.).

MAP 2: Oudekerksplein 23, tel. 020/625-8284, www.oudekerk.nl; visiting hours 10am-6pm Mon.-Sat., 1pm-5:30pm Sun.

Prostitute Information Center (PIC)

Run by a former sex worker and founder of the Dutch Union for Sexworkers (PROUD), the PIC aims to educate Red Light District visitors. The center offers books and brochures (mostly in Dutch) about the city's prostitution industry. Photographs, newspaper clippings, and art cover the walls. A small kitchen in the back is open for coffee and homemade cake. The owner also gives Red Light District tours on Wednesdays at 6:30pm and Saturdays at 5pm (€15, cash only).

MAP 2: Enge Kerksteeg 3, tel. 020/420-7328, www.pic-amsterdam.com; noon-5pm Wed.-Fri., noon-7pm Sat.; free

Fo Guang Shan He Hua Temple

Fo Guang Shan He Hua is a Chinese Buddhist temple that's been squeezed onto the Zeedijk since 2000. Its smooth golden exterior with large arches, red lettering, Chinese tiles, and perched statues replicate an authentic mountain temple. Once inside, wander around the peaceful room with its ornate reliefs, candles, and maroon marble floor. Light an incense stick and admire the shrine to Kuan Yin, a goddess said to see all suffering through her thousand hands and eyes. Monks and nuns still come to this monastery, and tours are available.

MAP 2: Zeedijk 106-118, tel. 020/420-2357, http://ibps.nl; visiting hours noon-5pm Tues.-Sat., 10am-5pm Sun.; free

Nieuwmarkt Square

Nieuwmarkt was originally a hub of old Amsterdam from which streets and alleys stretched like fingers to Chinatown, the Red Light District, the Old Jewish District, and the city center. Marked by the medieval De Waag gate, Nieuwmarkt expanded during the Golden Age, and Napoleon picked it as a prime place for guillotine beheadings. During this time, it was also an active marketplace for Sephardic Jews who lived nearby. Notice how all of the terrace seats at the square's cafés face toward the center of the square rather than being arranged around tables—a pleasant remnant of Napoleon's time.

There are still markets here on the weekends: one that sells trinkets and accessories and another selling organic and local food.

MAP 2: Intersection of Zeedijk, Geldersekade, Sint Antoniesbreestraat, and Kloveniersburgwal

The Scales (De Waag)

Part of medieval Amsterdam's fortifications, De Waag was once the main entrance to the city. In the Golden Age, De Waag became a weigh station that taxed goods brought in by ships. Today it sits in the center of Nieuwmarkt, resembling a small stubby castle—its short stature is because Nieuwmarkt Square was built up around it.

The corner turrets housed well-to-do guilds throughout the 1600s. In the southeast tower, the surgeon's guild conducted autopsies, offering public viewings of their work. Rembrandt's *The Anatomy Lesson of Dr. Nicolaes Tulp*, depicting an autopsy, was commissioned by the guild (and is now on display at the Mauritshuis in The Hague). The northwest tower still has windows framed by carefully placed brickwork, courtesy of the mason's guild.

Today, **Café in De Waag** (tel. 020/422-7772, www.indewaag.nl) is the building's main tenant, although there are also business offices upstairs. Inside the café, you can catch a glimpse of the building's part-medieval, part-renovated rustic interior, featuring high ceilings, traditional chandelier lighting, and original brick floors.

MAP 2: Nieuwmarkt 4

Trippenhuis

This building was once home to the Trip family, successful merchants that traded in weaponry. The broad building was designed in a neoclassical style, with gray columns running up the front. Two crossed powder guns decorate the gable above, representing the family crest, and the chimneys are shaped like cannons. The mansion is actually two separate houses that each belonged to one of the Trip brothers. Inside is the Royal Netherlands Academy of Arts and Sciences. The building is closed to the public.

MAP 2: Kloveniersburgwal 29

Pinto House (Huis De Pinto)

The late Isaac de Pinto was a wealthy Portuguese Jew, a published scholar, and one of the Dutch East India Company's main investors in the 1600s. As one of the only historic houses on the street to survive demolition during the famine of 1944, the Huis De Pinto is now preserved as a national monument. The inside retains a rich interior, with an ornate fireplace and grand ceiling murals painted to replicate the work of 17th-century Dutch masters. Wander through the building's foyer, front room, and library to see an authentic layout of a wealthy merchant's house from the 1600s. Pinto House now functions as a library and community center for intellectual readings and acoustic music performances.

MAP 2: Sint Antoniesbreestraat 69, tel. 020/370-0210, www.jhm.nl; 10:30am-5:30pm Mon.-Fri., 1pm-5pm Sat.; free

Cannabis College

While it isn't a true university, this information center offers an education in the history, politics, and cultivation of marijuana in its small space. The college is run by knowledgeable volunteers, who also train coffeeshop employees. Glass cases display innovative hemp creations, from car parts to snowboards. Shelves are stuffed with binders, books, DVDs, and articles about everything ganja. There's even a box of shame, which warns of coffeeshops that sell fake marijuana. The cannabis garden downstairs is open for viewing and photos for €3.

MAP 2: Oudezijds Achterburgwal 124, tel. 020/423-4420, www.cannabiscollege.com; 11am-7pm daily; free

Warmoesstraat

The 13th-century Warmoesstraat, beginning at Dam Square and extending toward Amsterdam Centraal Station, is Amsterdam's oldest street. Originally hosting wealthy merchants, fancy bars, and lace shops, Warmoesstraat transformed into a rowdy Red Light locale, home to specialty sex shops, touristy pubs, backpacker hostels, and pizza counters. Between the sex toy designers and

S&M accessory shops, Warmoesstraat has a ribald reputation.

MAP 2: Dam Square to Amsterdam Centraal Station

East India House (Oost Indisch Huis)

The Dutch East India Company (VOC), which dominated international sea trade from 1600 to the mid-1800s, had its original Amsterdam headquarters inside this building. The small entryway on the east side of the building leads to a quiet courtyard, where visitors can admire the Renaissance-era brick walls decorated with engravings of VOC members. The building now belongs to the University of Amsterdam; its interior is closed to the public.

MAP 2: Oude Hoogstraat 24

Our Lord in the Attic (Ons' Lieve Heer Op Solder)

During the Reformation, when Catholicism was illegal, many Catholics held mass in secret. As one of the city's two hidden churches (the other is inside the Begijnhof), Ons' Lieve Heer Op Solder hosted these covert worshippers in the attic of a former house of a Catholic merchant. Now a museum, the interior, from the original marble and metal beams to the replica gas lamps and hemp floor mats, is intended to reconstruct the clandestine church. An audio guide fills visitors in on the church's detailed history and its intricate construction.

MAP 2: Oudezijds Voorburgwal 40, tel. 020/624-6604, www.opsolder.nl; 10am-5pm Mon.-Sat., 1pm-5pm Sun.; €9

Schreierstoren

This short, stout tower dates from 1480, and once functioned as an entry into the city. The name translates to "sharp corner tower," but locals also call it the Tower of Tears, from tales of women crying farewell to departing sailors. A replica gable stone (decorative stone tablet) on the inner wall of the tower depicts a woman who wept so much for her absent lover that she went insane. An original gable stone on the outer wall depicts Henry Hudson leaving to discover Manhattan from this very tower. The interior of the Schreierstoren is now a traditional brown bar and café, **De Schreierstoren** (tel. 020/428-8291, www.schreierstoren.nl; 10am-1am Sun.-Thurs., 10am-2:30am Fri.-Sat.).

MAP 2: Prins Hendrikkade 94-95

Basilica of Saint Nicholas (Sint Nicolaasbasiliek)

The neo-baroque domes and neo-Renaissance facade of Sint Nicolaasbasiliek are easy to spot from Amsterdam Centraal Station. The inside of this Catholic basilica is a treasure trove of colorful stained-glass work, detailed statues, an impressive high altar, and an ornate dome ceiling. On Sunday evenings, vespers are held in Gregorian chant.

MAP 2: Prins Hendrikkade 73, tel. 020/330-7812, www.nicolaas-parochie.nl; visiting hours noon-3pm Mon., 11am-4pm Tues.-Fri., noon-3pm and 4:30pm-5:45pm Sat., 9:45am-2pm and 4:30pm-5:30pm Sun.; free

Zeedijk (Sea Dike)

Zeedijk is a pedestrian-only street that was originally the city's first sea wall, formed by sand and wood piles, protecting 14th-century Amsterdam from the North Sea. The city's elite originally settled on this strip of high ground, but by the 18th century, Zeedijk transitioned to a collection of pubs and brothels for sailors gallivanting through the Red Light District.

In the early 1900s, Zeedijk had an influx of Asian residents and the area coalesced into the city's Chinatown—Chinese lettering under the street name spells "Kindness and Virtue Street." The 1970s dragged in hard drugs and street crime, lending the street a rough reputation. Police initiatives have since swept the area clean, and now Zeedijk is a melting pot of past and present, with takeout restaurants, quirky shops, gay-friendly pubs, and 15th-century brown bars.

MAP 2: Prins Hendrikkade to Nieuwmarkt

Canal Belt South — Map 3

Leidse Square (Leidseplein)

Leidseplein, best described as a party square, is where tourists, visitors, and locals find themselves on weekends and weeknights for concerts, restaurants, bar-hopping, and clubbing. The square sits at the end of the pedestrian shopping street Leidsestraat, near the large Stadsschouwburg. Half of the square is covered by terraces belonging to touristy cafés. A few alleys off the square extend the nightlife options—some of the best places (and local spots) are here, rather than directly on Leidseplein. Try heading down Korte Leidsedwarsstraat and pop into Jazz Café Alto, L&B Whiskeycafe, or Café de Spuyt. On weekend nights, the well-used public urinals lend an unrefined aspect to the party atmosphere.

MAP 3: Intersection of Marnixstraat, Weteringschans, Vondelstraat, and Leidsestraat

Krijtberg Church

This 19th-century church doesn't look like much from the outside, with its two tall, slim, neo-Gothic towers and bland brick facade. Step inside, though, and be greeted by hand-painted emerald green, golden yellow, and royal blue columns and walls. The ornate decorations and wood-carved confessionals are impressive, and almost all windows are decorated with vivid stained glass. Free audio tours are available on request, and mass in English is held every Sunday at 5:15pm.

MAP 3: Singel 446, tel. 020/623-1923, http://krijtberg.nl; visiting hours noon-6pm Tues.-Sat., 9am-6:30pm Sun.; free

Metz & Co Building

One of the most striking structures on the Leidsestraat is the former headquarters of department store Metz & Co. This multistory stone building was built in 1891 and is topped by a distinctive cupola from 1933 designed by Dutch architect Gerrit T. Rietveld. Metz & Co was open from 1740 up until 2013, making it the longest-running and oldest department store in the country.

MAP 3: Leidsestraat 1-3

Amstelkerk

One of the few churches in the city still made from wood, Amstelkerk doubles as a cultural event center and reception space. Its whitewashed exterior and stout height stand out from the rest of the neighborhood. The original Amstelkerk was built in 1668 by Daniel Stalpaert, the architect who also designed the Scheepvaartmuseum and rendered the final exterior of the Royal Palace. The wooden structure was temporary at first, meant to be replaced with stone, though this never happened. The church was revamped in 1840, but by World War II it was in poor condition. The city bought the church and restored it to its original appearance.

Inside is a large open room with brick flooring surrounded by tall, white lancet arches. The building now houses the Stadsherstel Amsterdam, an organization that restores historic buildings. Concerts and weddings take place here about once a week, and there is a relaxing café that overlooks a small brick square, leafy trees, and the narrow Reguliersgracht canal. The church still offers Sunday services (10:30am), and there is always a small art exhibition on display.

MAP 3: Amstelveld 10, tel. 020/520-0090, www.amstelkerk.net; 9am-5pm daily or later depending on event

De Duif

De Duif is a Roman Catholic church built in 1858. Its neo-baroque facade can be seen in its stout shape and the columns installed in the front. The interior employs a neoclassical style, with clean, white arches and decorative columns. De Duif hosts live music and events, including monthly organ concerts (free), as well as a Sunday mass (in Dutch) at 10am.

MAP 3: Prinsengracht 756, tel. 020/520-0090, http://deduif.net; visiting hours noon-4pm first Wed. and third Sun. of the month

Frederiks Square (Frederiksplein)

The small green Frederiksplein, nestled in the middle of crossroads and tramlines, is a leafy oasis with a grand fountain and birds chirping in the trees. The square is wedged between the Netherlands National Bank and the end of the shopping street Utrechtsestraat, and is a common thoroughfare for those exploring the neighborhood. Find it and be charmed.

MAP 3: At intersection south of Utrechtsestraat, west of Sarphatistraat and east of Weteringschans

Golden Bend (Gouden Bocht)

The Gouden Bocht is a strip of grand canal houses known for being the crème de la crème of mansions, including some of the largest houses built in the Golden Age. These lots were sold two at a time so that the city's richest citizens could build double-width properties with deeper gardens and wider canalways. Nowadays, many of the buildings are law offices, banks, insurance companies, and cultural establishments. Look for the gold-and-white striped awnings starting at Herengracht 466, which run around the canal's curve.

MAP 3: Herengracht, between Leidsestraat and Vijzelstraat

Rembrandt Square (Rembrandtplein)

Rembrandtplein is another of the city's party squares, lined with cafés, bars, coffeeshops, and dance clubs. In the center is a cast-iron sculpture of Rembrandt from 1852, Amsterdam's oldest public statue. Below it is an entire bronze-cast installation of the artist's famous painting *The Night Watch*, which visitors like to use as a photo op. Street musicians play nearby as caricaturists offer their skills for €5 portraits, all with a backdrop of a giant LED screen (one of the largest in Europe), which plays commercials nonstop. On Thursdays to Saturdays, the area becomes a nightlife hub, with pub crawls through late-night bars and disco dance clubs; local party animals join in the tourist ruckus. In winter, a gimmicky but cute Christmas market sells German-style food, like brats and spiced wine.

MAP 3: Bordered by Reguliersdwarsstraat, Amstelstraat, Utrechtsestraat, and Vijzelstraat

Gijsbert Dommer Huis

Gijsbert Dommer Huis, also called the House with the Bloodstains, requires getting up close to see how its name came to be. The smooth stone building once belonged to Coenraad van Beuningen, a six-time mayor of Amsterdam during the late 1600s. Possibly due to either a bad marriage or a loss of shares from the Dutch East India Company, Van Beuningen's mental health deteriorated and he became known as the "mad mayor." He was bound by chains and monitored by his staff in his home. He broke free once, scribbling strange inscriptions and Hebrew characters on the building's facade with blood. To the side of the left entrance column at about eye level, the centuries-old bloodstains are still discernible. Gijsbert Dommer Huis is now an office building and closed to the public.

MAP 3: Amstel 216

Canal Belt West

Map 4

TOP EXPERIENCE

✪ Anne Frank House

As one of the most famous stories to come out of World War II, *The Diary of Anne Frank* is known as the heart-wrenching account of a Jewish girl who spent two years hiding in a building in Amsterdam before being captured and exterminated by Nazis. The building in which the Frank family hid is now the Anne Frank House. Over one million visitors per year come to visit, walking through the small rooms that once offered protection from discovery by Nazi forces.

The museum is split into two buildings, with the modern museum on one side and the house where the Frank family hid on the other side. The historic canal house was built in 1635 as a private residence, then was converted into business offices before the Frank family moved in.

Anne and her family escaped to Amsterdam from Germany just as Nazis began to take power in the early 1930s. Nazis invaded the Netherlands in 1940, and by 1942 Amsterdam Jews were being sent away to work camps. The Frank family went into hiding that summer in an annexed part of this canal house, disguising the secret entrance with a bookshelf. For nearly two years, the Franks and another family, the Van Pels, lived together in near silence, entrusting non-Jewish friends to bring supplies and reports of the outside world. In 1944, an unknown informer turned the families in to the Gestapo. Anne Frank died from typhus at the Bergen Belsen concentration camp in Germany one month before its liberation in April 1945.

the original diary of Anne Frank

Her father, Otto, was the family's only survivor.

Upon discovering Anne's diary after his return to Amsterdam, Otto published it in 1947. Her diary has since been published in over 60 languages. In 1960, Otto opened the former hiding area as the Anne Frank Huis Museum. Most of the families' belongings were destroyed or taken from the building, so many of the items in the museum are reproductions.

The museum is self-guided, taking visitors through the building's ground floor, upstairs, and into the Secret Annex, as the Franks referred to the hiding space. A small booklet with a map offers information about each room. While there is no official limit to the amount of time that can be spent in each room, visitors tend to follow a single file line while moving through the house, which makes for slow progress. Be prepared to spend an hour here. Photography is not allowed.

To avoid the notoriously long wait (up to three hours) to get into the museum, buy a timed ticket online. Tickets are issued from 9am to 3:30pm daily. After 3:30pm, the museum allows non-ticketed guests to enter. Plan to buy your tickets several months in advance.

For more information about the Nazi occupation of Amsterdam and the fate of Dutch Jews during World War II, visit the Jewish Historical Museum, the Dutch Resistance Museum, the Portuguese Synagogue, and the National Holocaust Memorial in the Plantage.

MAP 4: Prinsengracht 263-267, tel. 020/556-7105, www.annefrank.org; 9am-10pm daily Apr.-Oct., 9am-7pm Sun.-Fri., 9am-9pm Sat. Nov.-Mar.; €9 adults, €4.50 ages 10-17, free under 10; online reservations required for entry 9am-3:30pm

NEARBY:

- **Westerkerk** is the largest Protestant church in the country (page 53).
- The **Homomonument** honors the

homosexual people who perished during World War II (page 53).

- **West Market (Westermarkt)** is a cobblestoned, tree-lined square (page 54).
- Dine on traditional Dutch foods at **Bistro Bij Ons** (page 84).
- Cruise the city's waterways on a pedal-controlled raft from **Canal Bikes** (page 168).
- Across the canal in the Jordaan, **Galleria D'Arte Rinascimento** sells iconic Delftware (page 204).
- Also in the Jordaan, **Kitsch Kitchen** offers two floors of fun housewares (page 209).

Westerkerk

Although most churches in Amsterdam were originally Catholic, Westerkerk was built as, and still remains, the largest Protestant church in the country. The prominent 17th-century architect Hendrick de Keyser built Westerkerk in the Dutch Renaissance style, combining brick and sandstone with Gothic vertical lines and a rectangular body. The artist Rembrandt van Rijn, his lover Hendrickje, and son Titus were buried here, but Westerkerk is most famous for its carillon bells, which Anne Frank wrote about in her diary while in hiding two buildings away. The church's 51 perfectly tuned bells are played every 15 minutes, with a live carillonneur performing on Tuesdays from noon to 1pm.

Jutting up from the main entrance facing the Prinsengracht canal is the Westertoren (West Tower). Its spire reaches almost 280 feet, making it the tallest church tower in Amsterdam. At the top sits a giant red and gold crown, a replica of the crown of Maximillian I of Austria, a thank you gift to the Dutch for protection during a series of revolts in the 1400s. Perched atop the crown is a weather vane in the shape of a rooster. For €7.50, visitors can walk up the tower's 186 steps for a bird's-eye view of the city.

For as big as it seems outside, the church's interior is surprisingly sober, with white walls, 36 large windows, replica 17th-century chandeliers, and a wooden vaulted nave and ceiling. But the massive baroque organ is stunning, with biblical paintings on its shutters dating from the 1600s. Above the exit are two cherubs holding Amsterdam's coat of arms. A remembrance stone on one of the columns details Rembrandt's burial. As a poor man when he died, his remains were placed in an unidentified tomb, then removed after 20 years to make way for others.

MAP 4: Prinsengracht 281, tel. 020/624-7766, www.westerkerk.nl; 11am-4pm Mon.-Fri., 11am-3pm Sat., 10:30am-noon (services only) Sun. Apr.-Oct., 11am-4pm Mon.-Fri., 10:30am-noon (services only) Sun. Nov.-Mar.; tower access 10am-8pm Mon.-Sat. Apr.-Sept.

Homomonument

Behind Westerkerk sits the Homomonument, three pink triangles set into the ground, connected to each other by thin lines of stonework, resulting in an outline of one large triangle with filled pink corners. This 1987 installation by Karin Daan was the first monument in the world to commemorate homosexuals who perished under the Third Reich in World War II, as well as all who have been persecuted throughout history.

Each point on the large triangle has a symbolic reference. The northern triangle points to the Anne Frank Huis Museum. Etched in bronze are the words, "Verlangen naar vriendschap zuik een mateloos" ("Such an endless desire for friendship"), from the work of the gay Jewish poet Jacob Israel de Haan. The southwest triangle, raised two feet above street level, points toward the headquarters of the Dutch gay rights group COC. The most noticeable point is the southeast triangle, which juts out onto the Keizersgracht canal. Its tip points to the National Monument, a war memorial, on Dam Square and is often covered by bouquets of flowers.

MAP 4: Westermarkt and Keizersgracht, www.homomonument.nl

West Market (Westermarkt)

The open cobblestone area around Westerkerk is called Westermarkt—although markets rarely occur here, outside of the King's Day holiday. The square is dotted with trees, a few benches, and freestanding shacks that sell pickled herring, cone fries, fresh flowers, and tacky souvenirs. The Homomonument is here, just behind Westerkerk, as well as a small bronze of Anne Frank by Mari Andriessen, an artist known for his Holocaust memorial sculptures. Most of the time, Westermarkt is crowded with visitors waiting to enter the Anne Frank Huis Museum.

MAP 4: Intersection of Raadhuisstraat and Rozengracht, between Keizersgracht and Prinsengracht

Tower Lock (Torensluis)

Torensluis is the city's widest and oldest bridge, dating from 1648. Though it looks like a simple cobblestone road, the bridge held a tower until 1829. Today, with its many benches and chairs, Torensluis is one of the best spots in the city to lounge. The large bronze bust of Multatuli, on the northwest side of the bridge, was installed in 1987 as a tribute to colonial writer Edward Douwes Dekker (Multatuli was his pen name). The bridge is next to one of the narrowest houses in the city, Singel 166. Below the bridge are former underground dungeons that occasionally double as pop-up exhibitions and live music venues.

MAP 4: Spanning the Singel Canal, between Torensteeg and Oude Leliestraat

TOP EXPERIENCE

Rijksmuseum

The massive medieval backdrop to Museumplein is the Rijksmuseum, a stunning national art and history museum with exquisite artwork from 17th-century Dutch masters and more than 8,000 relics. It's easy to spend an entire day roaming its hallways and gardens, absorbing the rich collection that spans 800 years. The structure itself is a wonder, designed by 19th-century architect Pierre Cuypers, who also designed Amsterdam Centraal Station. The neo-Gothic and neo-Renaissance brick facade is decorated with statues and friezes related to significant events and figures in Dutch history. It opened in 1885 after almost 10 years of construction.

The museum is a chronological circuit, starting with the special collections and 1200s on the ground floor, and ending with the 21st century on the third floor. Each floor has two wings that exhibit a specific era via a dozen display rooms.

One of the museum's highlights is on the second floor: *Nachtwacht*, or *The Night Watch*, by Rembrandt van Rijn. With its dark background and portrayal of action, it's arguably the artist's most famous and innovative masterpiece. It was also the most criticized and a thorn in Rembrandt's side, leading to his end as a famous painter. The painting shares a bright

interior of the Rijksmuseum

and airy space with a collection of other Rembrandts and the works of his pupils.

Also on the second floor, the **Gallery of Honor** is a stunning neo-Gothic hallway with eight alcoves exhibiting Dutch masterpieces of the 17th century. Vermeer, Steen, Ruysdael, Hals, and Rembrandt have some of their best and most famous portraits, landscapes, and everyday life scenes here. The Gallery of Honor is behind Rembrandt's *Nachtwacht*.

Works by Breitner, Gabriel, and Van Gogh are grouped together in one large room on the first floor. There are only a few Van Goghs, so the focus is instead on Amsterdam impressionist painters like George Breitner, Jan Toorop, and Isaac Israëls. Their style of rapid, thick, visible brushstrokes depicted working-class people and street and harbor scenes inspired by the city during the late 1800s.

The exhibit **Netherlands Overseas,** on the first floor, provides insight into life at sea during the 17th and 18th centuries, with replica ships, wool caps from 17th-century skeletons, and spectacular paintings of battles at sea.

Dozens of other rooms exhibit works from the Enlightenment, colonial Indonesia, and the romantic period. There are also special collections, like Delftware, high-society dollhouses, and weaponry. The small third floor includes a few relatively contemporary works from Karel Appel, the Gerrit Rietveld Academie, and the art nouveau period.

The museum's attached ***bibliotheek*** **(library)** is the largest art history research library in the country. In it, a spiral iron staircase winds

up four floors, as researchers work diligently on the first floor. The polychrome walls, arched windows, painted brick, and cast-iron railings and colonettes lend a sense of antiquity to the space.

Before leaving, take time to wander around the museum's gardens to see elaborate topiaries and outdoor installations alongside lively fountains, tall trees, and wooden benches.

The best way to beat the lines is to come in the late afternoon. The glass-roofed atrium holds the ticket desk, information desk, storage lockers (free), audio guides, café, gift shop, and restrooms. The museum's vastness can be overwhelming; use one of the free maps at the information desk to make the most of your time. Visit the must-sees first, and allow yourself at least 90 minutes to explore the museum.

MAP 5: Museumstraat 1, tel. 020/674-7000, www.rijksmuseum.nl; 9am-5pm daily; €17.50 adults, free 17 and under

NEARBY:

- Splash around the indoor pool at **Zuiderbad** (page 170).
- Browse the selection of imported European shoes at **Meyer** (page 198).

TOP EXPERIENCE

✪ Van Gogh Museum

The Van Gogh Museum holds the largest collection of post-impressionist painter Vincent van Gogh's works in the world. The collection boasts over a thousand paintings, drawings, and letters from the artist. Van Gogh was only 37 when he died; more incredibly, his prolific career spanned only a decade. Over a million visitors come to the Van Gogh Museum annually, and it competes with the Rijksmuseum as the most visited art museum in the country.

Van Gogh Museum

The museum layout is open and intuitive. A single staircase leads to each floor, and the exhibition is arranged in chronological order. A collection of self-portraits on the ground floor marks the beginning of the exhibition. The first floor holds the bulk of the collection (1883-1889), starting with Van Gogh's early works depicting rural life. His early inspiration came from observing the hardship of peasant life. *De Aardappeleters,* or *The Potato Eaters,* is a highlight from this time; Van Gogh considered it the most successful work of his career.

From 1886 to 1889, Van Gogh's life in Paris and the south of France led to avant-garde experiments with color, brushwork, lines, and planes. His fixation on bright tones and blossoming flowers is evident in works like the famous *Tournesols (Sunflowers)* series, displayed on the second floor. To perfect the art of portraiture, Van Gogh created 28 self-portraits during his two-year residence in Paris. *The Bedroom* and *The Yellow House,* also located on the museum's second floor, are well-known works he made of the home he shared with fellow artist Paul Gauguin in Arles.

On the second floor are displays of some of Van Gogh's correspondence, a collection of handwritten letters to his brother Theo and fellow artists like Claude Monet. The letters are in Dutch, French, and English. A rotating exhibit of Van Gogh sketches and drawings are on display, as well as a closer look at his tools and mediums.

The third-floor exhibits pull from Van Gogh's final years, 1889-1890, including the time when he checked himself into a psychiatric ward in Saint-Rémy-de-Provence, France. Both *Irissen (Irises)* and *De Tuin van de Inrichting Saint Paul (The Garden of Saint-Paul Hospital),* works Van Gogh painted while looking out the window of his hospital room, are displayed here. *Korenveld met Kraaien*

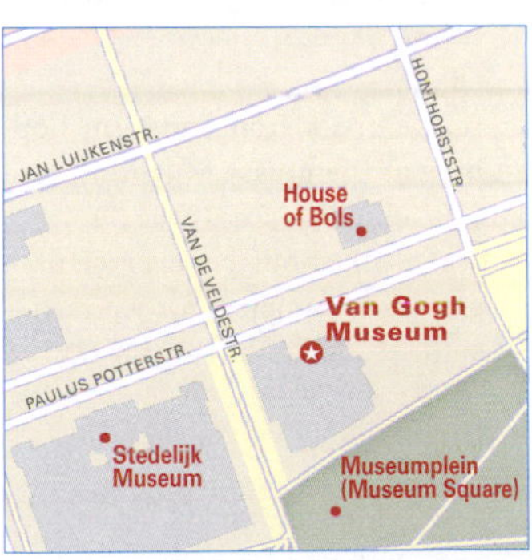

(Wheatfield with Crows) is one of the final pieces he finished before a self-inflicted gunshot wound led to his death in 1890.

While the museum's primary focus is on Van Gogh, a series of works by contemporaries like Monet, Gauguin, and Millet are also on display. The adjoining Kurokawa building hosts shows by other artists with a Van Gogh theme. A library on the third floor sells art books on Van Gogh and his contemporaries.

The modern rectangular museum, designed by influential Dutch architect Gerrit Rietveld, is on the west side of Museumplein. During high season (Apr.-Sept.), get here before opening time to avoid a long wait. The ticket desk and admission are through a modern, glass-covered entryway, next to the Stedelijk.

Photography is not allowed near any of the paintings. The museum holds Friday night events with free guided tours, a pop-up bar, and live performance art and music until 10pm.

MAP 5: Paulus Potterstraat 7, tel. 020/570-5200, www.vangoghmuseum.nl; 9am-6pm Sat.-Thurs., 9am-10pm Fri.; €17 adults, free 17 and under

NEARBY:

- For a taste of modern art, head to the **Stedelijk Museum** (page 58).
- Take a break from museum-hopping at the grassy **Museumplein (Museum Square)** (page 59).
- Learn all about *genever* (Dutch gin)—and sample it for yourself—at the **House of Bols** (page 60).

TOP EXPERIENCE

✪ Stedelijk Museum

Amsterdam's colossal Stedelijk Museum combines spectacular milestones from the masterminds of contemporary and modern art and design from 1850 to today. It's a prized gem, with one of the best abstract art collections in Europe. The museum occasionally rotates their 90,000-piece collection, with big names like Monet, Chagall, Mondrian, Warhol, and Lichtenstein on permanent display.

bird's-eye view of Museumplein

The Stedelijk is housed in a 19th-century neo-Renaissance building. A modern glass addition is covered by oversized white roofing (which locals say resembles a bathtub). The building makes up the southwest corner of Museumplein, next to the Van Gogh Museum.

The interior is bright and spacious, with minimal decor. There are two levels: the main ground floor and an

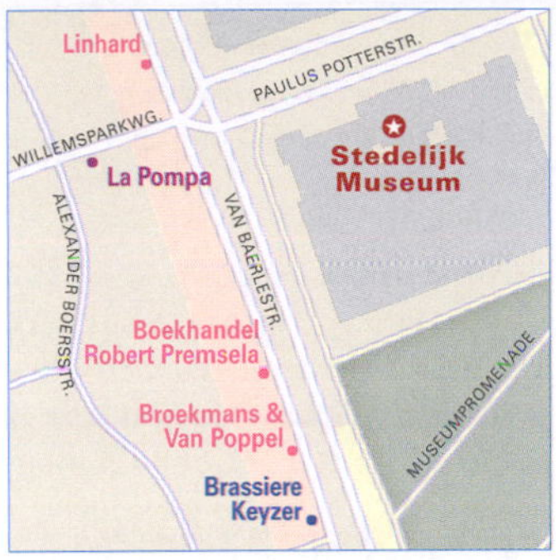

upper floor. Pre-1960 (modern) art and the design collection are on the ground floor and post-1960 (contemporary) art takes up the entire upper floor.

Works by recognizable blue chip artists like Vincent van Gogh, Henri Matisse, Marc Chagall, and Pablo Picasso are in the ground floor's right wing. Also here are artists from the CoBrA (Copenhagen, Brussels, Amsterdam) movement like Karel Appel. In contrast, the left wing is dedicated to influential designs like Holland's De Stijl and Germany's Bauhaus, both of which focused on avant-garde form and primary colors. Large display cases hold everything from old electronics and living room settings to political posters and advertisements from as early as the 1900s.

On the upper floor, the must-see is *As I Opened Fire*, a triptych by Roy Lichtenstein, which shares a room with a print collage by Andy Warhol. Large pieces by both Jackson Pollock and Willem de Kooning are also featured on this floor, along with vibrant works from current artists, like *Wall Drawing #1084*, the vivid wall of thick lines by Sol LeWitt.

Below the main entrance is a lower floor, accessed via a separate stairwell that's located across from the ticket desk. This space holds temporary exhibitions from smaller and more obscure movements that occurred post-World War II in Europe and around the world. The Stedelijk excels here, with a thorough and impressive roster of temporary exhibitions, from Matisse to Marlene Dumas, Yves Klein, and Andy Warhol.

One of the museum's most notable curators and directors was Willem Sandberg, whose modernist typography and graphic design work for the museum are part of the design collection. Sandberg was active in the Dutch resistance movement and forged documents for Jewish artists and others wanted by the Gestapo before he became museum director in 1945.

MAP 5: Museumplein 10, tel. 020/573-2911, www.stedelijk.nl; 10am-6pm Sat.-Thurs., 10am-10pm Fri.; €15 adults, €7.50 students 19-29, free 18 and under

NEARBY:

- Savor Mediterranean cuisine at **La Pompa** (page 88).
- Unwind with a glass of wine at the grand café **Brasserie Keyzer** (page 128).
- Browse clothing from Dutch designers at **Linhard** (page 198).
- Gain inspiration from the many art books for sale at **Boekhandel Robert Premsela** (page 199).
- Buy some classical sheet music from **Broekmans & Van Poppel** (page 199).

Museumplein (Museum Square)

The grassy, rectangular field at Museumplein is the best place to take a breather after doing the rounds at the Stedelijk Museum, Van Gogh Museum, and Rijksmuseum, which all border the square. The U.S. embassy is located on the southeast corner.

Museumplein hosts a number of

free festivals in the summer, and by winter the square's shallow pond turns into an ice-skating rink with a pop-up chalet café. On the east side of the park sits a Holocaust memorial comprised of stainless steel panels and a column that emits sound and light at night. Giant six-foot-tall red and white letters spell out "I amsterdam," making for a great photo op. There might be a few skateboarders or inline skaters testing out the steel vert ramps nearby. **MAP 5:** Bordered by Van Baerlestraat, Paulus Potterstraat, and Johannes Vermeerstraat

House of Bols

The House of Bols, in a historic building off of Museumplein, is all about *genever* (Dutch gin). On the self-guided tour, wander through a maze of rooms that tell the history of the Bols brand of spirits. There is some intense marketing happening along the way, but the fun part is the history lesson in *genever,* the Dutch gin that the British developed into modern-day gin. Among the rooms are sensory experiences, where visitors try to identify different scents in the alcohols on display. A small hallway displays a painting by one of Rembrandt van Rijn's pupils, given to the Bols family to pay an outstanding debt.

The best part is the Mirror Bar at the end of the tour, where visitors receive a free cocktail of their choice made with Bols spirits. Professional bartenders (trained at the Bols Bartending Academy upstairs) show off their skills, juggling bottles as they mix drinks. An automated kiosk helps you pick a drink based on flavor and strength. Once you have your drink, head to the black leather lounge and enjoy a cocktail whose history you've just learned all about. Visitors must be 18 or older.

MAP 5: Paulus Potterstraat 14, tel. 020/570-8575, www.houseofbols.com; 1pm-6:30pm Sun.-Thurs., 1pm-9pm Fri.-Sat.; €16

✪ Vondelpark

As the country's most famous park and the city's largest, Vondelpark is to Amsterdam what Central Park is to New York City. Over 10 million visitors come yearly to picnic by the ponds, barbecue on the grass, and kick back at the terrace cafés dotting the park's 100 green acres.

The park stretches over a mile long and a half-mile wide. A two-mile asphalt track winds around the park for running, bicycling, and roller-skating (especially at the year-round Friday Night Skate). Most people come to soak up rays and stroll among the waterfowl, outdoor art, and sweet-scented roses. Trees line the small ponds, and sculptures are scattered throughout the park. In the park's center is the Open Air Theater Vondelpark, which hosts free music, dance, and children's shows in the summer.

The park, built atop marshy grasslands in 1865, must undergo renovations every few decades because it is always sinking. Its name was originally Nieuwe Park, but it was later renamed after the poet Joost van den Vondel, whose statue was installed in the park in 1867.

During the flower power movement of the 1960s and 1970s, the park was a hub for hippies, which led to the opening of hostels around the park. A few hostels, like Flying Pig Uptown and Stayokay Vondelpark, continue the tradition today.

Vondelpark's main entrance gate is just behind Leidseplein on Stadhouderskade.

MAP 5: Off Stadhouderskade, between Vossiusstraat and Zandpad, www.hetvondelpark.net; dawn-midnight daily

Vondelkerk

The main feature of this neo-Gothic, 19th-century brick church is a trio of stunning towers that reach up to 150 feet. Vondelkerk was designed by Pierre Cuypers, the architect behind both Amsterdam Centraal Station and the Rijksmuseum. It features an ornate tiled vault, long lancet windows set with stained glass, and a rounded nave. Though this compact church is inactive, the inside is open to the public every first Wednesday and third Sunday of the month from noon to 4pm. It's mainly used as an event space for weddings and concerts.

MAP 5: Vondelstraat 120-A, tel. 020/520-0090, www.stadsherstel.nl; visiting hours noon-4pm first Wed. and third Sun. of the month; free

De Pijp — Map 6

Heineken Experience

The Heineken Experience offers visitors an education in the history of beer and some amusing gimmicks to pass the time. A self-guided tour takes visitors through the former Heineken brewery, easily identified by the giant brass sign hanging from the high brick walls.

The tour begins with the story of the Heineken family and features video clips, old photographs, and documents that led to the creation of the Heineken pilsner business in 1864. Next, visitors can see copper brewing vats used from 1867 to 1988. The brewery even has stables housing horses that still clop around the city towing a wagon full of beer barrels. Enjoy a short tasting, then view a short video shot from the point of view of a Heineken bottle on the assembly line. The tour ends at a modern bar serving Heineken on tap.

The hour-long tour is interspersed with blatant marketing, but beer fans may not mind too much. Tickets include two free beer vouchers. This is a busy attraction, so buy tickets online and get here before the afternoon hours. From here, the Heineken Shuttle Boat (one-way, free) takes visitors to the Heineken Brand Store just off of Rembrandtplein in the city center.

MAP 6: Stadhouderskade 78, tel.020/523-9222, www.heinekenexperience.com; 11am-7:30pm Mon.-Thurs., 10:30am-9pm Fri.-Sun.; €16 adults, €12.50 ages 12-17, free 11 and under

House with the Gnomes (Huis met de Kabouters)

The most impressive building in De Pijp is the Huis met de Kabouters, built in 1884. The facade is three buildings wide, backed by brick and sandstone, with Renaissance-style windows, Gothic-style doors, and a roof reminiscent of a Swiss chalet, with ornate wood carvings.

The house, which consists of 12 apartments, gets its name from the two green gnome statues on the rooftop. They are about eight feet high with red noses and matching hats. They straddle wooden beams, and appear to be playing catch with a red ball. Locals say the ball moves from one gnome to the other on New Year's Eve and every leap day.

MAP 6: Ceintuurbaan 251-255

Jordaan

North Church (Noorderkerk)

Noorderkerk, a short but picturesque church along the Prinsengracht, was built in 1623 for Jordaan's working-class residents. Its layout differs from typical Amsterdam churches, with its four short, stout arms emerging from its center. The brick facade and charming white-framed windows create a nice backdrop to the nearby cafés and weekly markets in the surrounding Noordermarkt square.

Two bronze plaques are installed on the church's south wall. One is dedicated to Jordaan residents who died in World War II and the other is dedicated to Jordaan's working class, who initiated the February Strike of 1941—one of only two general strikes that occurred during Nazi occupation.

Inside, the church tower, organ, and iron light fixtures are replicas that resemble the 17th-century style of the originals. The marble base of the pulpit, the wall plaster, and the dark oak pews are original. The church holds classical music concerts on Saturdays at 2pm from mid-September to mid-June (except Christmas holidays). Sunday services are held at 10am and 6:30pm in Dutch. Translators are available.

MAP 7: Noordermarkt 48, tel. 020/626-6436, www.noorderkerk.org; visiting hours 10:30am-12:30pm Mon., 11am-1pm Sat.; free

Haarlemmer Square (Haarlemmerplein)

This pleasant modern square is an open, airy space. The towering structure at its western end is Haarlemmerpoort (officially named Willemsspoort), a city gate that has existed since 1618. It was rebuilt in 1837 out of sandstone in a neoclassical style, seen in the eight Corinthian columns and symmetrical sides. Above the columns is a clock and border of rosettes. The gate, originally part of the fortified city walls, now borders spacious Westerpark and the city's western neighborhoods. In summer, a water feature installed in the ground is a playground for kids.

MAP 7: Intersection of Haarlemmerweg and Korte Marnixstraat

Johnny Jordaanplein

This tiny, funky square camouflaged within the Jordaan is a memorial to Johnny Jordaan, an important Dutch musician, and other Dutch pop folk singers from the 1950s. With statues of the musicians taking up most of it, the square is painted with flower power murals and scenes of the city. Jordaan residents regard this square with adoration and nostalgia.

MAP 7: Intersection of Elandsgracht and Prinsengracht

Plantage

Map 8

TOP EXPERIENCE

National Holocaust Memorial (Hollandsche Schouwburg)

The Hollandsche Schouwburg was originally a popular theater, producing Dutch-written plays during the Plantage's time as a lively entertainment district from the 1890s until 1941. In 1942, the Nazis turned it into a holding prison and deportation center for Jews being sent to the Westerbork and Vught transit camps—the last stop before extermination camps. The Hollandsche Schouwburg now serves as a national Holocaust monument and memorial museum.

Through video and photographs, the museum tells the building's—and the city's—ill-fated history. On one wall is a list of the over 100,000 deported Jews who lived in the Netherlands; almost half of them were at one point stationed in this theater. Interactive tools allow visitors to select names from the list and view a profile containing information gathered by the museum about that person. Upstairs is a permanent installation of news clippings, letters from deportees, and a silent film showing Jews boarding trains bound for Auschwitz.

In the courtyard, a tall monument stands enclosed by original brick walls that once held a theater stage. The often-overlooked theater gives immense insight into the dark and disturbing treatment of Amsterdam Jews by Nazis.

MAP 8: Plantage Middenlaan 24, tel. 020/531-0310, http://jck.nl; 11am-5pm daily; free, donations accepted

NEARBY:

- At the **Dutch Resistance Museum (Verzetsmuseum),** learn about the people who lived through the Nazi occupation of the Netherlands (page 63).
- View some of the 6,000 plants at the **Botanical Gardens (Hortus Botanicus)** (page 64).
- Order a gourmet burger at **Burgermeester** (page 100).
- Sip an Irish coffee and people-watch at the brown bar **Café Koosje** (page 136).
- Check out the sphinx-topped pillars at **Wertheimpark** (page 172).

Dutch Resistance Museum (Verzetsmuseum)

The Dutch Resistance Museum raises the ultimate question: "What would you have done?" With an endless display of posters, photographs, letters, clothing, and other memorabilia, the museum tells the story of the 300,000 people (both Jews and non-Jews) that lived in hiding in the Netherlands during the occupation and their acts of resistance.

Learn how underground printers

coordinated with spies to report on SS forces, as well as the techniques resistance supporters used to hide weapons in ordinary items like books and strollers. The Dutch banded together to form the only recorded act of resistance against Nazis during the Strike of February 1941.

The Junior wing, aimed at children nine and older, focuses on the lives of four children who lived in the Netherlands during the occupation. The exhibit allows visitors to walk through life-size sets made to look like rooms where the children and their families lived (and hid). Signs in Dutch and English guide visitors to look inside cupboards, press buttons to hear sounds, activate visual media, and illuminate window cases of WWII resistance tools.

The walls and installations of this small museum are overloaded with text and imagery from Nazi-occupied Holland. Use the free audio guide to focus on the most important elements of the museum.

MAP 8: Plantage Kerklaan 61A, tel. 020/620-2535, www.verzetsmuseum.org; 10am-5pm Mon.-Fri., 11am-5pm Sat.-Sun.; €10 adults, €5 ages 1-16

Entrepotdok

The Entrepotdok was once a warehouse complex for the hundreds of ships that made the Dutch East India Company a strong force during the height of the Golden Age. One of the largest storage areas in Europe during its heyday, the insides have since become apartments, offices, and cafés with exposed iron beams and antique wood foundations. The building stands out thanks to its uniform red brick exterior, roofline, and window facades. For the best view, walk down the Entrepotdok canal quayside.

MAP 8: Parallel to Hoogte Kadijk and Plantage Kerklaan

Botanical Gardens (Hortus Botanicus)

What began as an herb garden in 1638 has blossomed into a collection of 6,000 different plants, both native and foreign. Three large greenhouses hold a butterfly garden, a variety of palm trees, and plants from the desert, tropics, and subtropics. Highlights include a 350-year-old Eastern Cape giant cycad and a coffee plant that is a parent to all coffee growing in South and Central America. Placards, with both common and Latin names, label each plant. This is a great spot for families, nature loves, and visitors looking for a laid-back attraction.

MAP 8: Plantage Middenlaan 2a, tel. 020/625-9021, http://dehortus.nl; 10am-5pm daily; €9 adults, €5 students, seniors, and ages 5-14, free under 5

✪ Rembrandt House (Rembrandthuis)

Built in 1606, the Rembrandt House was owned for nearly 20 years by Rembrandt van Rijn, the famous Dutch artist. It now serves as a historic house and art museum highlighting his 17th-century life. While there are just two paintings by Rembrandt here (more are at the Rijksmuseum), the top floor holds his etchings, and the house is decorated with everything from 400-year-old antiques to work by well-known Golden Age artists like Jan Lievens.

Pick up a free audio guide before touring the eight rooms of the house. The guide's gossipy narration style keeps things fun, with stories about squabbles between Rembrandt and his mistress and intriguing trivia about life in the 17th century. Travel

etching lessons outside the Rembrandt House

through his studio, then see where Rembrandt conducted his job as an art dealer in his business room and where he taught in his pupil room. Rembrandt's props room displays his collection of exotic animal tusks and alligator taxidermy, which he asked models to pose with.

After viewing the last room, filled with Rembrandt's largest collection of ink etchings, head to the pupil room for the hourly live demonstration of the etching and ink process. Workshops, offered three times a day, teach visitors how to use a traditional etching press.

MAP 8: Jodenbreestraat 4, tel. 020/520-0400, www.rembrandthuis.nl; 10am-6pm daily; €13 adults, €4 ages 6-17, free 5 and under

Portuguese Synagogue

This grand, historic synagogue was built in 1675 by Spanish Jewish refugees posing as Portuguese Jews to avoid death during the Eighty Years' War between Spain and the Netherlands. The building still stands in its initial rectangular brick body with 72 square-paned windows and its original wooden pews. Also known as the Esnoga, it's the second-oldest synagogue in Europe, with a traditional Sephardic layout of seats and ornaments, and sand on the floor to muffle footsteps.

The free audio guide explains the setting and the synagogue's significance in Nazi-occupied Amsterdam. The outside chambers hold a treasure room and the oldest operating Jewish library in the world. Try to come in the late afternoon, when the lit candles on the grand chandeliers lend an eerie but beautiful touch. Tickets to the synagogue are also good at the Joods Historisch Museum and the Hollandsche Schouwburg.

MAP 8: Mr. Visserplein 3, tel. 020/624-5351, http://jck.nl; 10am-4pm Sun.-Thurs., 10am-2pm Fri. winter, 10am-5pm Sun.-Thurs., 10am-4pm Fri. spring, 10am-5pm daily summer, 10am-5pm Mon.-Thurs., 10am-4pm Fri. fall; €15, includes admission to Jewish Cultural Quarter attractions

Jewish Historical Museum (Joods Historisch Museum)

The Jewish Historical Museum is comprised of four synagogues woven into a modern museum campus devoted to the history of Jewish culture, from its origins to present day. One section of the museum outlines the history of Passover, Hanukkah, and the origins of Judaism. Another section concentrates on life as a Jew throughout the history of the Netherlands. As early as the 1500s, Jews emigrated from Western and Eastern Europe to find refuge in Amsterdam, a city rumored to offer tolerance and liberty toward minorities. Exhibits track the important developments and struggles of Amsterdam's Jewish residents, from the life of famous philosopher Baruch Spinoza in the 1600s to the community that established the diamond trade in the years leading up to World War II.

The standout here is the depiction of Jewish life in Nazi-occupied Holland. Relics include forged identification papers and fabric panels of the Star of David that Jews were forced to sew on their clothes. Survivors, in video interviews, relate accounts of life in hiding, how towns resisted the occupation, and the hardship of returning after the war without a home or family.

The museum offers a free self-guided audio tour. Museum tickets are also good for entry at the Portuguese Synagogue and the Hollandsche Schouwburg.

MAP 8: Nieuwe Amstelstraat 1, tel. 020/531-0310, http://jck.nl; 11am-5pm daily; €15, includes admission to Jewish Cultural Quarter attractions

Gassan Diamonds

At this diamond factory and retailer, visitors get an inside look at how the Gassan business shapes and sells the world's strongest mineral. In-house guides lead groups upstairs, where cutters shape diamonds with magnifying glasses and large plates greased with olive oil. After explaining diamond processing and polishing, guides move to the next room, a small showcase of diamonds and their pricing based on the four Cs: clarity, color, cut, and carat.

Although there's no pressure to buy, the rest of the tour is comprised of four small rooms showcasing diamond jewelry for sale. The grand finale, in a large room, is a display of high-end watches and jewelry encased in glass. Attracting mostly bus tour groups on European package trips, Gassan is interesting to those curious about the basics of the diamond industry.

MAP 8: Nieuwe Uilenburgerstraat 173-175, tel. 020/622-5333, www.gassan.com; 9am-5pm daily; free

Blue Bridge (Blauwbrug)

Blauwbrug connects Rembrandtplein to Waterlooplein over the Amstel River and is longer, wider, and more decorative than the city's other brick-and-cobblestone bridges. Made of gray stone, the bridge features sculpted piers that are modeled after ship bows, atop of which are ornate streetlamps made of maroon marble. Blauwbrug's design took its inspiration from the bridges over the Seine in Paris. Built in 1883, the bridge offers great views of the Stopera building and residences along the Amstel River.

MAP 8: Between Amstelstraat and Waterlooplein

Skinny Bridge (Magere Brug)

Considered the most famous bridge in Amsterdam, the Skinny Bridge sits across the Amstel River and is a unique example of 1930s drawbridge architecture. Its nine arches and thin passageway are composed of white-washed wooden beams, linked chains, and over 1,000 lightbulbs that illuminate boats passing in the night.

Walking across the bridge is like something out of a noir film: It's been a backdrop for many movies, including *Diamonds Are Forever,* the 1971 James Bond movie. Limited to pedestrians and cyclists, the bridge offers a city view to the north and a distant scene of the Amstelsluizen (Amstel Locks) to the south. The bridge is said to have gotten its name from its commissioners, two sisters named Magere, who lived across the canal from each other and wished to have a bridge in order to visit each other.

MAP 8: Amstel and Nieuwe Kerkstraat

Amstel Locks (Amstelsluizen)

The Amstel Locks don't look like much, but they are part of a complex control and pump system of the city's 60-mile canal structure. A few times a week these locks are closed while others around the city are opened to let old water out to the North Sea, then the action is reversed to bring fresh water in from the Amstel and IJ Rivers. The locks are a great spot to picnic and watch boats cruise by, and they are prime real estate for watching the Amsterdam Pride boat parade in August.

MAP 8: Amstel and Nieuwe Prinsengracht

Kadijks Square (Kadijksplein)

Next to an old drawbridge sits tiny, quiet Kadijksplein. An entry point for ships in the 1500s, the square now hosts a handful of petite B&Bs and charming cafés with terraces ideal for a cozy *koffie* or *wijn*. Oddly impervious to heavy tourist traffic, the area is a dainty crossroads offering a blend of Plantage greenery and views of the waterfront.

MAP 8: Southeast of Prins Hendrikkade where it intersects with Schippersgracht

Muiderpoort City Gate

Just past Artis Zoo, at the end of Plantage Middenlaan, stands the Muiderpoort City Gate, the only one of five entrances to the city still standing from the Golden Age (circa 1771). The Muiderpoort City Gate was the entry point for Napoleon and his troops when they arrived in Amsterdam and demanded supplies and food. The dome and clock tower at the top of the gate make it an eye-catching classical structure. Today, the gate serves as a marker of Alexanderplein, a major tram intersection. The city gate should not be confused with Muiderpoort train station, a national train stop in the nearby Oost (East) neighborhood.

MAP 8: Sarphatistraat 500

IJ River

Map 9

Eastern Docklands

Amsterdam's Eastern Docklands are a cluster of artificially constructed peninsulas that were once shipyards and are now a modern residential area. Owned by the Royal Dutch Steamboat Company in the early 1900s, the area was where passenger steamboats docked. Located east of Amsterdam Centraal Station, the quiet Docklands have a peaceful vibe, with wide waterways and modern bridges.

The Oostelijke Handelskade (Eastern Quay), built in the 1880s, is an entry point when coming from the city center. The long, narrow strip starts at the Muziekgebouw aan 't IJ concert hall and ends at Verbindingsdam bridge. Its main building is the historic **Lloyd Hotel,** but a walk down the waterside Veemkade, a peaceful boardwalk with sweeping views of the city, is an essential experience in the Eastern Docklands.

Javaeiland (Java Island) is one of Amsterdam's most prized pieces of unique architecture. It was transformed in the 1990s into a neighborhood with tiny canals, charming pedestrian bridges, and some of the most striking postmodern apartments around. Walk between the narrow canal streets of Brantasgracht, Lamonggracht, Majanggracht, and Seranggracht for an up-close look at peculiar and distinctive buildings, which often feature details like all-glass facades and wood paneling. On the east side of Javaeiland is KNSM (the Royal Dutch Steamboat Company), a complex with many of its original brick and industrial buildings still standing, though they now function as residential buildings and cultural centers.

One of the most striking architectural additions to the Eastern Docklands is the flaming red Python Bridge. This 295-foot-long steel crossbeam bridge was built in 2001, with a stepped design passable only by foot or bicycle. The bridge joins Sporenburg with Borneo Island via its unusual snaking curves.

With a spacious layout, small grassy areas, and interesting sights, the Docklands make for a great bike excursion close to the city center.

MAP 9: Northern terminus of Jan Schaeferbrug

De Gooyer Windmill

This is the most convenient windmill for a photo op. In operation since 1725, the windmill, with its thatched trunk and tiny windows, holds four sails with traditional green and white wind boards and crisscrossed hem laths. It once served as a corn mill, but nowadays it's a private home.

MAP 9: Funenkade 7

✪ NEMO

This five-story emerald building resembling a futuristic blimp is Amsterdam's science and learning center, one of the best kid-centric attractions in the city. Exhibits are laid out by age and explain in English the scientific properties of the various hands-on experiments that the museum presents.

Mechanics, engineering, and alternative energy are the main focus of the second floor. A massive array of tubes and conveyor belts send colorful balls zipping around the room, so kids can learn the logistics of worldwide shipping. And there are interactive brain teasers, from cranking windmills to pressing water through a model treatment system, which explains water filtration.

The third floor is designed for teens, focusing on evolution, sex education, and the brain. A section called Search for Life goes into the evolution of cells, life on Earth, and the unknown. Another section digs into the brain's functions with puzzles, illusions, and games. The most mature section is a crash course on sex and drugs aimed at a teenage audience. From diagrams of erogenous zones to detailed explanations of the effects of narcotics, visitors might feel shocked at the candor, but it's typical of the Dutch culture of frankness.

Don't miss the city view from the top floor café. The café's outdoor deck is accessible in summer without having to enter NEMO by climbing the steps from the entrance.

MAP 9: Oosterdok 2, tel. 020/531-3233, www.nemosciencemuseum.nl; 10am-5:30pm daily Apr.-late Aug., 10am-5:30pm Tues.-Sun. late Aug.-Mar.; €16.50

RESTAURANTS

Dutch cuisine has always been rooted in mild and hearty ingredients: dairy, meat, and produce. This is evident from the national dish, *stamppot*. Generally served in winter, it consists of mashed potatoes and greens served with sausage and gravy. The farm-to-table movement is ever-present in the city, focusing on local, organic ingredients. Locals favor fresh-squeezed fruit juices, melt-in-your-mouth gouda, and seafood directly from the North Sea.

a cake from bakery De Taart van m'n Tante

The Dutch don't shy away from indulging their taste buds. Many bars and food carts serve fried snacks like *bitterballen* (fried meatballs), fried croquettes, and thick cut Belgian fries (served with a heaping dollop of mayonnaise). Visitors with a sweet tooth should be on the lookout for *stroopwafel* (sandwich-style waffle cookies) and *appeltaart met slaagroom* (Dutch apple pie with whipped cream) at local cafés.

Amsterdam has an extensive variety of international cuisines. Some of the Netherlands' colonial history is evident in the many Indonesian and Surinamese restaurants, many of which are small takeout joints. Asian restaurants are especially dense in the Red Light District, with offerings ranging from Cantonese roast duck to Thai curries. De Pijp is home to several Middle Eastern eateries, and the Jordaan is known for its Italian cafés.

HIGHLIGHTS

- **BEST SEAFOOD IN THE CITY:** Whether you're a fan of ceviche, fish-and-chips, or oysters, you'll find the most delicious version at **The Seafood Bar** (page 73).
- **BEST BURGERS:** Burgers are a big deal in Amsterdam—and the place that does them best is **Cannibale Royale** (page 74).
- **BEST DIM SUM EXPERIENCE:** Immerse yourself in the seemingly endless baskets of dumplings, meat-filled buns, and more at **Oriental City** (page 77).
- **BEST FOR DATE NIGHT:** Cozy **Cafe Bern** is the perfect setting for a romantic night out, complete with the best fondue (page 77).
- **BEST BAKED GOODS:** Head to **De Bakkerswinkel** for freshly baked pastries, breads with homemade jam, and cakes (page 78).
- **MOST AMAZING RIBS:** The mouthwatering aroma of grilled meat wafting from **Café de Klos** is a preview of their flavorful pork ribs (page 81).
- **MOST CHARMING BREAKFAST:** Soak up the nostalgic ambience at **The Pancake Bakery,** set inside a historic canalside warehouse (page 84).
- **BEST CONTEMPORARY INDONESIAN: Blauw** is a modern update of the city's many Indonesian joints, offering family recipes in a sleek setting (page 86).
- **MOST AUTHENTIC ETHIOPIAN CUISINE:** Amsterdammers love **Lalibela** for its real-deal Ethiopian dishes and its wine, which comes from Ethiopia's Rift Valley (page 88).
- **BEST PLACE FOR SURINAMESE: Warung Spang Makandra** has the most flavorful Surinamese dishes, so it's a great place to try this cuisine for the first time (page 91).
- **MOST UPSCALE SUSHI:** Spend an evening at **Izakaya** for sashimi and sushi rolls in an edgy, modern setting (page 92).
- **BEST CHEF'S MENU:** Enjoy seven courses of fine French cuisine at **Daalder** (page 96).
- **BEST SPLURGE:** Savor a multicourse meal at **Gebr. Hartering,** featuring creative and innovative dishes (page 101).

PRICE KEY

$	Entrées less than €15
$$	Entrées €15-25
$$$	Entrées more than €25

Old Center

DUTCH

D'Vijff Vlieghen $$$

The lavishly decorated dining area of this traditional Dutch restaurant stretches across five 17th-century canal houses full of stained glass, antique wood furnishings, and flowers. Each room has its own theme: The Breitner Room has authentic Breitner oil paintings and the Rembrandt Room has real etchings by the Dutch artist. The restaurant serves a nightly three-course seasonal menu for a set price on its white cloth-covered tables. Mains are Dutch dishes, like pan-fried halibut and braised beef with bay leaf gravy. The restaurant's library of guest books is shelved around the rooms, signed by celebrities like Walt Disney and Franklin D. Roosevelt.

MAP 1: Spuistraat 294-302, tel. 020/530-4060, www.vijffvlieghen.nl; 6pm-10pm daily

Haese Claes $$

From the Delft plates decorating the walls to the exposed brick and wooden beam interior, Haese Claes drips with authenticity throughout its three-story space. The 300-person capacity is almost always maxed out, mostly with passengers of bus tours looking for a traditional Dutch meal. Coming here, with the smells of herbs and horseradish, feels like walking into an old dining hall. Loaves of brown bread are served on cutting boards, preceding local specialties of meat, fish, potatoes, cream sauces, and seasonal vegetables. Flavors are

Haese Claes

tame, but service is speedy. As this is a known tourist destination, beware of pickpockets.

MAP 1: Spuistraat 273-275, tel. 020/624-9998, www.haesjeclaes.nl; noon-midnight daily

Van Kerkwijk $$

This modest, simple-looking restaurant is tucked away on a quiet alley just behind Dam Square. Two sisters opened the spot in 1998 to serve up large Dutch meals with a tasty twist. There is no printed menu, so servers take time to explain the day's dishes. For lunch, try the Indonesian meatloaf or mackerel mousse salad with homemade horseradish. Dinner ranges from juicy chicken satay to steak on goat cheese with strawberry sauce. The owners' mother makes the dessert: The pear cake with whipped sour cream is a must. Though busy, the staff are friendly and attentive. Reservations are not accepted.

MAP 1: Nes 41, tel. 020/620-3316, www.caferestaurantvankerkwijk.nl; 11am-1am daily

SEAFOOD

✪ The Seafood Bar $$$

This top seafood restaurant is on Spui Square in a big and bright corner building with white marble columns, tiled flooring, and contemporary lighting. The open kitchen is huge, confined only by the cases that show off the catch of the day. Although the fish-and-chips here are killer, try the ceviche, crab cakes, or oysters. Dinners range from king crab to a chef's choice from the grill. Worldly white wines, from Italian pinot grigio to New Zealand chardonnay, are available. Reservations are suggested.

MAP 1: Spui 15, tel. 020/233-7452, www.theseafoodbar.nl; noon-10pm daily

Lucius $$$

This is a small, quaint, and romantic option for an intimate night at a long-standing local's choice. Some of Lucius's staff has been working here since the restaurant opened in 1975. The style is simple, clean, and consistent, from the long, elegant saltwater aquarium to the seafood menu. Lucius prides itself on its quality fresh fish made any way you like it—pan-fried, grilled, or poached. The soft taco with king prawns is a great starter. Mains range from blackened halibut to flounder braised in fish velouté sauce with shrimp.

MAP 1: Spuistraat 247, tel. 020/624-1831, www.lucius.nl; 5pm-midnight daily

INDONESIAN

Kantjil & De Tijger $$

Remnants of the Netherlands' colonial past can be found in the food at this Indonesian hot spot. The large restaurant brings in big groups, mostly Hollanders but also foreigners. The large and budget-friendly menu can be overwhelming. Try the *rijsttafel* (literally, rice table), a series of small portions of side dishes. The satay meats and spicy sambal sauce plates are also delicious. Newbies to Indonesian spice will like the mild approach here, which embraces flavor, with notes of coconut, peanut, cilantro, ginger, and lemongrass.

MAP 1: Spuistraat 291-293, tel. 020/620-0994, www.kantjil.nl; noon-11pm daily

GASTROPUBS

Hoppy Days $

Hoppy Days is a gastropub focused on Italian microbrews. The somewhat hidden corner location rarely sees a full house, which makes it a great find for a few rounds and dinner with large groups. Exposed brick walls and colorful pop art give things a fresh tavern feel. The menu includes classic dishes like fish-and-chips and pork shoulder slow-cooked in beer and applesauce. Wash it down with one of the microbrews from Turin, Milan, or Lazio, each of which is poured in a signature glass.

MAP 1: Koggestraat 1A, tel. 064/673-5212, www.hoppydays.nl; 5pm-1am Sun.-Thurs., 4pm-3am Fri.-Sat.

BREWPUBS

Bierfabriek $$

Bierfabriek (beer factory) is known for its centerpieces of beer taps on the tables, rotisserie chicken on long spits, and peanut shells on the floor. The home-brewed pilsners, ruby ales, and dark porters are served in frosty mugs. Burlap sacks of peanuts hang waist high on the walls, while copper brewing kettles and steel vats decorate the front and back rooms. Go for the BBQ farm chicken with a home-brewed mug of ruby Rosso. Businesspeople, couples, and friends come here for the trendy American-style layout and atmosphere.

MAP 1: Rokin 75, tel. 020/528-9910, www.bierfabriek.com; 3pm-1am Mon.-Thurs., 3pm-2am Fri., 1pm-2am Sat., 1pm-midnight Sun.

BURGERS

✪ Cannibale Royale $$

Welcome to the late-night tavern that serves some of the best burgers around. Aiming to look like a scene from an American horror flick, the place has photos of criminals from the 1920s on the wall, high wooden chairs and tables, and old dolls hanging from the ceiling. The effect is a little creepy, but it's easily overlooked when the food arrives. The house special is Le Cannibale Royale, a half-pound beef patty topped with sauerkraut, English cheddar, roasted pulled pork, fried onions, and bourbon barbecue sauce. The burgers are thick, juicy, and grilled to perfection. Choose from sides like Waldorf salad or baked potatoes. The full bar offers traditional cocktails and a beer list featuring the house blond.

MAP 1: Handboogstraat 17, tel. 020/233-7160, www.cannibaleroyale.nl; 6pm-3am Sun.-Thurs., 6pm-4am Fri.-Sat.

BREAKFAST AND BRUNCH

Upstairs Pannenkoeken $

This tiny nook of a Dutch pancake house has been the smallest restaurant in Europe since 1962. It feels like eating in the cook's house with 10 of your friends, and it makes the pancakes look massive. People wait outside to be called from the upstairs window. Once up the narrow, carpeted stairs, you'll be seated at one of four tables. Over 100 teapots hang from the ceiling, and the cook mixes pancake batter in the tiny kitchen. It doesn't get cozier than this.

MAP 1: Grimburgwal 2, tel. 020/626-5603, www.upstairspannenkoeken.nl; noon-6pm Tues.-Sat., noon-5pm Sun.

CAFÉS AND BISTROS

Stadspaleis $

This happy yellow cottage looks like it was dropped on the sidewalk by a tornado. Once an old police station, this spot houses a homey lunch café with a small garden and an organic menu. The place is run by a friendly and easygoing family. The inside features a small kitchen with communal cushioned benches and small handbuilt tables. The seasonal menu never strays far from soups, salads, and sandwiches. Try the homemade marinated chicken or the Vegan Dream (grilled vegetables on hummus). The owner recommends the burgers, claiming his butcher's meat is hard to beat.

MAP 1: Nieuwezijds Voorburgwal 277, tel. 020/625-6542, www.stadspaleis.com; 11am-7pm daily

BELGIAN FRIES

Vlaams Friteshuis Vleminck $

Since 1957 this small *frites* (fries) shop has scooped cones of piping hot fried potato to a line of tourists and locals. Over 25 sauces can be smeared on top, from classic Belgian *andalous* (tomato, garlic, peppers, and mayo) to yellow curry and spicy green pepper sauce. An Amsterdam favorite is the *oorlog*, half mayonnaise and half peanut satay sauce with diced onions on top. Fries are served to go with a small fork.

MAP 1: Voetboogstraat 33, tel. 065/478-7000, www.vleminckxdesausmeester.nl; noon-7pm Sun.-Mon., 11am-7pm Tues.-Wed. and Fri.-Sat., 11am-8pm Thurs.

BAKERIES

Gebroeders Niemeijer $

This traditional French bakery, started by brothers Marco and Issa Niemeijer, sells handmade breads and pastries with simple and natural ingredients. The brick oven downstairs is visible from the entrance and inside it's usually bustling. The one-room space is airy and bright with a high, art deco ceiling and an open floor plan. Don't be afraid to wave down a server to order. Get in before noon to try the *petit dejeuner extra*, an ideal sampling of fresh breads, homemade jam and butter, fresh cheese and ham, coffee, and orange juice. For lunch, try the high tea or walnut bread with homemade fig jam. Take a macaron to go.

MAP 1: Nieuwendijk 35, tel. 020/707-6752, www.gebrniemeijer.com; 8:15am-5:30pm Tues.-Fri., 8:30am-5pm Sat., 9am-5pm Sun.

baked delights at De Laatste Kruimel

De Laatste Kruimel $

This bustling bakery and sandwich shop is a tiny slice of French bliss in the heart of Amsterdam. Brimming with sweet and savory delights, the menu ranges from half a dozen quiches to scones, muffins, and pies. The long blackboard inside lists savory sandwiches like tuna melts and turkey with truffle mayo on white, brown, or spelt bread. It feels like eating inside a baker's kitchen, from the bags of flour to the baker sharing his workspace with patrons. The counters are made from wooden pallets, lamps are upside-down colanders, and the chairs are crates with floral cushions on top. Try to grab a sunny spot at the small balcony in the back that overlooks the canal.

MAP 1: Langebrugsteeg 4, tel. 020/423-0499, www.delaatstekruimel.nl; 8am-8pm Mon.-Sat., 9am-8pm Sun.

Van Stapele $

Step inside this tiny bakery and breathe in the smell of sugar and cocoa. The antique wooden furnishings, patched window panes, and crystal chandelier give this shop a 17th-century feel. Van Stapele bakes the best chocolate cookie in Amsterdam—and that's the only item they sell. Dough made with Valrhona cocoa is injected with a gooey white chocolate. The cookies are crispy on the outside, but dense and soft inside. They are served warm and made twice an hour. The shop also sells coffee or tea to go.

MAP 1: Heisteeg 4, tel. 065/424-1497, www.vanstapele.com; noon-6pm Mon., 10am-6pm Tues.-Fri., 11am-6pm Sat.-Sun.

Red Light District and Nieuwmarkt

Map 2

DUTCH

Dwaze Zaken $

Around the corner from the north end of Warmoesstraat sits this bright art-deco-style café with large windows and a sunny atmosphere. The reasonably priced Dutch menu offers organic, fair trade, and locally produced dishes, like Amsterdam-smoked sausage, portobello burgers, or baked goat cheese with walnuts and red onions on sourdough. This safe bet is surrounded by tourist cafés and is close to Amsterdam Centraal Station.

MAP 2: Prins Hendrikkade 50, tel. 020/612-4175, www.dwazezaken.nl; 9am-midnight Mon.-Sat., 9am-5:30pm Sun.

Skek $

Blending rustic charm and a cozy atmosphere, Skek is a student-run brown bar and restaurant catering to a laid-back and modern crowd of locals, creative professionals, and internationals. Dine on gourmet burgers and hearty stews made in a slow food kitchen. In the lounge and bar, a small corner stage with an old piano hosts acoustic acts and open mic nights. Skek is close to Centraal Station.

MAP 2: Zeedijk 4-8, tel. 020/427-0551, http://skek.nl; noon-1am Sun. and Tues.-Thurs., 4pm-1am Mon., noon-3am Fri.-Sat.

DUTCH-EUROPEAN FUSION

Lastage $$$

An interesting twist on fine dining, Lastage is a Michelin-starred fusion of French and seasonal local cuisine. The intimate and tranquil setting is complete with a canal view and candlelit tables. The knowledgeable staff explain the courses available from the 12-item menu, from cheeses and onion soup to mains like grilled sole and smoked eel from the North Sea. Reservations are required.

MAP 2: Geldersekade 29, tel. 020/737-0811, www.restaurantlastage.nl; 6:30pm-9:30pm Tues.-Sun.

Blauw aan de Wal $$$

Blauw aan de Wal is tucked away in a 17th-century warehouse identified by a blue-and-white sign. Wooden beams and exposed brick imbue a historic appeal, while chefs create two- and four-course meals that fuse Dutch, French, and Mediterranean flavors. From veal tongue to risotto, the seasonal menu changes twice a month. A terrace wraps around the tranquil courtyard to complement the relaxed dining space. Reservations are suggested.

MAP 2: Oudezijds Achterburgwal 99, tel. 020/330-2257, www.blauwaandewal.com; 6pm-11:30pm Tues.-Sat.

Hemelse Modder $$$

This busy but calm place is named after its most famous dessert, *hemelse modder* (literally, heavenly mud; chocolate pudding), and has been a local favorite for years—it even publishes its own cookbook. The ingredients used in the restaurant's dishes are Dutch, but the recipes are a blend of French, German, and Scandinavian. Aromas of the day's specialties fill the air: rillettes of oxtail, veal cheek, mackerel, or crab bisque. Service is slow but very friendly, so plan for a relaxing evening enjoying the superb and unpretentious wine collection and intimate ambience, all while overlooking a charming canal. The restaurant takes up two old houses, with a simple wooden floor, fresh blue walls, and desk lamps and tabletop candles for lighting. A back terrace is open in summer. Reservations are suggested.

MAP 2: Oude Waal 11, tel. 020/624-3203, www.hemelsemodder.nl; 6pm-10pm daily

CHINESE

New King $$

Rows of whole crispy duck hang in the front windows of Zeedijk's New King, a busy, multiroom Mandarin Chinese restaurant. Diners, mostly locals, start with crispy wontons and shrimp dumpling soup, then move on to specialties like crispy pork or flambéed lamb chops. Wooden walls with bamboo prints and a small gong provide calm to counteract the hectic vibe. Expect a wait on weekends.

MAP 2: Zeedijk 115-117, tel. 020/625-2180, www.newking.nl; 11am-10:30pm daily

✪ Oriental City $

This is Amsterdam's top spot for dim sum. Dig into dumplings, duck feet in oyster sauce, crispy bean curd rolls, and roast pork buns. Servers move swiftly around the dozens of tables, offering Cantonese dishes from Hong Kong chefs. Roasted meats and steamed or fried dishes are the typical dinner staples. Enjoy the view of a bustling street corner from the large, floor-to-ceiling windows. Reservations are suggested.

MAP 2: Oudezijds Voorburgwal 177-179, tel. 020/626-8352, www.oriental-city.com; 11:30am-10:30pm daily

THAI

Bird Thais $$

Quick service and filling meals have earned Bird Thais a top recommendation for dining out on Zeedijk. Generous servings of traditional Thai food range from thick red and green curry dishes to crispy baked fish and saucy pad Thai. The large restaurant has three levels of seating with a typical Thai decor of gleaming statues and tropical plants. It's great for groups, but come early on weekends to avoid the lines. Across the street is the restaurant's takeout outpost.

MAP 2: Zeedijk 72-74, tel. 020/620-1442, www.thai-bird.nl; noon-11pm daily

FONDUE

✪ Cafe Bern $$

This restaurant is a hidden pleasure on Nieuwmarkt, offering a soothing warmth that only a simmering Swiss fondue, entrecôte steak, and glass of house wine can evoke. A peek through

The fondue flame is ready at Cafe Bern.

the fogged white-framed windows reveals a typical Dutch café brimming with comfort. Inside, the small handwritten menu offers quality over quantity. The usual order for two is a mixture of meat and cheese, and first-timers will appreciate the brief how-to from their server. The romantic tones, antique decor, and friendly staff make it easy to spend hours soaking in the smell and taste of *fromage*. Reservations are suggested.

MAP 2: Nieuwmarkt 9, tel. 020/622-0034, www.cafebern.com; 4pm-1am daily (kitchen 6pm-11pm daily)

CAFÉS AND BISTROS

Latei $

A snug, kitschy café, Latei serves up wholesome egg-on-toast breakfasts and homemade apple pie. All the fixtures and knickknacks are for sale, from the china plates piled high to the old-school lamps and endless shelves of mugs. Locals come for a late-morning bite from the organic menu.

MAP 2: Zeedijk 143, tel. 020/625-7485, www.latei.net; 8am-6pm Mon.-Wed., 8am-10pm Thurs.-Fri., 9am-10pm Sat., 10am-6pm Sun.

BAKERIES

✪ De Bakkerswinkel $

De Bakkerswinkel is a cheerful bakery stocked with fresh pastries and sandwiches on rye, sourdough, gingerbread, and more. Scones with homemade jams and fresh orange juice are a popular order. Lunch brings quiche and hot rolls from the oven, stuffed with Dutch favorites like mackerel or caponata. Service is on the relaxed side, and the space is big enough for groups and great for families.

MAP 2: Warmoesstraat 69, tel. 020/489-8000, www.debakkerswinkel.com; 8am-5:30pm Mon.-Fri., 9am-6pm Sat.-Sun.

Betty Blue $

Betty Blue is a large and modern patisserie/café in a long-standing building near Nieuwmarkt. The café offers chai lattes and coffee alongside red velvet Bundt cake, pastries, and light entrées. Baked goods and chocolate truffles come fresh from the ovens and the chocolate machine on display downstairs. The retro furniture, potted plants, and colorful mounted cardboard animals conjure a vibe of a chic, feminine clubhouse. Try the selection of spongy and decadent éclairs, like raspberry, passion fruit and lime, or rosewater and mint. High tea reservations are available. The café doubles as a boutique, selling T-shirts and tote bags.

MAP 2: Snoekjessteeg 1-3, tel. 020/810-0924, www.bettyblueamsterdam.nl; 8:30am-6pm Mon.-Sat., 9:30am-6pm Sun.

Metropolitan $

Go cuckoo for cacao at this bakery and chocolatier. Everything, including the chocolate espresso and chocolate beer, is made from imported Dominican cacao beans that are peeled, roasted, and crushed in the store. And all of it satisfies the chocoholic, from milk chocolate pistachio cake, Nutella pastries, and truffles of chocolate-dipped whipped cream to cocoa-based lotions and soaps.

MAP 2: Warmoesstraat 135, tel. 020/330-1955, www.metropolitandeli.nl; 9am-10pm daily

COFFEE AND TEA

Quartier Putain $

Quartier Putain is a funky coffee bar serving espresso drinks with an upstairs lounge showcasing weekly local talent like musicians and writers. The lounge delivers a view of the Oude Kerk, and the vintage seven-inch jukebox still plays tunes. Outside, a picnic table offers a view of two busy areas.

MAP 2: Oudekerksplein 4, tel. 020/895-0162, www.quartierputain.nl; 8am-6pm Mon.-Fri., 10am-6pm Sat.-Sun.

Canal Belt South — Map 3

DUTCH-FRENCH FUSION

Breitner $$$

The founder of Amsterdam impressionism would take delight in the leisurely fine dining at this eponymous restaurant, as well as the spectacular city views of the Amstel River and Blauwbrug. Well-to-do locals and visitors come to experience a modern Mediterranean fusion of seasonal European elements over red carpet and white tablecloths. Choose between a four-course meal (€45), à la carte starters like grilled fish with asparagus and marinated mushrooms, and mains like baked Ibérico pig stewed with red onions. Winter offers venison sautéed with red cabbage and apple, and haddock with langoustine. Don't forget to order the crème brûlée.

MAP 3: Amstel 212, tel. 020/627-7879, www.restaurant-breitner.nl; 6pm-10pm Tues.-Sat.

SEAFOOD

RED $$$

Immaculate surf and turf awaits in this narrow, dark restaurant with emerald walls and zebra-print rugs. A giant mural of a woman on the ceiling watches as servers take orders of steak and Canadian lobster, served with fries and salad. While the appetizers are limited to caviar, the popular dessert menu is extensive. RED is the ideal spot for a classy night out; the lengthy international wine list tempts with a few spendy bottles. Reservations are suggested.

MAP 3: Keizersgracht 594, tel. 020/320-1824, www.restaurantred.nl; noon-3pm and 6pm-11pm Mon.-Wed., noon-3pm and 6pm-midnight Thurs.-Sat., noon-3pm and 5pm-11pm Sun.

INDONESIAN

Tempo Doeloe $$$

Tempo Doeloe is famous in the city for bringing Indonesian cuisine to a fine dining level with its white linen tablecloths and antique wooden furnishings. The *rijsttafel* (literally, rice table) is a colorful array of six fresh and spicy small plates, like beef *rendang*, tofu, coconut veggies, and sautéed green beans. Smells of curry, sesame oil, and coconut sauce swirl around the two-person tables and paintings on the walls. Venture beyond the usual samplers and go for the mains, but be sure to voice your preferred spice level (mild, medium, or very spicy). For dessert, cool down with a fresh fruit platter served with ice cream.

MAP 3: Utrechtsestraat 75, tel. 020/625-6718, www.tempodoeloerestaurant.nl; 6pm-midnight Mon.-Sat. (kitchen closes 10:30pm)

SPANISH TAPAS

Pata Negra $$

The original of three Pata Negra locations sits stout and cozy like a slice of Seville in Amsterdam. Tile mosaics of Spanish conquistadors and bullfighters adorn the walls, while fairy lights decorate brick walls with scratched-in hearts and initials. Bundles of dried pepper, strings of garlic, and legs of ham hang above the bar and counters. Nearly 50 tapas (€4-7 each) fill the menu. Skip the ordinary *patatas bravas* (french fries) and opt for the shrimp, squid, empanadas, or ceviche samplers. The pitchers of sangria keep groups here long into the evening. While the other two locations have their perks, this location is always buzzing.

MAP 3: Utrechtsestraat 124, tel. 020/422-6250, www.pata-negra.nl; noon-11:30pm daily

ITALIAN

Segugio $$$

Romantic, cute, and with innumerable flavorful dishes, Segugio will satisfy any gastronome. The elegant interior is accented by dark wood floors, exposed ceiling beams, and spotless white linen. Almost every item is made in house, from the pasta to the pastries. Let their seasonal menu guide you to culinary specials like ricotta gnocchi with arugula and walnuts or goose breast with shallots and pomegranate. The menu is laid out in the traditional Italian order of antipasti, *paste* (pasta), *secondi* (second course/meat dishes), and *dolci* (sweets). The wine list is divided into 20 Italian regions, with at least a dozen bottles under each section. Go for the risotto of the day—it's some of the best in town. Reservations are suggested.

MAP 3: Utrechtsestraat 96, tel. 020/330-1503, www.segugio.nl; 6pm-11pm Mon.-Sat.

Ponte Arcari $$

Ponte Arcari is a cozy and cherished bistro with an Italian chef whose patience and passion can be enjoyed with every plate of pasta and fish of the day. The smell of basil and oregano surround the cozy tables. Away from the crowds, enjoy fresh caprese salad, antipasti, linguini with clams, and truffle ravioli. Get a seat by the candlelit windows, start with the house Italian red, and take in the canal scenery, which is especially delightful at sunset.

MAP 3: Herengracht 534, tel. 020/625-0853; noon-10pm Tues.-Fri., 5pm-10:30pm Sat.-Mon.

Uliveto $

A bright corner trattoria frequented by locals, Uliveto is a spacious and modern find somewhere between a Mediterranean deli and an Italian takeout restaurant. Canisters of olive oil rest on shelves as freshly made casseroles and authentic dishes are sliced, served, and packed for takeout. Match your meal with Italian wine, fresh espresso, or juice. Options usually include chicken, veal, risotto, pasta, and a vegetarian dish. Spices change with the season. Uliveto also sells olive oil by the half and full liter, as well as balsamic vinegars and other products imported from Italy. Take your food to go or enjoy it at the communal wooden table.

MAP 3: Weteringschans 118, tel. 020/423-0099, www.uliveto.net; 11am-8pm Mon.-Fri., noon-6pm Sat.

MEDITERRANEAN

Van Vlaanderen $$$

The French-Mediterranean plates at Van Vlaanderen are classic and chic, like the restaurant's tranquil waterside terrace that locals have tried to keep to themselves. The terrace is matched by a sunny and spacious interior. The menu offers 2-5 courses, with options like beef entrecôte or a half lobster with avocado, orange, and tomato. Venison and stewed veal are top winter choices. Opt for one of their unique desserts, like tarte tatin with goat yogurt and almond milk. And don't forget the wine: The sommelier can recite their lengthy wine list, featuring bottles from Bordeaux to South Africa.

MAP 3: Weteringschans 175, tel. 020/622-8292, www.restaurant-vanvlaanderen.nl; noon-3pm and 6pm-10pm Tues.-Fri., 6pm-10pm Sat.

BREWPUBS

✪ Café de Klos $$

The best ribs in town are in this dusty and dark tavern that's been a city staple for decades. The servers and bartenders, with their odd senses of humor, are genuine souls, so the best seats are at the U-shaped bar that takes up most of the restaurant. Pork ribs, steak, and chicken sizzle on the grill in the open kitchen, while baked potatoes wrapped in foil cook on the side. Ribs are served with raw onions, two sauces, and a lightly dressed coleslaw—the best meaty meal in town. Pair it with red wine or draft beer. The usual wait is about an hour, which you can pass easily at the bar across the street, Café Genootschap der Geneugten (a server will come fetch you when your table is ready). For a minimal wait, come before 6pm or after 10pm.

MAP 3: Kerkstraat 41-43, tel. 020/625-3730; 4pm-11:30pm daily

Coco's Outback $

After a night out on the party squares, sometimes a greasy meal is just what the doctor ordered. Enter Coco's Outback, an Aussie pub serving up burgers, wings, and beer. There isn't any other place on Rembrandtplein that can match the hearty kangaroo burgers, dense beef patties, meat and Guinness pies, and mounds of nachos. International sports games play on flat screen TVs, with a chalkboard announcing the daily broadcasts. Daily happy hour specials offer buckets of beer bottles in addition to discounts on food. It has a classic sports pub vibe with a pool table and worn-looking leather sofas.

MAP 3: Thorbeckeplein 8-12, tel. 020/627-2423, www.cocosoutback.com; noon-3am Sun.-Thurs., 11am-4am Fri.-Sat.

BREAKFAST AND BRUNCH

De Sneeker Pan $

De Sneeker Pan won't turn foodie heads, but the wide range of breakfast and lunch options at affordable prices are satisfying in this spot just off the busy Leidsestraat. The bright and airy two-story café, adorned with still life paintings and homey chairs, mostly attracts tourists. A long list of egg and pancake dishes are available until 5pm daily, from bacon, mushrooms, and onions omelets to *uitsmijters* (fried eggs on toast with toppings of your choice). Pancake toppings range from sweet raisins to savory ham.

MAP 3: Kerkstraat 48, tel. 020/622-3660, www.restaurantdesneekerpan.nl; 9am-10pm daily

CAFÉS AND BISTROS

Brasserie Nel $$

Want a breather over a drink or a small bite with a view? Café Nel's picket fence terrace stretches out to a peaceful cobblestone square, offering a picturesque respite on a sunny afternoon. Somewhat apart from the tourist paths and nestled under the historic Amstelkerk, Café Nel serves lunch items like pulled duck with barbecue sauce and red peppers and traditional Dutch dinner picks like mussels or *stamppot*, a mashed potato dish mixed with rib eye and sauerkraut. Come after 4pm for happy hour and join the locals diving into crisp beers and fried *bitterballen* (breaded meat snacks) at this neighborhood hidden gem.

MAP 3: Amstelveld 12, tel. 020/626-1199, www.nelamstelveld.nl; 11am-1am Sun.-Thurs., 11am-3am Fri.-Sat.

Lavinia $

Escape the tourist eateries on Leidseplein and find Lavinia, a bright and eco-minded gourmet retreat for breakfast and lunch. Inside, large wooden shelves are filled with decorative boxes, glass jugs, plants, cookbooks, and spice racks. The shop's menu items are locally produced and free from additives, and include French toast and banana bread with roasted almonds, and savory options like mini sourdough pizzas with truffled sour cream and chives. Creative types sip ginger and pear juice at the communal wood tables while enjoying the earthy atmosphere.

MAP 3: Kerkstraat 176, tel. 020/626-1432, www.laviniagoodfood.nl; 8:30am-4pm Mon.-Fri., 9:30am-5pm Sat.-Sun.

Café Kale $

Modern Café Kale's stripped furnishings and open windows are a great setting for lunch on the sunny terrace, after-work drinks, or a weekend lounge under the red awning. This is where nearby residents go for a typical Dutch lunch on the cheap, like cheddar with fig jam or warm ham with tarragon mustard paninis and *uitsmijters* (fried eggs on toast). Cheerful soul and Motown tunes play as servers mingle with regulars. Café Kale is an uncomplicated and affordable find away from the nearby tourist traps.

MAP 3: Weteringschans 267, tel. 020/622-6363, www.cafekale.nl; 10am-1am Sun.-Thurs., 11am-3am Fri.-Sat.

Zuivere Koffie $

Checkered tiles, a tucked-away terrace, hanging fruit baskets, and delicious blueberry shakes are just a few reasons homey Zuivere wins hearts over. This warmly lit nook off trendy Utrechtsestraat holds a few small tables, simple decor, and a little corner kitchen serving up light breakfast and lunch items. Fresh-squeezed orange juice sits beside espresso shots. Be sure to try a slice of the artichoke cheese tart. In the back, the upper deck holds a cozy patio with berry vines and a countryside feel. Zuivere, where French meets Dutch, is authentic and inexpensive.

MAP 3: Utrechtsestraat 39, tel. 020/624-9999; 8am-5pm Mon.-Sat., 9am-5pm Sun.

DELICATESSEN

Loekie $

Step into Loekie and let the helpful staff guide you through the dozens of wheels of cheese and rows of fresh deli meats stuffed into this closet-sized sandwich shop. Loekie's sandwiches are made on fresh French baguettes, with fillings like shrimp and eel, smoked beef with boiled eggs, and smoked salmon with dill and horseradish. Affordable French, Portuguese, and Italian wines are for sale alongside salads, liver pâtés, and more. Look for the red awning off Utrechtsestraat and squeeze on in.

MAP 3: Utrechtsestraat 57, tel. 020/624-3740, www.loekie.net; 9am-6pm Mon.-Tues., 9am-1pm Wed., 9am-5pm Thurs.-Sat.

COFFEE AND TEA

Bocca Coffee $

Bocca Coffee jumps aboard the city's movement toward organic and fair trade coffee by offering fresh-roasted beans imported from Ethiopia, Kenya, and Colombia. This former garage has been transformed into a minimalist coffee bar with an industrial edge. Grab a seat at the bar or table, choose from the simple menu, and watch the expert baristas pull shots, steam milk, and drop knowledge about their beloved beans. Branch out and go for the *cascara,* a tea made from the fruit of the coffee plant, or try the trendy coffee tonic, a combination of cold-brewed coffee and tonic water.

MAP 3: Kerkstraat 96, tel. 032/131-4667, www.bocca.nl; 8am-6pm Mon.-Fri., 9am-6pm Sat.-Sun.

Greenwoods $

This expat hangout is as close as you can get to a modern-day tea house with muffins, scones, and hearty breakfasts. As the first English tearoom to grace Amsterdam, Greenwoods is the place to get extraordinary poached eggs with cottage cheese, avocado, and organic chicken over soda bread. Also popular are open-faced sandwiches piled high with fresh greens, grilled meats, and crumbly cheeses. Greenwoods is a homey place, with earthy green colors and wood decor, tea cups-turned-lights, jars of loose leaf teas, and fresh flowers.

MAP 3: Keizersgracht 465, tel. 020/623-7071, www.greenwoods.eu; 9am-5pm Mon.-Thurs., 9am-6pm Fri.-Sun.

Canal Belt West

Map 4

DUTCH

Struisvogel $$$

Many people walk into Struisvogel because of its charming canalside location. This restaurant is set in a rustic 17th-century kitchen with dark wooden furnishings, warm with candlelight. The friendly staff bustles around the limited seating, in a cozy atmosphere that feels like a local's find. The set, three-course menu, posted on the daily changing blackboard, is a mix of Dutch and French with an emphasis on organic ingredients. Start with pear salad or Dutch shrimp bisque before moving to a main like veal cheek stewed in red wine or roasted pumpkin risotto with sage. Dessert can be a cheese platter or warm apple crumble.

MAP 4: Keizersgracht 312, tel. 020/423-3817, www.restaurantdestruisvogel.nl; 5:30pm-midnight Sun.-Fri., 5pm-midnight Sat.

Bistro Bij Ons $$

This traditional Dutch café, whose name means "with us," is just across from Westerkerk in a cozy basement and serves traditional Dutch soul food. Grab a seat on the canal-side terrace in summer, or sit inside and enjoy the crimson wallpaper, old photographs, and moody red lighting from old chandeliers. The café offers simple, filling, and seasonal recipes that are best at dinner, although they're also open for breakfast and lunch. Go for the Shipper's Delight: split peas, bacon, onions, and pickles, or pan-fried mussels with fries. For dessert, try the Tante Leen (named after a Dutch singer popular in the 1950s)—ice cream with eggnog liqueur and chocolate sauce. Get bold and go for a round of *genever* (Dutch gin) shots. The staff is friendly and the prices are decent, despite the touristy crowd.

MAP 4: Prinsengracht 287, tel. 020/627-9016, www.bistrobijons.nl; 10am-10pm Tues.-Sun.

EURO-INTERNATIONAL

Envy $$$

Envy's narrow and industrial-chic setting offers European fusion meals cooked in an open kitchen. Inspired by Italian delicatessens, Envy seats its guests at one long communal table. Eating here is like sampling creative concepts, rather than feasting on a heavy meal. Watch the chefs spice delicacies with European herbs and cheeses pulled from the small see-through refrigerators that line the walls. The dishes are a circus of flavor, like zucchini risotto, Anjou pigeon with beetroot, or a creamy brill filet. This is a great find for sociable foodies.

MAP 4: Prinsengracht 381, tel. 020/344-6407, www.envy.nl; 6pm-11pm Mon.-Thurs., noon-3pm and 6pm-11pm Fri.-Sun.

FRENCH-BELGIAN

Chez Georges $$$

Chez Georges is a locals' favorite thanks to its heavenly blend of Flemish and French Belgian cuisine. French cooking methods, divine sauces, and tender meats come to play with seasonal and regional dishes like rabbit filet in a béarnaise sauce or prawns poached in white wine and escargot butter. Known for its attentive and wine-savvy staff, the restaurant has intimate warm lighting and white-tableclothed tables staggered elegantly over three floors. Towers of wine bottles lean against the floral wallpaper, cast-iron railings, and wooden trim. Reservations are recommended.

MAP 4: Herenstraat 3, tel. 020/626-3332, www.chez-georges.nl; 6pm-11pm Tues.-Sat.

BREAKFAST AND BRUNCH

✪ The Pancake Bakery $$

There are plenty of pancake houses around Amsterdam, but The Pancake Bakery, set inside a 17th-century canalside warehouse, is a top pick for its creative crepes and nostalgic ambience. The busy café is two floors high, with a cozy vibe that has attracted celebrities Miley Cyrus and Paris Hilton, among others. Pancakes come loaded with toppings like banana, rum, and whipped cream. First-timer visitors should try one of the sweet or savory specialties, like apple cinnamon or cheese and ham. The international selection is for the adventurous eater and includes the Indonesian pancake topped with chicken, onions, mushrooms, leeks, bean sprouts, and prawn crackers with a spicy peanut sauce. After a visit here, you won't look at crepes the same way again. Reservations are suggested.

MAP 4: Prinsengracht 191, tel. 020/625-1333; 9am-9:30pm daily

Koffiehuis De Hoek $

Think of it as more of an old-fashioned coffee shop, with checkered tablecloths, walls decorated with old currency, and pots of coffee simmering in the back. The all-day breakfast options include fried eggs, hearty pancakes, and omelets. Lunch is comprised of cheap and uncomplicated sandwiches, like egg salad and roast beef. Most people come here for the affordable brunch or to warm up with a *koffie verkeerd* (latte) and a slice of homemade *appletaart* (apple pie) or cheesecake with *slagroom* (whipped cream). This spot is cash only.

MAP 4: Prinsengracht 341, tel. 020/625-3872; 8am-5pm Mon.-Fri., 9am-5pm Sat.-Sun.

CAFÉS AND BISTROS

Singel 404 $

This cute canalside sit-down lunch spot is a great find and local favorite for its simple, fresh, and satisfying sandwiches. The inside is cramped but cute, filled with small tables. Singel 404's most buzzworthy items have always been their open-faced sandwiches, including four types of club sandwiches, toasted pita tuna melts, and fried eggs with roast beef and aged cheese. Wash it down with a fresh-pressed orange juice. Noon finds both the café and its terrace packed, so come late morning or after 1:30pm to avoid the rush.

MAP 4: Singel 404, tel. 020/428-0154; 10:30am-7pm daily

SWEETS

Chocolaterie Pompadour $

Welcome to the cutest tearoom and chocolatier in the city. It's impossible to pass under Pompadour's candy cane awning and not ogle the storefront packed with desserts. The adorable shop mimics a vintage tearoom, with elegant blush and brass wallpaper, wooden paneling from 1795, and a small set of marble tabletops. Choose from bonbons, chocolate truffle cake, and quiche, or opt for one of the delicate berry tarts or candied oranges. Add a cup of Catalan coffee and soak in the cuteness.

MAP 4: Huidenstraat 12, tel. 020/623-9554, www.pompadour-amsterdam.nl; 10am-6pm Mon.-Fri., 9am-6pm Sat., noon-6pm Sun.

COFFEE AND TEA

Screaming Beans $

From the pour-over setup to the high-tech AeroPress brewer, the coffee quality is what makes modern Screaming Beans such a hit. Their mild and fruity Arabica bean comes mostly from small coffee farms near Mount Kilimanjaro in Africa. They also serve a few items of food: Breakfast includes scrambled eggs and fresh baked goods; lunch is soft cheeses, smoked meats, and homemade spreads on thick slices of bread. Order your flat white (a smaller version of a latte) with a slice of lemon meringue pie.

MAP 4: Hartenstraat 12, tel. 020/626-0966, www.screamingbeans.nl; 8am-5pm Mon.-Fri., 9am-5pm Sat., 10am-5pm Sun.

Museumplein

DUTCH

Restaurant Happ-Hmm $$

This neighborhood diner, located off a quiet residential street next to Museumplein, offers hearty Dutch comfort food. Not much has changed at Happ-Hmm since its opening in 1935, but this consistency is what attracts its loyal customers. The menu emphasizes meat, potatoes, and boiled greens in simple but fun dishes like chicken cordon bleu or butter-braised beef and seasonal veggies. Dessert is ice cream with whipped cream and a choice of sweet sauces. The friendly staff buzzes about the warmly lit space, serving customers seated at small wooden tables.

MAP 5: Eerste Helmersstraat 33, tel. 020/618-1884, www.hap-hmm.nl; 5pm-9:15pm Mon.-Fri.

La Falote $$

Under the green awning off Van Baerlestraat is a neighborhood tavern serving traditional Dutch food in a small rustic setting. A mix of tourists and older locals sit at plaid-tableclothed tables, deciding between the daily specials on the blackboard. From the ingredients to the preparation, La Falote is as Dutch as it gets, from rib eye and saucy veal to boiled potatoes with rhubarb sauce, and garlic-buttered and steamed vegetables. A closer look at the decor reveals that every photo, thank you letter, and trinket mounted on the wall has a tear-jerking story to accompany it. Just ask Peter, the sociable owner livening up the place with conversation and spontaneous accordion performances. The kitchen, which Peter renovated himself, is run by an efficient staff of young Dutch residents. This is a great place to get cozy with a plate of comfort food; it's cash only.

MAP 5: Roelof Hartstraat 26, tel. 020/662-5454, www.lafalote.nl; 3pm-9pm Mon.-Fri., 5pm-9pm Sat.

INDONESIAN

✪ Blauw $$$

Welcome to one of the freshest and most contemporary Indonesian spots in the city. Unlike the usual mom-and-pop joints, Blauw offers sleek modern dining with extras, like a balcony and in-table hot plates to keep dishes warm, all while serving recipes passed down through generations. One wall features a giant black and white portrait of an Indonesian family during Dutch colonial times. While the wines are delightful and the mains explode with taste, the *rijsttafel* (literally, rice table), an assortment of spicy and savory dishes, wows diners with over a dozen items. The spectacle of stewed meats and vegetables in exotic sauces can be meaty, seafood-centric,

rijsttafel, an Indonesian sampler platter

or vegetarian-friendly with tofu and tempeh options.

MAP 5: Amstelveenseweg 158-160, tel. 020/675-5000, www.restaurantblauw.nl; 6pm-10pm Mon.-Wed., 6pm-10:30pm Thurs.-Fri., 5pm-10:30pm Sat., 5pm-10pm Sun.

Kartika $$

A top pick with locals and travelers because of its friendly prices, extra spices, and generous servings, Kartika is a solid choice for Indonesian food on Overtoom. The tight quarters encourage sharing tables, which are scattered between the decorative Javanese tribal decorations. The authentic and cozy vibe is friendly, and it's usually packed. The large *rijsttafel* (rice table, in English) offers an array of Indonesian tapas. Order an Indonesian beer, snack on some rice, and let the smells of coconut, saffron, and sambal tickle your taste buds.

MAP 5: Overtoom 68, tel. 020/618-1879, www.restaurantkartika.com; 5pm-10:30pm daily

FRENCH

Brasserie van Baerle $$$

As one of the more posh but reasonably priced restaurants in the area, Van Baerle is a sophisticated Dutch take on a French brasserie. The long-established eatery is in a historic house with a small but classy art nouveau dining room and a peaceful garden patio. An experienced sommelier pairs wines with the menu of fish and meat. Choose between two or three courses, with chic options like shrimp croquettes with shallot mayonnaise or classic entrecôte with green walnut salad.

MAP 5: Van Baerlestraat 158, tel. 020/679-1532, www.brasserievanbaerle.nl; noon-11pm Tues.-Fri. and Sun., 5:30pm-11pm Mon. and Sat.

L'Entrecôte et les Dames $$$

Dinner here is either entrecôte steak or sole fish, and your second helping is on the house. This modern steakhouse impresses patrons with competitive prices and a less touristy feel compared to the surrounding restaurants. Wine is served by the carafe. Choices are more numerous come dessert, from crème brûlée to crepes made with Grand Marnier. Lunch offers a choice of the popular steak sandwich or steak tartar. The restaurant's two rooms are full of simple white-tableclothed tables, with black and white photos on the walls and some balcony seating. Reservations are not accepted for groups smaller than seven, so come before 9pm, when the Concertgebouw crowd across the street starts to converge here.

MAP 5: Van Baerlestraat 47-49, tel. 020/679-8888, www.entrecote-et-les-dames.nl; noon-3pm and 5:30pm-midnight daily

Le Garage $$$

See and be seen at this high-end Dutch-French bistro with its flair for attentive service and upbeat vibe. The open kitchen is staffed with half a dozen bustling chefs preparing entrées like ceviche, baked foie gras, escargot, and rib-eye steak. The two owners are local celebrities: Marie Cecile Thijs is a well-known chef and television personality, and Erwin Walthaus is an award-winning sommelier. The dining room highlights an enormous floral arrangement, with white tablecloth settings and rose-colored wraparound booths. Mirrored walls enhance the spotlights circling on the low ceiling. The loyal customer base, which has been returning to Le Garage since it opened in 1985, appreciates the upscale look and feel.

MAP 5: Ruysdaelstraat 54-56, tel. 020/679-7176, www.restaurantlegarage.nl; noon-2pm and 6pm-11pm Mon.-Fri., 6pm-11pm Sat.-Sun.

ITALIAN

De Italiaan $$

De Italiaan is a classic corner café where everything is an authentic slice of Italy, from the truffles to the fluffy mozzarella. Pizzas are large and topped with fresh cheeses, thinly sliced meats, fresh arugula, and bubbling tomato sauce. The antipasti are served on wood boards, and the homemade desserts range from strawberries and cream with pistachio to tiramisu. The place is big and casual with floor-to-ceiling windows and a relaxing terrace. Kick back under the red awning on this quiet corner and end the day with a filling meal over a beer. Reservations are suggested.

MAP 5: Bosboom Toussaintstraat 29, tel. 020/683-6854, www.deitaliaan.com; 5:30pm-10pm daily

MEDITERRANEAN

La Pompa $

La Pompa is just off Museumplein, offering big Mediterranean lunches and dinners in a setting less touristy than its neighbors. The airy but small interior has three staggered levels, with wide windows and a wraparound terrace. A friendly and patient staff buzzes around the small tables, refilling glasses of sangria and afternoon coffees. Dive into a Greek salad with grilled eggplant, bell peppers, feta cheese, and kalamata olives, or go for the seafood pasta or tapas, like the lamb chops or fried clams with aioli.

MAP 5: Willemsparkweg 6, tel. 020/662-6206, www.pompa-restaurant.nl; 9am-10pm daily

GREEK

I Kriti $$

This quirky Crete and Greek kitchen off Van Baerlestraat draws a local crowd who love its large portions and authentic Greek dishes. Traditional food, music, and decorations fill the space. Bright blue and pink hues with lanterns and art on the walls aim for an ancient Greek theme. The friendly owners are fond of playing Greek music and socializing with patrons. Go for the large Greek salad, moussaka, or hearty stews served in terracotta bowls. Wash the meal down with a glass or two of the house red.

MAP 5: Balthasar Floriszstraat 3, tel. 020/664-1445, www.ikriti.nl; 5pm-midnight daily

ETHIOPIAN

✪ Lalibela $$

Locals rave about Lalibela (named after a holy city in 12th-century Ethiopia) because of its authentic Ethiopian dishes. The hot, flavorful entrées are served on spongy injera (a pancake-style bread), used for scooping up the food. Smells of cinnamon and cumin waft by as African music plays. Try the deblek, a combination of meats and vegetables stewed in cardamom and cloves. A few wines come from Ethiopia's Rift Valley, like the dry cabernet sauvignon. Order a post-meal coffee made in the traditional boiling pot method.

MAP 5: Eerste Helmersstraat 249, tel. 020/683-8332, www.lalibela.nl; 5pm-11pm daily

MOROCCAN

Paloma Blanco $$

Just past the cluster of Ethiopian eateries on the corner of Overtoom and Jan Pieter Heyestraat is a small Moroccan café serving flavorful tagines to locals.

It gets rave reviews for its subtlety and charm, where warm tones and authentic Moroccan lamps set the stage for the menu of warm couscous and exotic spices. Whether it's the fish of the day or chicken with candied lemons and olives, the tagines are a true taste of Morocco. The prices are reasonable, the baklava is tasty, and the Arabian coffee is one of a kind. This spot is cash only.

MAP 5: Jan Pieter Heyestraat 145, tel. 020/612-6485, www.palomablanca.nl; 6pm-10pm Tues.-Sun.

TEX-MEX

Tomatillo $

Just off Overtoom is a small joint offering fresh and organic Tex-Mex cuisine via gut-busting burritos, tostadas, fajitas, and quesadillas. Tomatillo is the only place in town for a huevos rancheros breakfast burrito, but expats mostly come here for the carnitas and habanero salsa. Big eaters should try a *kip* (chicken) burrito with organic chicken, lime and garlic rice, black beans, a choice of salsa, cheddar, and guacamole. Seating is limited to just a few tables, so take your meal to go and head to Vondelpark. Don't forget to pick up a bag of homemade Mexican hot chocolate cookies.

MAP 5: Overtoom 261, tel. 020/683-3086, www.tomatillo.nl; 4pm-10pm Mon.-Thurs., noon-10pm Fri.-Sun.

VEGAN

De Peper $

De Peper (The Pepper) is a vegan café housed in a community center. It's a *volkskeuken* (people's kitchen) run by a volunteer staff and offering a set dinner menu in a convivial atmosphere. Prices are on a sliding scale (€7-10), so people pay what they can afford. Starters vary from miso soup to borscht, and mains can be tempura sushi, lasagna, or seasonal veggies roasted over a bed of grains. Dessert is a worthy slice of apple or chocolate pie. This is a homey, alternative place that resembles a typical Amsterdam café, with a wooden floor and long bar. Rotating artwork on the walls displays the range of local artists. Dinner reservations (by phone) are a must; call the day of to book a table. Dinner is served 7pm-8:30pm; outside these hours, the café functions as a bar. Note that De Peper is closed Monday, Wednesday, and Saturday.

MAP 5: Overtoom 301, tel. 020/412-2954, www.depeper.org; 6pm-1am Sun., Tues., and Thurs., 6pm-3am Fri.

GASTROPUBS

Café Parck $

This stylish English gastropub is off Overtoom and is a great place for some good grub and a pint. Locals come for Monday pub quizzes (8:30pm, in Dutch and English) or to watch soccer games. The usual order is two sliders with parmesan white truffle fries, a beer, and maybe a few *bitterballen* (fried meatballs). The wood-heavy look and decor give the place a tavern feel, with purposely graffitied walls, chesterfield couches, and glazed tables. Café Parck makes for a warm escape on a rainy night or after an afternoon at Vondelpark.

MAP 5: Overtoom 428, tel. 020/412-5335, www.cafeparck.nl; 3pm-1am Sun.-Thurs., 3pm-3am Fri.-Sat. (kitchen closes 10pm Mon.-Sat. and 9pm Sun.)

CAFÉS AND BISTROS

Café Touissant $$

This neighborhood café has a French look and feel that's ideal for a relaxing coffee or post-Museumplein lunch. Patrons love the homey chalkboard menus and hanging pots, quaint terrace tables, and fairy lights. French toast with cinnamon sugar is served until 3pm, while lunch boasts open-faced sandwiches like smoked wild salmon or Coppa di Parma with artichoke, parmesan, truffle mayo, and pine nuts. Wash it down with a Dutch blond beer on tap.

MAP 5: Bosboom Toussaintstraat 26, tel. 020/685-0737, www.cafe-toussaint.nl; 9am-10pm daily

Valerius Eten & Drinken $

This corner lunch café is a hit with locals for brunch and lunch, from its crispy croissants to the towering open-faced sandwiches. The coffee, freshly ground and pressed through a steel espresso machine with each order, is complemented by a slice of apple pie or dense chocolate brownie. The modern decor and pastel walls can be seen through the windows along the outdoor covered terrace. Friendly service and low prices make Valerius a great pit stop in the neighborhood.

MAP 5: Banstraat 14, tel. 020/471-3976, www.valeriusetenendrinken.nl; 8:30am-6pm Mon.-Fri., 10am-6pm Sat.-Sun.

Blauwe Theehuis $

Smack-dab in the center of Vondelpark is this two-story café surrounded by ponds and leafy trees. Its flying saucer look uncannily resembles something from *The Jetsons*, but people come here mostly for its terrace, which is said to be the largest in Europe. The wraparound balcony on the second floor gives diners a bird's-eye view of the trees. A decent lunch menu of sandwiches is available until 4pm, and snacks and cakes are an all-day affair. Relax with a few drinks and soak up the scenery.

MAP 5: Vondelpark 5, tel. 020/662-0254, www.blauwetheehuis.nl; 9am-10pm daily

Vondelpark3 $

Although Vondelpark3 has an indoor dining area, the best experience is relaxing on the large terrace, which offers a great view of busy, leafy Vondelpark. All three meals are served here, but the most popular order is a round of drinks with a snack, like Spanish ham with tapenade or a meat and cheese platter. The café is housed in a late 19th-century Italian Renaissance pavilion. Sharing the building are several radio stations, one of which actually broadcasts in a windowed radio booth inside the café itself. Outside, the terrace spans the building's facade, with long benches, small tables, and large sun umbrellas. There's a lot of activity passing by in summer, from picnickers to roller skaters, cyclists, and dog walkers, so it's a great spot for people-watching.

MAP 5: Vondelpark 3, tel. 020/639-2589, www.unlimitedlabel.com; 10am-6pm Mon.-Tues., 10am-11pm Wed.-Sat., 10am-8pm Sun.

DELICATESSEN

Peperwortel $

This is the go-to neighborhood *traiteur* (delicatessen) for healthy eats and fresh takeout, made by a small group of chefs. Check out the large blackboards hanging on the walls to see what's in the display case. Options range from hearty sandwiches and seasonal specials to veggie burgers with thick portobello mushrooms, homemade pesto ravioli, and deep dish lasagna. Try the Basque-inspired *piperrada*, with soft, round goat's cheese enclosed by carrots, celery, tomatoes, and roasted red pepper. In summer, the front patio has

Peperwortel is a great choice for lunch alfresco.

a few chairs to enjoy lunch under the leafy vines.

MAP 5: Overtoom 140, tel. 020/685-1053, www.peperwortel.nl; noon-9pm daily

BAKERIES

Arnold Cornelis $

This tiny bakery and sweet shop on Van Baerlestraat bakes heavenly cakes, chocolate éclairs, and pralines against a backdrop of colorful floral decor, as well as offering tasty treats ranging from marzipan to jars of jelly. The friendly, bubbly staff serves up cakes and miniature tarts for sweet-toothed customers to enjoy inside or at a quaint table outside. Another location in the Jordaan (Elandsgracht 78) is just as delightful.

MAP 5: Van Baerlestraat 93, tel. 020/662-1228, www.cornelis.nl; 8am-6pm Mon.-Fri., 8am-5pm Sat.

De Pijp — Map 6

SURINAMESE

✪ Warung Spang Makandra $

Since 1978, this tiny Surinamese joint has been the prime place for flavorful, spicy dishes. A blend of herbs and meat rubs brings a savory surprise to every plate. Dishes, made with love and that extra kick of seasoning, include the Javanese tempeh, chicken satay, and roti with lamb and vegetables. If the few tables and tall lounge booths are too cramped, take your meal to go and enjoy it at nearby Sarphatipark (Ceintuurbaan, between Eerste Jan Steenstraat and Tweede Jan Steenstraat). This spot is cash only.

MAP 6: Gerard Doustraat 39, tel. 020/670-5081, www.spangmakandra.nl; 11am-10pm Mon.-Sat., 1pm-10pm Sun.

VIETNAMESE

Pho 91 $$

This small and friendly noodle joint on Albert Cuypstraat takes Vietnamese street food and adds a modern twist to traditional pho and *bun* (rice vermicelli) recipes. The sauces and starters, like hoisin-peanut sauce and crispy spring rolls, are made with fresh ingredients from Albert Cuypmarkt. The nourishing noodle soups blend beef broth with sliced meat, bean sprouts, cilantro, onions, and herbs. Noodle dishes *(bun)* feature stir-fried meats or tofu in lemongrass with veggies, herbs, crushed peanuts, and fish sauce. Don't forget the *caphe sua da*, an iced coffee with condensed milk. The limited seating is always full for dinner, so try to come early.

MAP 6: Albert Cuypstraat 91, tel. 020/752-6880, www.pho91.nl; 5:30pm-10pm Tues.-Thurs., noon-10pm Fri.-Sun.

INDIAN

Balti House $$

This small corner restaurant is known as one of the best spots in the city for authentic and flavorful Indian, Bangladeshi, and Pakistani dishes. Orders are served in small *balti* bowls (thin woks), accompanied by naan and plate warmers. The restaurant has a simple wood interior with a Taj Mahal mural and ample seating. The terrace stretches across a leafy street corner, perfect for an intimate or casual dinner. Try the tandoori mixed grill, butter chicken curry, or a prawn mushroom *balti* with spices from northwest India. Service is quick and attentive.

MAP 6: Albert Cuypstraat 41, tel. 020/470-8917, www.baltihouse.nl; 4pm-11pm daily

JAPANESE

✪ Izakaya $$$

The ultramodern Izakaya blows most of its competition out of the water with its cosmopolitan take on the sushi bar. The metallic bar, long counters, and windows that wrap around the restaurant bestow an edgy and modern look, attracting celebrities like Rihanna and Lionel Richie. While the pricey cocktails are made by well-trained bar staff, it's the avant-garde take on ordinary Japanese plates that are worth paying for. Three Japanese chefs create inventive sashimi, tempura, and temaki dishes that melt in your mouth. Look for tasty rolls like Alaskan king crab or jalapeño octopus. This place to see and be seen is unforgettable.

MAP 6: Albert Cuypstraat 2-6, tel. 020/305-3090, www.izakaya-amsterdam.com; 10am-1am Sun.-Thurs., 10am-2am Fri.-Sat.

SPANISH TAPAS

Vamos a Ver $$

Vamos a Ver, a classic Spanish tapas joint, is a hidden gem where the sangria and paella rival most places in Spain. The decor evokes Spain, with dark maroon walls, and a few sporadically placed guitars and flowers. Spanish expats come here for the *costillas* (ribs) and the *pata negra* (black ham). Mains are diverse, from tonguefish with fruit to baked chicken with Spanish herbs. To find the entrance, look for the little yellow sign with the two flamenco dancers. This spot is cash only.

MAP 6: Govert Flinckstraat 308, tel. 020/673-6992, www.vamosaver.nl; 5:30pm-10:30pm Wed.-Mon.

ITALIAN

District V $$

Located on a shady square south of Sarphatipark, District V offers pizza that Italians rave about. The Sicilian-style dough rests for a strict 48-hour period before being rolled to a thin 13-inch crust and topped with fresh ingredients. The seasonal toppings change every two weeks, but fresh basil, authentic olive oil, and ripe tomatoes are permanent fixtures. The interior feels like an Italian tavern, with an open kitchen next to tables set against exposed brick and windows, and a romantic, rustic dining room downstairs. In summer, the outside terrace expands through the square under a canopy of old plane trees. Locals come for the real-deal Italian pizza kitchen and charming Roman ambience.

MAP 6: Van der Helstplein 17, tel. 020/770-0884, www.district5.nl; 5:30pm-10:30pm daily

TURKISH

Saray $

White wine, warm mezes (Mediterranean finger foods), and wood-fired trout are just some of the traditional items found at this eatery representing the Eastern Anatolia region of Turkey. Spacious and airy, the overall look is upscale, while the prices are budget friendly. Turkish music plays softly throughout the restaurant, and warm lighting and stained wood furnishings make for an intimate and relaxed atmosphere. Flavorful specialties from the owner's hometown of Malatya, Turkey, include tender grilled chicken cutlets, minced lamb with garlicky mint yogurt, and stuffed eggplant. This is a peaceful stop for lunch or an early evening snack.

MAP 6: Gerard Doustraat 33, tel. 020/671-9216, www.saraylokanta.nl; 10am-midnight Tues.-Sun. (kitchen closes 10pm)

LEBANESE

Artiste $$

Artiste's owner, Simon, opened this Lebanese restaurant in 1977 and named it after a trait his entire family carries. The former jazz musician once led an orchestra, and now he puts his creativity into cuisine from his homeland. Inside, the upstairs dining area is adorned with old Lebanese posters and carpets that create a homey feel. Guests dine at low tables, cushioned stools, and sofas. Jazz plays softly in the background while mezes (small dishes) of pitas with hummus and eggplant with tahini and tomato sauces are served. Try the meze combo for two, a blend of warm and cool dishes from kebabs to grilled okra and veggie couscous. An older, cultured clientele comes here for long nights of conversation.

MAP 6: Tweede Jan Steenstraat 1, tel. 020/671-4264, www.libanees-artist.nl; noon-midnight daily

NORTH AFRICAN

Mamouche $$

This intimate tavern offers upscale and authentic cuisine from Morocco and Algeria with a twist of French inspiration. The kitchen is decorated with ornate teapots hanging next to strings of garlic. Menus are bound in leather, and white tablecloths garnish the small tables, with tall taper candles and a slightly formal setting. Start with *brik a l'oeuf*, a flakey filo dough with tuna, capers, parsley, and quail's egg. Try one of the savory tagines, chicken with lemon confit and artichokes or the lamb shoulder with *ras el hanout* spices, green beans, and plums. The wine list includes Moroccan reds, like cabernet sauvignon, but make sure to try their homemade house aperitif made from roses of the High Atlas Mountains. Romantic and tucked away, this place gets raves from local couples and intimate groups.

MAP 6: Quellijnstraat 104, tel. 020/670-0736, www.restaurantmamouche.nl; 5pm-11pm Tues.-Sun.

Bazar $

The 19th-century Buiten-Amstelkerk was converted from a church into a two-story Moroccan restaurant with floor-to-ceiling tiled murals, mosaic-topped tables, and ornate chandeliers in 2002. Gold-plated columns interrupt green walls, with strings of fairy lights hanging above large groups, families, and dinner dates. The visible kitchen is two floors high with a colorful elevator shaft that runs orders up and down. The North African menu has a flood of options, from falafel salad with fresh tabouleh to steamed lamb with chickpeas and almonds. Wash it down with a Turkish Efes beer or Moroccan mint tea.

MAP 6: Albert Cuypstraat 182, tel. 020/675-0544, www.bazaramsterdam.com; 8am-midnight Mon.-Thurs., 8am-1am Fri.-Sat., 9am-midnight Sun.

VEGETARIAN

De Waaghals $$

Vegetarians will be thrilled to see an entire menu dedicated to organic, seasonal, and contemporary veggie dishes in this small and informal eatery. Not your run-of-the-mill crunchy hippie joint, the sleek dining area is simple and modern and attracts mostly local diners. The chefs deliver innovative items, like udon noodles with smoked tofu, and sautéed eggplant with ginger-lime sauce, seaweed, and coconut. The Classic is a hearty mushroom pie with red onion chutney and chard roulade served with a buttery, garlicky baked potato and crispy onion rings.

MAP 6: Frans Halsstraat 29, tel. 020/679-9609, www.waaghals.nl; 5pm-9:30pm daily

BURGERS

The Butcher $$

Eating at The Butcher feels like dining at a chic butcher shop, with its wood furnishings and diagrams stenciled on the white tile walls. This small joint has a few high tables with one long bench and a picnic table outside. Around a dozen options are on the menu, mostly towering burgers held together by a giant toothpick. Go for The Daddy, a half-pound patty of Aberdeen Angus beef with Dutch edam cheese, bacon, barbecue sauce, and grilled onion. Fried fish, grilled chicken, and veggie burgers are also available.

MAP 6: Albert Cuypstraat 33-35, tel. 020/470-7875, www.the-butcher.com; 11am-1am Mon.-Fri., 11am-3am Sat.-Sun.

BREAKFAST AND BRUNCH

Bakers and Roasters $$

Here, brunch recipes from a Kiwi and a Brazilian blend into a healthy and hearty combination. In a small, diner-style space decorated in teals and with wooden crates of citrus, the counter shows off heavenly frosted cakes and pies. The bright and narrow shop is busy with expats and creative types ordering coffee while waiting for their generous plates. Sweet tooths love the banana nut bread French toast, while fans of the savory go for the egg dishes. The Navajo eggs are a yummy bowl of pulled BBQ pork, avocado, mango salsa, chipotle cream, and two poached eggs.

MAP 6: Eerste Jacob van Campenstraat 54, tel. 020/772-2627, www.bakersandroasters.com; 8:30am-4pm daily

Little Collins $$

The Aussie-owned Little Collins is known for its signature Bloody Marys and hearty egg dishes. Locals, international tourists, and Aussie expats grab a seat on the terrace to watch Albert Cuypmarkt shoppers pass by while sipping bellinis and Tom Collins. Inside is a mix of high tables and counters. The Cumberland sausage is a hit, and the surf 'n' turf combines pan-fried prawns, scrambled eggs, roasted pork belly, and kimchee. Little Collins is also open for dinner Wednesday-Saturday, but brunch is its most popular meal.

MAP 6: Eerste Sweelinckstraat 19-F, tel. 020/673-2293, www.littlecollins.nl; 10:30am-4pm Mon., 10:30am-10pm Wed.-Fri., 9am-10pm Sat.-Sun.

Scandinavian Embassy $$

This Nordic brunch spot and coffee bar is a modern-meets-rustic take on food and bean culture. The tiny kitchen is run by a Swedish and Norwegian staff in a whitewashed wood cottage that's quiet and moody. Dishes are thoughtfully designed with a contemporary take on traditional Scandinavian ingredients. The menu varies but can include poached eggs with cured salmon and authentic Danish rye bread, or homemade liver and herb pâté with an egg yolk dropped on top. The slow-filtered coffee comes from Scandinavian roasters. The staff is friendly and patient, and at times painstakingly meticulous. This is a perfect spot for hipsters and foodies.

MAP 6: Sarphatipark 34, tel. 061/951-8199, www.scandinavianembassy.nl; 7:30am-6pm Mon.-Fri., 9am-6pm Sat.-Sun.

CAFÉS AND BISTROS

Wasserette $

This former laundromat kept its original name but otherwise converted into a breakfast, brunch, and lunch café. The inside is rustic, with low tables and floor-to-ceiling windows overlooking the street corner. The eggs Benedict are stacked high, the stainless-steel espresso machine turns out lattes three at a time, and open-faced sandwiches tower with fresh and flavorful combos. Try the grilled chicken and bacon with avocado, freshly sliced parmesan and truffle mayo on sourdough, or the roast beef with spicy tomato salsa and cashews. Looking for a typical Dutch snack? Try the fried shrimp croquette with lemon mayo and deep fried parsley.

MAP 6: Eerste van der Helststraat 27, no phone, www.dewasserette.com; 7:30am-6pm daily

BAKERIES

De Taart van m'n Tante $

This corner bakery-café, whose name in English is The Pie of My Aunt, began in 1990 with two confectionary connoisseurs with extraordinary styles of cake-making. Visiting this place is like attending the Mad Hatter's tea party. Three-tiered cakes decorated with violet, yellow, and turquoise fondant sit in giant birdcages as table centerpieces and in the storefront windows. Festive and colorful lights garnish the ceiling, and loud placemats adorn every table. Visitors enjoy the gaudy decor and absolutely love the cake. About 20 cakes and pies occupy the glass display case each day, from pecan to banana rum raisin and sour cherries baked with cream. The parlor has a chirpy and cheerful vibe, as locals and tourists take their cake with coffee and good company.

MAP 6: Ferdinand Bolstraat 10, tel. 020/776-4600, www.detaart.com; 10am-6pm daily

Jordaan

DUTCH

Moeders $$

Moeders (Mothers, in English) serves up hearty Dutch comfort food. The inside of this always-busy restaurant is fun and homey, with hundreds of framed family photos on the walls. Everything on the menu—divided into recipes from three mothers, Anne, Betty, and Corrie—comes in large portions. A popular dish is *stamppot,* a traditional mash of potatoes and vegetables topped with meat and brown gravy, or go for the spare ribs or calf liver. The food will leave you stuffed. Reservations are suggested.

MAP 7: Rozengracht 251, tel. 020/626-7957, www.moeders.com; 5pm-midnight Mon.-Fri., noon-midnight Sat.-Sun.

typical Dutch dish of sliced ham and root vegetables at Moeders

FRENCH

✪ Daalder $$$

Foodies looking to be pampered with a chef's choice dinner of up to seven courses will find Daalder a perfect match. This fine dining restaurant is a cross between a French bistro and a casual Dutch café, with art deco light fixtures set in a breezy space, giving off an unassuming atmosphere. Ingredients like scallops, edamame, flank steak, and pork belly are local and seasonal. The experienced staff know their wine pairings, and the courses are served with perfect timing. Come with an open mind and trust the chefs—though vegetarians may not find enough choices here. Reservations are suggested.

MAP 7: Lindengracht 90, tel. 020/624-8864, www.daalderamsterdam.nl; noon-2:30pm and 6pm-10pm Sun. and Fri., 5:30pm-10pm Mon.-Thurs. and Sat.

De Belhamel $$$

De Belhamel is the neighborhood spot for an intimate, quiet canalside dinner. The romantic art nouveau restaurant features oversized floral decor and emerald walls, setting the tone for serene ambience. The creative menu and seasonal selection, served by a friendly staff, have garnered acclaim throughout the industry. Oxtail soup, foie gras French toast, and candied orange flan are just some of the inventive entrées. There is a two-hour limit for tables on busy nights; a weekday reservation is best to avoid feeling rushed.

MAP 7: Brouwersgracht 60, tel. 020/622-1095, www.belhamel.nl; noon-4pm and 6pm-10pm Sun.-Thurs., noon-4pm and 6pm-10:30pm Fri.-Sat.

De Groene Lanteerne $$$

De Groene Lanteerne (The Green Lantern) is a hidden-in-plain-sight restaurant, situated on Haarlemmerstraat with an entrance that looks like a residence. A few steps inside this charming lounge reveals wood furnishings made from remnants of an old church, red-patterned wallpaper, and 1920s figurines, model ships, and art deco books. The ever-changing menu is French, with starters like lobster salad and shrimp tartar and mains like rack of venison and a tender rib eye. The welcoming owner, Roberto, is a wine specialist, and his wife, Yvonne, ensures the menu is made with seasonal, organic ingredients. Reservations are suggested.

MAP 7: Haarlemmerstraat 43, tel. 020/624-1952, www.degroenelanteerne.nl; 6:30pm-11pm Mon.-Sat.

ITALIAN

Cinema Paradiso $$

There is no way to tell from the outside what's in store for diners at Cinema Paradiso. Walk through the hallway of vintage posters of starlets to a dramatic fish tank and the sound of clinking glasses. Behind the aquarium, a gigantic dining room awaits with semicircular booths on one side and a large bar on the other. The long tables and spacious setting make this spot perfect for large groups. Scenes from James Bond movies play on a large projector on the back wall. The Italian menu offers pizza, seafood pasta, and meat dishes like tenderloin and veal. For dessert, go for the *sgroppino*, a frozen cocktail similar to lemon sorbet.

MAP 7: Westerstraat 186, tel. 020/623-7344, www.cinemaparadiso.info; 6pm-11pm Tues.-Sun.

Koevoet $$

From the outside, Koevoet appears to be a Dutch brown bar tucked away in the Jordaan, but it's actually a petite Italian restaurant. The menu is traditional Italian, serving dishes like mozzarella burrata and al dente pear cheese ravioli, as well as tiramisu, wine, and San Pellegrino. Everything tastes as if you stumbled into Italy, and the friendly staff is passionate about the work. The antique wooden furnishings, tarnished brass chandeliers, and sepia photographs feel rustic and European. Prices are reasonable, the ambience is intoxicating, and locals love to come here because it's hidden from the rest of the world. Reservations are suggested.

MAP 7: Lindenstraat 17, tel. 020/624-0846, www.koevoetamsterdam.com; 5:30pm-10pm Tues.-Sun.

AFGHAN

Mantoe $$

The latest destination for foodies is this small and modern Afghani restaurant off a narrow side street. The menu is a set-course meal (but dishes can be altered to suit most diets). Starters are soup and light snacks like hummus, dumplings, and olives. Mains are small plates of meats made with exotic spices and herbs and vegetable stews with ingredients like turnips, spinach, and eggplant. The dining room is simple and plain, but the friendly service and unique food are more than satisfying. Reservations are suggested.

MAP 7: Tweede Leliedwarsstraat 13, tel. 020/421-6374, www.restaurantmantoe.nl; 5pm-11pm Wed.-Sun.

ARGENTINIAN

Salmuera $$$

There are many Argentinian steakhouses in the city, but Salmuera is the best. Enter through the courtyard and try to catch a glimpse of the day's pig on a spit. The attentive and helpful staff will seat you in one of the many rooms decorated with traditional painted wood horses and old Argentinian farming tools. Candles give off an intimate glow, illuminating a big selection of cocktails and wine in this large and open building. Most diners come here for the tender meat matched with flavorful salsas. The ceviche and empanada starters are a plus; for a main, try the *chuletón* cut with chimichurri, and bring some mints along to fight the garlic.

MAP 7: Rozengracht 106, tel. 020/624-5752, www.sal-amsterdam.nl; 5pm-1am daily

STEAKHOUSES

Venus & Adonis $$

The steak scene in Amsterdam is often a tourist trap, but Venus & Adonis is the real deal, set in a romantic 17th-century canal house overlooking the Prinsengracht canal. Opt for a table for two, the communal table, or the white marble bar. The simple decor is highlighted by a tiled floor, modern lighting fixtures, and Scandinavian furniture. Meat and seafood are prepared over a charcoal grill and served family-style on a wooden board. Mains include varied portions of steak, soft-shell crab, and lobster tail. The lighter lunch menu is a short list of burgers, pitas, soups, and salads.

MAP 7: Prinsengracht 274, tel. 020/421-1848, www.venusadonis.nl; noon-4pm and 5pm-11pm daily

CAFÉS AND BISTROS

Café Kobalt $

Kobalt is a long-established neighborhood café with an open space that comfortably fits large groups while keeping its 17th-century canal house charm. Original wooden ceiling beams and pillars lend the space historic integrity, and the large window lets in natural light ideal for cups of morning coffee and afternoon hot chocolate. The light menu is a modest mix of croissants, toasted sandwiches, and typical fried Dutch snacks. The crowd of locals usually opt for a homemade Italian soda, *koffie verkeerd* (latte), or a post-work beer. Its location at the end of the Singel means it's perpetually busy, but locals love it all the same. There are live music performances every Sunday at 4pm.

MAP 7: Singel 2A, tel. 020/320-1559, www.cafekobalt.nl; 8am-1am Mon.-Thurs., 8am-3am Fri.-Sat., 10am-1am Sun.

G's $

G's was opened by a Canadian couple determined to bring brunch and Bloody Marys to Amsterdam. This cozy, cute café charms with Roy Lichtenstein tablecloths, menus on old vinyl, beaded chandeliers, and mismatched plates. On the menu, the towering French toast is heavenly (get the bacon), and the eggs Pedro are poached on cornbread with jalapeño hollandaise. Don't miss out on one of their Bloody Mary masterpieces, especially the Bloody Caesar. Reservations are suggested.

MAP 7: Goudsbloemstraat 91, no phone, http://reallyniceplace.com; 10am-4pm Fri.-Sun.

P96 $

P96 is one of the best lunch cafés around simply because of its terrace—an old red barge that's been converted into a patio—on the Prinsengracht canal. The place is run by two friendly women who move fast as they fill orders. Try the open-faced sandwiches, like a tuna melt with cheddar, capers, and red onions. Wash it down with Leffe Blonde and soak in the view as the boat slowly rocks back and forth.

MAP 7: Prinsengracht 96-98, tel. 020/622-1864, http://p96.nl; 11am-3am Sun.-Thurs., 11am-4am Fri.-Sat.

Vinnie's $

This two-story corner café with its simple, whitewashed look boasts an organic menu. Order at the bar and have a seat at one of the small wooden tables. Breakfast features a small selection of oats, poached eggs, and homemade pastries, like carrot walnut cake and brioche. Lunch includes Mediterranean salads and sandwiches. Order a fair-trade espresso or flat white and unwind from the bustle outside.

MAP 7: Haarlemmerstraat 46, tel. 020/771-3086, http://vinnieshomepage.com; 7:30am-6pm Mon.-Fri., 9am-6pm Sat., 9:30am-6pm Sun.

DELICATESSEN

Raïnaraï $

There isn't much space at this Algerian *traiteur* (delicatessen), but if you find a seat, your taste buds will thank you. The usual order is a freshly prepared stewed meat, vegetable, and couscous combination. The day's choices are on colorful display in the deli case. Order, and the chef will serve your meal at your table, amid Arabian lamps and the scent of cumin. A visit to this small, warm space is like visiting another world.

MAP 7: Prinsengracht 252, tel. 020/624-9791, www.rainarai.nl; noon-10pm daily

SWEETS

Monte Pelmo IJs $

This is one of the best gelato shops in town. Open late, the place is quaint and only big enough to hold the gelato case and a small crowd of customers. The homemade gelatos range from pistachio to white chocolate passion fruit, and the flavors are authentic with no added preservatives. A mural of Mount Pelmo wraps around the walls, and gelato cups are stacked on an ancient Roman Pantheon lookalike. This is a perfect after-dinner stop to sweeten a walk around the scenic neighborhood.

MAP 7: Tweede Anjeliersdwarsstraat 17, tel. 020/623-0959, http://montepelmo.nl; 1pm-9pm daily fall-spring, 1pm-10pm daily summer

Petit Gateau $

At this adorable French patisserie off Haarlemmerstraat people stop to buy minicakes and tarts to share. A color wheel of pastel macarons, chocolate glazed éclairs, spongy madeleines, and savory quiches are all on display in an assortment of flavors. The pristine white setting of the shop looks a little like a cake laboratory, but things here are just too cute for that.

MAP 7: Haarlemmerstraat 80, tel. 020/737-1585, www.petitgateau.nl; 10am-6pm daily

Plantage

Map 8

SEAFOOD

Een Vis Twee Vis $$

Unpretentious Een Vis Twee Vis is a quaint seafood joint with a simple menu of North Sea fare, prepared in a humble galley-size kitchen. The focus is on quality over quantity, with a small list of entrées, like baked Dover sole and flakey sea bass with fresh spices, and sides like wild spinach. The attentive staff can help with wine pairings in this intimate, cozy spot. Reservations are suggested.

MAP 8: Schippersgracht 6, tel. 020/623-2894, www.eenvistweevis.nl; 6pm-10pm Tues.-Sat.

INDONESIAN

Café Kadijk $$

Café Kadijk serves up authentic Indonesian food to faithful regulars from a kitchen the size of a cubicle. This quaint two-level spot offers spicy specialties like stink beans, shrimp, and coconut; eggs Auntie Bea; and stewed beef Rendang Padang. The family recipes have been passed down from generation to generation.

MAP 8: Kadijksplein 5, tel. 061/774-4411, www.cafekadijk.nl; 4pm-1am Sun.-Thurs., 4pm-3am Fri.-Sat. (kitchen closes 10pm daily)

BURGERS

Burgermeester $

Burgermeester has a modern feel, with an open kitchen and counter service. Choose from a solid list of gourmet burgers made of beef, lamb, chicken, falafel, and tuna. Forget fries: Sides are homey selections like potato salad, corn on the cob, and coleslaw. Take a seat at the cherry-red booths or outside on picnic benches. Look for specials like mango salsa and pigeon patties. There are multiple locations around Amsterdam.

MAP 8: Plantage Kerklaan 37, tel. 0900/287-4377 (€0.10 per minute), www.burgermeester.eu; noon-11pm daily

BAKERIES

Bakhuys Amsterdam $

Known for its sheer size and variety of goods, Bakhuys Amsterdam is an organic bakery and a destination for brunch and lunch. It's three buildings wide, with over a dozen bakers slicing bread and rolling out pizza dough for the giant iron oven. Sweet treasures like apple tarts are for sale, and salad and sandwich orders are served at the wooden tables. This spot is great for an on-the-go grab or a family lunch.

MAP 8: Sarphatistraat 61, tel. 020/370-4861, www.bakhuys-amsterdam.nl; 7am-7pm Mon.-Sat., 8am-5pm Sun.

DUTCH-EUROPEAN FUSION

✪ Gebr. Hartering $$$

This is a top choice for foodies who can commit an evening to modern Dutch dining. From the open kitchen, the restaurant's cooks create innovative courses that are served like artistic tapas. Dishes may include flamed rump steak, marinated anchovy spines, roasted nutty endives, French cheese, and crème brûlée. One of the owners often works as a server and is knowledgeable about the ingredients, cooking method, and best wine to match each dish. The four- or seven-course menu is served over a long evening in a small canal house with a cozy ambience. If it's warm, try to reserve a place on the canal boat docked outside. This place is worth the splurge. Reservations are suggested.

MAP 9: Peperstraat 10, tel. 020/421-0699, www.gebr-hartering.nl; 6pm-10:30pm Tues.-Wed., 6pm-11pm Thurs.-Sat., 6pm-10pm Sun.

SEAFOOD

Frank's Smoke House $

Enter this small smoked organic meat and fish deli and you immediately notice the strands of Alaskan salmon and North Sea mackerel drying out behind the counter next to industrial steel smokers. The deli case displays large smoked fish filets, king crab cakes, herring caviar, and sticks of beef jerky. The sandwich list is a good place to start, where smoked meats, like Alaskan halibut, black cod, and wild boar, are stacked between halves of a bread roll. Seating is limited to a small bar and a tiny table that folds out when there are more than two customers. This is a great lunchtime pit stop with a friendly staff and neighborhood feel.

MAP 9: Wittenburgergracht 303, tel. 020/670-0774, www.smokehouse.nl; 9am-4pm Mon., 9am-6pm Tues.-Fri., 9am-5pm Sat.

FRENCH

Choux $$$

One of Amsterdam's most-talked-about contemporary dining spots features a multicourse menu in an industrial, chic setting with a lively atmosphere. The restaurant's open layout is minimalist, with tiled pillars and red metal railings standing out among small, low tables. Choux's menu of local produce comes in five or seven courses, including a few of the chef's special plates. Each course offers a choice of meat, fish, or a vegetarian option. Starters feature dishes like fresh cheese with artichokes, kohlrabi, and poppy seeds. Halibut with chard, hazelnut, and pied-de-mouton mushrooms is an example of a typical entrée. Reservations are suggested.

MAP 9: De Ruijterkade 128, tel. 061/651-2364, www.choux.nl; noon-2pm Mon.-Fri., 6pm-10pm Tues.-Sat.

Hotel de Goudfazant $$$

Hotel de Goudfazant is a fine dining restaurant in a former warehouse with rusted vintage cars and motorbikes stacked against brick walls. The space is industrial chic, with steel beams and large chandeliers hanging from high ceilings. Two- and four-person white tablecloth settings convey elegance. Innovative, seasonal, and ever-changing entrées include stewed meats with sprouts and asparagus, tender steaks with bacon-wrapped potatoes, and lobster tail. Chocolate mousse, a great house wine, friendly staff, and the lively atmosphere are more reasons to choose this out-of-the-way place. Take the free ferry to IJplein; from there, it's an easy 15-minute walk.

MAP 9: Aambeeldstraat 10-H, tel. 020/636-5170, www.hoteldegoudfazant.nl; 6pm-11pm Tues.-Sun.

CAFÉS AND BISTROS

La Place $

On the top floor of the OBA public library is a cafeteria-style café with spectacular views of Amsterdam and a variety of freshly prepared fare. Grab a tray and peruse the different gourmet food stations, from the personalized wok-cooked curries to the towering open-faced sandwiches. Brick oven pizzas are made on the spot. Choose between an assortment of fruit smoothies or grab a coffee and cake from the café bar. Prices are reasonable, and there is ample seating at the tables, couches, and open terrace. The crowd is a mix of students, library patrons, and visitors who know this is one of the best spots for fresh, cheap eats with a view.

MAP 9: Oosterdokskade 143, tel. 020/523-0870, www.laplace.com; 10am-10pm daily

COFFEE AND TEA

Al Ponte $

Al Ponte started in 2007 as just an espresso machine and a small takeout window at the IJplein ferry dock. It has since expanded into a full-blown Italian café with the slogan "Make coffee not war." It continues to serve expertly crafted espresso and coffee in some of the tightest quarters in the city. One of the best ways to enjoy the waterfront on the cheap is by ordering a coffee and grabbing a seat on the nearby benches while waiting for the ferry to Amsterdam Centraal Station. A short list of sandwiches—Italian ham, provolone with grilled red peppers, and vegan options—is also on offer.

MAP 9: Meeuwenlaan 2 (IJplein), tel. 064/208-7482, www.alponte.nl; 8am-6pm Mon.-Fri., 10am-6pm Sat.-Sun. summer, 8am-3pm Mon.-Fri., 10am-4pm Sat.-Sun. winter

The Coffee Virus $

The Coffee Virus offers coffee for everyone, whether it's cheap drip, AeroPress-filtered, or trendy Japanese-style iced. The café is located in the large brick building just behind the A'DAM tower and is populated by the young freelancers and creative minds of Amsterdam. It offers a lunch menu that includes sandwiches like roast beef teriyaki with wasabi mayo, chorizo toasted with young cheese and spicy sambal, and a basil panini with zucchini and mozzarella. Minimalist, with bare wood boards for the bar and burlap sacks on the wall, The Coffee Virus has an undeniable trendy Brooklyn coffeehouse vibe.

MAP 9: Overhoeksplein 2, tel. 062/870-9872, www.thecoffeevirus.nl; 9am-4:30pm Mon.-Fri.

NIGHTLIFE

Amsterdam's nightlife is legendary. You've most likely heard of its Red Light District, but it's in the other neighborhoods that you'll find the best parties, cocktails, and beats.

Most clubs and live music halls are spread across the two main party squares, **Rembrandtplein** and **Leidseplein,** both of which are located in the southern section of the Canal Belt. Every kind of dance club is represented here, from small corner discos to larger stages with a DJ, turntables, and expensive sound systems. Between the clubs are rows of bars and restaurants, most of which cater to tourists. Out of the two, Rembrandtplein is smaller, with a heavier concentration of locals and students. It's home to clubs like Air and Club Escape. Leidseplein has more live music halls, like Paradiso, Melkweg, and Café in De Balie.

Genever (Dutch gin) is a staple in Amsterdam's bars.

Nieuwmarkt and the infamous Red Light District have the oldest watering holes, which have been open since the 1400s. Rustic **brown bars** link back to their roots as *genever* (Dutch gin) distilleries and old breweries. The few **coffeeshops** and gay bars in this area echo the district's well-known liberalism.

The Jordaan and the western part of the Canal Belt are perfect for visitors seeking authentic brown bars. De Pijp is the best spot to go bar-hopping among the young and trendy.

HIGHLIGHTS

- **MOST POPULAR PATIO: Café de Jaren** has the best waterfront terrace in the city, a perfect spot to kick back with a drink (page 106).
- **BEST PLACE TO TRY *GENEVER*:** There are more than 100 types of this Dutch gin at **Wynand Fockink** (page 112).
- **GREENEST HIDEAWAY:** Come to **Coffeeshop Bluebird** to get a sense of the greener side of Amsterdam (page 113).
- **BEST BEER SELECTION:** At the brown bar **Café de Spuyt,** you can choose from over 100 European and Dutch beers (page 116).
- **BEST LIVE MUSIC VENUE: Paradiso** is one of Europe's top places to see a show, thanks to its acoustics and intimate size (page 119).
- **FINEST WHISKEY:** Pop into **L&B Whiskeycafe** to peruse the seemingly endless list of single malt scotches, bourbons, and other whiskies from around the world (page 124).
- **FRIENDLIEST GAY BAR: Café Montmartre** is known for its convivial atmosphere and fun regulars (page 124).
- **SMOKER'S PARADISE: Grey Area** often has a line out the door thanks to its award-winning weed (page 125).
- **MOST PATRIOTIC BEER BAR:** Over 100 Dutch brews are served at **Arendsnest** (page 126).
- **WHERE TO FIND THE COOLEST BANDS: OCCII** hosts obscure indie bands that play everything from electro to metal (page 128).
- **BEST MIX OF ACTS:** On any given night at **OT301,** you might see local bands, acrobats, or belly dancers (page 128).
- **BEST BROWN BAR FOR A DRINK AND A MEAL:** At **Festina Lente,** make yourself comfortable at one of the cozy couches with a beer, or order a full dinner (page 131).
- **BEST PLACE FOR A DRINK IN THE SUN:** At trendy **Waterkant,** soak up the summer sunshine on a waterfront terrace (page 134).
- **BEST CHANCE TO SPOT AN A-LISTER:** Some of the customers at **Green House** are visiting celebrities curious about the city's cannabis culture (page 137).
- **MOST DUTCH BREWERY:** At **Brouwerij 't IJ,** craft beer fans can sip a fresh pour under an old windmill (page 138).
- **BEST ROOFTOP BAR:** Enjoy the views from swanky **SkyLounge** by day or night (page 140).

BROWN BARS

Café het Schuim

Café het Schuim is a roomy, retro spot that doubles as a mellow afternoon terrace café and a funky dive bar at night. Murals from the latest urban artist wrap the interior walls. The flea market collection of vintage sofas adds a homey feel. At night, DJs spin in the corner under a disco ball, and a dance floor usually starts beside it. The crowd is a mix of travelers and locals who seem to have come straight out of the city's bohemian hangouts from the 1960s.

MAP 1: Spuistraat 189, tel. 020/638-9357; 11am-1am Mon.-Thurs., 11am-3am Fri.-Sat., noon-1am Sun.

Café Hoppe

Café Hoppe is one of Spui's oldest brown bars, dating from 1670. Inside are antique wooden *genever* (Dutch gin) barrels lining the back bar. The sand on the floorboards protects the floor from beer spills. A second room, built in the 1930s, is the only place to enjoy a seat, but most people at Hoppe stand and socialize. By late afternoon the covered terrace is always full with workers looking to unwind with a crisp Dutch pilsner. It's the most popular café on the Spui, hands down.

MAP 1: Spui 18-20, tel. 020/420-4420, www.cafehoppe.com; 8am-1am Sun.-Thurs., 8am-2am Fri.-Sat.

Café de Jaren

Café Van Zuylen

This well-known brown bar's terrace stretches across Torensluis, the widest bridge in Amsterdam. In fact, the area is so large that service takes time, but why go elsewhere when good views and vibes are all around? This place is great on a sunny day, complete with entertaining people-watching. While the food menu is not outstanding, the large interior, with its tavern atmosphere, is a great place for a beer at night.

MAP 1: Torensteeg 8, tel. 020/639-1055; 10am-1am Sun.-Thurs., 10am-3am Fri.-Sat.

De Doelen

De Doelen is a go-to spot for an afternoon beer or a *genever* (Dutch gin) nightcap. The cozy feel is completed by candles, worn wooden walls and furniture, and a resident cat. The sand on the floor is a traditional way to keep floorboards from getting soggy from spilled drinks. The awning-covered terrace offers a canal view perfect for people-watching. The Duvel Tripel Hop is a favorite option among Belgian beer fans.

MAP 1: Kloveniersburgwal 125, tel. 020/624-9023; 9am-1am Mon.-Thurs., 9am-3am Fri.-Sat., 10am-1am Sun.

GRAND CAFÉS

✪ Café de Jaren

Jaren has one of the best waterfront terraces overlooking the Amstel River. Inside are high ceilings, large windows, and a colorful, tiled floor. The place is popular for a few intimate drinks, small bites, or weekend lunch. Upstairs becomes a restaurant after 5:30pm, serving Mediterranean entrées. Jaren is beloved by locals and tourists, so it may take patience to find a seat.

MAP 1: Nieuwe Doelenstraat 20-22, tel. 020/625-5771, www.cafedejaren.nl; 8:30am-1am Sun.-Thurs., 8:30am-2am Fri.-Sat.

1e Klas

Located on the second platform of Amsterdam Centraal Station, this is the only place to get a decent drink while you wait for your train. The inside is a large, two-room space with lavish art nouveau wallpaper, furnishings, and windows. In the late 1800s, this used to be the waiting room for first class passengers. At the bar is a cute cockatoo named Elvis, but watch out—he bites. A daily two-for-one special on beer and wine (4pm-7pm) helps to offset the otherwise pricey drinks.

MAP 1: Amsterdam Centraal Stationsplein 15, tel. 020/625-0131, www.restaurant1eklas.nl; 8:30am-11pm daily

The Tara

What began as a simple English pub expanded to a six-room contemporary tavern on the grounds of a former convent. Four bars guarantee there's always someone to pour a pint of lager, cider, or Guinness. On game nights a dozen flat-screens are tuned into the latest soccer or rugby match. The crowd is a mix of international businesspeople, sports fans, and regulars. Go for the sofas near the fireplace, take a seat at the long bars, or settle yourself in one of the big six-person tables. The pub food menu is a mix of fish-and-chips, burgers, and ribs.

MAP 1: Rokin 85-89, tel. 020/421-2654, www.thetara.com; 10am-1am Sun.-Thurs., 10am-3am Fri.-Sat.

COFFEESHOPS

De Dampkring

At this coffeeshop, whose name means "earthy atmosphere," blown-glass lamps

TOP EXPERIENCE

BROWN BARS

Café In 't Aepjen

One of the best ways to experience Amsterdam as a local is by visiting one (or several) of the city's brown bars. These combination bar-cafés have been populating the city's neighborhoods since the 1500s—and the interiors of most are a testament to this fact, with walls stained by centuries of tobacco smoke; gritty, sandy floors; and creaking stools. Brown bars are known for their homey atmosphere: Some are partially lit by candles, while others are occupied by a snoozing resident cat.

By day, brown bars are where locals come for a cup of coffee; by night, they function as pubs, serving beer. They're a popular destination during cold or rainy weather, as locals come seeking *gezellig*, a warm and cozy feeling, at any time of day.

The standard coffee order at a brown bar is *koffie verkeerd*, a traditional Dutch drink made of half drip coffee and half milk. Most brown bars stock a fair selection of beer by the bottle and on tap, as well as some hard liquor, wines, and soft drinks. The Dutch drink beer in smaller portions than is standard in North America. Order a *biertje* (small beer) and you'll blend right in.

★ Café Hoppe (page 105)
★ Café Van Zuylen (page 106)
★ De Doelen (page 106)
★ Café In 't Aepjen (page 111)
★ Café de Spuyt (page 116)
★ Café Genootschap der Geneugten (page 117)
★ De Pieper (page 118)
★ Festina Lente (page 131)
★ Café De Prins (page 131)
★ Café De Druif (page 136)

illuminate swirling murals and burl wood tables. The vibe is psychedelic and chilled out, with a laid-back, helpful, and friendly staff. The resident cat is usually spread out on one of the barstools. Outside and above the entrance is a famous Max Zorn mural made only of brown tape, depicting a scene from Golden Age Amsterdam. The coffeeshop's claim to fame is that George Clooney, Brad Pitt, and Matt Damon all came here to film a scene for the movie *Ocean's Twelve*. But locals know the true highlights here are the Cannabis Cup award-winning products.

De Dampkring

MAP 1: Handboogstraat 29, tel. 020/638-0705, www.dampkring-coffeeshop-amsterdam.nl; 10am-1am daily

De Tweede Kamer

According to the owner, this small coffeeshop is named after the Dutch House of Representatives because both places have people "sitting and chatting to each other about nothing." The single-room shop holds several tables, a bar, and a few stools. It feels like a brown bar inside, with large windows that overlook a busy alley. One of the tin canisters above the bar holds the remains of an American whose dying wish was to have his ashes at this coffeeshop. Some of the bestsellers here include Pineapple Haze, AK47, and Big Buddah Cheese. Nonsmokers might like the cakes and muffins. The crowd is a mix of locals of all ages.

MAP 1: Heisteeg 6, tel. 020/422-2236; 10am-1am daily

Kadinsky

This simple and small coffeeshop is two floors high, with a clean layout and sleek furnishings. The attraction of Kadinsky is its products, the uncrowded space, and the friendly staff. Customer favorites include Blue Cheese, Super Silver Haze, and Maui Haze. No chemicals or fertilizers are used in organic Highrise. Patrons rave about the homemade chocolate space cakes. There's a second location on Zoutsteeg.

MAP 1: Rosmarijnsteeg 9, tel. 020/420-4686; 9:30am-1am daily

LIVE MUSIC

Bitterzoet

Little Bitterzoet knows how to bring people together for an intimate performance or all-out dance party. Admission is cheap, and the space can hold about 250 people. Some of the best views are from the small balcony upstairs. Everything is crammed together, from the soundboard to the merch stand. Check out the red stained-glass art of the devil on the side wall. After the headliner finishes, DJ sessions last until the late hours, spinning everything from hip-hop to house and soul. A cigarette smoking room is just past the balcony bar.

MAP 1: Spuistraat 2, tel. 020/421-2318, www.bitterzoet.com; 8pm-3am Thurs.-Sun.; cover €10

BEER BARS

Beer Temple

This bar was the first in Amsterdam to offer American microbrews. The taps rotate among 30 beers, with another 300 available by bottle. The place feels like a tavern, with U.S. license plates, rusted beer signs, and empty beer bottles decorating the walls. Grab one of the red booths in the back, or swap stories with travelers at the bar. The staff are savvy beer connoisseurs who help match patrons with their perfect pint. The import tax means prices are higher than at other bars, but it's the only place with a long list of American favorites.

MAP 1: Nieuwezijds Voorburgwal 250, tel. 020/627-1427, www.beertemple.nl; noon-midnight Sun.-Thurs., noon-2am Fri.-Sat.

Belgique

One of the smallest bars in Amsterdam, grungy and popular Belgique is a laid-back scene specializing in strong Belgian beers. Over 50 Belgian beers are sold in this tiny, dusty space; also crammed inside are two DJ turntables, a cozy bar, and two window-side tables. Go for the 9 percent La Chouffe blond and try to squeeze onto one of the benches out front (a space that's also marijuana-friendly).

MAP 1: Gravenstraat 2, tel. 020/625-1974, www.cafe-belgique.nl; 3pm-1am Mon.-Wed., 1pm-1am Thurs. and Sun., 1pm-3am Fri.-Sat.

Bloemen Bar

This tiny late-night bar pulls in a younger party crowd who want to knock back beers after most bars have closed. The hippie-inspired decor features a colorful mural, retro lamps, and kitschy floral wallpaper. Bloemen is tucked into an alley, a hidden gem offering cheap drinks, fun music, and a casual crowd of young locals and internationals. There is a cigarette smoking room upstairs.

MAP 1: Handboogstraat 15, no phone, www.bloemenbar.nl; 8pm-4am Sun.-Thurs., 8pm-5am Fri.-Sat.

Café Gollem

This is the original location of the first Belgian beer bar in Amsterdam. The look of this dark, brown bar is inspired by its former status as a liquor distillery. Now the walls are decorated with Belgian beer signs from the 1970s and dozens of different beer glasses. It's well loved by local and international beer fans, and offers 200 different beers. The selection ranges from trappist varieties to a selection of Dutch microbrews. An older, relaxed, and beer-savvy crowd come here for a few rounds with friends in a rustic setting. If you're overwhelmed by choice, the bartender can recommend some good picks.

MAP 1: Raamsteeg 4, tel. 020/737-0273, www.cafegollem.nl; 4pm-1am Mon.-Thurs., noon-3am Fri.-Sat., noon-1am Sun.

De Buurvrouw

Down a quiet alley, De Buurvrouw can be spotted by the green Grolsch beer sign jutting out from the entrance. Through the double doors is an offbeat late-night bar attracting off-the-clock bartenders and local partygoers. The namesake *buurvrouw* (neighbor) is the styrofoam cutout of an older woman grouchily watching over the entrance. A long accent wall features designs painted by a rotation of well-known international urban artists. After 1am, ashtrays are set out as patrons pull out cigarettes (and possibly a spliff or two) and light up, despite laws that call for separate smoking rooms in bars.

MAP 1: Sint Pieterspoortsteeg 29, tel. 020/625-9654, www.debuurvrouw.nl; 10pm-3am Sun.-Thurs., 10pm-4am Fri.-Sat.

In de Wildeman

In de Wildeman is housed in a spacious former distillery from the 1600s. The inside gives off an antique charm, with old beer barrels stacked against the walls, a checkered tile floor, worn wooden furniture, and cozy lighting. There is a worldly selection of 18 beers on tap and over 250 beers by the bottle. Belgian and Dutch beers are prominent, but don't miss the list of German lagers and English ales. In de Wildeman was one of the first bars to bring more beer variety to Amsterdam. Take a look at the chalkboard menu above the entrance to see what's on tap, and try some traditional Dutch cheese with your brew.

MAP 1: Kolksteeg 3, tel. 020/638-2348, www.indewildeman.nl; noon-1am Mon.-Thurs., noon-2am Fri.-Sat.

COCKTAIL BARS

Tales & Spirits

The friendly and good-humored bartenders at this upbeat and buzzing cocktail bar and small restaurant serve speakeasy-style drinks, shaken or stirred. The interior resembles an upscale saloon, with an authentic 1920s wooden bar and cocktail shaker collection. Come for a cocktail, but stay for a few bites of modern international dishes like poached crayfish or truffle risotto.

MAP 1: Lijnbaanssteeg 5, tel. 065/535-6467, www.talesandspirits.com; 5:30pm-1am Sun. and Tues.-Thurs., 5:30pm-3am Fri.-Sat.

GAY AND LESBIAN BARS

PRIK

This small and narrow gay bar has one of the best reputations for its friendly atmosphere. The inside is a funky pink lounge with a long sleek bar, retro lamps, and disco balls. PRIK knows how to make an after-work drink fun, a night out lively, and a Sunday brunch relaxing, with champagne on tap and a street-side terrace. Quality cocktails, snacks, and groovy DJ beats—what else do you need?

MAP 1: Spuistraat 109, tel. 020/320-0002, www.prikamsterdam.nl; 4pm-1am Mon.-Thurs., 4pm-3am Fri.-Sat., 3pm-1am Sun.

The Cuckoo's Nest

The Cuckoo's Nest has gotten tamer since it opened as a leather bar in 1984. Nevertheless, it's still not for the faint-hearted or prude; its patrons, a mix of locals and tourists, would agree. The Cuckoo's Nest is the gateway to Amsterdam's raucous underground gay scene. The ground floor, with its simple bar, stays busy with cheap drinks and approachable staff. The basement is divided into two parts: A cigarette smoking room in the front, and a maze of smaller areas that make up one of the biggest dark rooms in Europe in the back. Free condoms are available at the bar.

MAP 1: Nieuwezijds Kolk 6, tel. 020/627-1752, www.cuckoosnest.nl; 1pm-1am Sun.-Thurs., 1pm-2am Fri.-Sat.

WINE BARS

Bubbles & Wines

Wine lovers who find this narrow, hidden gem behind Dam Square are in luck. Over 550 still wines and 100 sparkling ones are stored in this intimate, modern lounge. The bar is stocked with bottles from innumerable regions, from Bordeaux to Lebanon. Smooth and buttery, or sparkling and dry—there is something for everyone. Most of the wines are sold by the bottle, but 54 are available by the glass and poured from a high-tech tap system. Have a seat at the bar to socialize, or try a romantic two-person table in the front. Epicurean small plates range from flights of caviar to honey-drizzled parmesan "bee stings." Meet the owner, Rob, a passionate wine lover who's attentive and welcoming.

MAP 1: Nes 37, tel. 020/422-3318, www.bubblesandwines.com; 3:30pm-1am Mon.-Sat., 2pm-9pm Sun.

Red Light District and Nieuwmarkt

Map 2

BROWN BARS

Café de Engelbewaarder

Due to its location near the University of Amsterdam campus, Engelbewaarder (Guardian Angel in English) draws a literary crowd of PhD students, professors, and writers who come for the unfiltered Belgian beers at this classic brown bar. Rotating photo exhibitions and poster-style ads for upcoming jazz concerts around town decorate the walls. In summer, the picnic tables on the terrace offer a great canal view. On Sunday afternoons, the bar hosts jazz ensembles who play for an audience of sociable and laid-back locals. There is a lunch and dinner menu available.

MAP 2: Kloveniersburgwal 59, tel. 020/625-3772, www.cafe-de-engelbewaarder.nl; 10am-1am Mon.-Thurs., 10am-3am Fri.-Sat., 11am-1am Sun.

Café In 't Aepjen

The inside of this brown bar is like traveling back to when sailors populated the city streets. Old-fashioned liquor barrels stand alongside antique trinkets and old brass taps. One of the oldest brown bars in the city (and one of two buildings with a circa-1400s wooden facade), Café In 't Aepjen has a legend about a sailor using an *aapje* (monkey) as down payment for an unpaid tab. After many months at sea, the sailor returned to find the bar full of apes because other customers had used his method of payment. Others say the bar name comes from sailors scratching their skin like monkeys.

MAP 2: Zeedijk 1, tel. 020/428-8291; noon-1am Sun.-Thurs., noon-3am Fri.-Sat.

Café Stevens

The long bar inside this unpretentious spot is where journalists convene for bar snacks and glasses of La Chouffe, a Belgian tripel ale. Visitors kick back at one of the tables against the large windows that overlook Nieuwmarkt. A small menu of snacks and sandwiches is available.

MAP 2: Geldersekade 123, tel. 020/620-6970; 10am-1am Sun.-Thurs., 10am-3am Fri.-Sat.

Lokaal 't Loosje

At the turn of the 20th century, this brown bar was once a stable for carriage horses. What's left of the original structure are tile mosaics depicting scenes of Golden Age Amsterdam. A friendly and talkative mix of locals and visitors come for the cozy vibe. Find an empty wicker chair on the terrace to sip wine and people-watch under the burgundy awning. Small morning bites and a lunch menu are available.

MAP 2: Nieuwmarkt 32-34, 020/627-2635, www.loosje.nl; 8:30am-1am Sun.-Thurs., 8:30am-3am Fri.-Sat.

Mata Hari

Mata Hari was a Dutch courtesan and exotic dancer executed by a French firing squad for espionage during WWI. This brown bar is a Red Light District pearl, with lavish decor from taxidermy fowl to black and white photos of Hari herself. Patrons sit at high tables and on vintage sofas, drinking from oversized wine glasses in dim lighting. The long list of cocktails on the chalkboard downstairs are what most people come for, but the upstairs kitchen also serves a full lunch and dinner menu.

MAP 2: Oudezijds Achterburgwal 22, tel. 020/205-0919, www.matahari-amsterdam.nl; noon-1am Sun.-Thurs., noon-3am Fri.-Sat.

The Old Sailor

Entering The Old Sailor feels like walking into the captain's quarters of a 17th-century trading ship, full to the brim with locals and British expats. In this authentic maritime pub, decor consists of wooden helms, rusty chains, and anchors hanging from the ceiling. The view of nearby brothel windows adds to the endearing squalor of this joint.

MAP 2: Oudezijds Achterburgwal 39-A, tel. 020/624-7739, www.cafeoldsailor.eu; 11pm-1am Sun.-Thurs., 11pm-3am Fri.-Sat.

BREWERIES AND DISTILLERIES

✪ Wynand Fockink

Amsterdam's only operational and authentic 17th-century Dutch liquor distillery, Wynand Fockink is cherished by locals. What matters here is the sheer variety of the 100 *genever* (Dutch gin) types available. Dusty wooden shelves behind the bar have held liquor jugs for centuries, and windows just beyond the tasting room reveal the antique distillery, which offers weekly tastings (Sat.-Sun., multiple sessions, €17.50). The staff are incredibly pleasant, patient, and helpful.

MAP 2: Pijlsteeg 31, tel. 020/639-2695, www.wynand-fockink.nl; 3pm-9pm daily

copper kettles on display at De Bekeerde Suster

De Bekeerde Suster

De Bekeerde Suster (The Converted Nun) gets its name from its location on the grounds of a former convent. With a wood-heavy interior and shiny copper kettles, the brewery has taps that pour 4 in-house beers and another 10 Dutch brews. Multiple levels keep the space open, while old beer signs on the exposed brick walls create a tavern feel. A hearty Dutch dinner menu is available, with beer tours and tastings offered by reservation.

MAP 2: Kloveniersburgwal 6, tel. 020/423-0112, www.debekeerdesuster.nl; 3pm-midnight Mon., 3pm-1am Tues.-Thurs., noon-2am Fri.-Sat., noon-midnight Sun.

De Prael

Tucked down a Red Light District alley is the sizable De Prael tasting room. The pub is themed after late Dutch folk singers, and walls are decorated with their old records and posters. Hops lovers will appreciate the Bitterblond and the IPA, while the Weizen (wheat beer) refreshes the palate. Live jazz performances occur every Sunday 2pm-5pm. Bottles are available for purchase at the gift store (Oudezijds Voorburgwal 30) around the corner. De Prael is run by an organization that helps adults with learning disabilities maintain jobs.

MAP 2: Oudezijds Armsteeg 26, tel. 020/408-4470, www.deprael.nl; noon-midnight Mon.-Wed., noon-1am Thurs.-Sat., noon-11pm Sun.

In de Olofspoort

The cheerful In de Olofspoort has a knowledgeable staff who pour young, old, and fruity *genever* (Dutch gin) varieties from 17th-century recipes. Customers sit around small tables among rows of antique liquor bottles and photographs of old Amsterdam. A tiny window downstairs peers into a 14th-century cellar that houses about 200 different liquors, which are available both in full and sample pours.

MAP 2: Nieuwebrugsteeg 13, tel. 020/624-3918, www.olofspoort.com; 4pm-12:30am Tues.-Thurs., 3pm-1:30am Fri.-Sat., 3pm-10pm Sun.

COFFEESHOPS

✪ Coffeeshop Bluebird

Resembling a treehouse hidden in a jungle, Bluebird consists of rainforest murals and tropical plants. The vibe is quaint and groovy, with a friendly staff who serve up homemade soups and apple pie. Smokers can flip through two thick binders called Book of Dreams and Plant of Gods, which detail the different strains of marijuana and hash available. The menu is posted on a laminated card near the bar. Blue Cheese is a popular choice.

MAP 2: Sint Antoniesbreestraat 71, tel. 020/622-5232, www.coffeeshopbluebird.nl; 9:30am-1am daily

Greenhouse Effect

Blending in with its surroundings on the corner of Nieuwmarkt and Bloedstraat, this small and simple spot prides itself in its spacious terrace, which is great for people-watching. Curious about edibles? Their chocolate-flavored and banana-flavored space cakes are well-known for their excellence.

MAP 2: Nieuwmarkt 14, tel. 020/624-4974, www.greenhouse-effect.nl; 9am-1am daily

The Bulldog

One look at the round signs running down the length of Oudezijds Voorburgwal, a main street in the Red Light District, and it's easy to tell

TOP EXPERIENCE

CANNABIS CULTURE

The Bulldog is a Red Light District landmark.

Amsterdam is known for its lenient drug laws, which allow for the existence of coffeeshops—combination cannabis dispensaries and cafés. Here, customers can buy marijuana to smoke or in edible form, then hang out in the shop to enjoy their purchases.

Several million tourists a year come to Amsterdam solely to experience the city's cannabis offerings. Less than 7 percent of Amsterdam residents use marijuana regularly, so coffeeshops rely on tourism to stay afloat. All in all, the city is home to about 150 coffeeshops, most in the Old Center, the Red Light District, and Nieuwmarkt. Most coffeeshops are mellow, with friendly employees.

The bar features a menu listing different strains of marijuana, along with hash and edible cannabis products. Each menu entry notes the type of high the product induces, the product's origin, and prices for different quantities (up to five grams). The shop's budtender helps customers decide, offering recommendations and information. Most coffeeshops have equipment like vaporizers and pipes available for use. The café setup encourages customers to enjoy their purchases over a cup of coffee or tea.

Coffeeshops can always be identified by the small green-and-white window decal that reads "coffeeshop." Each shop can only sell up to 5 grams of cannabis per customer each day, with a maximum of 500 grams allowed in their inventory at a time. Coffeeshops cannot sell alcohol and weapons are not allowed inside. It's common for proprietors to ask that customers show ID, as you must be 18 or older to enter a coffeeshop. No establishment in the city sells hard drugs, which are illegal. Possession of cannabis is technically illegal, but having five grams or less is considered a decriminalized offense and is tolerated by authorities. It's illegal to smoke marijuana anywhere outside of a coffeeshop.

★ Coffeeshop Bluebird (page 113)
★ The Bulldog (page 113)
★ Grey Area (page 125)
★ Amnesia (page 125)
★ Katsu (page 129)
★ Barney's (page 133)
★ Paradox (page 133)
★ Green House (page 137)

that The Bulldog is a dominant chain in the city. In addition to this coffeeshop, its properties include a brown bar, a nightclub, and a hostel. The coffeeshop stands out from its surroundings, with its hippie mural painted on the exterior and cowhide barstools inside. Staff friendliness levels fluctuate, the vibe is touristy, and the products may not be of the highest quality. This is one of the few coffeeshops left in the Red Light District.

MAP 2: Oudezijds Voorburgwal 90, no phone, www.thebulldog.com; 8am-1am daily

NIGHTCLUBS

The Winston

The Winston draws in backpackers and partygoers with its variety of DJs, low-cost covers, and late-night hours. A bit of a dive and a bare-bones venue, the club is small, but the crowd is sociable. The only spot in the Red Light

District with regular club nights, The Winston hosts drum and bass Monday nights, R&B Tuesdays, and open-mic Wednesdays. Weekends see both live gigs and DJs playing club tracks.

MAP 2: Warmoesstraat 131, tel. 020/623-1380, www.winston.nl; 9pm-4am Mon. and Wed.-Thurs., 9pm-5am Fri.-Sat., 10am-4pm Sun.; cover €7

BARS

Ton Ton Club

Once home to the first peep show in Amsterdam, Ton Ton now draws customers looking to play nostalgic arcade classics like Atari, Pac Man, Mortal Kombat, and more. Five pinball machines are set up side by side, while air hockey, board games, and even a 360-degree Ping-Pong table are all included in this miniature rec room. This is a fun alternative to hitting the bars. A short menu of hot dogs, nachos, and a few fridges of craft beers are at the snack bar.

MAP 2: Sint Annendwarsstraat 6, tel. 063/441-2913, www.tontonclub.nl; 4pm-midnight Mon.-Tues., 11am-midnight Wed.-Sun.

WHISKEY BARS

Café Zilt

An inconspicuous, sophisticated breath of fresh air, Café Zilt holds over 90 whiskies from all regions of Scotland. The owner suits up his knowledgeable staff in black vests and ties to accompany the retro setting. From smooth to smoky, each glass of whiskey is served with a glass of water and dropper to open its full-bodied aroma. The relaxed vibe is part of the reason locals and expats come here for a more refined nightcap.

MAP 2: Zeedijk 49, tel. 020/421-5416, www.cafezilt.nl; 5pm-3am Sun.-Thurs., 5pm-4am Fri.-Sat.

GAY AND LESBIAN BARS

Café 't Mandje

Café 't Mandje is considered to be the first gay bar in the Netherlands. First run by famed lesbian Bet van Beeren, who motorcycled down Zeedijk dressed in leather, the bar opened in 1927 and is considered a historic landmark for the gay scene. The ties hanging from the ceiling were cut off men's suits and hung up by Bet herself. This vintage look of this small and sometimes-cramped dive bar gives it a boost of charm and character.

MAP 2: Zeedijk 63, tel. 020/622-5375, www.cafetmandje.nl; 4pm-1am Tues.-Thurs., 4pm-3am Fri., 3pm-3am Sat., 3pm-1am Sun.

Queen's Head

Knock back a few pilsners with Dutch drag queens at this small brown bar on the Zeedijk. A mic and small stage are set up in the back for impromptu karaoke performances and Tuesday night bingo games hosted by drag queens. The cozy inside is lit up like a cabaret, with glittery red curtains, a few stage lights, and chandeliers. The usual Dutch folk songs and traditional party tunes are a friendly invitation to step inside and join the occasion.

MAP 2: Zeedijk 20, tel. 020/420-2475, www.queenshead.nl; 4pm-1am Sun.-Thurs., 4pm-3am Fri.-Sat.

KARAOKE

The End

A hole-in-the-wall karaoke bar popular with college students, young backpackers, and partygoers, The End is home to sing-along camaraderie and thunderous applause. Over 5,000 songs are available, from R&B soul to rock and pop.

MAP 2: Nieuwebrugsteeg 32, tel. 064/904-8839, www.theendkaraoke.nl; 10pm-3am Sun.-Thurs., 9pm-3am Fri.-Sat.

STRIP CLUBS

Bananenbar Amsterdam

A hefty cover charge greets customers at the door of this themed strip club. The downstairs has a small number of cushioned tables, where topless women serve clients bananas in any possible arrangement. The upstairs strip club is more like a small dance floor, where a few dancers and many clients interact. This spot is not for prudish first-timers. It gets busy on weekends.

MAP 2: Oudezijds Achterburgwal 37, tel. 020/627-8954, www.bananenbar.nl; 8pm-2am Sun.-Thurs., 8pm-3am Fri.-Sat.; cover €25-60

SEX SHOWS

Casa Rosso

The first Amsterdam venue to show live sex on stage in 1969, Casa Rosso mixes adult entertainment with amusing skits for a one-hour show. Performances vary from couples having sex on a rotating stage to performers executing a variety of titillating tricks. The crowd is a mix of stag parties, couples, and curious visitors, and the interior of the club resembles an old movie theater.

Casa Rosso

MAP 2: Oudezijds Achterburgwal 106-108, tel. 020/627-8954, www.casarosso.nl; 7am-2am Sun.-Thurs., 7am-3am Fri.-Sat.; cover €40-50

Canal Belt South — Map 3

BROWN BARS

✪ Café de Spuyt

Spuyt is a one-room brown bar with a dusty but cozy feel, and one of the best beer selections around Leidseplein. Order from the 100-plus Dutch or European beers on tap. Their extensive bottled selection is written on the chalkboard wall, but the young staff are familiar enough to recommend good picks. While the playlist blares indie tunes, find a seat at the small bar, the few high tables, or outside under the awning for a great people-watching spot. Thursdays and weekends are busiest, and the crowd is always casual and chatty. Cash is preferred.

MAP 3: Korte Leidsedwarsstraat 86, tel. 020/624-8901, www.cafedespuyt.nl; 4pm-3am Mon.-Thurs., 3pm-4am Fri.-Sat., 3pm-3am Sun.

Café de Wetering

A local's brown bar that's increasingly discovered by visitors, Café de Wetering has the pub feel locked down with simple beers, minimal decor, and a relaxed ambience. This low-key neighborhood bar is quiet and quaint. The upstairs is charming, with a fireplace and an atmosphere that feels more authentic than nearby party bars. Its open-minded owner and regulars extend an inviting vibe to all whom enter. It's cash only here.

MAP 3: Weteringstraat 37, tel. 020/622-9676; 4pm-1am Mon.-Thurs., 4pm-3am Fri., 3pm-2am Sat., 3pm-1am Sun.

a Belgian trappist beer at Café Eijlders

Café Eijlders

This unassuming brown bar is tucked just enough behind Leidseplein to keep tourists at bay and attract local bohemians and worldly travelers. The red and white marble floor is populated with leather booths and stripped-down furniture leading out to a small, heated terrace. The well-dressed bartender is happy to serve the usual *bier van de tap* (tap beer) or *genever* (Dutch gin) under flickering candlelight. Eijlders opened in 1940, and started as an artists', writers', and poets' bar and anti-Nazi hangout.

MAP 3: Korte Leidsedwarsstraat 47, tel. 020/624-2704, www.cafeeijlders.com; 4:30pm-1am Mon.-Wed., noon-1am Thurs. and Sun., noon-2am Fri.-Sat.

Café Genootschap der Geneugten

Café Genootschap der Geneugten (Society of Delights Café) is a hidden gem serving up a healthy list of Belgian beers and fruit *genever* (Dutch gin) just off busy Leidsestraat. The brown look comes from the dark wooden furnishings; a tavern atmosphere is enhanced by chalkboards on the walls listing the available spirits. For fruit liquors, try the blood orange *bloedsinaasappel*, or get real Dutch about it and head straight for the black licorice *drop*. Or try a little of everything: €30 will buy you a 12-shot sampler. This bar is where patient patrons wait for a table at nearby Café de Klos.

MAP 3: Kerkstraat 54, tel. 020/625-0934; 6pm-1am Tues.-Thurs., 6pm-2am Fri.-Sun.

Café Langereis

This place feels more like a student's living room, with antique lamps, bookshelves full of tattered books, and board games stacked on an upright piano. The aged wooden furniture, old barstools, and cheerful bartenders contribute to the cozy atmosphere. Acoustic jazz or folk music performers play on Sundays around 6pm, and the pub is busiest a few hours later when the younger generations of bohemian artists and writers head over for a *biertje* (small beer) or *huiswijn* (house wine).

MAP 3: Amstel 202, tel. 020/785-0641, www.cafelangereis.nl; 11am-3am Sun.-Thurs., 11am-4am Fri.-Sat.

Café Slijterij Oosterling

Just at the end of Utrechtsestraat is Café Slijterij Oosterling, a family-run locals' spot brimming with history. Large wooden casks that once held brandy wine hang from the ceiling, and the interior walls date from 1735, way before the building was used as a distillery in 1877. The bar sells an assortment of liquors and *genever* (Dutch gin). Regulars and visitors in need of a break head here for a *biertje* (small beer) or two. The bar is supposedly haunted, and the owners have some convincing stories to prove it.

MAP 3: Utrechtsestraat 140, tel. 020/623-4140, www.cafeoosterling.nl; 3pm-midnight Mon.-Wed., noon-1am Thurs.-Sat., 1pm-8pm Sun.

De Pieper

This brown bar has stood since 1665, making it one of the oldest spots for a drink in the city. De Pieper was built during the time the Prinsengracht was buzzing with merchants and traders; this corner café and bar is still a good spot for people-watching. The squeaky floorboards, stained-glass window patches, cramped room, and tiny bar are reminders of the building's origins. In good weather, try for a seat on the terrace overlooking the Prinsengracht. A mix of tourists and a handful of older, local regulars frequent this bar.

MAP 3: Prinsengracht 424, tel. 020/626-4775; noon-1am Mon., 4pm-midnight Tues., noon-1am Wed.-Thurs., noon-2am Fri.-Sat., 2pm-10pm Sun.

GRAND CAFÉS

Café Americain

This bar at the Hampshire Hotel—Amsterdam American feels like 1920s Amsterdam. The grand café and long bar have kept an art nouveau tone with cast-iron stained glass, peacock feathers, and stunning Tiffany-style lamps in a dark wood setting. A giant vase spouting a full bouquet sits on a grand piano, and a large window overlooks a water fountain. Arches in the ceilings are bricked in white and emerald, and the mural behind the bar is an original 1930 oil painting of Shakespeare's *A Midsummer Night's Dream*. Many people come to indulge in an early evening glass from the extensive wine list while absorbing the gorgeous interior, but a full menu of food is also served here.

MAP 3: Leidsekade 97, tel. 020/556-3010, www.cafeamericain.nl; 6:30am-10:30pm daily

Café in De Balie

Situated in the lobby area of a grand cinema is this elegant, charming café, spacious and lively enough to visit even if you're not in the mood for a movie. A former 19th-century courthouse, the building sports high ceilings and windows flooded with light. During the day, it's an unassuming bistro; by night, Café in De Balie attracts a cultured yet unpretentious crowd. Dozens of small wood tables sit under a dazzling chandelier, at the foot of a grandiose staircase. This is a perfect spot to begin or end an evening with a few rounds in a refined manner. DJs play ambient beats on Thursdays and Fridays.

MAP 3: Kleine-Gartmanplantsoen 10, tel. 020/553-5100, www.debalie.nl; 9am-1am Mon.-Thurs., 9am-3am Fri., 10am-3am Sat., 10am-midnight Sun.

COFFEESHOPS

Boerejongens Centre

The Boerejongens Centre is something of a hipster coffeeshop, resembling an 1800s-era pharmacy and featuring a marble floor. The budtenders behind the counter wear white shirts that look like lab coats. Small, clear plastic containers filled with marijuana are set on shelves behind the bar like old medicine jars. The menu is decent, featuring strains like AK Bio Flower, Grape Ape, and Sour Diesel Kush, and there are also pre-rolled joints and space cakes available. Small, with no chairs or space to hang out, this gimmicky

Gatsby-style coffeeshop is a big hit with locals who like their smokes to go.

MAP 3: Utrechtsestraat 21, no phone; 7am-1am daily

The Dolphins

Quirky, tacky, and aggressively ocean-themed, The Dolphins is a novel addition to Amsterdam's coffeeshop culture. While the upstairs is bejeweled with coral decorations, a simpler and more subdued smoking lounge is downstairs. Novices are fond of the space tea or space cake; smokers prefer the White Dolphin and Royal Dolphin.

MAP 3: Kerkstraat 39, tel. 020/774-3336; 10am-1am daily

LIVE MUSIC

✪ Paradiso

The best venue for live music in the country (some bands would say in all of Europe), this former 19th-century church turned concert hall has hosted every musician from Queens of the Stone Age to B. B. King. The dramatic Gothic stained-glass windows and white wraparound balconies are the backdrop for an intimate stage. There is a smaller room in the back that hosts lesser-known acts, and the cellar functions as a post-gig bar and hangout spot. Paradiso also doubles as a nightclub after 11pm, and their indie nights are huge with students. Buy tickets online; expect a €3.50 mandatory membership fee.

MAP 3: Weteringschans 6, tel. 020/626-4521, www.paradiso.nl; hours and ticket prices vary by event

Bourbon Street

Adorned with the iconic figures of the Blues Brothers dancing about the entrance, Bourbon Street is Amsterdam's answer to a boozy and bluesy New Orleans bar. The large, rundown ballroom is lined with posters of The Rolling Stones, Jimi Hendrix, and other rock legends, with street lanterns hanging above the massive oak bar. The weekly lineup includes house bands jamming to rock, funk, reggae, and blues and the occasional touring band. Depending on the night, the crowd varies from Grateful Dead fans to younger partygoers looking for a cheap night out. With the right group on the right night, the vibe resembles a Mardi Gras party.

MAP 3: Leidsekruisstraat 6-8, tel. 020/623-3440, www.bourbonstreet.nl; 10pm-4am Sun.-Thurs., 10pm-5am Fri.-Sat.; cover €5

Jazz Café Alto

For decades, Alto had a reputation as a hot spot for rebellious jazz musicians who wouldn't conform to the established "rules" of music. Things have tamed a bit since its heyday in the 1990s, but Jazz Café Alto is still a sultry and low-lit jazz club hosting nightly gigs with local and international trios, quintets, solo singers, and sax players. Get here before 11pm to avoid the cover charge, and grab a seat at one of the small tables in front. Amstel on tap is the drink of choice. As bands squeeze themselves onto the tiny stage, check out the photos and posters on the walls and ceiling, warped from years of sweat and smoke. When the place is packed and the music is hot, you'll want to groove to the beat.

MAP 3: Korte Leidsedwarsstraat 115, tel. 020/626-3249, www.jazz-cafe-alto.nl; 9pm-3am Sun.-Thurs., 9pm-4am Fri.-Sat.; cover €0-5

Rock out at The Waterhole.

Melkweg

This former milk factory has become a concert venue and cultural hub hosting a mix of nightly gigs, club nights, film screenings, and photography shows. A neon sign reading *Melkweg* (Milky Way) marks the entrance's two doors. The larger concert hall, The Max, is on the left, and the smaller, Oude Zaal (Old Hall), is on the right. Both stages have a star-spangled roster, featuring acts like At The Drive-In, U2, and Jack White. In the back is a photography exhibition wing. A modern addition next to the front entrance acts as a cinema, screening indie and offbeat films. Club nights see an all-ages crowd. Buy tickets online and expect a €3.50 mandatory membership fee.

MAP 3: Lijnbaansgracht 234A, tel. 020/531-8181, www.melkweg.nl; hours and ticket prices vary by event

The Cave

Any rocker seeking heavy metal should come to The Cave, Amsterdam's only metal bar. Set in a basement, The Cave hosts live hardcore acts through the week. CDs are stacked behind the bar, and the layout is limited to a few tables and a long bar. A small stage in the back is where bands play everything from stoner rock to thrash metal; the cover charge is rarely more than €10. Dark and dirty like its namesake, but with the inviting and friendly atmosphere of a tavern, The Cave is upbeat despite the headbanging.

MAP 3: Prinsengracht 472, tel. 020/626-8939, www.thecave.nl; 8pm-3am Sun.-Thurs., 8pm-4am Fri.-Sat.; cover €10

The Waterhole

This disheveled saloon and rock bar dishes out cover bands belting classic favorites to a crowd swaying and singing. There are old rock posters, guitars, and signs on the walls. Favorite rock tunes, like top hits from Queen, Guns N' Roses, and the Red Hot Chili Peppers, hum through the air. A few old pool tables are in the back, and the favored drink at the long, busy bar is cheap beer in a wide glass mug. The

cheap cover is mostly for crowd control, and the crowd here is a mix of tourists, international students, and locals who have a thing for American rock in a gritty, country tavern setting.
MAP 3: Korte Leidsedwarsstraat 49, tel. 020/620-8904, www.waterhole.nl; noon-3am Sun.-Thurs., noon-4am Fri.-Sat.; cover €1

NIGHTCLUBS

AIR

Five bars occupy the sleek and modern AIR, one of the largest clubs on Rembrandtplein. The main room is spacious, with a tiered layout and a stage hosting the latest DJs who play electronic dance and house music. A smaller room has a separate sound system that plays more obscure R&B and hip-hop tracks. A downside here is the expenses after admission: AIR runs on prepaid cards, where customers load up money (starting with more than €30 is encouraged) to pay for drinks, which some say makes their money go faster than at a cash bar.
MAP 3: Amstelstraat 16, tel. 020/820-0670, www.air.nl; 11:30pm-4am Sun. and Thurs., 11pm-5am Fri.-Sat.; cover €10-20

Chicago Social

This corner club is the only spot for dancing on Leidseplein and was once the venue for English stand-up comedy club BOOM Chicago. The crowd is international, a bit touristy, and fun. The club itself is a room with a tall ceiling and black walls, and a stage that rarely gets used. Amsterdammers come for the trendy DJs playing different genres of electronic music. Many skip the cover fee by stopping for a cocktail in the adjacent bar and lounge in the front of the building.
MAP 3: Leidseplein 12, tel. 020/760-1171, www.chicagosocialclub.nl; 8pm-4am Sun.-Thurs., 8pm-5am Fri.-Sat.; cover €10

Club Escape

It's impossible to miss Club Escape, the focal point of Rembrandtplein, luring in clubbers who come to Amsterdam searching for something resembling a night out in Ibiza. Inside, multicolored strobes flash and smoke and confetti ribbons fly from every corner. DJs amp up the crowd's energy, and in-house dancers vogue to the rhythm on stage and on platforms across the space. VIP balconies overlook the dance floor. This place is a hit-or-miss spot that survives mainly thanks to its location. Still, the DJ lineup is strong and appealing to fans of the electronic scene. International students get in for free on Thursdays.
MAP 3: Rembrandtplein 11, tel. 020/622-1111, www.escape.nl; 11pm-4am Sun. and Thurs., 11pm-5am Fri.-Sat.; cover €10-16

Club Up

The inconspicuous entrance at Club Up is noticeable only by the long line of partygoers waiting to enter. Find it and enjoy the Brooklyn feel of hip-hop, classic house, and techno music, which draws in stylish twentysomethings. The lineup features up-and-coming DJs. The simple setup of a dance floor, disco balls, and visual projections makes for a straightforward and casual vibe. A lounge upstairs has a cigarette smoking room and a few tables to take a breather when it gets stuffy.
MAP 3: Korte Leidsedwarsstraat 26, tel. 020/623-6985, www.clubup.nl; 11pm-4am Thurs., 11pm-5am Fri.-Sat.; cover €6-10

Jimmy Woo

Jimmy Woo is at the forefront of Amsterdam's club scene, a place to see and be seen by the city's hottest partygoers and DJs. Its two-floor location features a pricey bar and bottle service lounge upstairs. The basement level is a dance floor with a low ceiling illuminated by 12,000 bare bulbs pulsating to the beat. Despite the clique of regulars and the entrance fee and bar tab, those who love to flaunt it on the dance floor to disco, R&B, and house music will fit right in.

MAP 3: Korte Leidsedwarsstraat 18, tel. 020/626-3150, www.jimmywoo.com; 11pm-4am Thurs.-Sun.; cover €15

Sugar Factory

From live indie rock to underground hip-hop, Sugar Factory wears many hats. Weekdays and early weekend nights host live bands on an intimate stage, while late nights transform the space into an electronic, house, and synth pop scene. The bare-bones dance floor has a few spots to lounge. On Sundays, when everywhere else in town is quiet, Wicked Jazz Sounds heats up the space with soulful funk and jazz jams until very late. The crowd includes college students, tourists, and longtime clubbers.

MAP 3: Lijnbaansgracht 238, tel. 020/627-0008, www.sugarfactory.nl; 11pm-4am Thurs., 11pm-5am Fri.-Sun.; cover €8-15

BARS

Coco's Outback

Aussie expats, international students, and young locals who have a thing for Oz all come to Coco's for live sports games (soccer, rugby, American basketball, and more) during the day and the party at night. It's fun here, with rounds of flaming sambuca shots, overflowing pints of ale, and loud, thumping dance hits blasting across a sweaty dance room (that doubles as a restaurant by day). When it comes to carefree dancing on the cheap with a crowd of blissful dancers, Coco's is it.

MAP 3: Thorbeckeplein 8-12, tel. 020/627-2423, www.cocosoutback.com; noon-3am Sun.-Thurs., 11am-4am Fri.-Sat.

De Duivel

Lovers of rap and old-school rhymes will find a new favorite at De Duivel, Amsterdam's funk, soul, and hip-hop bar. Small, narrow, and with not much more than a long bar, De Duivel is a place to chill out and soak in the music from Dutch DJs to The Pharcyde and everything in between. Despite the music playing, it's not a nightclub. The walls exhibit artwork from the latest stars of the local street art scene. The crowd is low key, and there have even been sightings of The Black Eyed Peas. The popular order here is a Jager shot washed down with Amstel beer.

MAP 3: Reguliersdwarsstraat 87, tel. 063/083-2404, www.cafededuivel.nl; 8pm-3am Sun.-Thurs., 8pm-4am Fri.-Sat.

BEER BARS

De Zotte

De Zotte is a favorite among beer lovers in Amsterdam because of its casual, tavern feel, hidden location, and the hundreds of Belgian beers on the menu. Rusted beer signs cover the walls, the chalkboard lists daily beers on tap, and classic and indie rock play over the sound system. If you're not sure which of the many brews to order, choose from the different types of beer glasses displayed behind the bar; there's even a beer that comes in a glass shaped like a horn. Come early and grab some rays on the small bench outside, or come for dinner or a Belgian cheese plate to match your trappist, tripel, dubbel, or blonde. These brews can get potent, with ABV averages of 7-8 percent.

MAP 3: Raamstraat 29, tel. 020/626-8694, www.dezotte.nl; 4pm-1am Sun.-Thurs., 4pm-3am Fri.-Sat.

Mulligans

Just behind Rembrandtplein sits the most authentic Irish bar in the city. Live Irish folk music? Guinness and Murphy's Stout on tap? Irish crowd, owner, and bartenders? Check, check, and check. This spot gives off a warm welcome and enough charm to feel like Ireland. Bands usually set up on a small platform near the entrance, where Irish expats and locals enjoy a pint and watch the soccer game. The upstairs balcony offers a great bird's-eye view of the energy below and the Amstel River outside.

MAP 3: Amstel 100, tel. 020/622-1330, www.mulligans.nl; 4pm-1am Mon.-Thurs., 4pm-3am Fri., 2pm-3am Sat., 2pm-1am Sun.

COCKTAIL BARS

Door 74

This spot started the speakeasy trend with innovative concoctions created by trained mixologists who have won international awards (most of which are on display in a glass cabinet here). The long, minimalist lounge fits a maximum of 30 patrons among its tables and horseshoe-shaped booths. The main feature is the fully stocked bar, illuminated by antique lamps. To find Door 74, look for a dim green light above an unmarked door. Reservations (by phone only) are suggested, but walk-ins are accepted if there's space—usually after 11pm.

MAP 3: Reguliersdwarsstraat 74, tel. 063/404-5122, www.door-74.com; 8pm-3am Sun.-Thurs., 8pm-4am Fri.-Sat.

LOUNGES

Bar Weber

Bar Weber is a narrow bar just behind Leidseplein, about the size of a train car and resembling a chic cabin. It attracts a crowd of creative locals and fashionably cool groups who prefer to party on the outskirts of Leidseplein. While the place can turn into a party, the attitude here is too nonchalant to get crazy.

MAP 3: Marnixstraat 397, tel. 020/422-1412, www.barweber.nl; 7pm-3am Sun.-Thurs., 7pm-4am Fri.-Sat.

Café Brecht

This is a favorite among trendsetters looking for a Berlin-style bar. The vintage wallpaper, mismatched second-hand furniture, and 1940s look lend a welcoming feel. Café Brecht pulls it off, complete with a selection of Czech and German beers on tap and by bottle, soft pretzels, and smooth cocktails like the tangy Aperol Spritz. A good mix of locals and internationals of all ages fill the place, making for a friendly atmosphere and a boisterous terrace. The location makes it easy to find.

MAP 3: Weteringschans 157, tel. 020/627-2211, www.cafebrecht.nl; noon-1am Sun.-Thurs., noon-3am Fri.-Sat.

Lux

This retro-cool bar, just next door to Bar Weber, attracts its trendy clientele with leopard-print seats, a sleek black color scheme, and other mod decor elements. A projector above the bar screens old movies as bartenders serve up cocktails and craft beers. DJs play here on weekend nights, when the bar fills with locals and international creative types.

MAP 3: Marnixstraat 403, tel. 020/422-1412, www.barlux.nl; 7pm-3am Sun.-Thurs., 7pm-4am Fri.-Sat.

WHISKEY BARS

✪ L&B Whiskeycafe

Seen through fogged-up windows is this cozy and quaint brown bar overflowing with its inventory of 1,500 whiskies and brimming with a mellow character. Bottles are stacked in the cupboards, hang from the bar, and are stored in the cellar, and the staff seems to know a little something about each one of them. Order your favorite neat, and it will come with a small glass of water and a dropper to open the whiskey. Sit back, sip along with the sophisticated crowd, and absorb the rustic feel of the place. The lengthy menu can be daunting, so let the staff guide you to a perfect match.
MAP 3: Korte Leidsedwarsstraat 82-84, tel. 020/625-2387, www.whiskeyproeverijen.nl; 8pm-3am Mon.-Thurs., 5pm-4am Fri.-Sat., 5pm-3am Sun.

GAY AND LESBIAN BARS

✪ Café Montmartre

This gay bar has been voted the city's best many times over for its friendly atmosphere and fun clientele that pack the small space nearly every night. Much of its cheery ambience comes from the Dutch pop and *shlager* (Dutch folk music) that the locals and regulars know by heart. Montmartre is set in a narrow room with a long bar and a tiny dance floor at the back. Order a Heineken on tap and let the good times roll. Happy hour is 6pm-8pm daily.
MAP 3: Halvemaansteeg 17, tel. 020/625-5565; 5pm-3am Sun.-Thurs., 5pm-4am Fri.-Sat.

Club NYX

This modern club is three floors high, and each floor has its own bar and music system. The gay and straight crowd is young and energetic. The dazzling interior adds to the contemporary chic feel, with steel beams and colorful illuminated walls. Different DJs play each night, and it's not uncommon to see a line out the door on weekends. It's very trendy, but unpretentious and fun.
MAP 3: Reguliersdwarsstraat 42, no phone, http://clubnyx.nl; 11pm-4am Sun. and Thurs., 11pm-5am Fri.-Sat.; cover €10

Exit Après Chique

This small gay bar, part of Club NYX and formerly known as Club Exit, has no chairs—perfect for the gotta-dance vibe that lasts until the late hours of the night. As its name implies, the theme here is après-ski, evidenced by the old ski posters hanging on the walls. The crowd is a mix of young gay men and women, who pack the place after 2am. Go for a watermelon vodka shot during the 1am-2am happy hour. Sundays are karaoke days.
MAP 3: Reguliersdwarsstraat 42A, no phone, 9pm-4am Sun.-Thurs., 9pm-5am Fri.-Sat.

Lellebel

Lellebel is a semi-hidden, dive-y drag bar that is just as fun as it sounds. At this cramped, gaudy nook just off Rembrandtplein, drag queens are the bartenders and the sound system blasts pop hits from Madonna to Men at Work. The oldest drag bar in the city hosts theme nights and live shows. Everyone is welcome, which is why it's such a good time here.
MAP 3: Utrechtsestraat 4, tel. 020/233-6533, www.lellebel.nl; 9pm-3am Mon.-Thurs., 9pm-5am Fri., 3pm-5am Sat., 3pm-3am Sun.

Canal Belt West Map 4

BROWN BARS

Café de II Prinsen

Café de II Prinsen is a lively brown bar with a charismatic student crowd. The no-frills atmosphere is offset by antique chandeliers and historic portraits on the ceiling. Dutch beers made by Lindeboom are on tap next to small café tables and large wooden barrels doubling as bar tables. Loud conversations over pop music are the norm at night as the room quickly becomes standing-room only. On sunny days, the terrace is a great spot for a beer break.

MAP 4: Prinsenstraat 27, tel. 020/624-9722, www.heffer.nl; 11am-1am Sun.-Thurs., 11am-3am Fri., 10am-3am Sat.

De Admiraal

The hidden-in-plain-sight De Admiraal was originally a 17th-century distillery. The space contains various antique copper tools and distillery equipment from the 1800s and earlier; the water pump behind the bar is one of a kind. Even the bathroom doors are made from giant barrels from the 1600s. The leather-bound menu has a full list of liquors and wines, and they also serve a full dinner menu, though service is sometimes slow.

MAP 4: Herengracht 319, tel. 020/625-4334, www.proeflokaaldeadmiraal.nl; 4:30pm-midnight Mon.-Fri., 5pm-midnight Sat.

Van Puffelen

Van Puffelen is a neighborhood pub on a quiet part of the Prinsengracht canal, perfect for relaxing with a few drinks as the day turns to dusk. A couple tables outside are a great place to settle in, and the roomy inside is a charming surprise. Beyond the first room with the bar are two larger dining areas, complete with a mezzanine and candlelight. Sketches on the walls depict local plants. Though the menu and service are hit-or-miss, locals come for a break to soak in the alluring ambience before moving on for the evening.

MAP 4: Prinsengracht 375-377, tel. 020/624-6270, www.restaurantvanpuffelen; 4pm-1am Mon.-Thurs., noon-3am Fri.-Sat., noon-1am Sun.

COFFEESHOPS

✪ Grey Area

This hole-in-the-wall coffeeshop is the smallest in town, and one of the more famous ones, attracting celebrities like Snoop Dogg, Willie Nelson, and members of Phish. The space can only fit three tables, and its walls are covered in skateboarding and snowboarding stickers. Their products often win awards, no surprise for a place opened by two Americans from Colorado. Among the 20 varieties, Double Bubble Gum, Stonehedge, and the Grey Mist Crystal are all Cannabis Cup award winners. Glass bongs are available to use, and the coffee is bottomless. Weekends can sometimes see a line out the door, but the vibe stays friendly and social in the tight quarters.

MAP 4: Oude Leliestraat 2, tel. 020/420-4301, www.greyarea.nl; noon-8pm daily

Amnesia

Don't let the name intimidate you: Amnesia is a local's favorite, a modern coffeeshop that's not the average hippie hideaway. The main feature is a sleek purple lounge area with swirling gray and gold wallpaper and a purple illuminated bar. The quaint terrace outside has a canal view that's both peaceful and uncrowded. The clientele is a mix of visitors, internationals, and backpackers. The vanilla kush with fresh mint tea is a favorite with locals.

MAP 4: Herengracht 133, tel. 020/427-7874; 9:30am-1am daily

Siberië

Operating since 1984, the genuine vibe at Siberië comes from the chilled-out locals sipping herbal teas by the canal. The simple yet satisfying menu of about a dozen indica, sativa, and hybrid strains of marijuana are explained by a system of smiley faces, indicating each option's effects. Siberië has an artsy side, with rotating local exhibitions, bohemian light fixtures, and a staff who are also musicians and artists. The atmosphere is tranquil, and the space is comfortable, unassuming, and away from the tourist swarm.

MAP 4: Brouwersgracht 11, tel. 020/623-5909; 9am-11pm Mon.-Thurs., 9am-midnight Fri.-Sat., 10am-11pm Sun.

BARS

Café Louis

With exposed brick beams and a minimalist look, Café Louis looks like an abandoned 17th-century space that's been turned into a slightly discovered bar. The look is bare bones, with a few tables, worn furniture, and a small bar. Its corner location offers a view of the canal and a few red light windows. The laid-back crowd is comprised of mostly locals and trendy expats; the place is ideal for an afternoon weekend coffee.

MAP 4: Singel 42, tel. 020/752-6328, www.louis-amsterdam.nl; 11am-1am Mon.-Thurs., 11am-2am Fri.-Sat., 11am-11pm Sun.

De Vergulde Gaper

Corner bar De Vergulde Gaper was once a pharmacy. It still resembles one, with old medicine advertisements from the 1920s hanging on original brick walls and shelves decorated with large mixing bottles and glass beakers. Groups of friends and couples look out the large windows to the Prinsengracht canal while enjoying a few rounds on black leather benches and a long wraparound booth in the back. The atmosphere is lively and busy. This is a great stop for a drink after a day of exploring the neighborhood.

MAP 4: Prinsenstraat 30, tel. 020/624-8975, http://deverguldegaper.nl; 10am-1am Mon., 11am-1am Tues.-Thurs. and Sun., 11am-3am Fri., 10am-3am Sat.

Tabac

On busy nights, the crowd at Tabac spills out to the canal. Inside, the quarters are tight, but a warm camaraderie pervades. The red Tabac sign is the main decor; otherwise it's a simple spot, nicer than a brown bar but just as casual, cozy, and easygoing. By day, the best seating is outside on the cushions. These little perches are covered by an awning that keeps patrons shaded as they gaze at the Prinsengracht canal.

MAP 4: Brouwersgracht 101, tel. 020/622-4413, www.cafetabac.eu; noon-1am Mon.-Thurs., noon-3am Fri., 11am-3am Sat., 11am-1am Sun.

BEER BARS

✪ Arendsnest

This is Amsterdam's first and only Dutch beer bar that serves a menu of

130 brews from some of the 300 breweries in the Netherlands. Look at the blackboard to see what's on tap; the beer tenders can also help pick your match. The place is decked out with antique Dutch beer signs, bottles, and posters along its wood-paneled walls, with an impressive brass tap at the bar. The canalside terrace has a great view, and the cheerful tavern atmosphere inside is infectious. The beer drinkers here are a fun and talkative mix of locals and visitors.

MAP 4: Herengracht 90, tel. 020/421-2057, www.arendsnest.nl; noon-midnight Sun.-Thurs., noon-2am Fri.-Sat.

LOUNGES

Brix

Anyone looking for a posh place to sip cocktails in the Nine Streets shopping district should duck into small, stylish Brix. The neighborhood's young people come for weekend day drinking or a few glasses of white wine after work. Large photographs hang on the exposed brick walls, and the back area is lit by skylights. DJs play here on occasion.

MAP 4: Wolvenstraat 16, tel. 020/639-0351, www.cafebrix.nl; 9am-1am Sun.-Thurs., 9am-3am Fri.-Sat.

WHISKEY BARS

J. D. William's Whiskey Bar

J. D. William's is Amsterdam's third whiskey bar, with a contemporary, chic edge and over 250 whiskies on the menu. Orange fairy lights illuminate bottles on the shelves; martini glasses and tumblers spill onto the bar counter. The whiskey cocktail menu is a healthy list for anyone wanting a Manhattan or an old-fashioned. Kick back at the bar or look out to the street while ambient house music plays in the background. The kitchen serves a pan-Asian list of bites, including spring rolls, meatballs, Korean-style beef tacos, and bourbon-glazed pork ribs.

MAP 4: Prinsenstraat 5, tel. 020/362-0663, http://jdwilliamswhiskybar.com; 5pm-1am Tues.-Thurs., 5pm-2am Fri., 3pm-2am Sat., 5pm-midnight Sun.

WINE BARS

Vyne

This casual yet stylish wine bar is made to look like a barrel that one of its 270 wines was aged to perfection in. The narrow wooden interior, long bar, and dark lighting are more modern than old-fashioned, with a cool and classy vibe. Its location, away from the most tourist-trodden areas, makes for a calm and relaxing atmosphere, and it's never crowded. A long list of Old and New World reds and whites are represented, along with Italian proseccos and French champagnes. Try a flight of three half glasses with the added bonus of an explanation of each from the bartender.

MAP 4: Prinsengracht 411, tel. 020/344-6408, www.vyne.nl; 6pm-midnight Mon.-Thurs., 5pm-1am Fri.-Sat., 4pm-11pm Sun.

Museumplein

BROWN BARS

Café Welling

Thanks to its location tucked behind the grand Concertgebouw, this brown bar from 1928 brings in post-show crowds for a few glasses of Dutch gin, wine, or beer. It's also a popular locals' spot during the day, with patrons chatting over *biertjes* (small beers). Its rustic look comes from worn lamps and a sign on the door that reads *Sterk drank in oude zuid* (A strong drink in the Old South). Live jazz happens every Sunday around 4pm, drawing an older, local crowd.

MAP 5: Jan Willem Brouwersstraat 32, tel. 020/662-0155, http://cafewelling.nl; 4pm-1am Mon.-Thurs., 4pm-2am Fri., 3pm-2am Sat., 3pm-1am Sun.

GRAND CAFÉS

Brasserie Keyzer

Wine lovers and concertgoers alike unwind at this stately brasserie just next to the Concertgebouw music hall. In the dining and lounge areas are iron chandeliers, a grand piano, white tablecloths, and an art deco bar. In summer, the terrace, under a white awning, is a great spot for people-watching and cooling off with a glass of white wine. The seafood lunch and dinner menu is tasteful, albeit high-priced. The steady flow of customers is a blend of Museumplein visitors and well-to-do locals.

MAP 5: Van Baerlestraat 96, tel. 020/675-1866, www.brasseriekeyzer.nl; 10am-11pm daily

Wildschut

This locals' favorite grand café is nestled under a unique 1920s brick building overlooking Van Baerlestraat and is home to a packed terrace in summer. People come here to lounge over post-work drinks or for casual dates, drawn by the café's spaciousness and classy decor. Long tables complement the art deco look of the original light fixtures, antique-looking chairs, and lavish chesterfield benches. A full lunch and dinner menu is available.

MAP 5: Roelof Hartplein 1-3, tel. 020/676-8220, www.cafewildschut.nl; 9am-midnight Mon., 9am-1am Tues.-Thurs., 9am-2am Fri., 10am-2am Sat., 10am-midnight Sun.

LIVE MUSIC

✪ OCCII

OCCII (pronounced oh-key) is a concert hall for independent music with roots in obscure rock, electro, new wave, and metal, from a mix of local and international acts. The affordable cover and beer selection bring in Amsterdammers looking for something different. The facade of OCCII looks like a wooden cuckoo clock. It was built in 1883 as storage and stables for the city's horse-drawn trams. The room is small with a low and intimate stage in a casual setting.

MAP 5: Amstelveenseweg 134, tel. 020/671-7778, http://occii.org; 8pm-2am Sun.-Thurs., 8pm-4am Fri.-Sat.; cover €0-10

✪ OT301

This former film academy is a destination for small bands, urban art shows, DIY workshops, and classes ranging from yoga to acrobatics and belly dancing. It's a full house on weekends and gig nights, and easily spotted off Overtoom with its tall steel doors that lead to a small courtyard with rusty bikes and street art on the walls. The vegan café De Peper resides in the front, while the concert hall and bar are through the doors to the back. A staircase covered in graffiti leads upstairs to artist studios and classrooms. The overall feel is friendly, artsy, and alternative.

MAP 5: Overtoom 301, tel. 020/412-2954, http://ot301.nl; 7pm-2am Sun.-Thurs., 6pm-4am Fri.-Sat.; cover €0-10

De Pijp — Map 6

GRAND CAFÉS

Braque

The open layout, high ceiling, and oversized mirrors make classy Braque something of a cross between a classic French brasserie and an old New York café. The red booths are low, while large windows overlook the street and higher windows sparkle with stained glass. Locals come to unwind on weekend afternoons or before the dinner rush with a glass of Italian carmanere or Austrian chardonnay. Nibble on the well-known starters like bouillabaisse or Burgundy snails. The creamy *scroppino* (an Italian dessert cocktail) with grapefruit is heavenly. Though it's named after a 20th-century French painter, Braque carries a double meaning: In Dutch, *braque* is a tongue in cheek term for feeling hungover.

MAP 6: Albert Cuypstraat 29-31, tel. 020/670-7357, www.caferestaurantbraque.nl; 5pm-1am Tues.-Thurs., 4pm-3am Fri.-Sat., 4pm-1am Sun.

De Kleine Valk

The most cosmopolitan lounge and restaurant in De Pijp is De Kleine Valk, situated in the middle of Marie Heinekenplein behind the Heineken Experience. The look here is all zebra print and turquoise. The vibe is modern rustic, with dark wood walls, cowhide rugs, animal print chairs, and enormous glossy black and white photographs. The fireplaces flicker digital flames and embers. The area is massive enough to hold two bars, a dining area, and an equally sharp terrace to enjoy summer drinks and small bites.

MAP 6: Marie Heinekenplein 5-8, tel. 020/223-2096, www.dekleinevalk.nl; 11am-1am daily (kitchen noon-10pm)

COFFEESHOPS

Katsu

Older locals and young internationals come to this little, canopied, hippie oasis for its high-quality products and a vibe that's more peaceful than most coffeeshops. Squeezed between a boutique and a café bar, the location is bustling with Albert Cuypmarkt shoppers by day and bar-hoppers by night. Take a seat in the earth-toned front area or in the back room, which features a glass roof. The terrace draws a mix of locals reading newspapers and chatting. The groovy artwork on the walls goes with the coffee bar, illuminated by fluorescent and black lights. The menu is on the blackboard; the Kush is a favorite pick.

MAP 6: Eerste van der Helststraat 70, no phone, www.katsu.nl; 10am-midnight Mon.-Thurs., 10am-1am Fri.-Sat., 11am-midnight Sun.

Yo-Yo

Dr. Weed, the main supplier for Yo-Yo, has been delivering organic, chemical-free hybrid strains of cannabis to this shop since it opened in 1986. She is also the main draw for the older local smokers who frequent the coffeeshop. The shop's two rooms have just a few modern red couches with a coffee bar in the back. If it weren't for the smell, you would think this is just someone's bare living room. The place is sunny and clean, and also serves as a gallery space for local artists and, after business hours, a small community center for book clubs, workshops, and painting classes. The mature staff are friendly and talkative. Their recommendations include Dr. Weed's Lavender, Northern Lights, and Master Kush strains.

MAP 6: Jan van der Heijdenstraat 79, tel. 020/233-9800; noon-7pm Sun.-Thurs., noon-8pm Fri.-Sat.

BARS

Café Bloemers

Out of all the cafés around Sarphatipark, Café Bloemers is one of the best in De Pijp. In summer, the terrace stretches around the corner with full tables of relaxed patrons on both sides of the bike path. Inside, the Berlin café meets cozy brown bar has groovy tunes, retro lampshades and chandeliers, exposed brick, and hunting relics like a buffalo head and stuffed pheasant. The beer list is a thoughtful mix of local and Belgian, and cocktails come in big sizes. A lunch and dinner menu of plentiful plates like fish, steak, and veggie stew is also available.

MAP 6: Hemonystraat 70, tel. 020/400-4024; 10am-1am Sun.-Thurs., 10am-3am Fri.-Sat., 10am-midnight Sun.

Het Paardje

Weekends at Gerard Douplein are swamped with single students looking to flirt and party, and Het Paardje (The Horse) is their most preferred pickup bar. Others come for a snack or a few drinks on the large and lively terrace, and end up staying for the whole night. The bar gets packed by early evening. The inside resembles a brown bar, while the outside covered terrace spills onto the streets and Gerard Douplein.

MAP 6: Gerard Douplein 1, tel. 020/664-3539, www.cafehetpaardje.nl; 10am-1am Sun.-Thurs., 10am-3am Fri.-Sat.

Kingfisher

Kingfisher is one of the original bars that made De Pijp cool and trendy. It could be because of the sleek nautical look with red retro fridges, thin diner stools, and a classic navy trim. Regulars have been coming since 1999 for an afternoon beer on the terrace or a long night out with friends. Unlike other De Pijp party bars, the vibe here is laid-back. A talkative and easygoing crowd of Dutch locals and some internationals congregates here at night. It's also possible to pop in at lunch for a quick sandwich or fresh smoothie.

MAP 6: Ferdinand Bolstraat 24, tel. 020/671-2395, www.kingfishercafe.nl; 10am-1am Mon.-Thurs., 10am-3am Fri.-Sat., noon-1am Sun.

MASH

MASH is a tiny bar on Gerard Douplein, the De Pijp party square, with a better-quality drink list than most. A thoughtful microbrew selection is available on tap and by bottle, and the house beer is the original Czech Budweiser pilsner. The small inside is basic, decked out in plywood with seating around the walls. The terrace is fun and trendy on a sunny weekend or a warm evening. The friendly and funny bar staff are social and casual. A huge perk is the selection of Thai bites, coming straight from the famous chef who created the very popular Bird Thais restaurant in the Red Light District.

MAP 6: Gerard Douplein 9, tel. 020/664-4428; noon-1am Sun.-Thurs., noon-3am Fri.-Sat.

COCKTAIL BARS

Twenty Third Bar

This posh and pricey cocktail and champagne bar is located on the 23rd floor of the classy Okura Hotel, with an amazing panoramic view of the city. Moody blue lighting illuminates the bar that serves upscale and unconventional cocktails, from martinis to champagne cocktails, cosmopolitans, and Singapore slings. Small bites, like mango, goose liver, and rose pepper macarons, fresh oysters, or caviar, come straight from the adjoining Michelin-starred Ciel Bleu Restaurant. Come dressed to the nines for this small and sleek bar.

MAP 6: Ferdinand Bolstraat 333, tel. 020/678-7111, www.okura.nl; 6pm-1am Sun.-Thurs., 6pm-2am Fri.-Sat.

Jordaan Map 7

BROWN BARS

✪ Festina Lente

This local spot is an old-fashioned brown bar with a modest but stylish vintage look. The canalside location is off the beaten path—a big perk, as are its modern soundtrack and mixed crowd of young couples, elderly locals, and groups of friends. A few tattered couches, stripped-down wooden tables and chairs, and large windows give off a cozy, sepia-toned ambience. It's one of the few brown bars in the area that's also an *eetcafe* (dinner café), and the options like red bell pepper risotto with sauerkraut or cod filet with fennel rise above the pub food norm.

MAP 7: Looiersgracht 40b, tel. 020/638-1412, www.cafefestinalente.nl; 9am-1am Mon.-Thurs., 9am-3am Fri., 10am-3am Sat., 10am-1am Sun.

Café De Prins

Café De Prins is a traditional brown bar with the best view of Westerkerk bell tower. Patrons come here because of the sunny and inviting terrace and the small interior with its nostalgic charm. The old wooden floor, clinking of glasses, and exposed wooden beams bring an effortless, cozy vibe. Even though the majority of customers are tourists, locals still come here for a drink or two in an authentic setting.

MAP 7: Prinsengracht 124, tel. 020/624-9382, www.deprins.nl; 10am-1am Sun.-Thurs., 10am-2am Fri.-Sat. (kitchen 10am-10pm daily)

Café De Tuin

This is the quintessential Jordaan spot that's not really old enough to be a brown bar but is casual enough to feel like one. The look here is of an old-fashioned saloon, with floral wallpaper, hanging stained-glass lamps, antique mirrors, and old signs on the walls. Laid-back locals come to sip from the local and Belgian beers, including seasonal microbrews. It's rare to find this friendly place empty.

MAP 7: Tweede Tuindwarsstraat 13, tel. 020/624-4559, www.cafedetuin.nl; 10am-1am Mon.-Thurs., 10am-3am Fri.-Sat., 11am-1am Sun.

Café Thijssen

Café Thijssen is all about location, and the trendy residents of the Jordaan come here to pass time on the sunny terrace or inside the simple and humming brown bar. Wedged along the Brouwersgracht and busy Lindengracht, the space is larger than most, with an authentic brown bar feel from its wooden fixtures and large windows. There is always a sports game on a few flatscreens during soccer season, otherwise classic rock tunes play in the background. Service is a bit on the slow side, but count on the beer selection and the Dutch bar snack menu to be tasty.

MAP 7: Brouwersgracht 107, tel. 020/623-8994, http://cafethijssen.nl; 8am-1am Mon.-Thurs., 8am-3am Fri., 7:30am-3am Sat., 8am-midnight Sun.

De Twee Zwaantjes

By day, this spot looks like a typical brown bar. The terrace sits on the Prinsengracht, with a beautiful view of the canal and Westerkerk bell tower. Inside, dripping candles set a tavern-like mood, pairing well with a classic Dutch bar snack like *bitterballen* (fried meatballs). But at night, get ready for a rollicking time belting out Dutch folk songs. This café was featured in Anthony Bourdain's *No Reservations*.

MAP 7: Prinsengracht 114, tel. 020/625-2729, www.cafedetweezwaantjes.nl; 3pm-1am Sun.-Thurs., 3pm-3am Fri.-Sat.

Finch

Out of the handful of brown bars that line the Noordermarkt, Finch is the one that pulls in regulars looking for a trendier vibe. The leafy front, outlined with plants and vines, is complete with a cute terrace that can only seat a dozen or so patrons. The inside is modern retro, with a sleek bar, exposed brick, photo art, and funky lampshades. The food menu is raved about, but the main draws are rounds of coffee or drinks while people-watching around the Noorderkerk.

MAP 7: Noordermarkt 5, tel. 020/626-2461; 9am-1am Mon.-Thurs., 9am-3am Fri., 7am-3am Sat., 10am-1am Sun.

Het Papeneiland

There are enough regulars occupying this brown bar and spilling out onto the corner terrace that it's impossible to not notice it. The name comes from an archaic slang term for the pope, and since 1642 this spot has thrived, with one of the best views in the neighborhood. Traditionally patched windows give an antique charm, with black and white photos of the neighborhood on the walls and high ceilings. The drinks of choice are coffee, wine, or Amstel beer, which pair well with the *ossenworst* and *leverworst* sausages.

MAP 7: Prinsengracht 2, tel. 020/624-1989, www.papeneiland.nl; 9am-1am Sun.-Thurs., 2pm-3am Fri.-Sat.

't Monumentje

This bar is a great spot to find a little local spirit and good-humored patrons—a motley crew of locals and retirees. It's cramped in a cozy way, decorated with photos of hippies and concert posters. The owner loves American and British classic rock, and even DJs here on occasion. The drink menu is on the cheaper side and every first Monday of the month sees a sing-along session with a live band.

MAP 7: Westerstraat 120, tel. 020/624-3541, www.monumentje.nl; 8:30am-1am Mon.-Thurs., 8:30am-3am Fri., 9am-3am Sat., 11am-1am Sun.

't Smalle

This brown bar is the perfect rustic and cozy stop after a long day of walking around the Jordaan. Remnants of this place's origins as a 1700s liquor distillery can still be seen in the old wooden barrels behind the bar and the liquor pump on the counter. The spiral staircase and stained-glass windows are from the 19th century, adding an authentic look that sends patrons on a nostalgic trip back to Golden Age Amsterdam. Upstairs has a bit more privacy, but the most special feature is the terrace—it is one of the few in Amsterdam that is at canal level.

MAP 7: Egelantiersgracht 12, tel. 020/623-9617, www.t-smalle.nl; 10am-1am Sun.-Thurs., 10am-2am Fri.-Sat.

COFFEESHOPS

Barney's

While checking IDs at the door feels a little extreme for a coffeeshop set in a basement, Barney's reputation for award-winning products keeps the place packed with visitors. The modern interior resembles an old pharmacy, with retro knickknacks on the walls, numerous screens, and a conspicuous absence of bohemian decor. Cookies Kush and Carmella Cream Hash are the popular picks at this mellow shop. Each table has a vaporizer ready for use (ask at the counter for a bag and mouthpiece). There is usually a line throughout the day to get in. For a snack, hop across the street to Barney's Lounge, its sister restaurant, bar, and DJ lounge.

MAP 7: Haarlemmerstraat 102, tel. 020/625-9761, www.barneysamsterdam.com; 9am-1am daily

La Tertulia

From the outside, La Tertulia looks more like a hippie residence, with its leafy entrance and flower power murals. Inside, though, the place feels like an exotic jungle café resplendent with tropical plants, crystals, and mellow reggae tunes. The atmosphere is relaxed and geared toward locals. The upstairs adds even more space to mellow out and gaze over the Prinsengracht.

MAP 7: Prinsengracht 312, tel. 020/623-8503, www.coffeeshoptertulia.com; 11am-7pm Tues.-Sat.

Paradox

One of the greatest examples of a neighborhood coffeeshop, Paradox is a bit hidden on a Jordaan canalside street. The vibe is easygoing and inviting, with newspapers to peruse, board games to play, and art hanging on the walls. The owner is approachable and friendly to newbies and experts. The menu is simple and straightforward, with smaller portions than other shops. Their hash cakes are some of the strongest in town.

MAP 7: Eerste Bloemdwarsstraat 2R, tel. 020/623-5639, http://paradoxcoffeeshop.com; 10am-8pm daily

LIVE MUSIC

Maloe Melo

Open since 1998, Maloe Melo has had a reputation as a late-night blues spot known only by the most die-hard fans and musicians. It's a small and dusty dive bar with chairs but no stage, which makes it feel more genuine. The long bar offers affordable drinks to a crowd of older locals. The place could easily be tucked away in some Tennessee town, and though its glory days may be behind it, it's still worth a visit.

MAP 7: Lijnbaansgracht 163, tel. 020/420-4592, www.maloemelo.com; 9pm-3am Sun.-Thurs., 9pm-4am Sat.; cover €5

Nieuwe Anita

One of the hot spots for indie crowds is Nieuwe Anita, a small concert hall with a vintage living room feel that's both casual and cool. The place hosts everything from funky rock bands to alternative film screenings. Housed in a residential building in former storage and boiler rooms, the first room is a bar and Berlin-style lounge. Old wallpaper and mismatched furniture found at thrift shops decorate the space. The performance space is in the back, and the balcony offers a great view of the small stage below. For the sake of nearby residents, keep quiet when you exit.

MAP 7: Frederik Hendrikstraat 111, tel. 020/774-4922, www.denieuweanita.nl; 8pm-1am Mon.-Thurs., 8pm-2am Fri.-Sat., hours vary Sun.; cover €3-8

BARS

✪ Waterkant

Waterkant (Waterside) is a summer hot spot for hipsters and students that sits next to the Marnix canal under two tall, white, and modern parking structures. The long terrace stretches a few hundred feet along the waterfront with colorful chairs and picnic tables, and gets a lot of sun. In slower times, it can be easy to find a spot on the blue patio; on busy nights, more blue stalls open to serve cocktails and beer to the large crowds. Fun and flirty, it's as close to a riverside party as this city gets.

MAP 7: Marnixstraat 246, tel. 020/737-1126, www.waterkantamsterdam.nl; 4pm-1am Mon.-Thurs., 11am-3am Fri.-Sat., 11am-1am Sun.

Bar Struik

A little bit of hip-hop and some funky style is what makes the small Bar Struik an attractive hangout. Creative types come here because of its casual vibe and old-school beats. Grab a seat at one of the tables or couches and don't let the cool crowd intimidate you. Graffiti on the back brick wall spells out the name of the bar.

MAP 7: Rozengracht 160, tel. 020/625-4863; 5pm-1am Mon.-Thurs., 5pm-3am Fri., 3pm-3am Sat., 3pm-1am Sun.

Checkpoint Charlie

Checkpoint Charlie combines German beer, a vintage look, and late-night *currywursts*. Named after the crossing point between East and West Berlin during the Cold War, this spacious and cool bar's exterior mural was created by street artists known as The London Police. Inside is a mix of illustrations, gig posters, and photo collages. There is a pool table and a giant bookshelf stocked with good reads and a few games.

MAP 7: Nassaukade 48, tel. 020/370-8728, www.cafecheckpointcharlie.nl; 1pm-1am Sun.-Thurs., 1pm-3am Fri.-Sat.

Soundgarden

It doesn't get much more grungy or dive-y than Soundgarden, one of the most alternative bars in Amsterdam. The roomy tavern has a pool table, foosball table, pinball machine, and a long bar serving Budels on tap. Dark, punk art is always on the walls, with street art outside; the sticker-laden toilets lack seat covers. On some nights, Soundgarden hosts cult film screenings, while other nights feature a live band or DJs spinning obscure rock. Soundgarden has a reputation for one of the best and most marijuana-friendly canalside terraces in town.

MAP 7: Marnixstraat 164-166, tel. 020/620-2853, www.cafesoundgarden.nl; 1pm-1am Sun.-Thurs., 1pm-3am Fri.-Sat.

BEER BARS

Tripel

Take a few hundred Belgian beers, add classic rock, and you have Tripel. The bar is great in winter, not as stuffy as a one-room brown bar, though it does get busy with beer lovers. The mixed crowd of students, internationals, and a few older locals love it here. The occasional acoustic act performs in the early evening, and by midnight the tables are full with different beer bottles, cheese plates, and pub food. The stained wood furniture, old beer signs, and array of glass goblets give Tripel an authentic Belgian atmosphere. Dinner is served until 10pm daily.

MAP 7: Lijnbaansgracht 161, tel. 020/370-6421; 4pm-3am Sun.-Thurs., 4pm-4am Fri.-Sat.

COCKTAIL BARS

Bar Oldenhof

Find the entrance to this speakeasy under a small yellow sign reading BAR, off the west side of Elandsgracht, then ring the bell. A well-dressed host will come to the door and, if there's room, allow you inside the 12-person cocktail lounge. A night here feels like a throwback to 1920s New York City: In this dimly lit space, patrons drink sophisticated cocktails and neat whiskies while relaxing on chesterfield couches and red velvet chairs. Oldenhof doesn't take reservations.

MAP 7: Elandsgracht 84, tel. 020/751-3273, www.bar-oldenhof.com; 6pm-1am Sun.-Thurs., 5pm-3am Fri.-Sat.

Vesper Bar

James Bond would appreciate this elegant boutique cocktail bar serving up creative concoctions by hipster mixologists. The warm lighting in this small space wraps around the bar. Still shots from James Bond films hang on the walls, and the large, tinted windows offer a private view to the outside. Go early to avoid a long wait and be patient—considerable time and care is put into each cocktail.

MAP 7: Vinkenstraat 57, no phone, www.vesperbar.nl; 8pm-1am Tues.-Thurs., 5pm-3am Fri.-Sat.

GAY AND LESBIAN BARS

Saarein

The great thing about this lesbian-friendly bar is that you don't have to have any specific sexual preference to feel welcome here. Regulars love it because the vibe is casual and social, the music is pumping, and the free pool table downstairs is a fun way to pass the time. It also has a great beer selection. The small corner spot is hidden from the tourist path. Look for the rainbow flag hanging in front of the entrance.

MAP 7: Elandsstraat 119, tel. 020/623-4901, www.saarein2.nl; 4pm-1am Tues.-Thurs., 4pm-2am Fri., noon-2am Sat., 2pm-1am Sun.

WINE BARS

Wijnbar diVino

One of the few wine bars in the Jordaan is off a quiet corner with a small terrace. DiVino specializes in reds and whites from family vineyards in Tuscany, Sicily, Venice, and Lombardy, Italy. Pair your selection with a platter of imported Italian hard cheeses and meat. Local wine connoisseurs come here for something relaxed. The large windows and wooden trim create an instant cozy ambience within a modern setting that's fashionably rustic with traces of Italian decor.

MAP 7: Boomstraat 41A, tel. 020/845-2207, www.wijnbardivino.nl; 5pm-midnight Mon.-Thurs., 5pm-2am Fri., 4pm-2am Sat., 4pm-midnight Sun.

Plantage — Map 8

BROWN BARS

Café De Druif

A few steps west from Kadijksplein is one of the oldest pubs in Amsterdam. In 1631, Café De Druif was a bar that sailors would frequent when the Red Light District closed at night. The pocket-size pub displays a 350-year-old liquor pump, while antique wooden barrels pour brandies from brass faucets. The crowd is a mix of older patrons and laid-back, cheerful locals. Slip back into the 1600s and warm up with a pour of *gember* (ginger) or *aprikoos* (apricot) liquor.

MAP 8: Rapenburgerplein 83, tel. 020/624-4530; 2:30pm-1am Sun.-Thurs., 2:30pm-2am Fri.-Sat.

Café Koosje

Across from Artis Zoo, Café Koosje is a corner café ideal for people-watching while slurping an Irish coffee. Relax on a chesterfield couch or at one of the small tables that abut the long brown bar and walls covered in the latest event posters. The daytime crowd is comprised of families (who come for lunch) and students. Evenings bring a mix of couples, internationals, and trendy city-dwellers for rounds of beer and house wine. Sunny days are packed, with locals lingering underneath the burgundy awning. The menu offers items like toasted sandwiches, salads, and traditional *stamppot* (meat with mashed potatoes and root vegetables).

MAP 8: Plantage Middenlaan 37, tel. 020/320-0817, htto://koosjeamsterdam.nl; 8am-1am Sun.-Thurs., 8am-3am Fri., 8am-2am Sat.

Café Sluyswacht is a great brown bar for a beer break.

Café Sluyswacht

Across from the Rembrandt House is a severely tilted house once owned by a Jewish metal dealer. Café Sluyswacht sits atop the 1602 Sint Antoine lock, with a back terrace exposing a beautiful canal view. Most patrons come for a round of Leffe Belgian beer and a snack of gooey *bitterballen* (fried meatballs). The second floor offers a view of the surrounding canals. Just be careful when opening the windows downstairs—the building leans so acutely they will swing shut on their own.

MAP 8: Jodenbreestraat 1, tel. 020/625-7611, www.sluyswacht.nl; 12:30pm-1am Mon.-Thurs., 12:30pm-3am Fri.-Sat., 12:30pm-7pm Sun.

Eetcafé De Magere Brug

Located right on the corner of the Amstel River and the Skinny Bridge, Eetcafé De Magere Brug is an old corner pub that has all the right outdoor views for an authentic, laid-back Amsterdam feel. Its usual customers are Carré theatergoers and locals seeking a drink in the sun on the outdoor terrace benches. Standard Dutch pub food like chicken satay and hamburgers are on the lunch and dinner menu.

MAP 8: Amstel 81, tel. 020/221-3400, http://demagerebrug.nl; 11am-1am Mon.-Thurs., 10am-3am Sat., 10am-1am Sun.

GRAND CAFÉS

Bar Lempika

The avant-garde Bar Lempika draws a blend of the luxury Amstel Hotel crowd and Carré theatergoers. The narrow room has floor-to-ceiling windows that overlook the Amstel River and luxurious Amstel Hotel. The marble bar complements mirrored shelves of liquor, and the overall effect is polished with a touch of chic. A daily menu offers typical Dutch-Euro cuisine like steak and salad.

MAP 8: Sarphatistraat 23, tel. 020/622-0209, www.barlempicka.com; 9am-1am Mon.-Fri., 9am-3am Sat.-Sun.

COFFEESHOPS

✪ Green House

Green House, a classic, groovy Amsterdam coffeeshop on the cusp of the Red Light District, pleases visitors (including some celebrities). The canalside shop, with its green awning and mural, is earthy but modern, with plush barstools and funky glass ceiling lamps. Their Cannabis Cup award-winning products are available in the back. Try to find a spot on the terrace overlooking the canals. There are three other locations in the city.

MAP 8: Oudezijds Voorburgwal 191, tel. 020/627-1739, www.greenhouse.org; 10am-1am daily

Het Ballonnetje

Het Ballonnetje (The Little Balloon) has been around since 1978. Its name refers to hot air balloons, as you can see with the display of hot air balloon figurines and the sky-blue trim along its big windows. Located near the University of Amsterdam's dorms, students often come here to study. The vibe is philosophical and literary. It's also a hangout for locals who are looking for low prices.

MAP 8: Roetersstraat 12, tel. 020/622-8027, http://coffeeshopballoon.com; 9am-midnight daily

IJ River

BROWN BARS

Koffiehuis KHL

A café and small concert hall fit inside this freestanding brick cottage, serving as a cozy and charming spot for a drink since 1917, a few blocks down from Lloyd Hotel. Most customers enjoy the atmosphere with a *biertje* (small beer), but a lunch and dinner menu is also available, offering standard and affordable Dutch dishes. The simple wooden tables, exposed brick walls, and rust-colored curtains give an old-fashioned feel in the front, while the back area has a larger room with high ceilings and space for a small stage. Live music sessions, from jazz to acoustic, take place around 8pm on various days of the week, entertaining cheerful neighborhood locals in a casual and homey setting.

MAP 9: Oostelijke Handelskade 44, tel. 020/779-1575, http://denieuwekhl.nl; noon-midnight Tues.-Sun.

GRAND CAFÉS

De Kompaszaal

This is a classic grand café tucked away on KNSM Island, offering evening dancing from Lindy Hop to tango. Kompaszaal hasn't changed much since the 1950s, with its seafarer decor of green trim, a large fish tank, and a sweeping outdoor terrace overlooking the waterfront. In the daytime, big band music plays softly as locals sip coffee or tea. On Friday nights, a live big band plays to an audience of swing dancers of all ages. There is tango on every third Sunday of the month, and every third Saturday features salsa.

MAP 9: KNSM-Laan 311, tel. 020/419-9596, www.kompaszaal.nl; 10am-5pm Wed., 10am-1am Thurs.-Fri., 11am-1am Sat.-Sun.

Kanis En Meiland

This locals' spot on Javaeiland is a perfect stop day or night for a drink or small bite overlooking the waterfront. Large windows look out onto houseboats and the outdoor terrace, while the chic nautical inside is illuminated by retro light fixtures and candles. Plants hang from the ceiling, and regulars catch up over drinks at the large communal wooden tables. Check out the Dutch beers from small breweries in Holland like SNAB and Emelisse. A full lunch and dinner menu is also available.

MAP 9: Levantkade 127, tel. 020/737-0674, www.kanisenmeiland.nl; 8:30am-1am Mon.-Fri., 10am-1am Sat.-Sun.

BREWERIES AND DISTILLERIES

✪ Brouwerij 't IJ

Brouwerij 't IJ is a Belgian-style microbrewery offering a short list of its own full-bodied craft beers. Underneath the Gooyer windmill, the brewhouse has a large island bar where servers pour drinks into small goblets. Find descriptions of the different beers on a chalkboard wall, and order snacks like sausage and gouda cheese dipped in beer barley. On busy afternoons, the place is packed with a few hundred beer lovers, both locals and tourists. The smell of yeast drifts out to the small beer garden in the front. There are always a few permanent beers on tap, like IJwit (a wheat beer) and Zatte (a

Belgian tripel), but seasonal brews like IJbok (a dark autumn beer) and Paasij (a hoppy spring beer) are big favorites.

MAP 9: Funenkade 7, tel. 020/622-8325, www.brouwerijhetij.nl; 2pm-8pm daily

Oedipus Brewery

Oedipus started with a group of young Dutch men brewing craft beer in their homes and selling six packs at neighborhood markets and festivals. In 2015, they established a tap house in the roomy warehouses of Amsterdam North. This is a place that prides itself on using unusual ingredients and creative labels. The look at this minimalist brewery is urban funk. Mannen Liefde has been their most successful beer, but on tap are other creative options like the cilantro, coriander, and chili pepper Thai Thai tripel or the light Slomo session saison with citrusy Czech hops.

MAP 9: Gedempt Hamerkanaal 85, no phone, http://oedipus.com; 5pm-9pm Wed.-Thurs., 2pm-11pm Fri.-Sat., 2pm-9pm Sun.

LIVE MUSIC

Tolhuistuin

Tolhuistuin is a two-story concert hall that hosts live bands, club nights, and cultural events across the IJ River from Amsterdam Centraal Station. The main hall fits just over 500 people on the main floor and balcony, hosting acts like Lee Fields, Neko Case, and many other indie rock bands. The acoustics are great here, as the room is spacious but with an intimate feel. The in-house café has a wide view overlooking the waterfront; downstairs, there is a smaller bar serving the riverside terrace. A garden behind the building hosts concerts and other events in summer. This is a credit card-only spot; they don't accept cash.

Hanneke's Boom

MAP 9: Tolhuisweg 5, tel. 020/763-0650, www.tolhuistuin.nl; 10am-1am daily, garden 9am-9pm daily summer; cover €15

BARS

Hanneke's Boom

Hanneke's Boom, on a tiny manmade island, is like a tiki bar set inside a trendy shack, where locals and young adults come for drinks and a few fried *hapjes* (Dutch appetizers). Outside are rows of picnic tables and a dock to dangle your feet as a few sloops dock nearby. The back area has long logs and a grassy patch, and the rooftop terrace is just up the stairs above the outhouse. Things get crowded inside when DJs play on weekend nights. It's quiet here in winter, and the big fireplace can be a cozy spot to hang out.

MAP 9: Dijksgracht 4, tel. 020/419-9820, www.hannekesboom.nl; 11am-1am Sun.-Thurs., 11am-3am Fri.-Sat.

COCKTAIL BARS

Hiding in Plain Sight

This cocktail bar sits snuggly on a corner slightly off the beaten path of the Old Center. Looking like a cross between an old-fashioned hunting club and a mad scientist's lab, the small space is attractive and private. Bartenders wear bow ties and suspenders, and this 1920s atmosphere is enhanced by the chesterfield furniture and warm hanging lamps. The high bar is well stocked, serving classic drinks like gin fizzes and Moscow mules, all with their own twist. The young staff are genuine, funny, and quick to help recommend a drink. The in-house band plays upbeat Balkan folk live on Thursdays. Reservations are suggested on weekends.

MAP 9: Rapenburg 18, tel. 062/529-3620, www.hpsamsterdam.com; 6pm-1am Sun.-Thurs., 6pm-3am Fri.-Sat.

LOUNGES

✪ SkyLounge

SkyLounge is a stylish lounge and a top choice for a swanky cocktail with the best rooftop view in the city. This top-floor hotel bar is sleek, long, and modern, with shiny, high tables lining the floor-to-ceiling windows. A lounge at the end of the bar sprawls out to a large outdoor terrace on one end of the space. The view is stunning both day and night. Ambient lounge music fills the room as hotel guests and posh locals sip on expensive cocktails and wine. The full dinner menu is pricey.

MAP 9: Oosterdoksstraat 4, tel. 020/530-0800, www.skyloungeamsterdam.com; 11am-1am Sun.-Tues., 11am-2am Wed.-Thurs., 11am-3am Fri.-Sat.

Roest

This café-lounge is an urban beach bar housed in a rundown industrial space that oozes cool Berlin vibes. Here, the alternative crowd digs their toes into a massive sandbox and relaxes in canalside beach chairs or picnic tables. At night, there are DJ dance sessions, featuring everything from hip-hop to '50s rock. A double decker bus out front serves up barbecue in the summer. Cocktails, local beers, and bottles of wine are on offer—a more interesting assortment than what's served in most club bars.

MAP 9: Jacob Bontiusplaats 1, tel. 020/308-0283, www.amsterdamroest.nl; 4pm-1am Thurs., 4pm-3am Fri., noon-3am Sat., noon-11pm Sun.

ARTS AND CULTURE

Amsterdam has had a harmonious relationship with art for over 400 years, most notably with artists like Rembrandt van Rijn, Vincent van Gogh, and Piet Mondrian. The city is also forward-looking, with cutting-edge performance art that will define music, dance, and stage for years to come.

Leading away from Museumplein, arguably one of the highest concentrations of famous art in the country, is Nieuwe Spiegelstraat, where you'll find the city's main strip of art galleries. Along this walkable street is every type of art imaginable, from ancient relics and European antiques to abstract and contemporary works.

Amsterdam also embraces music, dance, film, and theater arts, rivaling Europe's other cultural capitals. Large performance halls host international operas, ballet companies, and orchestras. Meanwhile, small theaters and cultural centers, many located near Leidseplein and Rembrandtplein, are home to lesser-known, avant-garde productions.

Felix Meritis

Many productions in the city are performed in Dutch; few are in English, with the exception of international acts. Confirm ahead before buying your tickets.

HIGHLIGHTS

- **MOST PHOTO-CENTRIC MUSEUM: Foam** houses works from the most iconic photographers, featuring genres ranging from street and portrait photography to documentary and photojournalism (page 147).
- **MOST FASHIONABLE COLLECTION:** Make your way to the **Museum of Bags and Purses** to glimpse bags and purses made of everything from steel to eel skin (page 147).
- **BEST GALLERY FOR ART LOVERS ON A BUDGET—OR A SPLURGE:** At **The Public House of Art,** customers can buy pieces that range from budget to sky-high prices (page 149).
- **BEST BET FOR AN ENGLISH-LANGUAGE PERFORMANCE:** See a classic drama or a modern musical in the **Stadsschouwburg,** where many performances are in English or include English subtitles (page 151).
- **MOST STUNNING MOVIE THEATER:** The art deco exterior and mesmerizing stained-glass windows at **Pathé Tuschinski** make for a one-of-a-kind moviegoing experience (page 152).
- **BEST UNDER-THE-RADAR PHOTOGRAPHY MUSEUM:** The **Huis Marseille Museum for Photography** contains edgy and artistic photography exhibitions in a restored 17th-century canal mansion (page 153).
- **SWEETEST ACOUSTICS:** Whether you're here to see a legendary rock band or a symphony orchestra, the **Royal Concertgebouw** offers the best possible way to hear it (page 155).
- **QUIRKIEST MUSEUM:** The psychedelic neon installations at **Electric Lady Land** aren't the usual museum fare (page 156).
- **MOST GRANDIOSE ART COLLECTION:** As the largest satellite of St. Petersburg's Hermitage, **Hermitage Amsterdam** possesses impressive artworks ranging from Dutch Golden Age paintings to 18th-century Russian place settings (page 158).
- **MOST SOPHISTICATED EVENING:** At the opulent **Dutch National Opera & Ballet,** let the elegant surroundings enhance your appreciation of the music and drama unfolding on the stage before you (page 159).
- **BEST VENUE FOR JAZZ:** In a cool, laid-back space, the sleek and intimate **Bimhuis** is the city's hot spot for performances by international and local jazz artists (page 162).
- **BEST LOCALE FOR CLASSICAL MUSIC:** At **Muziekgebouw aan 't IJ,** you're guaranteed both waterfront views and exceptional music (page 162).

MUSEUMS

Amsterdam Museum

Amsterdam's 800-year history is on display at the large and central Amsterdam Museum. Three floors of fascinating artwork and relics reveal the city's cultural evolution, from its medieval beginnings to its current status as a cosmopolitan capital.

The building that houses the museum dates from 1645 and was the city orphanage until the 1960s. What's left of this time is the main entrance on Kalverstraat: The building's original entrance gate features a relief depicting eight orphans and a dove.

An exhibit titled Amsterdam DNA chronicles Amsterdam's most prolific centuries, from the 1500s to pre-World War II, ending with a brief breakdown of modern-day drug laws, demographics, and the political climate. It takes about an hour to get through, and is a perfectly digestible overview.

The museum's best relics are downstairs, where the oldest surviving map of Amsterdam, circa 1538, is framed above a wooden casket said to have held the host from the **Miracle of Amsterdam.** Look for *The Anatomy Lesson of Dr. Deijman*, Rembrandt's (arguably disturbing) group portrait of a brain dissection. Farther on, a wing focuses on the 19th century—a time of bicycles, Napoleon, industrial feats, and impressionist art.

The museum's top floor encompasses Amsterdam from 1940 to today. A small World War II wing relates stories from Jews who survived the Nazi

Amsterdam Museum

occupation. Another section exhibits photos from underground news publications.

The Amsterdam Museum also has a children's wing. Het Kleine Weeshuis (The Little Orphanage) tells the city's history in a kid-friendly way through a replica of the 17th-century orphanage, with hands-on interactive displays, presentations, and animated characters.

MAP 1: Kalverstraat 92, tel. 020/523-1822, www.amsterdammuseum.nl; 10am-5pm daily; €12.50 adults, €6.50 ages 5-18, free under 5

Body Worlds: The Happiness Project

In 1977, German anatomist Gunther von Hagens invented a way to preserve human tissue by replacing the body's water and fat with plastic. This permanent exhibition, located off busy, touristy Damrak, displays preserved cadavers for an up-close view of human anatomy. Each showcased body has a significant role, such as displaying the nervous system or demonstrating physical characteristics of professional athletes like high jumpers and rugby players. Multimedia stations and informational placards explain the damaging effects of stress, smoking, cancer, and obesity on the brain, heart, and reproductive organs.

Since Body Worlds' first exhibition in 1995, over 13,000 people have donated their bodies to participate. The many displays can make sensitive viewers a little queasy, so visit before a meal rather than after.

MAP 1: Damrak 66, tel. 0900/8411 (€0.45 per minute), http://bodyworlds.nl; 9am-8pm Sun.-Fri., 9am-10pm Sat.; €20 adults, €14 ages 6-18, free under 5

Madame Tussauds Amsterdam

Housed in the colossal 1917 Peek & Cloppenburg building, Madame Tussauds attracts a steady crowd of visitors to its five floors of carefully crafted wax celebrity figures. At its dominating Dam Square location, each floor plays host to famous actors, pop stars, athletes, and models, from Lady Gaga to every James Bond. There's a great view of Dam Square from the fourth floor (right next to Heidi Klum). It's all about cheesy photos ops here, whether it's a selfie with Madonna or bicycling with E.T. over a moonlit backdrop. Wax displays can be hit-or-miss in terms of their resemblance to the original person, but the atmosphere is light and well-humored enough to be fun if you're into the whole celebrity thing.

MAP 1: Dam 20, tel. 020/522-1010, www.madametussauds.nl; 10am-6pm daily; €23.50 adults

Sex Museum

A stone's throw from Amsterdam Centraal Station, the Sex Museum is a combination of corny and naughty displays on the history of sex, which are more silly than smutty. Visitors are greeted with a tacky remake of the Red Light District, complete with mechanical Peeping Toms and couples fooling around behind public urinals. Mannequins wearing S&M outfits, complete with studded masks and whips, line the hallways. Display cases exhibit sex-themed sculptures from East Asia; the stairwell is decorated with explicit contemporary art. One room features an extensive collection of nude and pornographic photographs spanning 1860 to 1960. The museum, full of giggly teens and couples, is great for cheeky laughs on a rainy day.

MAP 1: Damrak 18, tel. 020/622-8376, www.sexmuseumamsterdam.nl; 9:30am-11:30pm daily; €4

Torture Museum

This unusual hole-in-the-wall across from the Singel Canal chronicles the history of human cruelty through a private collection of antique and replica medieval torture devices. Two creepy, dimly lit rooms contain a collection of instruments used for corporal punishment, public shaming, and persecuting witches and heretics. The tools on display—among them a rusty chastity belt, guillotine, and a spiked torture chair—were of popular use across Europe and North America until the 1800s. Copies of old photographs demonstrating actual use accompany each painful gismo. This is an intriguing stop for anyone wanting a quick dose of the heebie-jeebies.

MAP 1: Singel 449, tel. 020/320-6642, www.torturemuseum.nl; 10am-11pm daily; €7.50 13 and up, €5 12 and under

GALLERIES

Oode

While the art galleries on Nieuwe Spiegelstraat often feature intimidating prices, Oode sells orphaned art at heavy discounts (starting at €25). The owner, a designer with a master's degree in arts, has an eye for collecting, adopting canvases from closed museums, and acquiring pieces from young interior designers. The big collection in this small gallery features sleek tables and chairs, clever lamps, and countless artworks—an entire spectrum of contemporary pieces looking for a second life.

MAP 1: Singel 159A, tel. 061/410-0376, www.oode.nl; noon-6pm Tues.-Sun.

CULTURAL AND PERFORMING ARTS CENTERS

De Brakke Grond

The large space of De Brakke Grond is the headquarters for dynamic and modern Flemish theater, music, and cultural exhibitions and performances. Three rooms and their adjoining foyers also offer exhibitions ranging from architecture to new media. De Brakke Grond hosts a monthly event with Belgian DJs and live music. A typical evening here sees a variety of performances and exhibitions. The box office is located at Nes 63.

MAP 1: Nes 45, tel. 020/626-6866, www.brakkegrond.nl; prices vary by exhibition or event

THEATER

Frascati Theater

One of the most well-known stages for modern Dutch theater, Frascati offers fresh and progressive programming. About 15 productions a year blend urban cool with New Age ideas, featuring young and innovative dancers, directors, and choreographers. The building's four spaces are home to productions of Shakespeare's plays, politically themed works, and interpretive dance performances. Programs are offered in Dutch, with some in English.

MAP 1: Nes 63, tel. 020/626-6866, www.frascatitheater.nl; tickets €0-15

Red Light District and Nieuwmarkt

Map 2

MUSEUMS

Erotic Museum

The Erotic Museum is housed in an old Red Light District warehouse with three floors exhibiting a psychedelic jumble of tantalizing statues, trinkets, and drawings. Highlights include Picasso sketches, lithographs by John Lennon, and original Bettie Page photographs. Trending more sleazy than tasteful, the museum features a life-size mannequin riding a dildo-enhanced bicycle and a pornographic cartoon remake of *Snow White*.

MAP 2: Oudezijds Achterburgwal 54, tel. 020/627-8954, www.erotisch-museum.nl; 11am-1am Sun.-Thurs., 11am-2am Fri.-Sat.; €7

Hash Marihuana & Hemp Museum

This two-room museum holds a private collection of pot paraphernalia, like old wooden pipes, homeopathic hemp medicine bottles, and portraits of people smoking marijuana dating from 1660. There are anti-marijuana propaganda posters from 1950s America and vivid prints of giant cannabis buds on the walls. The grand finale is a small cannabis garden and a vaporizer demonstration. Aficionados will appreciate this jumbled shrine to Mary Jane.

MAP 2: Oudezijds Achterburgwal 148, tel. 020/624-8926, www.hashmuseum.com; 10am-10pm daily; €8.50

Red Light Secrets Museum of Prostitution

This museum takes visitors on an informative and entertaining journey through the experiences of a sex worker. The museum's rooms replicate different sex worker locales, including a luxury escort suite, an S&M chamber, and a Red Light District brothel window. Informative placards and interactive visuals deliver facts, personal stories, and insightful statistics about prostitution in Amsterdam. Visitors can sit in a real window and watch the reactions of passersby outside (from a distance). The museum's approach to infotainment makes for a fun education.

MAP 2: Oudezijds Achterburgwal 60, tel. 020/846-7020, www.redlightsecrets.com; 11am-midnight daily; €8

GALLERIES

W139

This nonprofit exhibition hall has been a magnet for edgy, fresh contemporary art since it opened in 1979. W139 strives to be the alternative to commercial galleries and museums, and does so by giving artists complete freedom, via curation, installation, and performance. Openings are popular with young creatives looking to mingle with like-minded artists.

MAP 2: Warmoesstraat 139, tel. 020/622-9434, http://w139.nl; noon-6pm daily; free

MUSEUMS

✪ Foam

Foam (Fotografiemuseum Amsterdam) is an internationally renowned leader in photography curation, exhibiting some of the best camerawork in history, from London in the 1960s to American farmers of the 1920s. Photographers Henri-Cartier Bresson, Vivian Maier, Richard Avedon, and Anton Corbijn have all had work on display here. Housed in a 19th-century mansion, Foam has a handful of rooms that flow easily from one to the next. The main exhibition is always in the Upper Gallery and usually lasts for about three months. Two rooms in the Front Gallery tend to include installation pieces. The museum's other rooms feature emerging photographers and change on a monthly basis, with a focus on street documentary, portraits, and artist retrospectives.

On the top floor is a small in-house gallery, where museum editions of photo prints are available for purchase starting at around €25. A café, coat check, and restrooms are on the ground floor. Try to arrive before 3pm to avoid a long line.

MAP 3: Keizersgracht 609, tel. 020/551-6500, www.foam.org; 10am-6pm Sat.-Wed., 10am-9pm Thurs.-Fri.; €11 adults, €8 students, free 12 and under

✪ Museum of Bags and Purses (Tassenmuseum Hendrikje)

At the Museum of Bags and Purses, visitors find themselves in the midst of 5,000 pieces of history. The exhibits begin in the 16th century: Before pockets were invented, people wore small bags made of beads or precious metals from a belt or girdle. From there, bags evolved and branched out, turning into the workbags of the 1700s, drawstring bags made of tortoiseshell or ivory in the 1800s, and even a brocade bag made from mother of pearl. The museum's pieces come from across the world, including Finland, Turkey, Italy, England, and the Americas. Materials range from art deco cut steel to exotic animal hides, like elephant, cobra, crocodile, and even eel. The collection includes a history of the suitcase, backpack, and vanity case.

The museum is housed in a 17th-century mansion whose bottom floor has retained its original style and doubles as the museum's café.

MAP 3: Herengracht 573, tel. 020/524-6452, http://tassenmuseum.nl; 10am-5pm daily; €12.50 13 and up, €3.50 ages 7-12

ceiling fresco at the Museum of Bags and Purses

Amsterdam City Archives (Stadsarchief Amsterdam)

One of the most eye-catching buildings on Vijzelstraat is Stadsarchief

Amsterdam, a giant brick expressionist building and the largest municipal archive in the world. The archive boasts 30 miles of protected historical documents about Amsterdam governance, businesses, people, and projects connected to the city. Though visitors cannot access the entire archive, a lot of free history is offered in its exhibition rooms. The archive hosts shows that cover everything from Van Gogh paintings to photography from the Dutch hippie protests of the Provo movement. Display cases in the building include a letter from Charles Darwin to the Artis Zoo, the excommunication of Spinoza, and a police report of a bike stolen from Anne Frank in 1942. There is also a section with historic pamphlets about the city's World War I army barracks and the efforts to preserve the Dutch coastline. A bookshop on the premises specializes in Amsterdam culture and history.

The early 1900s building that houses the archive is a marvel, a former bank originally called De Bazel, named after the architect who designed it. The unusual brick designs, stained-glass windows, mosaic floors, and exterior sculptures make a strong argument for visiting the Stadsarchief, even for those not interested in historical documents.

MAP 3: Vijzelstraat 32, tel. 020/251-1511, www.amsterdam.nl; 10am-5pm Tues.-Fri., noon-5pm Sat.-Sun.; free

Van Loon House

The Van Loon House is a 17th-century mansion, boasting original Golden Age furnishings, an impressive garden, and a coach house. The house, now a museum, is still owned by the Van Loon family. The patriarch, Willem van Loon, founded the Dutch East India Company in 1602, and his grandson would later be mayor of Amsterdam. In 1973, the family funded a restoration of the house and its conversion into a museum.

Although the Van Loons moved here in 1884, the double-width house was built in 1672. The entrance hall is a stunning introduction, featuring marble flooring that surrounds a grand staircase with a rococo brass bannister. Each room of the house is adorned with family portraits painted by famous artists like Jacob de Wit. Rooms are embellished with remarkable statues, fine linens, bookcases stuffed with old hardcovers, and antique lamps.

On the main floor, the Blue Drawing Room has a rare empire wood floor and 18th-century Asian decor, while the Red Drawing Room features a striking marble table and elegant yellow silk furnishings. The dining room exhibits a collection of fine Dutch porcelain, and the 18th-century table setting is still used by the family for special occasions.

Head upstairs to peek into the bedrooms. The Drakensteyn Room has a full wall mural of the Mediterranean countryside. The Bird Room contains an elegant harp and blue and white wallpaper peppered with exotic birds, while the Sheep Room features an intense wallpaper in the French-Indian chintz style.

The house's most stunning feature is outside. The Garden Room has full windows that look out at one of the most breathtaking gardens in the city. Evergreen box hedges look just as they did in the Golden Age, colorfully green even in winter and trimmed into various shapes. The garden is dotted with a 16th-century sundial and small, peaceful ponds. The coach house once held up to eight coaches. An original carriage with liveries and harness is on display inside.

The Van Loon family still resides on the upper floors above the museum; you might even run into one of them during your visit.

MAP 3: Keizersgracht 672, tel. 020/624-5255, www.museumvanloon.nl; 10am-5pm daily; €9

Willet-Holthuysen Museum

The Willet-Holthuysen Museum is the former mansion of wealthy couple Abraham and Louisa Willet-Holthuysen. In the late 1800s, the Willet-Holthuysens bequeathed their home, with its collections of fine art and European furnishings, to the city to be converted into a museum.

The mansion consists of three floors of rooms transformed into exhibits of the Willet-Holthuysen's hobbies and affairs or elegantly decorated with furnishings only a royal could rival. The double-width mansion was built in 1685, although the majority of the exterior was redesigned in 1739 in the style of Napoleonic classicism. Each room has paintings from the 1800s of the French countryside, still life objects, or portraits of Abraham and Louisa's dogs (they never had children). The ladies' salon and gentlemen's parlor are decorated with expensive Parisian furniture and silk curtains; the white marble in the hallway reaches to the ceiling. A French-inspired ballroom once hosted music and dancing.

The conservatory at the end of the corridor looks out onto the French garden in the back, with shrubs shaped in an elegant symmetrical design. There are bedrooms, a kitchen, a pantry, a den, and more rooms exhibiting the couple's ample fine art collection. A visit here grants a rare chance to explore one of the Golden Bend mansions and the life and culture it housed within.

MAP 3: Herengracht 605, tel. 020/523-1822, www.willetholthuysen.nl; 10am-5pm Mon.-Fri., 11am-5pm Sat.-Sun.; €9 adults, €4.50 ages 5-18, free under 5

GALLERIES

✪ The Public House of Art

This photography, sculpture, print, and painting gallery has a mission to reach people who want to buy art without breaking the bank. Enter this modern, four-story space, sit down for a drink at the bar, and listen to staff explain how pieces come in four price categories: House, Villa, Mansion, and Castle. Prices start at €375 and move up to €1,500, with styles like portraits, cityscapes, and illustrations. With its friendly yet straightforward approach to buying art, this is one of the coolest gallery spaces in town.

MAP 3: Nieuwe Spiegelstraat 39, tel. 020/221-3680, https://publichouseofart.com; noon-7pm Sun.-Mon., 10am-7pm Tues.-Sat.; free

Jaski Art Gallery

Jaski is a gallery specializing in contemporary artists inspired by the CoBrA (Copenhagen, Brussels, and Amsterdam) avant-garde movement, which was active in the years following World War II. The contemporary artworks are fun to admire, like those of Miguel Delie, who uses miniature doll heads and figures in his mixed-media pieces, or the dream-like digital illustrations by Danny van Ryswyk. Before you leave this inviting and friendly space, don't forget to grab one of the large postcards from the towering pile near the door.

MAP 3: Nieuwe Spiegelstraat 29, tel. 020/620-3939, www.jaski.nl; noon-6pm daily; free

Lionel Gallery

Lionel Gallery established itself in the city's popular consciousness with Banksy's solo show in 2015 and now seems to devote much of its walls to the urban and pop side of contemporary fine art. Lionel's exhibitions are inspired by artists like Mark Jenkins, Jean-Michel Basquiat, Andy Warhol, Salvador Dalí, and Damien Hirst. The main floor and basement have monthly rotating shows, which are worth checking out.

MAP 3: Nieuwe Spiegelstraat 64, tel. 020/233-8171, www.lionelgallery.com; noon-6pm daily; free

Okker Art Gallery

Founded by the son of a gallerist and former Dutch tennis pro, Okker Art Gallery offers the Amsterdam art scene edgy, sexy, and surreal photography and paintings in a large space with giant windows. Step inside and be wowed by striking portraits and works displaying irony, humor, and playfulness. Some of the artists represented here are part of the CoBrA (Copenhagen, Brussels, Amsterdam) modern art movement of 1950, like Karel Appel, while others are new to the scene. The common thread at this gallery is individuality.

MAP 3: Vijzelstraat 125, tel. 020/233-8842, http://okkerartgallery.com; 11am-6pm Tues.-Fri., 11am-5pm Sat.; free

Peter Pappot Art Gallery

Pop into the spacious Peter Pappot Art Gallery for a quick look at works by prominent Dutch, Belgian, and French painters of the 19th and early 20th centuries. In these six rooms are Dutch impressionist paintings, one or two works by Henri Matisse, and even some 17th-century paintings. While modern art and bronzes seem more their forte, they also exhibit a small collection of portraits of musicians, including David Bowie and John Lennon and Yoko Ono's Bed-In for Peace protest at an Amsterdam hotel.

MAP 3: Nieuwe Spiegelstraat 30, tel. 020/624-2637, www.peterpappot.com; 11am-5:30pm Mon.-Sat., 12:30pm-5pm Sun.; free

Reflex Gallery

Reflex, in a wide white space, hosts some of the freshest and youngest established artists in contemporary art, with a focus on photography. Shows range from nude photography to theatrical black and white portraits. A few painting exhibitions feature international artists who explore abstract pop art, digital art, and aerosol with mixed media. The gallery also has its own publishing imprint, producing coffee table books and lookbooks from house artists and exhibitions.

MAP 3: Weteringschans 79A, tel. 020/627-2832, www.reflexamsterdam.com; 11am-6pm Tues.-Sat.; free

CULTURAL AND PERFORMING ARTS CENTERS

De Balie

De Balie is a cultural center with an emphasis on screening innovative films and documentaries. Debates and political talks happen here—both independently and sponsored by national media outlets and NGOs. De Balie is housed in the city's 19th-century former courthouse, so the layout is grand, with high ceilings, a symmetrical brick facade, and a modern interior with a sparkling chandelier and an imperial staircase.

MAP 3: Kleine-Gartmanplantsoen 10, tel. 020/553-5151, www.debalie.nl; 9am-1am Mon.-Thurs., 9am-3am Fri., 10am-3am Sat., 10am-midnight Sun.; admission €10

De La Mar

Musicals, plays, and concerts take up most of the agenda at this theater. The grand facade is lined with contemporary red windows. The modern interior is sleek and sophisticated, with a theater space to match. A long and wide area of floor seating and a small balcony boast red velvet chairs. The theater was built in 1887; the newest part of the building was restored after the Dutch resistance bombed it in World Word II, as Nazis were storing documents about forced labor here. Since all plays are in Dutch, De La Mar attracts mostly Dutch visitors.

MAP 3: Marnixstraat 402, tel. 020/555-2627, https://delamar.nl; tickets €10-20

THEATER

✪ Stadsschouwburg

The Stadsschouwburg (Municipal Theater) is a prominent building on Leidseplein that hosts plays, musicals, and dance performances. The neo-Renaissance style of the building dates back to its completion in 1894; it is the former home of the Dutch National Opera & Ballet. There are plays like *Macbeth* (performed in English), English musical theater, and Dutch versions of plays (like an adaptation of a Woody Allen film) with English subtitles. The acoustics are phenomenal, and the interior is jaw-dropping: gracefully sweeping balconies, stately columns, and grand burgundy decor. While a majority of performances are in Dutch, there is an assortment of

The Stadsschouwburg often has performances in English.

English options to choose from and Thursdays often see performances with English subtitles. Check online to verify which performances will be in English or have subtitles.

MAP 3: Leidseplein 26, tel. 020/624-2311, http://stadsschouwburgamsterdam.nl; tickets €0-25

Theater Bellevue

Theater Bellevue hosts modern theater, musicals, and occasional dance performances. In one room, visitors can watch amateur cabaret (music, singing, dance, and drama), while another room holds matinee performances accompanied by a meal. An overwhelming majority of the acts are in Dutch. The building dates from 1840, when it was used by politicians as a conference center. It was renovated in 1938, resulting in its current boxy appearance.

MAP 3: Leidsekade 90, tel. 020/530-5301, www.theaterbellevue.nl; tickets €12-20

COMEDY

De Kleine Komedie

This comedy club, located on Rembrandtplein, is housed in a theater that dates back to 1788, one of the oldest in the city. It's known locally and nationally as a launching pad for Dutch comedians, and shows are fresh, inspiring, and almost always in Dutch. The 500-seat theater is an intimate setting, with two balconies and red plush seats.

MAP 3: Amstel 56-58, tel. 020/624-0534, www.dekleinekomedie.nl; box office 4pm-7:30pm daily; cover €9

CINEMA

✪ Pathé Tuschinski

Pathé Tuschinski is easily the most beautiful movie theater in the Netherlands. Abraham Tuschinski commissioned the theater in 1921 for €2 million and requested the building be a blend of iconic styles and architecture of the time: art deco for the exterior design, Amsterdam School for the ornate stained-glass windows, Jugendstil for the brass fixtures and lighting, and art nouveau for the elaborate detailing. Tuschinski, a Jewish man, was sent to his death at a concentration camp in World War II. His spirit carries on in the dramatic, Gothic wonder of this theater, where blockbuster movies have their premieres. Walk inside, if only for a moment, and admire this unique work of art.

MAP 3: Reguliersbreestraat 26-34, tel. 0900/235-7284 (€0.90 per minute), www.pathe.nl; tickets €5-10.50

Canal Belt West

Map 4

MUSEUMS

✪ Huis Marseille Museum for Photography

This labyrinthine museum, occupying two 1665 merchant mansions, exhibits modern photography in a dozen quiet and spacious rooms. White marble floors and stucco give off a pristine museum vibe, while the 18th-century ceiling frescoes by Jacob de Wit nod to the Golden Age. The photography here is up and coming, from emotionally revealing portraits to fresh and unique visual storytelling. Exhibitions change seasonally. The courtyard garden is perfect for soaking in the imagery, and the small library is stocked with photography books. Marseille and Foam are the only permanent photography museums in Amsterdam.

MAP 4: Keizersgracht 401, tel. 020/531-8989, www.huismarseille.nl; 11am-6pm Tues.-Sun.; admission €8

Bible Museum and Cromhouthuizen

The Bible Museum (Bijbels Museum) is on the top floor of Cromhouthuizen, a collection of four mansions built in 1662 for the wealthy Cromhout family. The museum consists of the private collection of a 19th-century reverend, its few rooms displaying everything from an ancient Egyptian mummy to intricately detailed models of the Tabernacle and Ark of the Covenant. Other exhibits include biblical paintings and the country's oldest bible, dating from 1477.

The remaining areas make up the public sections of Cromhouthuizen. Wander through white marble hallways and see kitchens from the mid-1600s, a tranquil courtyard garden, and a large saloon covered with portraits and ceiling frescoes. Theology buffs and anyone curious about Golden Age mansions should visit. The admission fee includes entry to both the museum and mansion, and a free audio guide is included.

MAP 4: Herengracht 366-368, tel. 020/624-2436, www.bijbelsmuseum.nl or www.cromhouthuis.nl; 11am-5pm Tues.-Sun.; €8.50 adults, €4.25 ages 5-18, free 4 and under

Brilmuseum

Brilmuseum, also known as the National Museum of Spectacles, is one family's private collection of eyeglasses, started in the 1970s. The museum has since grown to occupy three floors, showcasing an abundant collection of antique frames, including items dating as far back as ancient Greece. From the aviator goggles to handiwork Elton John would kill for, the array of spectacles here is unlike anything else. It's free to poke around the museum's old-fashioned optician shop and admire the remarkable collection of eccentric eyeglasses and sunglasses for sale. Frames in antique vanity cabinets and drawers are vintage and usually unworn, with some still in their original advertising stands.

MAP 4: Gasthuismolensteeg 7, tel. 020/421-2414, www.brilmuseumamsterdam.nl; 11:30am-5:30pm Wed.-Fri., 11:30am-5pm Sat.; €4.50 13 and over, €2.25 12 and under

House of the Canals Museum (Grachtenhuis Museum)

The Grachtenhuis Museum, set in a polished 1665 mansion, is all about the engineering feats that went into the creation of the Amsterdam Canal Belt. The museum's five rooms span 400 years of history, beginning when Amsterdam was in desperate need of expansion to accommodate an influx of merchants; from this crisis, the idea for the Canal Belt was born. The museum examines one of the most complex challenges of its time at a level the general public can understand.

The self-guided tour lets visitors learn how 17th-century engineers tackled the project while examining scale model construction sites, dollhouse-sized mansions, and canal blueprints. Small and uncrowded, the museum is great for architects, kids, and even those who don't typically like museums.

A ticket also allows visitors to wander around the rest of the 17th-century mansion and courtyard. The foyer boasts red tapestry, inlaid wood floors, elegant chandeliers, and gold-painted walls. The Painting Room harkens back to its 18th-century origins with a countryside mural painted in 1776.

MAP 4: Herengracht 386, tel. 020/421-1656, www.hetgrachtenhuis.nl; 10am-5pm Tues.-Sun.; €10 adults, €5 ages 6-17, free 5 and under

CULTURAL AND PERFORMING ARTS CENTERS

De Rode Hoed

Hidden behind a row of houses, De Rode Hoed (The Red Hood) is a cultural center originally built in 1631 as a hidden church (one of several structures built to avoid religious persecution). Today, the large neoclassical hall serves as a platform for lectures and debates, hosting speakers like Dutch Prime Minister Mark Rutte. On occasion, there are English-language events and music performances. Two stories of white balconies are connected by white columns under a wooden nave, with red curtains as an elegant backdrop. If you happen to pass by when the doors are open, take a peek at the interior and the basilica. The center's name comes from a time when a milliner ran his hat-making business here. Look outside above the middle set of doors for the gable stone (stone tablet) with a small red hat.

MAP 4: Keizersgracht 102, tel. 020/638-5606, www.rodehoed.nl; 8:30am-5:30pm daily; €7-20

Felix Meritis

Felix Meritis is a cultural space for concerts, symposiums, and theater and dance performances. The building has changed hands and purpose several times: During the Enlightenment, it was home to Amsterdam's scientific academy. By the 1960s, it was the headquarters for the Communist Party, and in the 1970s, it transitioned into a platform for avant-garde theater, led by well-known actor Ramses Shaffy. Today, its concert rooms are well known for their acoustics. Most of the center's events are in Dutch; check the online program to see what's on.

MAP 4: Keizersgracht 324, tel. 020/627-9477, www.felixmeritis.nl; 9am-6pm Mon.-Fri.; €10-20

Museumplein Map 5

MUSEUMS

Dutch Equestrian School Museum (Hollandsche Manege)

Since the late 1800s, this chic riding school, hidden among the wealthy surroundings of Vondelpark, has taught equestrians to groom, saddle, and ride traditional sidesaddle with one of the school's 50 horses and ponies. Adolf Leonard van Gendt, the same architect behind the Royal Concertgebouw, designed the school's neoclassical building. The white sandstone walls and balustrade balconies were inspired by the well-known Spanish Riding School in Vienna, Austria.

Visitors come to admire the elaborate interior and watch classic horse riding. The entrance fee includes a drink at the upstairs café that overlooks the horse arena. A small shop sells souvenirs and snacks to feed the horses. For horse lovers, this is a great inside peek at a unique European tradition.

MAP 5: Vondelstraat 140, tel. 020/618-0942, www.dehollandschemanege.nl; 10am-11pm Mon.-Fri., 10am-5pm Sat.-Sun.; €8

MUSIC

✪ Royal Concertgebouw

The neoclassical concert hall facing the south side of Museumplein is Royal Concertgebouw, boasting spectacular acoustics for a range of performances since 1888. Its facade has tall columns and a neo-Renaissance style with symmetrical patterns made out of bricks. The roof has a giant, gold-plated lyre on top, representing Apollo, the Greek god of music, poetry, and art. Inside is a breathtaking oval hall with about 2,000 red velvet seats. A grand organ from 1890 is the backdrop of the stage. A smaller recital hall and choir hall host more intimate performances.

At classical performances, tuxedoed maestros conduct musicians with passionate fervor. During intermission, concertgoers sip beverages and mill around the multiple foyers. Groups like Led Zeppelin and Pink Floyd played here in the 1960s, but the program has always leaned heavily on classical, from Wagner to Beethoven. Additionally, the hall embraces jazz ensembles, world music, and opera performances. Almost 1,000 concerts are held here each year.

MAP 5: Concertgebouwplein 10, tel. 020/573-0573, www.concertgebouw.nl; ticket prices vary by performance

Open Air Theatre Vondelpark

Since 1974, this open air theater has held live music performances every summer weekend in the heart of Vondelpark. Performances range from classical to big band music and ballet to children's theater. The look is simple, with a covered stage and seating area composed of folding chairs and bleachers. Drink stands in the back serve cold beverages, wine by the bottle, and light snacks. With over 100 shows throughout the five-month program, the theater offers many opportunities to be entertained—all for free. Shows start Friday afternoons and run periodically through Sunday night. Some productions are one-offs, while others recur throughout the weekend.

MAP 5: Vondelpark, tel. 020/428-3360, www.openluchttheater.nl; Fri.-Sun. early May-mid-Sept.; free

Jordaan

MUSEUMS

✪ Electric Lady Land

Opened in 1999, Electric Lady Land is a small, psychedelic installation museum dedicated to fluorescent arts, a unique hidden gem for art lovers. A visit here starts with a greeting from the American owner and artist. Visitors swap out their shoes for slippers in the museum's entryway, which is a mix between an art studio and gift shop.

The owner leads visitors downstairs to a neon installation that occupies the whole basement level. This floor-to-ceiling fluorescent cave glows with vivid hues from black lights and UV lights. Display cases with various minerals and inventions represent a timeline of discoveries and artifacts in the history of fluorescence.

The installation is hands-on, and visitors are encouraged to press buttons and flip different switches around the room that demonstrate the effects lighting has on fluorescence while Jimi Hendrix songs play in the background.

When you arrive, ring the doorbell for entry. Allow 30 minutes to experience this trippy spot. The owner can accommodate only a small number of visitors at a time, so groups may be asked to wait in the entrance room.

MAP 7: Tweede Leliedwarsstraat 5, tel. 020/420-3776, www.electric-lady-land.com; 1pm-6pm Tues.-Sat.; €5 ages 13 and up, free 12 and under

Houseboat Museum

Opened in 1997, this museum, set within an 860-square-foot houseboat and run by the boat's owner, offers an insight into the lives of those who inhabit Amsterdam's canals. From the living room to the small sleeping quarters, the *Henrika Maria*, built in 1914, is furnished in the typical Dutch style of the 1950s, an era when houseboats first became popular in Amsterdam. During this time, the city gave away mooring rights for free, so houseboats were seen as an affordable solution to a housing shortage. Most of the boats are connected to electricity, gas, and sewers.

At the museum, a few lounge chairs, an old hope chest, and nostalgic illustrations make for a homey vibe. Take a close look at water depth charts, model houseboats, and vintage Dutch knickknacks. Even the bathroom is part of the show, with placards explaining how modern houseboat plumbing connects to the city's sewer system. A video with clips of the ups and downs of houseboat life, like ice-skating and ice fishing on canals, is shown in its own small theater room. Lastly, the visiting crew are urged to enjoy a coffee and absorb the charm either inside or above on the houseboat garden and upper deck.

MAP 7: Prinsengracht 296-K, tel. 020/427-0750, www.houseboatmuseum.nl; 10am-5pm Tues.-Sun. Jan.-June and Sept.-Dec.; 10am-5pm daily July-Aug.; €4.50 16 and up, €3.50 ages 5-15, free 4 and under

Pianola Museum

In the heart of the Jordaan is this quaint, one-room museum doubling as a small performance hall, crammed with bulky pianolas (self-playing pianos) from the turn of the 20th century. Listen as the curator describes the history of the pianola (originally invented in the United States), the different playing styles, and the evolution of these spirited instruments. Over 20,000 pianola music rolls (paper with holes punched in it, representing the notes of a song) are stored in small wooden boxes throughout the museum. The Roaring '20s decor of old ruby rugs, stage bulbs, and tasseled lamps give off a vintage brilliance. Intimate piano recitals are held every weekend September to June. This is a great stop for music history lovers and pianists, though it's only open on Sundays.

MAP 7: Westerstraat 106, tel. 020/627-9624, www.pianola.nl; 2pm-5pm Sun.; €5

Tulip Museum

At first the Tulip Museum looks like any other tulip souvenir shop, but beyond the gift shop lies an ode to Holland's tulip history. The museum is separated into sections on the history of tulips via enlarged photos; traditional cultivation tools from East Asia; and even, from April to late May, blooming tulips. A section called Tulipmania tells of a time when the Dutch were in a tulip-induced frenzy, and bulbs sold for tons of beer, acres of land, and much gold. Today, one-quarter of the Netherlands' flower exports (over 900 million bulbs each year) are destined for the United States.

Back in the gift shop, ask at the counter for certified bulbs that you can bring back home. Each bag comes with 8-10 bulbs, from "spring green" to "flaming parrot"; information about the color, height, and treatment; and a plant-to-bloom timeline.

MAP 7: Prinsengracht 116, tel. 020/4210095, www.amsterdamtulipmuseum.com; 10am-6pm daily; €5 adults, €3 students

GALLERIES

Go Gallery

Oscar and Farud, the managers of this longest-running urban art gallery in Amsterdam, have a passion for street art. The gallery holds monthly exhibitions, bridging urban art with new contemporary works and providing a platform for local and international street artists. The small two-room gallery is in a historic canal house, and can be easily identified by the four-story mural painted by The London Police next door. Not only do Oscar and Farud know every urban artist in town, they are down-to-earth and welcoming businesspeople.

MAP 7: Prinsengracht 64, tel. 020/422-9581, www.gogallery.nl; noon-6pm Wed.-Sat., 1pm-5pm Sun.; free

Rock Archive

This is the only place in Amsterdam for authentic prints of rock stars doing what they do best—rocking out on and off stage. What began as a photo gallery of rock and jazz icons slowly grew into a collection so powerful it stops many people walking along the Prinsengracht. Stills feature the likes of Marvin Gaye, Bob Marley, Janis Joplin, Billie Holiday, and more current artists like Daft Punk. Prints here are not cheap, but die-hard fans can easily overlook that.

MAP 7: Prinsengracht 110, tel. 020/423-0489, http://rockarchive.nl; 2pm-6pm Wed.-Sat.; free

CULTURAL AND PERFORMING ARTS CENTERS

Roode Bioscoop

Classical soloists, folk musicians, poets, improv theater groups, and more perform in this charming and rustic neighborhood theater. The look is early 1900s, with ruby red walls, velvet curtains, tall cream and gold walls, and solid acoustics. The wooden chairs fit an intimate audience of about 100. This theater setting has featured mainly Dutch performers since its opening in 1913. The in-house café is open daily, with a terrace boasting a scenic view of Haarlemmerplein.

MAP 7: Haarlemmerplein 7, tel. 020/625-7500, http://roodebioscoop.nl; tickets €18-20

COMEDY

BOOM Chicago

Big with expats and locals who love American humor, this comedy club features a small group of improv and sketch actors offering a fun, energetic, and creative night, along with a pizza dinner. The cast members are usually Americans living in Amsterdam—Seth Meyers and Jordan Peele have both performed here—so BOOM Chicago is the only consistent spot for a comedy show in English. Show times run about two hours, including dinner and intermission. Drinks can be ordered at the bar before and after the show, and during intermission—take them back to your seat to enjoy, as there's no drink service in the theater. BOOM Chicago is located at the historic Rozentheater, which was built in 1913.

MAP 7: Rozengracht 117, tel. 020/217-0400, www.boomchicago.nl; show times vary; €15 and up

Plantage — Map 8

MUSEUMS

Hermitage Amsterdam

The Hermitage Amsterdam is a satellite of one of the largest art and culture museums in the world, the original Hermitage in St. Petersburg, Russia. The artwork and installations at Hermitage Amsterdam are a fraction of some three million pieces exhibited at the original museum. The museum displays elegant and rich exhibits, ranging from Dutch Golden Age paintings to the dinnerware of 18th-century Russian czars.

The building itself was originally a 17th-century almshouse. Its west side delivers a sparkling view of the Amstel River. The large, modern corridors lead visitors from room to room with a flow of informative placards. The crowd can be large, but moves steadily, even on weekends. The Hermitage is definitely for classical art lovers and Russian history buffs. In the hallway along the river, informational cards relate amusing tidbits about the tenants who lived in the 17th-century homes across the water.

MAP 8: Amstel 51, tel. 020/530-8755, www.hermitage.nl; 10am-5pm daily; €17.50 13 and up, free 12 and under

THEATER

Koninklijk Theater Carré

Originally created for a circus company, this stunning neo-Renaissance theater has delivered musical theater and vaudeville performances to audiences since 1887. Programs feature musicians, comedians, singers, and actors, from David Sedaris to Cirque du Soleil. Floor seats are prime, but the balcony offers a bird's-eye view of

audience at the Dutch National Opera & Ballet

the grand, wine-red theater, which can hold over 1,700 people.

MAP 8: Amstel 115-125, tel. 020/524-9452, www.carre.nl; tickets €25-90

MUSIC AND DANCE

Dutch National Opera & Ballet

Housed in the modern, white Stopera building (a portmanteau of *stadhuis*, or city hall, and opera), the Dutch National Opera & Ballet sits between Waterlooplein and the Amstel River. Enchanting productions from *Cinderella* to *Macbeth* boast spectacular acoustics within the tiered 1,600-seat auditorium. The studded ceiling lights illuminate a velvety red interior, while the foyer's windows overlook the Amstel River. Opera subtitles are offered in Dutch and English.

MAP 8: Waterlooplein 22, tel. 020/551-8117, www.operaballet.nl; tickets €30-130

IJ River

MUSEUMS

Amsterdam Center for Architecture (ARCAM)

ARCAM is a small three-story museum focused on the history of Amsterdam's architecture, set in a swooping aluminum building designed by architect René van Zuuk. The main floor has rotating exhibits on different Amsterdam buildings. Also on this floor are architecture books for sale, many in English. Downstairs is a presentation room for lectures, as well as a timeline of Amsterdam architecture styles and explanations of Dutch design. Free to the public, this is a great find for architecture lovers or those curious to learn more of Dutch design.

MAP 9: Prins Hendrikkade 600, tel. 020/620-4878, www.arcam.nl; 1pm-5pm Tues.-Sun.; free

National Maritime Museum (Het Scheepvaartmuseum)

The National Maritime Museum is for anyone wanting to understand how the Dutch created their country from the sea, became global traders, and continue to thrive as leaders in boat and water engineering to this day. The museum has over 400,000 artifacts, plus an entire wing for kids with dozens of interactive stations, including a replica of a ship that visitors can board and explore.

The museum's waterfront building dates back to 1656 and is navigable via compass, as each direction, differentiated by color, leads visitors to various wings and exhibits. The entrance, via the green Zuid (South) wing, leads into a courtyard covered by a stunning 1,200-piece glass roof with crossbeams resembling an old nautical map. Seafaring fans should grab a free audio guide.

The orange Oost (East) wing ranges from model ships dating back to 1560 to scaled industrial wharves and ship engines. Upstairs are ship decorations, like 17th-century carved figureheads and historic navigational instruments.

The magenta West wing on the two top floors is a maritime playground for kids. The exhibit See You in the Golden Age has visitors meet Dutch captains, sailors, and other key figures through sets mimicking 17th-century naval and oceangoing scenes.

Children will also love the interactive rooms of the blue Noord (North) wing, which include a 25-minute virtual seafaring voyage complete with visual and sound effects. Head outside for a close-up look at the Christiaan Brunings icebreaking steamship from 1900 and the Royal Barge built in 1818 for King Willem I. Visitors can even board the replica of the 18th-century VOC ship *Amsterdam* and explore the different decks.

Most adults spend at least an hour here, although families can spend an entire day at this museum. A café downstairs can help refuel for lunch.

MAP 9: Kattenburgerplein 1, tel. 020/523-2222, www.hetscheepvaartmuseum.nl; 9am-5pm daily; €15 adults, €7.50 ages 4-17, free 3 and under

The Kromhout Shipyard (Museum Werf 't Kromhout)

Museum Werf 't Kromhout is an active shipyard turned outdoor museum and monument that documents the history of Amsterdam's shipyards. This shipyard, one of just two left in the city, began in 1757 and today continues to repair boats, barges, modern ships, and historic sailboats. Inside the warehouse, which consists of two large iron halls, is an impressive collection of diesel and steam engines dating back to the turn of the 20th century. The museum has a historic feel, with iron beams, glass-paned walls, and brick floors. While all information is in Dutch, the museum is great for anyone with an interest in shipping and mechanical engineering. Note that it's only open on Tuesdays.

MAP 9: Kruithuisstraat 25, tel. 020/627-6777, www.kromhoutmotorenmuseum.nl; 9:30am-3:30pm Tues.; €6 ages 14 and up, free 13 and under

GALLERIES

Rademakers Gallery

Any contemporary art lover exploring KNSM Island should pass through Rademakers Gallery for a look at emerging and established Dutch artists excelling in visual art and design. Two spacious floors, minimal and white, exhibit monthly shows ranging from unique portrait photography to hanging statues made of beads. With a keen eye for the different, striking, and stunning, Rademakers has a strong presence in some of the most highly esteemed art fairs in the world, like Art Karlsruhe and PAN Amsterdam.

MAP 9: KNSM-Laan 291, tel. 020/622-5496, www.rademakersgallery.com; noon-6pm Fri., noon-5pm Sat.-Sun.; free

CULTURAL AND PERFORMING ARTS CENTERS

De Appel

Since 1975, De Appel, an eclectic art exhibition house in a historic canal building, has been showcasing modern and postmodern visual and performance art by international artists. Conceptual art fans appreciate the cutting-edge shows and installations within De Appel's large, sterile white rooms overlooking the waterfront. Dutch and international artists use these rooms to exhibit works that go far beyond paint on canvas. A small pamphlet in English describes the concepts of each piece, like the jars of pulverized bicycle parts or contorted doors. A library on the top floor holds an impressive collection of contemporary art magazines and books categorized by country and focus. De Appel is best enjoyed by experimental art fans.

MAP 9: Prins Hendrikkade 142, tel. 020/625-5651, www.deappel.nl; 11am-6pm Tues.-Sun.; €7 adults, €4.50 ages 12-17, free under 12

MediaMatic

MediaMatic is an exhibition hall, open-kitchen café, and greenhouse all wrapped into one eco-minded concept. Hidden along the train tracks just east of Amsterdam Centraal Station with a waterfront view, its offerings include lectures, performances, and workshops on topics ranging from social experiments to urban farming.

MAP 9: Dijkspark 6, tel. 020/638-9901, www.mediamatic.net; 9am-10pm Mon.-Wed., 9am-midnight Thurs.-Fri., 11am-midnight Sat., 11am-10pm Sun.; free

Mezrab

Mezrab is a small performing arts venue in the Eastern Docklands. Here, something quirky is always happening, and it's usually free and in English. The one-room space has a small stage and an intimate vibe. Mezrab hosts European folk dances with a live band on Thursdays; live storytelling and improv performances in English on Fridays; live music from local and international bands on Saturdays; and a mixed bag of performances, like poetry readings and live jam sessions, on Sundays. Drawing an international crowd, Mezrab is a cool destination for an unusual evening out.

MAP 9: Veemkade 576, no phone, www.mezrab.nl; show times generally 8pm Wed.-Sun.; donations accepted

MUSIC

✪ Bimhuis

The iconic heart of Amsterdam's jazz and world music scene is Bimhuis, a modern black box concert hall on stilts, which is connected to Muziekgebouw aan 't IJ. Equipped with high-tech acoustics, Bimhuis provides an intimate setting for international artists to perform nightly. Performances may feature instruments like a grand piano, baby saxophone, stand-up bass, or tubas. Wide windows behind the stage show the lights and trains of the city.

MAP 9: Piet Heinkade 3, tel. 020/788-2150, http://bimhuis.nl; ticket prices vary

✪ Muziekgebouw aan 't IJ

There is no better place to see contemporary classical music in Amsterdam than the stunning waterfront concert hall Muziekgebouw aan 't IJ. Designed by Danish architects in 2008, the building has a distinctive roof that juts out over glass walls, covering a large deck that overlooks the IJ River. Inside, concrete walls and

performance at Muziekgebouw aan 't IJ

wide, wooden stairs contribute to an industrial but classic look. The concert hall has tiered red bucket seats and thousands of thin wooden pilings evenly placed across the walls, giving off a faint scent of cedar. Here, musicians perform an eclectic mix ranging from postmodern world music to experimental electro. Audience members hang around the classy foyer for a post-show drink and to absorb the stunning river views. Some concerts are free; check the website. Jazz hub Bimhuis is on the second floor.

MAP 9: Piet Heinkade 1, tel. 020/788-2000, www.muziekgebouw.nl; ticket prices vary

Conservatorium van Amsterdam

This conservatory is the largest of its kind in the country. Audiences enjoy daily (and usually free) recitals and presentations by the conservatory's students, from opera and classical to jazz and pop performances. The students are an international mix of composers and musicians studying under some of Europe's finest musical professors and theorists. Performances are spread out among four concert halls, each holding 50-450 seats.

MAP 9: Oosterdokskade 151, tel. 020/527-7550, www.ahk.nl/conservatorium; usually free

CINEMA

Eye Film Institute

Eye Film Institute is a stunning cultural hub that combines cinema with exhibitions dedicated to the history and art of filmmaking. Housed in a white, modern, and uniquely shaped building on the banks of the IJ River, the institute screens unique films and offers breathtaking views of the waterfront. The institute's four screens offer a good balance of Hollywood blockbusters, independent films, documentaries, and classic flicks. Special screenings revolve around exhibitions dedicated to the likes of Stanley Kubrick and Alfred Hitchcock.

In the main hall is an open café with floor-to-ceiling windows overlooking the river. Downstairs is a permanent multimedia exhibit, Panorama, chronicling the history of film with clever and creative installations and an interactive green screen. The second floor holds temporary exhibitions, often featuring unconventional short films and work by film students.

MAP 9: IJpromenade 1, tel. 020/589-1400, www.eyefilm.nl; exhibition admission €10 adults, €5 ages 12-18, free under 12; cinema €10.50 ages 13 and up, €8 ages 12 and under

SPORTS AND ACTIVITIES

Recreation in Amsterdam comes most often in the form of fun modes of transportation: biking and boating. Both can be enjoyed independently or on one of the city's many tours. In winter, ice-skating is a national pastime, whether it be on ice in rinks or frozen canals.

boating on one of the city's many canals

Creating and maintaining green spaces is a central feature in Dutch urban planning. Even in the 1600s, when canalside mansions were being built, ample space was left for grand backyard gardens. Parks are essential to life in Amsterdam. Over 30 parks are within the city limits, including the famous Vondelpark, which sees nine million visitors a year. Maybe it's the grand, leafy trees or the waterfront views, but even the smallest parks give the feel of being away from the city. In summer, Amsterdammers spend as much time outdoors as possible. The city's parks are packed with locals and visitors alike enjoying the precious warm summer days.

HIGHLIGHTS

- **BEST INSIDER BIKE TOUR:** Get an Amsterdammer's taste of the city on a cycling tour with one of the local guides at **We Bike Amsterdam** (page 166).
- **BEST PLACE TO KEEP WARM ON A COLD DAY:** Fight off the chill at **Sauna Deco** with a Turkish steam bath or a Finnish dry sauna (page 168).
- **MOST ROMANTIC ACTIVITY:** Glide across the ice and under the stars on a winter evening at **ICE Amsterdam,** an outdoor ice-skating rink (page 170).
- **BEST PLACE TO RACK 'EM UP:** The largest and most casual place to shoot pool is **Plan B,** a pool hall equipped with 14 professional billiard tables, darts, large screens showing sports games, and a bar serving up pitchers of Amstel (page 170).
- **FUNNIEST BOAT TOUR: Those Dam Boat Guys** offer hilarious guided tours of Amsterdam's canals (page 171).
- **BEST RENTAL BOATS FOR BEGINNERS:** Captain one of the unsinkable rentals from **Canal Motorboats** and cruise the city's waterways (page 173).
- **MOST AFFORDABLE RENTAL BIKES:** Visit friendly **Star Bikes** for some of the cheapest rentals of authentic Dutch bikes (page 173).
- **BEST PLACE TO CLIMB THE WALLS:** Get vertical at **De Klimmuur,** an indoor climbing gym for both beginners and advanced rock climbers (page 173).

Old Center

Map 1

BOAT TOURS

Open Boat Tours

While most boat tours play a multilingual audio recording, Open Boat's tours boast a skipper who also acts as a guide, pointing out the historic sights of the city. The boats cruise on quiet, ecofriendly electric motors and are open-topped for great photo ops. Each tour is 75 minutes, and there's a 20-passenger maximum, allowing for a cozy experience. Tours leave from Damrak 6, the first dock south from Amsterdam Centraal Station.

MAP 1: Damrak 6, tel. 020/217-0501, www.canal.nl; 10am-4:20pm daily; €20

BIKING

BIKE TOURS

✪ We Bike Amsterdam

Thijs and Jasper, two Amsterdam locals, offer intimate bike tours that highlight off-the-beaten-path destinations, from hidden gardens to small parks and local cafés, and point out historic sites and museums along the way. Groups never exceed 12 people; private tours are also available. The three-hour tours start at 10am daily, and the meeting point is at the northernmost lion statue at Dam Square. Booking online in advance is recommended.

MAP 1: Dam Square 1, tel. 061/007-1179, www.webikeamsterdam.com; 10am daily; €28

Limo Bike

This party on wheels, a multi-rider bike with four wheels, echoes through the city streets as its passengers sing, laugh, and drink beer. The bikes emulate a limousine, boasting beer from an onboard tap, a detachable roof, and red leather seats for up to 17 passengers (up to 10 can pedal at a time). Multiple ride themes are available, from the VIP Belgian Beer Bike to the BBQ Bike. Every 90-minute trip includes beverages, snacks, and a sober driver.

MAP 1: Spuistraat 74A, tel. 020/642-3927, www.limobike.nl; €400-450 for 6-17 people

Yellow Bike

This outfitter offers rentals of bright and easy-to-ride bikes as well as city and countryside tours. The yellow bikes definitely stand out—a good thing for those less experienced with biking in a crowded city, as they increase your visibility to cars and other vehicles. Tours stop at major attractions like Vondelpark and Museumplein. Along the way, guides dish out historical facts about the city. The tours last 3-4 hours and take a maximum of 12 people. Private tours are also available. Book in advance online.

MAP 1: Nieuwezijds Kolk 29, tel. 020/620-6940, www.yellowbike.nl; rentals 9:30am-5pm daily, tours 1:30pm daily; tours €22.50-32.50, rentals €12/day

BIKE RENTALS

Damstraat Rent-a-Bike

This small bike rental shop, down a narrow alley near Dam Square, has a friendly and professional staff. It rents everything from the classic fixed-gear bike to tandem bikes for kids. To try and pass as a local, rent one of the basic black bikes without the company's insignia—just don't forget which is yours in the sea of bike racks. To find the

TOP EXPERIENCE

BICYCLES

bike tour

There is nothing more liberating than feeling the wind on your face as you glide around Amsterdam on two wheels. Amsterdam is known as the bicycle capital of the world, with over half the city's population biking on a daily basis. Cycling remains the fastest and most convenient way to get around because the landscape is so flat. Designated bike paths, traffic lights, and easy-to-ride bicycles make it easy to join locals as they effortlessly cruise their way through the city.

The bicycle industry took off in the Netherlands in the 1880s and became very popular among the upper and middle classes. When World War II ended, there was a huge drop in cycling as the automotive industry leapt ahead, but pollution and traffic accidents spiked to an intolerable level. Activists garnered enough support in the 1970s to revamp bike transit, expanding bike paths and creating bike parking lots.

Two styles of bikes dominate the city: the women's *omafiets* (grandma bike, with a step-through frame to prevent skirts from tangling) and the men's *opafiets* (grandpa bike, with a standard, straight cross bar).

Though many cities have recently launched bike share programs (where you can rent a bike from one of many stations for a short period of time), Amsterdam has no plans for such a program due to the city's problem with bicycle theft; tens of thousands of bikes are stolen annually. Amsterdammers often joke that their bike lock cost more than the bike itself. Never leave a bike unlocked, and lock it like a local: through the frame, the front wheel, and attached to a metal rail.

BIKE TOURS

★ We Bike Amsterdam (page 166)
★ Limo Bike (page 166)
★ Yellow Bike (page 166)

BIKE RENTALS

★ MacBike (page 172)
★ Star Bikes (page 173)

shop, look for the cartoon of a superhero cyclist.

MAP 1: Damstraat 20-22, tel. 020/625-5029, www.rentabike.nl; 9am-6pm daily, rentals €10-14/day

Holland Rent-A-Bike

This bike rental shop is in the cellar of the Beurs van Berlage building. A bike shop since 1900, it rents out bikes, does repairs, and sells bikes. The bikes are sturdy and feature either hand or pedal brakes, and some include a baby seat in the back. These bikes are much nicer than the average Amsterdam rental bike.

MAP 1: Damrak 247, tel. 020/622-3207, www.holland-rentabike.nl; 8am-7pm Mon.-Fri., 9am-6pm Sat.-Sun.; rentals €8.50-13.50/day

BILLIARDS

The Poolbar

Amsterdam's most central pool hall doubles as a small American-style sports bar, located in a basement decorated with vinyl records on the ceiling and dollar bills pinned on the sides of the bar. Classic rock blares from the speakers as patrons play cheap games of pool and darts while drinking pitchers of Heineken. If pool isn't your thing, check out the shelves of board games. Snacks like *bitterballen* (fried meatballs) and *lumpia* (small egg rolls) are served. This is a popular, dive-y hangout for University of Amsterdam students.

MAP 1: Voetboogstraat 3-B, tel. 020/330-0813, www.thepoolbar.nl; noon-2am Sun.-Thurs., noon-3am Fri.-Sat.; €3/game or €12/hour

Canal Belt South — Map 3

BOAT TOURS

Amsterdam Canal Bus

Probably the coolest way to get around the city is by boat, and this hop-on, hop-off cruise offers three routes around the city. All the main sights and popular squares are on the route: Anne Frank House, Van Gogh Museum and Rijksmuseum, and Waterlooplein. The boats are the average tourist putters; it's a fun, relaxing, and picturesque way to get around. In addition to the standard ticket, there are also 24- and 48-hour options. Boats hit the pickup points every hour and an audio guide informs passengers what's coming up next. The boats have onboard bathrooms and also offer free Wi-Fi. There's a maximum passenger limit of 80 people.

MAP 3: Weteringschans 26, tel. 020/217-0501, www.canal.nl; 9:30am-6pm daily, €19-21

Canal Belt West — Map 4

BOAT RENTALS

Canal Bikes

These white floating rafts that look like water-bound bumper cars are powered and controlled by pedals. They might make an easy target for jokes, but "canal biking" is a fun way to cruise around the canals. There are three rental locations around the city, with the most popular spot just in front of the Anne Frank House. Every passenger is equipped with a canal map, a boat hood for bad weather, and access to free Wi-Fi. The boats are easy to control and nearly unsinkable. Go to the white ticket box to rent a boat, or make a reservation online.

MAP 4: Anne Frank Huis Museum, Prinsengracht 263-267, tel. 020/217-0501, www.canal.nl; ticket stand 10am-6pm daily; €8/hour

SPAS AND SAUNAS

✪ Sauna Deco

The secret to keeping warm on a cold day in Amsterdam is Sauna Deco. Like the name implies, the sauna boasts a 1920s Parisian art deco style. Everything is original, from the stained-glass windows to the gilded brass railings and ornate light fixtures. There are innumerable chairs, couches, and sauna beds to relax on between Turkish steam baths, Finnish dry saunas, tanning

TOP EXPERIENCE

CANALS

About 165 canals, adding up to about 60 miles in length, are within the city of Amsterdam. These canals are as much a part of the city as the rest of its infrastructure. With more bridges than Venice, the city's famous Grachtengordel (Canal Belt) has been a UNESCO World Heritage Site since 2010. The 2,500 houseboats permanently docked on the canals add even more charm. Large parts of the canals have attracted enough cranes and great blue herons to be considered nature preserves. To better understand the complex feats of engineering that went into designing and building the Canal Belt, be sure to visit the **House of the Canals Museum** (page 154). To experience a houseboat as it might have appeared in the 1950s, check out the **Houseboat Museum** (page 156).

You don't have to get in a boat to experience the charm of Amsterdam's canals. Waterfront bars and restaurants expand their terraces in good weather, giving customers a chance to get up close to the water. You can also just sit down at one of the hundreds of canalside benches to take a break or have a picnic lunch.

typical Amsterdam tour boat

WATERFRONT BARS AND RESTAURANTS

- ★ Van Vlaanderen (page 81)
- ★ Bistro Bij Ons (page 84)
- ★ P96 (page 98)
- ★ Gebr. Hartering (page 101)
- ★ De Doelen (page 106)
- ★ Café de Engelbewaarder (page 111)

BOAT RENTALS AND TOURS

- ★ Open Boat Tours (page 166)
- ★ Amsterdam Canal Bus (page 168)
- ★ Canal Bikes (page 168)
- ★ Those Dam Boat Guys (page 171)
- ★ Canal Motorboats (page 173)

booths, and cold plunge baths. Unwind with one of their unique massages, from Swedish to shiatsu, or go for the facials, manicures, and pedicures. There is no modesty here: Swimsuits are not allowed and all spaces—including the dressing rooms and saunas—are co-ed. Cash is preferred.

MAP 4: Herengracht 115, tel. 020/623-8215, http://saunadeco.nl; noon-11pm Mon. and Wed.-Sat., 3pm-11pm Tues., 1pm-7pm Sun.; day pass €24

Museumplein

ICE-SKATING

ICE Amsterdam

In winter, the long, rectangular pond at Museumplein morphs into one of the most popular ice rinks in town. Families, couples, and tourists come to spend some time in the rink with a fabulous backdrop of the Rijksmuseum. At night, the rink is illuminated with a charming, festive glow. Skating lessons, ice hockey sessions, and curling also occur here, but it never gets too crowded. Take a break from the ice at **Brasserie Winters** (10am-10pm Sun.-Thurs., 10am-11pm Fri.-Sat.), the pop-up wooden chalet next door. A range of warm Dutch dishes, drinks, and desserts are on the menu throughout the day.

MAP 5: Museumplein, tel. 020/470-1069, www.iceamsterdam.nl; 10am-9pm Sun.-Thurs., 10am-10pm Fri.- Sat. mid-Nov.-early Feb.; admission and rental €10-12/two hours

SWIMMING

Zuiderbad

Zuiderbad (South Baths) is an indoor pool housed in a historic monumental brick building where locals come by the thousands each year for a swim during the cold months. Most of the exterior and interior are preserved from 1897 (when the building was first built). The spacious interior, with the mosaic fountain and modest 80-foot rectangular pool, feels nostalgic. At its opening in 1912, the Zuiderbad's central heating and electrical systems were seen as ultramodern. It exists thanks to a University of Amsterdam professor who insisted on better hygiene for the city's pool-goers. Nowadays, the water is cleaned by a combination of a purifier and filtering system, which pushes the water through seven layers of sand. Whirlpools and tanning beds are also available. There are children-specific swimming hours each day from 10am to 12:30pm.

MAP 5: Hobbemastraat 26, tel. 020/252-1390; 7am-6pm Mon., 7am-10pm Tues.-Fri., 8am-3pm Sat., 10am-3:30pm Sun.; day pass €4

BILLIARDS

Plan B

This pool hall off Overtoom has 14 full-size tables in a large, laid-back space with a full bar, lounge, and cigarette smoking room. The hall is two stories high, with lamps hanging low from the high ceiling, urban art murals, and a wall-size flat-screen television for live sports games. Three dartboards are mounted on the walls, and you can find a full poker set and board games near the lounge. The full bar pours pitchers of beers and mixes drinks for customers. Two more pool tables are in the smoking lounge upstairs. Tournaments on Mondays (beginners) and Thursdays (advanced players) draw a full house.

MAP 5: Overtoom 209, tel. 020/845-6221, www.planbovertoom.nl; 2pm-1am Mon.-Thurs., 2pm-3am Fri., noon-3am Sat., noon-1am Sun.; €13/hour, second hour free until 6pm

De Pijp

Map 6

PARKS

Sarphatipark

This is a quaint urban park in De Pijp with tranquil ponds, willow trees, ducks, and 19th-century statues. The park takes up just two blocks, but locals come here for its oasis feel and to picnic near Albert Cuypmarkt.

Dominating the landscape is a temple-like structure with fountains and a bronze bust of Samuel Sarphati. Sarphati was a Dutch Jew who worked as a physician and city planner in the mid-19th century. During World War II, Nazis removed the statue and renamed the park; this action was reversed soon after the war. The surrounding houses are historic monuments, where city officials and artists like Piet Mondrian lived in the early 1900s.

MAP 6: At Ceintuurbaan between Eerste Jan Steenstraat and Tweede Jan Steenstraat, tel. 020/664-1350; 24 hours daily

ZOOS

De Pijp Petting Zoo (Kinderboerderij de Pijp)

In the middle of an urban setting, this petting zoo resembles a miniature farm, where the staff wear wooden clogs and teach kids about the resident goats, sheep, rabbits, birds, and one big pig. Kids can check out the aquarium and terrarium, swing in the playground next to peacocks, or take a ride on one of the Shetland ponies (2:30pm Wed.). The cutest attraction is cuddle time (4pm-4:30pm Mon.-Tues., 2pm-2:30pm Wed., 3pm-3:30pm Sat.-Sun.), where kids can snuggle with some of the animals.

MAP 6: Lizzy Ansinghstraat 82, tel. 020/664-8303, www.kinderboerderijdepijp.nl; 11am-5pm Mon.-Fri., 1pm-5pm Sat.-Sun.; free

Jordaan

Map 7

BOAT TOURS

✪ Those Dam Boat Guys

This private tour is run by three extroverted North Americans with a knack for history and a sense of humor. Bring your own food and drink for this funny, casual, and nearly two-hour-long trip through the city. The guides are knowledgeable about the city's history and may accommodate floating by specific sights. The maximum capacity for each tour is 11 people. Walk-up guests are accepted as space permits, but it's possible to book in advance.

MAP 7: Pickup location Cafe Wester, Nieuwe Leliestraat 2, tel. 061/885-5219, www.thosedamboatguys.com; 1pm, 3pm, and 5pm daily; €25

Plantage

BIKING

BIKE RENTALS

MacBike

MacBike is the bicycle rental king of Amsterdam, thanks to its distinctive red bikes, ideal for cyclists wanting to cruise around town. The shop also offers bike tours, repairs, and accessories. Out of the four locations throughout the city, Waterlooplein and Centraal Station are the most central. Though they're not the cheapest, reliable MacBikes are easy to ride and perfect for the novice cyclist.

MAP 8: Waterlooplein 199, tel. 020/620-0985, www.macbike.nl; 9am-5:45pm daily; rentals €10-15/day

PARKS

Wertheimpark

Named after the 19th-century Jewish philanthropist A. C. Wertheim, this tennis-court-sized park marks its entrance with sphinx-topped pillars. A stone water fountain functions as the centerpiece of the park. The west side is made up of the Nieuwe Herengracht canal. On the east side, an Auschwitz monument titled *Broken Mirrors* is installed on the ground: six large, shattered mirror panels reflect the movement in the sky.

MAP 8: Plantage Middenlaan 1, no phone; dawn-dusk daily

giraffes at Artis Zoo

ZOOS

Artis Zoo

In this snug city, Artis Zoo is something of a surprise. The perimeter is a compact jungle: Black spider monkeys are caged next to a herd of elephants, who eat grass near a pool of North Sea seals. The campus also contains an aquarium, insectarium, and planetarium, along with a new microbe museum, which exhibits the microscopic aspects of nature. It's cramped, but the animals are grouped by natural habitat and it's loaded with exotic trees and plants. The top kids' attraction in the country, Artis is packed with stimulation.

MAP 8: Plantage Kerklaan 38-40, tel. 020/523-3694, www.artis.nl; 9am-6pm daily Mar.-Oct., 9am-5pm daily Nov.-Feb.; €21.50 10 and up, €18 ages 3-9, free 2 and under; parking €9

BILLIARDS

In De Gracht

In De Gracht is a hidden pool hall with 14 pool tables, eight dart lanes, and a poker table. The place is simple with a student vibe, and the staff are friendly pool pros. Small chandeliers, a wooden bar, and paneled walls give off a brown-bar feel. Busy nights pull in a local crowd of billiard devotees. During the week, from noon to 6pm, your second hour at the pool tables is free, and solo players pay half price. Poker tournaments are held every second Saturday of the month.

MAP 8: Nieuwe Achtergracht 110-112, tel. 020/620-1908, www.indegracht.nl; noon-1am Sun.-Thurs., noon-3am Fri.-Sat.; €12/hour, darts €5/hour

IJ River — Map 9

BOAT RENTALS

Canal Motorboats

Canal Motorboats is a family-run boat rental business offering 18-foot aluminum boats that fit up to seven people for a cruise along Amsterdam's canals, ranging from one hour to a full day. No license is required on these electro-motorboats, and the owners supply operation instructions, a waterproof map, and tips on which waterways are the easiest to navigate. Passengers can bring their own food and drink onboard to boat like a true Amsterdammer. Boats are docked on Prinseneiland just west of Amsterdam Centraal Station.

MAP 9: Zandhoek 10A, tel. 020/422-7007, www.canalmotorboats.com; 10am-10pm daily; €90/two hours, €140/four hours

BIKING

BIKE RENTALS

Star Bikes

Star Bikes is a reliable bike rental shop with some of the best rates in town, set in a funky space. Bikes are the typical black *omafiets* (fixed-gear bikes, called granny bikes), which are easy to ride and blend in with the sea of bikes in the city. There are also tandem bikes, bikes with an attached picnic basket, cruising bikes, and bikes for people with disabilities. The café upstairs offers affordable espresso and snacks. The service is friendly and welcoming, and quirky vintage furniture adds a rustic look. The shop is tucked behind Amsterdam Centraal Station and a few blocks east.

MAP 9: De Ruijterkade 143, tel. 020/620-3215, www.starbikesrental.com; 8am-7pm Mon.-Fri., 9am-7pm Sat.-Sun.; €7/day

De Klimmuur

ROCK CLIMBING

De Klimmuur

The jagged and windowless building east of Amsterdam Centraal Station and adorned with giant letters spelling out Klimmuur Centraal is the city's destination for indoor climbing. Run by climbers since 1992, De Klimmuur boasts a massive climbing wall and bouldering area. Take a stab at the routes, varying from beginner to expert. The roof opens in summer to give an outdoor feel, and the slabs are over 25 feet tall, with enough space for over a dozen climbers and belayers on each side. The in-house shop has everything from chalk and slacklines to top climbing shoes, which you can test out before buying. Lessons and rentals are offered and there is even a café here. De Klimmuur draws a mix of internationals and locals and is welcoming to newbies and experts alike.

MAP 9: Dijksgracht 2, tel. 020/427-5777, www.deklimmuur.nl; 1pm-10:30pm Mon.-Wed., 11am-10:30pm Thurs.-Fri., 10am-10:30pm Sat.-Sun.; day pass €9-13, equipment rental €9

BOWLING

Powerzone

The Powerzone offers a funhouse trifecta of bowling, miniature golf, and laser tag. Six lanes are illuminated by a glowing rainbow of LED and black lights. The 12-hole minigolf course is a glow-in-the-dark adventure with a pirate and deep-sea theme. The laser tag arena is almost 5,000 square feet of industrial obstacles and murals set under black lights. The price tag here is high, but this is definitely a fun time for kids and teens.

MAP 9: De Ruijterkade 153, tel. 020/760-7600, www.powerzone.amsterdam; noon-10pm Sun.-Wed., noon-midnight Thurs., noon-1am Fri.-Sat.; €28-30/lane per hour, 12-hole minigolf €7-8, laser tag €8-10/game

SHOPS

The Dutch are known both as thrifty types that love picking through secondhand shops and as trendsetters pursuing the latest fashions. Amsterdam is home to dozens of secondhand and vintage thrift shops; it's also where the fashion industry congregates for Amsterdam Fashion Week, and where Tommy Hilfiger, G-Star, Chanel, Scotch & Soda, and Calvin Klein have their European headquarters.

Henk Comics

A destination for all things vintage is Waterlooplein Market. Secondhand shops surround this market's namesake square. But, really, you can't stroll the city without running into a hidden gem stuffed with unique used threads. The young and trendsetting De Pijp is brimming with locally made clothing stocked in indie boutiques.

Shoppers looking for local and international designers shouldn't miss the quaint alleyways of The Nine Streets (De Negen Straatjes) at Canal Belt West. Here, you can find a mix of specialized denim, designer clothing, and accessories. Nearby, within the Jordaan, are charming Dutch shops selling everything from chocolate to handmade children's clothes, all tucked between Italian bistros and brown bars.

Head to the shopping streets of Kalverstraat and Nieuwendijk for two- and three-story shops overflowing with the latest European and global trends. The stores have seasonal sales with discounts of 50 percent or more—people flock from across the Netherlands to shop here. The highest-end fashions are found on P. C. Hooftstraat, a shopping street featuring clothing and shoes fresh off the catwalk.

HIGHLIGHTS

- **BEST SELECTION OF DELFTWARE:** The widest range of the iconic blue and white pottery can be found at **Heinen Delfts Blauw** (page 178).
- **MOST COLORFUL:** Head to the **Bloemenmarkt (Flower Market)** during spring and be amazed at the rainbow of tulips on display (page 187).
- **BEST JEANS EXPERIENCE:** Whether you're looking for the perfect denim or waiting at the coffee bar while your significant other browses, **Denham Concept Store** offers a memorable way to buy jeans (page 191).
- **BEST LINGERIE:** Nab one of the eye-catching corsets or swimsuits from Dutch designer **Marlies Dekkers** at her eponymous boutique (page 191).
- **BEST EUROPEAN DESIGNER WEAR:** Bring home an outfit (or two) by one of the chic European designers stocked at **Van Ravenstein** (page 192).
- **MOST DELICIOUS CHEESES:** Sample different ages of gouda at **De Reypenaer,** an award-winning cheese shop (page 195).
- **MOST FASHIONABLE KIDS' CLOTHES:** If you've ever wanted a tot-sized tuxedo, **'t Schooltje** is the place to buy it (page 197).
- **MOST FUTURISTIC SHOE STORE:** At sleek and ultramodern **Shoebaloo,** browsing high-end footwear feels like being on a spaceship (page 198).
- **BEST TRAVEL BOOKSTORE:** Venture into **Pied a Terre,** a beautiful bookstore with the city's most expansive collection of travel guides, exploring every part of the planet (page 199).
- **BIGGEST OUTDOOR MARKET:** The huge **Albert Cuypmarkt** is also the city's most famous outdoor market (page 200).
- **BEST POP-UP MARKET:** The businesses at **Hutspot** rotate every few months, so there's always something new and different (page 201).
- **BEST SHOP FOR SNEAKER FANS:** Visit **Baskèts** to browse creative and colorful high-end sneakers (page 201).
- **BEST FLEA MARKET: Waterlooplein Market** is a daily outdoor market where you can easily spend an afternoon rummaging through clothes and knickknacks (page 210).
- **TRENDIEST SECONDHAND STORE: Episode** is a thrift shop that takes ordinary clothes and upcycles them into fashionable pieces (page 210).

SHOPPING DISTRICTS

Kalverstraat

Starting from Dam Square and ending at Muntplein, Kalverstraat is one half of the Old Center's shop-'til-you-drop pedestrian street, with European styles, sales, and crowds. Familiar brands like Crocs, Levi's, Vans, and Kiehl's are here. There are a few American chain stores like Claire's and Foot Locker, and European brands like Zara and Topshop.

MAP 1: Dam Square to Muntplein, www.kalverstraat.nl

Nieuwendijk

The other half of the Old Center's main shopping street, Nieuwendijk stretches from Dam Square toward Amsterdam Centraal Station. Like its twin, Kalverstraat, the pedestrian shopping street offers big brands like Timberland, Jack Jones, and Hunkemöller lingerie. The H&M flagship store is on the corner of Nieuwendijk and Dam Square. The other end of Nieuwendijk has touristy coffeeshops, cannabis souvenirs, and a few smartshops (places that sell "soft" drugs like mushrooms).

MAP 1: Dam Square to Haarlemmerstraat, www.nieuwendijk.nl

The Nine Streets

Within the charming alleys known as the Nine Streets are a mix of specialized denim, designer clothing, and accessory shops. This is a popular shopping area in the Canal Belt.

MAP 4: Bounded by Singel Canal, Rozengracht, Marnixstraat, and Leidsegracht

P. C. Hooftstraat

Head to this high-end shopping street for the city's top designer wear. This is where fashion houses sell the hottest trends that have just been seen at Fashion Week.

MAP 5: Stadhouderskade to Van Baerlestraat

Old Center Map 1

MARKETS AND SHOPPING CENTERS

Artplein-Spui

Since 1988 this art market has been run by the Amsterdam International Artists Foundation. The market's stands are run by about 25 Dutch and foreign artists. Artwork varies from jewelry and glass to sculptures and oil on canvas. Stands rotate, so new artists are presented weekly.

MAP 1: Spui, no phone, www.artplein-spui.com; 10am-6pm Sun. Mar.-Dec.

Magna Plaza

This neo-Gothic, neo-Renaissance former post office was built in 1899 and was eventually renovated into a two-floor shopping center in the 1990s. The historic structure contains about 40 stores. A dozen upscale trendy clothing stores like Mango and Men at Work are here, as well as a Toni & Guy salon, a Swarovski jeweler, and a few gift shops.

MAP 1: Nieuwezijds Voorburgwal 182, no phone, www.magnaplaza.nl; 11am-7pm Mon., 10am-7pm Tues.-Wed. and Fri.-Sat., 10am-9pm Thurs., noon-7pm Sun.

TOP EXPERIENCE

OUTDOOR MARKETS

During the Golden Age of the 17th century, Amsterdam was a trade hub, known as the busiest port city in Europe. Today, outdoor markets still thrive on seemingly every corner. City squares fill up on weekends with specialized markets selling books, local organic goods, or nostalgic knickknacks. Neighborhoods around the Grachtengordel (Canal Belt) each have their own outdoor market, set along a bustling main drag, selling everything from fresh produce and meat to clothing and tulips.

shoes for sale at Waterlooplein Market

- **Artplein-Spui** has the best art (page 177).
- **Spui Book Market (De Boek Markt op het Spui)** is where bookworms will be happiest (page 180).
- **Bloemenmarkt (Flower Market)** sells iconic Dutch tulips and tulip bulbs (page 187).
- **Albert Cuypmarkt** has been in business since 1904 (page 200).
- **Hutspot** is an indoor pop-up market that features a rotating selection of vendors (page 201).
- **Noordermarkt Organic Farmers Market** features booths full of produce, dairy, meat, and pastries (page 204).
- **Waterlooplein Market** is a flea market offering the city's most random treasures (page 210).

DELFTWARE

✪ Heinen Delfts Blauw

Heinen Delfts Blauw prides itself on having the country's largest stock of 17th-century Delftware. Step into their flagship store under the Munttoren and take in the spectacle of intricate blue designs on white porcelain. The shop stocks Delftware makers, including New Delft, Blue D1653, Heinen, Makkum, and Koninklijke, the royal family's top choice. Upstairs, there is a small private collection. For €5, you can walk around a showroom of unique, collectible Delft pieces and watch a master Delft painter at work. There's a second location in the Old Center and a third on the Canal Belt.

MAP 1: Muntplein 12-14, tel. 020/623-2271, www.delftblueshop.com; 9:30am-9pm daily Apr.-Oct.; 9:30am-6pm daily Nov.-Mar.

SHOES

Betsy Palmer

This independent shoe store was named after the American actress from the 1950s who shared the silver screen with the likes of Jackie Gleason and Jack Lemmon. The store's inventory is an homage to Palmer's classic, feminine, and bold style. Shoes are from European brands, displayed on racks that resemble pedestals. The shop focuses on the latest trends, including ballerina flats, funky sneakers, ankle boots, suede pumps, and platform sandals. The collection is a unique combination of creativity, color, and design at decent prices.

MAP 1: Rokin 15, tel. 020/422-1040, www.betsypalmer.com; noon-6pm Sun.-Mon., 10am-6pm Tues.-Wed., 10am-7pm Thurs., 10am-6pm Fri.-Sat.

United Nude

This shoe store looks like *Vogue* magazine's idea of outer space. United Nude is a designer shoe brand that attracts fashionistas and runway models. The store is dark with illuminated cubbies that each hold one impressive shoe. It's an odd fit against the surrounding Old Center. It makes people stop in their tracks, which is why it's worth a look.

MAP 1: Molsteeg 10, tel. 020/626-0010, www.unitednude.com; 11:30am-6pm Sun.-Wed., 10:30am-7pm Thurs.-Sat.

ACCESSORIES AND JEWELRY

Lyppens Jewelier

Minus the security man at the door, this is one of the most understated jewelry stores around. Inside a 17th-century canal house, the shop is a sea of gold, silver, and precious stones, displayed on the walls and in cabinets. Sterling silver spoons rest next to antique jewelry and Victorian diamonds. A workshop upstairs houses a small team who fix stones and metals. From rare rose-colored diamonds to freshwater pearls and strings of red coral, this shop offers every jewel imaginable. The friendly, unpretentious treatment is a pleasant surprise.

MAP 1: Langebrugsteeg 8, tel. 020/627-0901, http://lyppens.nl; 12:30pm-5:45pm Mon., 9am-5:45pm Tues.-Fri., 9am-4:45pm Sat.

DEPARTMENT STORES

De Bijenkorf

This department store is the Neiman Marcus of Holland. It's one of the main buildings on Dam Square, selling top-dollar brands from Louis Vuitton to Chanel. Open since 1870, De Bijenkorf has become a destination for shopping sprees for locals and visitors. The first four floors have everything from accessories and clothing to luggage and housewares, while the fifth floor has an upscale cafeteria with great views of Dam Square.

MAP 1: Dam Square 1, tel. 0800/0818, www.debijenkorf.nl; 11am-8pm Sun.-Mon., 10am-8pm Tues.-Wed., 10am-9pm Thurs.-Fri., 9:30am-8pm Sat.

GIFTS AND SOUVENIRS

Chimera Fantasy Shop

Fairies and dragons and trolls, oh my! Entering Chimera is like walking into an enchanted forest and strolling among trees with friendly faces. A few racks offer fairy-style dresses, Gothic outfits, lace skirts, and coats. Throughout the shop are displays of trolls, mushrooms, owls, and forest creatures. Figurines like howling wolves, dragons, and fairies are for sale next to dreamcatchers, daggers, and leather-bound notebooks. Upstairs, there is a store with a focus on Buddhism and Asian Taoism, accessible from within Chimera.

MAP 1: Damstraat 7, tel. 020/624-6199, www.fantasyshopchimera.com; 10am-6pm Mon.-Wed. and Fri.-Sat., 10am-9pm Thurs., 11am-5pm Sun.

De Posthumus Winkel

This gift store has specialized in rubber stamps since 1865. The collection is impressive, from a wall of stamps to

SHOPS

OLD CENTER

wax kits where buyers pick their initials or family crests. Complementing the stamps are Italian stationery, quill pens with ink, and embossing powder in 100 shimmering colors. Don't see what you're looking for? They do custom-made stamps, invitations, and business cards.

MAP 1: Sint Luciensteeg 23-25, tel. 020/625-5812, www.posthumuswinkel.nl; 10am-5:30pm Tues.-Fri., 11am-5:30pm Sat.

Totalitarian Art Gallery

As one of the most peculiar shops in town, Totalitarian Art Gallery specializes in selling original Communist propaganda art and historic memorabilia from World War II and earlier eras. Walk into this dusty corner shop and wonder at how one person could grow such a collection. Beware: The shop does not hold back on selling swastikas, Soviet Union war hero trophies, and posters of Fidel Castro.

MAP 1: Singel 87, tel. 065/369-3694, www.sovietart.com; noon-6pm Thurs.-Sun.

BOOKS

Athenaeum Nieuwscentrum & Bookstore

This impressive collection of niche magazines and international newspapers is one of the most diverse in town. Shelves of magazines range from eco-design, architecture, and contemporary art to local self-published zines and academic periodicals. News buffs will appreciate the stock of various daily papers, from the French *Le Monde* and German *Die Zeit* to the *International New York Times* and *Wall Street Journal.*

MAP 1: Spui 14-16, tel. 020/514-1470, www.athenaeum.nl; 9am-8pm Mon.-Sat., noon-6pm Sun.

Boekenmarkt Oudemanhuispoort

In the mid-1700s, Oudemanhuispoort was a retirement home for men. Today, it's a building on the University of Amsterdam campus known for its daily book market, which has been held here since 1879. Sellers sit in folding chairs as bookworms peruse countless used paperbacks and hardcovers in Dutch and English, prints, postcards, and sheet music. The adjacent green courtyard only serves to enhance the market's peaceful atmosphere. Access the market through the arched entrance at the south end of Oudezijds Achterburgwal or Kloveniersburgwal.

MAP 1: Oudemanhuispoort, no phone; 9am-5pm Mon.-Sat.

books at Boekenmarkt Oudemanhuispoort

Spui Book Market (De Boek Markt op het Spui)

This small book market hosts a few dozen stands from booksellers across the country every Friday. Stands offer an obscure collection of used books, many out of print and hard to find. The books are mostly in Dutch and English, with some French. Also on offer are posters, prints, postcards, and old magazines.

MAP 1: Spui, no phone, www.deboekenmarktophetspui.nl; 10am-6pm Fri.

The American Book Center

The American Book Center (ABC) is your go-to place for English-language books at decent prices. The ground floor holds a wall of American magazines and trendy art books, while the stairway is packed with travel guides to every country. The second floor has a few dozen fiction genres, and the top floor stocks over 20 types of nonfiction.

MAP 1: Spui 11, tel. 020/625-5537, www.abc.nl; noon-8pm Mon., 10am-8pm Tues.-Sat., 11am-6:30pm Sun.

The Book Exchange

Over 60,000 used English-language books are stacked on a sea of shelves that wrap around this small shop. A range of genres are for sale, from American history to science fiction. The shop has been in business since 1978 and is run by an American expat.

MAP 1: Kloveniersburgwal 58, tel. 020/626-6266, www.thebookexchange.nl; 10am-6pm Mon.-Sat., 11:30am-4pm Sun.

MUSIC

Rush Hour Records

Since 1999, this hole-in-the-wall off Spuistraat has been a record label and distributor of rare techno, house, and disco LPs. While the small store has a fair collection of pop, rock, and reggae, their stock spans into more eclectic genres, like new soul, dubstep, and obscure electronic subgenres. Browse the new vinyl, or check out the used records, usually below the cupboards.

MAP 1: Spuistraat 116, tel. 020/427-4505, www.rushhour.nl; 1pm-7pm Mon., 11am-7pm Tues.-Wed. and Fri.-Sat., 11am-9pm Thurs., 1pm-6pm Sun.

SPECIALTY FOOD AND DRINK

Amsterdam Kaashuis

The Amsterdam Kaashuis (Amsterdam Cheese House) is run by the reputable dairy Henri Willig. A few of the shop's walls are lined with long wooden shelves stacked with wheels of farm-fresh cheese. The smaller wheels for sale are the size of a softball, and popular flavors are cumin, herbs and garlic, and yearlong aged varieties. They also sell homemade mustards, smoked sausages, and Dutch chocolates. On display are traditional farming machines that demonstrate how cheese wheels are made. Most cheeses are available to sample before buying. The shop is a bit touristy, but cute.

MAP 1: Haringpakkerssteeg 10-18, tel. 020/624-1006, www.henriwillig.com; 10am-8pm daily Mar.-Nov., 10am-8pm Sun., 10am-7pm Mon.-Fri. Dec.-Feb.

De Bierkoning

Over 1,500 beers are stacked in crates, buckets, and baskets at this specialty beer store. Since 1985 De Bierkoning (The Beer King) has sold imported bottled brews. The selection includes fruity beers from Africa, Californian IPAs, monk-brewed Belgian beers, and Scandinavian microbrews. Looking for a cold one to go? The fridges in the front have a good selection.

MAP 1: Paleisstraat 125, tel. 020/625-2336, http://bierkoning.nl; 11am-7pm Mon.-Sat., noon-6pm Sun.

Puccini Bomboni

One step inside and Puccini Bomboni hits you with the rich smell of cocoa and mounds of gourmet chocolate truffles. Chocolate shavings, jelly teardrops, and candied cranberry adorn the tops of chocolates in flavors like pecan, rhubarb, thyme, and fig marzipan. Truffles are made with all-natural ingredients and no preservatives. There's another location at Singel 184 (tel. 020/4278341; noon-6pm Sun.-Mon., 11am-6pm Tues.-Sat.).

MAP 1: Staalstraat 17, tel. 020/626-5474, www.puccinibomboni.com; noon-6pm Sun.-Mon., 9am-6pm Tues.-Sat.

CIGARS

P. G. C. Hajenius

In 1826, P. G. C. Hajenius opened its art deco doors, and it still stands today with the largest assortment of cigars in the city. A humidor room stores Cuban brands like Cohiba and Montecristo, as well as cigars from the Dominican Republic. Displays in the front room showcase different brands of Dutch cigars. The smoking lounge in the back has cozy leather chairs. Clients can personalize their own flavors and blends at the DIY tobacco counter. Small safes in the back room hold merchandise for VIP clients like Arnold Schwarzenegger and the Dutch king.

MAP 1: Rokin 92-96, tel. 020/623-7494, www.hajenius.com; noon-6pm Mon., 9:30am-6pm Tues.-Sat., noon-5pm Sun.

VINTAGE AND ANTIQUES

Bij Ons

Bigger than most secondhand boutiques, Bij Ons stands out thanks to more than just its size. This vintage store sells merchandise from the Netherlands, Germany, and the United States. Furniture from the art deco era is for sale next to leather clutch bags and new but vintage-inspired sunglasses. Men's leather dress shoes, baskets of hats, and hand-knitted pillow covers are part of this shop's superb mix of inventory spanning the 1960s to the 1990s.

MAP 1: Nieuwezijds Voorburgwal 150, tel. 061/187-1278, www.bijons-vintage.nl; noon-7pm Sun.-Mon., 11am-7pm Tues.-Wed., 10am-9pm Thurs., 10am-7pm Fri.-Sat.

HOUSEWARES AND FURNITURE

Dille & Kamille

At Dille & Kamille, the adorable spice racks, collectible tins of coffee and tea, and colorful candles make it feel as if Martha Stewart has put the finishing touches on the shop's displays. Homey cookbooks by locals, picnic sets, and assorted linens are on display. Kitschy aprons and table settings are organized by color. Treats like cinnamon *speculoos* (ginger cookies), infused olive oils, and mustards are ready for sampling. Even the kids' toy corner is stocked with tasteful dolls and books.

MAP 1: Nieuwendijk 16, tel. 020/330-3797, www.dille-kamille.nl; 11am-6pm Mon., 9:30am-6pm Tues.-Wed. and Fri.-Sat., 9:30am-9pm Thurs., noon-6pm Sun.

Scandinavian style at HAY

HAY

This contemporary Danish design store is expert at turning homes into über-cool spaces. The space is clever, highlighting products like forks shaped like hands, eclectic furniture, and chic lighting fixtures. Come by for a coffee at their in-store café and test out the sofas and lamps.

MAP 1: Spuistraat 281, tel. 020/370-8851, www.hay-amsterdam.com; noon-7pm Mon., 10am-7pm Tues.-Fri., 10am-6pm Sat., noon-6pm Sun.

Wonderwood

The owner of Wonderwood sells used and new wooden furniture and is always on the hunt for original pieces dating from the 1940s to the 1960s, resulting in a collection hailing from Italy, the United States, and Scandinavia. Modern sculptures hang on the walls next to vintage wooden stereos—all of which are for sale. The owner's love for clean and retro designs is even seen in the small collection of kids' toys.

MAP 1: Rusland 3, tel. 020/625-3738, www.wonderwood.nl; noon-6pm Wed.-Sat.

SPORTS AND OUTDOOR GEAR

COPA

This flagship store is a celebration of old-school soccer. COPA was founded in 1998 by a soccer fanatic selling retro jerseys, track suits, and official game balls from the 1950s, a business plan which continues to be successful today. Framed photos of soccer stars decorate the walls, while Astroturf covers the floor. The shop has a bar in the front with a coffee machine and a minifridge stocked with its own beer for sale. There's also a foosball table and a projector that shows live matches.

MAP 1: Prins Hendrikkade 20-B, tel. 020/620-1660, www.copafootball.com; 11am-7pm Mon.-Fri., 10am-6pm Sat., noon-6pm Sun.

Red Light District and Nieuwmarkt

Map 2

MARKETS AND SHOPPING CENTERS

Nieuwmarkt Antiques Market

While a few stands do sell antique figurines and traditional Dutch collectibles at this small summer market, it's more of a mix of random odds and ends, New Age clothing, and souvenir hats, and it has the advantage of being open on Sundays. From handmade decorations and housewares to cute jewelry, books, and records, the wares here are nice to browse for gifts or souvenirs.

MAP 2: Nieuwmarkt; 9am-5pm Sun. May-Oct.

Nieuwmarkt Farmers Market

Vendors have sold North Sea fish and Asian spices at this farmers' market since the 1600s. Nowadays, the Boerenmarkt (Farmers Market) is comprised of local farmers selling everything from fresh cheese to organic olive oils, marmalades and jams, and smoked meats—all of which make for good gifts to bring home. Customers peruse stalls and colorful crates of seasonal fruits, wild mushrooms, and homemade pesto. For a quick bite, head to the crepe stand, fresh juice counters, corn on the cob grill, or the organic bread stalls.

MAP 2: Nieuwmarkt; 10am-6pm Sat.

CLOTHING

Madchique by Chimera

This boutique mixes vintage with rockabilly, featuring dresses with fitted waists, petticoats, and pencil skirts. Faux leaves and vines on the walls curl around quill pens and punky heels imported from the United Kingdom. Fabrics come in colorful plaids, various polka dots, and red cherries. The shop radiates a fun and airy feeling. Antique headpieces like fascinators and floral hats offer an elegant finishing touch.

MAP 2: Zeedijk 80, tel. 020/774-7914, www.madchique.nl; 10am-6pm Mon.-Wed. and Sat., 10am-9pm Thurs., 11am-5pm Sun.

SHOES

Patta

Patta means shoes in Surinamese slang, and this small designer-sneaker shop stocks the latest men's releases, from Adidas and Asics to New Balance and Nike. Together with a selective line of streetwear and caps, the shop offers limited editions like Kanye West's collaboration with Adidas, which saw sneaker fanatics camped outside for days.

MAP 2: Zeedijk 67, tel. 020/331-8571, www.patta.nl; noon-7pm Mon.-Wed. and Fri.-Sat., noon-9pm Thurs, 1pm-6pm Sun.

ACCESSORIES AND JEWELRY

De Hoed van Tijn

This studio and hat shop showcases elegant hats for both men and women with a 1920s sensibility. The hats are handmade and imported from Italy, France, England, and Eastern Europe. The wall of occasion hats includes colorful bonnets woven out of banana leaves for a unique look. There are sun hats, sharp trilbies, and traditional caps made of Scottish wool, among many other styles. A small children's section is also available.

MAP 2: Nieuwe Hoogstraat 15, tel. 020/623-2759, www.dehoedvantijn.nl; noon-6pm Mon., 11am-6pm Tues.-Fri., 11am-5:30pm Sat. Jan.-Sept.; noon-6pm Mon., 11am-6pm Tues.-Fri., 11am-5:30pm Sat., noon-5pm Sun. Oct.-Dec.

BOOKS

Henk Comics

Over 100,000 comic books reside in a sea of cardboard boxes at this shop, where the owner, Henk, collects all of the newest releases, rare finds, action figures, and collectibles. From the entire catalog of Marvel comics to collectors' Star Wars posters, piles of mint-condition Batman comics, and small press magazines from Asia, this shop is a treasure trove for comics lovers.

MAP 2: Geldersekade 96, tel. 020/421-3688, www.comics.nl; 11am-7pm Mon.-Sat., noon-6pm Sun.

Pantheon Books

This shop has a small English-language section of Dutch history, international news, and magazines. However, the standout here is the photo gallery upstairs, with photography books on display stands, along with a small photography exhibition. Anyone with an interest in unusual photography will enjoy this hidden gem.

MAP 2: Sint Antoniesbreestraat 132-134, tel. 020/622-9488, www.pantheonboekhandel.nl; noon-6pm Mon., 9am-6pm Tues.-Fri., 10am-6pm Sat., noon-5pm Sun.

MUSIC

RecordFriend Elpees

At the entrance to this store is a cardboard cutout of Andy Warhol's famous yellow bananas from the 1960s Velvet Underground album. This two-room basement shop is stocked with over 35,000 used vinyl albums, with prices starting at around €1-2 per record. They sell a heavy list of rock and roll, soul, and obscure Amsterdam artists, though they have offerings from nearly every musical genre imaginable. The posters, refurbished record players, and collectors' items on display are also for sale. Directly next door, **RecordFriend** (Sint Antoniesbreestraat 46, tel. 061/660-4700) sells the latest in new indie rock, hip-hop, and live recording sessions.

MAP 2: Sint Antoniesbreestraat 64, tel. 020/620-0084, www.recordfriendamsterdam.nl; 11am-6pm Tues.-Sat., noon-6pm Sun.

SPECIALTY FOOD AND DRINK

Jacob Hooy & Co

Not much has changed inside Jacob Hooy & Co since its original iteration as a home remedy stand in 1743. Small wooden barrels hold lavender, anise, and a variety of salts. Original ceramic jars that once contained opium sit on display shelves, while pots of throat lozenges line the countertop. Organic teas, ointments, and cosmetics are also available, as are natural raw foods and plant powders like spirulina and wheatgrass.

MAP 2: Kloveniersburgwal 12, tel. 020/624-3041, www.jacob-hooy.nl; 1pm-6pm Mon., 10am-6pm Tues.-Fri., 10am-5pm Sat.

ARTS AND CRAFTS

Capsicum

In 1975, two Dutch hippies traveled to India to study music. While there, they met a silk maker and decided to open a shop selling linens and bolts of fabric. Creative customers come here for one-of-a-kind textiles, like handwoven bedspreads and tablecloths. Most of the limited production fabrics are handmade from cotton and natural fibers woven in India. The cozy silk cushions and shawls come in vibrant violets, brilliant pinks, and modern patterns.

MAP 2: Oude Hoogstraat 1, tel. 020/623-1016, www.capsicum.nl; 11am-6pm Mon., 10am-6pm Tues.-Sat., 1pm-5pm Sun.

Henxs

A graffiti artist's paradise, Henxs is the supplier for all the street art in Amsterdam. The owner, Henk, created and branded the first European spray paint to hit the market. Since 1992, Henxs has been the largest spray paint store in the country, even with its small storefront. Paint cans and markers are packed into cubby holes, while display cases feature detailed color palettes and sought-after specialty aerosols. Silk screen shirts made by local artists are also sold here. **Henxs Clothing** (Sint Antoniesbreestraat 136, tel. 020/638-9478), next door, has a healthy catalog of hoodies, leather jackets, and other urban wear.

MAP 2: Sint Antoniesbreestraat 138, tel. 063/109-4886, www.henxs.amsterdam.com; 11am-6pm Mon.-Sat., noon-6pm Sun.

TOYS AND GAMES

Joe's Vliegerwinkel

At this shop, which sells kites, Frisbees, party gags, and juggling balls, there's a lot of fun to be had. Kites range from basic to expert power and stunt varieties. Boomerangs and Hacky Sacks are next to New Zealand poi kits (lighted weights on ropes that are twirled through the air) and Hula-Hoops.

MAP 2: Nieuwe Hoogstraat 19, tel. 020/625-0139, www.joesvliegerwinkel.nl; noon-6pm Tues.-Fri., noon-5pm Sat.

Knuffels

Knuffels (cuddles, in Dutch) is a compact toy shop with handmade plush animals that smile and move invitingly in the display windows. Inside this space, a former metro entrance, is a mix of marionettes, collectible figures, bouncy toys, dragons, monkeys, mermaids, and more. Downstairs, there is a tiny corner where kids can watch a woodcarver make traditional Dutch clogs, which the shop sells in all sizes and colors. Adults have their own small section with cheeky card games and gifts.

MAP 2: Sint Antoniesbreestraat 51-A, tel. 020/427-3862, http://knuffels.nl; 10am-6pm Mon.-Sat., 11am-6pm Sun.

VINTAGE AND ANTIQUES

Bis!

Bis! began in 1991 as a one-room army surplus store selling rare Russian navy uniform shirts and German military fatigues. Since then, Bis! has expanded to three stores. This location still specializes in military items, but it also offers one-of-a-kind European vintage classics, including shelves of snakeskin heels, cowboy boots, and racks of coats, slacks, and berets.

MAP 2: Sint Antoniesbreestraat 25-A, tel. 020/620-3467; noon-8pm Mon., 11am-6pm Tues.-Fri., 11am-5pm Sat., noon-5pm Sun.

GARDEN

Jemi

Amsterdam's first stone-built house is now occupied by a charming florist specializing in seasonal flowers and plants. The ground floor can barely fit the hundreds of tulips for sale, and winter brings green vines and soft ferns. The upstairs is stocked with garden accessories, seashell chandeliers, wooden birdhouses, and dozens of shapely glass vases.

MAP 2: Warmoesstraat 83-A, tel. 020/625-6034, www.jemi.nl; 8am-5pm Mon.-Fri.

nature-themed decor at Jemi

ADULT

Condomerie

The world's first condom boutique is easily spotted by its storefront decorated with inflated condoms shaped like animals, vegetables, and even the Eiffel Tower. The shop sells 100 different styles of condoms in glass cases and jars, as well as lubricants and gag gifts like magnets in the shape of a condom. Most customers venture in for the novelties, but the shop deals in the serious, too, selling custom-fit varieties and condoms in bulk. Browse the white binders to see what's in stock.

MAP 2: Warmoesstraat 141, tel. 020/627-4174, https://condomerie.com; 11am-9pm Mon. and Wed.-Sat., 11am-6pm Tues., 1pm-6pm Sun.

DeMask

DeMask is a serious fetish boutique, specializing in leather and latex. DeMask prides itself on using high-quality heavy rubber to create catsuits and other gear. On display in the small shop are harnesses, masks, and other items made out of shiny latex and in a variety of colors. The downstairs has a small room with more kinky items, like bondage suits. Though the space may seem intimidating, the owner is often behind the counter and ready to put first-timers at ease—but this shop is generally geared toward serious customers. If they don't have what you're looking for, the shop allows for custom orders.

MAP 2: Zeedijk 64, tel. 020/423-3090, www.demask.com; noon-8pm Mon.-Sat.

RoB

Amsterdam's oldest leather shop for men, dating back to 1975, has its own workshop upstairs. In this large space, made to measure harnesses and belts are in the back room, and tamer options like leather vests and track pants are in the front. The shop is definitely aimed at kinky male Amsterdammers, but curious shoppers are welcome to stop by.

MAP 2: Warmoesstraat 71, tel. 020/428-3000, www.rob.nl; 11am-7pm Mon.-Sat., 1pm-6pm Sun.

SMARTSHOPS

Kokopelli

Kokopelli is a smartshop (a business that sells psychedelic mushrooms and herbal drugs) that feels like a friendly hangout. The large counter is stocked with truffles, hemp seeds, herbal aphrodisiacs, and natural hallucinogenic products. Tables display incense and Tibetan garb, while the walls feature psychedelic works by local artists. Grab a stool shaped like a Super Mario mushroom and browse reference books, or enjoy the central canal view over a cup of tea in the back lounge. Note that smartshops do not allow customers to consume their merchandise inside the store, unlike cannabis coffeeshops.

MAP 2: Warmoesstraat 12, tel. 020/421-7000, www.kokopelli.nl; 11am-10pm daily

Canal Belt South Map 3

MARKETS AND SHOPPING CENTERS

✪ Bloemenmarkt (Flower Market)

Bloemenmarkt (Flower Market) is the only floating flower market in the world. At this top attraction, which has been held on the Singel Canal since 1862, customers find dazzling bouquets and a sea of tulip bulbs that come in many colors, from golden yellow to deep violets, and even hybrids of red and white, with frayed-looking edges. The market today has around 15 stands, selling everything tulip related, from the flowers and bulbs themselves to souvenir trinkets like magnets, keychains, and carved wooden tulips.

This is the prime place to buy tulips (both bulbs and flowered versions), but there are a few things to know before you visit. This spot is a tourist destination first and foremost. Since tulips are a spring flower, you'll only be able to find them in bloom from mid-April to mid-May. Over the summer, other flowers and plants are sold here, like roses, daisies, and orchids. In winter, the stands might seem colorful at first glance, but a closer look shows photos of flowers on bulb bags and boxes instead. Souvenirs veer toward the cheap and cheesy, so look elsewhere for something original for friends back home. Finally, expect high prices; often the best deals on bouquets can be found in neighborhood markets like Albert Cuypmarkt.

Tulips are seasonal plants whose bulbs should ideally be planted in fall, soon after purchase. The best bulbs are the ones that have been harvested within one or two weeks. They should feel firm, with an exterior resembling the brown papery skin of an onion. Avoid buying bulbs that feel soft or look shriveled.

Hit the market in spring or summer to get the full experience of countless blooms on display. Compare prices, choose wisely, and read up on gardening with tulips before buying a bag of bulbs.

MAP 3: Singel 630-600; 8:30am-7pm Mon.-Fri., 8:30am-7:30pm Sat.-Sun.

CLOTHING

De Badjassenwinkel

At this store, shoppers will find every type of robe, whether it be a towel-like bathrobe, a silky kimono, or a warm flannel robe. The racks are filled with robes imported from Vietnam and Indonesia or made in Holland. They're made of soft silk, terrycloth, cotton, or fleece, and come in sizes from kids to men's XXL. They also sell towels, with the option of custom embroidery to add a name or monogram. Business has been booming since the owner's mother opened the shop in 1979.

MAP 3: Vijzelgracht 39, tel. 020/320-1617, www.debadjassenwinkel.nl; 11am-6pm Tues.-Fri., 11am-5pm Sat.

Shirt Shop

The colorful rows of crisp, unique men's shirts behind long storefront windows distract many who walk by Shirt Shop. Top quality T-shirts, one-of-a-kind dress shirts, and funky hoodies are just the beginning of what's in stock at this men's shirt store, which offers patterns as far-ranging as plaids and animal prints. Most of the inventory is purchased locally from independent designers in Germany, Denmark, London, and Italy, then brought back by staff and displayed on the shop's clean, sleek racks.

MAP 3: Reguliersdwarsstraat 64, tel. 020/423-2088, www.shirtshopamsterdam.com; 1pm-7pm daily

LUXURY GOODS

Tamago

Duck into this high-end designer and luxury consignment shop that sells clothing, shoes, bags, and jewelry from big names like Jean Paul Gaultier, Yves Saint Laurent, and Prada. The small boutique is lined with racks of must-haves, some—but not all—at jaw-dropping prices. A historic interior with exposed wooden beams and brick walls accentuates the classic picks on consignment here. The selection is screened by season, condition, and authenticity. Tamago also designs a small collection of its own clothing at reasonable prices.

MAP 3: Spiegelgracht 13, tel. 020/626-6054, https://tamago.co; 11am-6pm Tues.-Fri., 11am-5pm Sat., 1pm-5pm Sun.

GIFTS AND SOUVENIRS

Dick Meijer

This odd but interesting archaeological antiquity shop and gallery showcases artifacts from pre-Columbian, ancient Roman, and ancient Egyptian periods. Nothing can surpass rare finds like Peruvian statues from 1700 BC, ancient clay jugs, spears from 1500 BC in Mexico, masks, weapons, and small figurines. The owner seems to be in the business more out of passion than profit, so don't be afraid to stop in just to gape at this collection of relics.

MAP 3: Keizersgracht 539, tel. 020/624-9288, www.dickmeijer-antiquities.nl; 10:30am-9pm Tues.-Fri., noon-7pm Sat., noon-6pm Sun.

Maranon Hangmatten

Backpackers, kids, and hippies have loved this colorful and playful hammock store on Blomengracht since 1981. Just as vibrant and colorful as the nearby Bloemenmarkt (Flower Market), Maranon's earthy swinging beds are produced in South and Central America. Some hammocks are made of cotton, others canvas or denim, and some can hold up to 650 pounds. It also sells hanging chairs, handwoven hammocks from the deserts of Colombia, and mosquito nets (yes, sometimes in Amsterdam you need one). The staff urges people to swing away on one of the pre-hung hammocks inside. The shop also runs a small ice cream station in the same space.

Maranon Hangmatten

MAP 3: Singel 488, tel. 020/622-5938, www.maranon.net; 10am-6pm daily

BOOKS

International Theater and Film Books

Inside Leidseplein's Stadsschouwburg is a niche bookshop that any movie buff or theater fan would want to peruse. Its collection includes biographies and other books covering famous directors like the Coen brothers, Hitchcock, and Tarantino, acting tips, and stage theory. Other topics include stand-up comedy, stage management, puppetry, cabaret, and understanding Shakespeare.

MAP 3: Leidseplein 26, tel. 020/622-6489, http://theatreandfilmbooks.com; noon-6pm Mon., 11am-6pm Tues.-Sat., noon-5pm Sun.

MUSIC

Concerto

Known to many as the ultimate vinyl shop in town, Concerto is four buildings wide with a deeper stock of records, CDs, books, and DVDs than anywhere in the city. They sell graphic design books authored by ABBA, stories by Patti Smith, used CDs and DVDs for a couple bucks a pop, and a sea of new and used vinyl. Listening before buying is encouraged by the staff of this poster-laden record shop. It's easy to spend hours rummaging through the inventory of classical, jazz, third-wave punk, and second-wave pop. The coffee bar here is an invitation to kick back on an afternoon and catch a live acoustic performance by local or touring groups on the tiny stage in the back.

MAP 3: Utrechtsestraat 52-60, tel. 020/261-2610, https://concerto.amsterdam.com; 10am-6pm Mon.-Wed. and Sat., 10am-7pm Thurs.-Fri., noon-6pm Sun.

SPECIALTY FOOD AND DRINK

Hart's Wijnhandel Amsterdam

This wine shop with over 600 wines gets high ratings from customers for the employees' friendliness and knowledge, as well as the reliable stock of rare and vintage finds. The shop works with small, award-winning French vineyards and stocks both Old and New World wines from around the globe. They also sell a great selection of port, dating from 1935, and over 30 French champagnes. Sometimes the shop hosts tastings at the communal table upstairs. The whole look of the place is charming, thanks to its wooden wine crate decor.

MAP 3: Vijzelgracht 27, tel. 020/623-8350, www.henribloem.nl; 10am-6pm Mon., 9:30am-6pm Tues.-Fri., 9:30am-5pm Sat.

TOYS AND GAMES

Tinkerbell

Tinkerbell carries enough tradition and imagination in their toys to satisfy Peter Pan himself. Shelves of toys for everyone from babies to young teens line this tiny shop. With wooden trains and blocks, dolls, Swiss music boxes, and kaleidoscopes, the shop places a heavy emphasis on tradition and exploration. Games lean scientific, with educational puzzles and challenging brain teasers. Look for the teddy bear on a column outside the shop, dressed in costumes fit for the season and blowing bubbles.

MAP 3: Spiegelgracht 10, tel. 020/625-8830, www.tinkerbelltoys.nl; 1pm-6pm Mon., 10am-6pm Tues.-Sat., noon-5pm Sun.

VINTAGE AND ANTIQUES

Droomfabriek

Off the beaten path of galleries on Nieuwe Spiegelstraat lies this glittering and charming shop run by an actress selling antique jewelry, furniture, and fixtures. Costume jewelry and handbags dangle from ornate vanity tables. Chandeliers, mirrors, and footstools from the 1950s and 1960s give off as much glamour as the glass and crystal tables with large perfume bottles nearby. Be sure to check out the row of vintage Chanel shoes on the floor.

MAP 3: Nieuwe Spiegelstraat 9B, tel. 020/620-0760, www.droomfabriekantique.nl; 1pm-6:30pm daily

Kramer

Walking into Kramer is like discovering a treasure box of antiquities. The mountains of inventory include antique lamps, Delftware, and countless hand-painted Dutch ceramic tiles. In one corner are stacks of silver jewelry and bone china, and in another, crystal vases and wooden ships. The shop was once a grocery store, and remnants of this origin can be seen in the fruit-themed stained-glass windows. There is something for everyone here.

MAP 3: Prinsengracht 807, tel. 020/626-1116, www.antique-tileshop.nl; 11am-6pm Mon., 10am-6pm Tues.-Sat., 1pm-6pm Sun.

SPORTS AND OUTDOOR GEAR

Independent Outlet

The most well-known skateboard shop unsurprisingly happens to also be the largest of its kind in the city, selling boards, shoes, street clothes, outerwear, and a healthy collection of punk rock records. There are a slew of classic Vans and Converse here, button-up Dickies shirts and pants, all the big skate brands, and even some merchandise from bands like Suicidal Tendencies, Frank Zappa, and Metallica. Pro skateboarding films play on the flat-screen TV, music is always blasting, and there is a lot of room to rummage through everything.

MAP 3: Vijzelstraat 77, tel. 020/421-2096, www.skateboardsamsterdam.nl; 1pm-6pm Sun.-Mon., 11am-6pm Tues.-Sat.

ADULT

Mail & Female

Based on its artsy window display of scantily clad mannequins, Mail & Female could pass as a racy art gallery or futuristic lingerie store. In reality, Mail & Female is an erotic goods store, started by women as one of the first mail-order shops targeting women customers. Due to high demand, the shop opened a brick-and-mortar location and began releasing toys and lingerie under their own brand LOVE from HOLLAND. The best sellers are small, inconspicuous toys and vibrators.

MAP 3: Nieuwe Vijzelstraat 2, tel. 020/623-3916, www.mailfemale.com; 11am-7pm Mon.-Sat., 1pm-6pm Sun.

SMARTSHOPS

When Nature Calls

This quaint and well-known smartshop (a business that sells psychedelic mushrooms and herbal drugs) is located on a bustling corner where customers have purchased "soft drugs" since 1998. The employees know how to guide customers in the right direction, especially in finding the right truffles. A sophisticated chandelier hangs from the ceiling, and traditional stained-glass windows depict tobacco leaves, a nod to the shop's former status as a tobacco shop.

MAP 3: Keizersgracht 508, no phone, www.whennaturecalls.nl; 9am-10pm daily

Canal Belt West — Map 4

CLOTHING

✪ Denham Concept Store

The flagship store of the Amsterdam-founded Denham is a hipster men's boutique with a focus on fitting perfect jeans. Inside this concept shop, there's a coffee bar that serves up frothy lattes while clients peruse the latest jeans from Italy and Japan. There are over 30 styles of men's jeans here, from ripped to acid washed, skinny to relaxed, and black to light blue. These jeans are not for the thrifty traveler.

MAP 4: Prinsengracht 531, tel. 020/303-2825, www.denhamthejeanmaker.com; noon-6pm Sun.-Mon., 10am-6pm Tues.-Wed. and Fri.-Sat., 10am-8pm Thurs.

✪ Marlies Dekkers

Dutch designer Marlies Dekkers has a seductive and stunning flagship store selling her latest lines of award-winning lingerie. She started her first lingerie line at age 28 and has since developed an eye for plunging corsets, stylish strappy bras, and shimmering swimwear separates. The boutique itself is an experience, with chocolate and coffee to welcome clients to their red velvet lounge and fitting rooms.

MAP 4: Berenstraat 18, tel. 020/421-1900, www.marliesdekkers.com; 1pm-6pm Mon., 11am-6pm Tues.-Sat., noon-5pm Sun.

Van Ravenstein

Van Ravenstein sells chic, en vogue designer clothing from Dutch, Belgian, and French brands like Dries Van Noten and Viktor & Rolf. The sleek, white shop is like entering a model's fitting room, with gorgeous dresses, wraps, blouses, and handbags. Everything is high-end and pricey, but on the last Saturday of every month, they sell end-of-season items at outlet prices.

MAP 4: Keizersgracht 359, tel. 020/639-0067, www.van-ravenstein.nl; 1pm-6pm Mon., 11am-6pm Tues.-Fri., 10:30am-5:30pm Sat.

Exota

Fun, flowery, and funky are three words that describe the collection of women's, teens', and girls' clothing at Exota's flagship location. The shop is narrow but deep, with endless racks of vibrant dresses, skirts, pea coats, and blouses. Exota's wares are typical Dutch fashions, perfect for those who desire colorful, flowing pieces. Named after an old soft drink from the 1950s, the shop is covered in cocktail-inspired colors like raspberry, grenadine, champagne, and lemon. Sales racks are in the back near the fitting rooms. There's another location directly across the street.

MAP 4: Hartenstraat 10, tel. 020/344-9390, www.exota.com; 10:30am-6:30pm Mon.-Fri., 10am-6pm Sat., noon-6pm Sun.

The Pelican Studio

The Pelican Studio sells the latest Scandinavian threads from Stockholm and Copenhagen designers like Maison Kitsuné and Samsøe & Samoøe, with an eye for timeless cuts and looks. The high-ceilinged shop's 1950s Miami interior is decorated with peacock blues, blush tones, and pea green fitting rooms. Round out the shopping experience by ordering a coffee or juice at the shop's bar.

MAP 4: Raadhuisstraat 35, tel. 020/363-8024, www.thepelicanstudio.com; noon-7pm Sun.-Mon., 10am-7pm Tues.-Wed. and Fri.-Sat., 10am-8pm Thurs.

ACCESSORIES AND JEWELRY

Amsterdam Watch Company

The whimsical watchmakers at this unique watch shop specialize in buying, fixing, and reselling vintage watches from 1945 to 1985. Most are Swiss brands like Rolex and Omega, scooped up at auctions or brought in by owners. About 350 watches are for sale here, and repairs take two months on average. The married couple who own the shop met at a watchmaking school in 1990. Both take time to talk to customers and treat each purchase like an investment. Warranties are included, and prices range €1,000-10,000.

MAP 4: Reestraat 3, tel. 020/389-2789, http://awco.nl; 11am-6pm Tues.-Fri., 11am-5pm Sat.

Hester van Eeghen

This vibrant boutique selling handbags, clutches, wallets, and elegant duffel bags comes from Amsterdam designer Hester van Eeghen, a frontrunner in leather accessories. Van Eeghen began selling her designs at

Socks We Love

small market stands and eventually evolved her business into a cluster of high-end shops. She's been knighted for her contribution to Dutch design, and her creations are a permanent feature in the city's Museum of Bags and Purses. Another location down Hartenstraat specializes in her line of colorful shoes.

MAP 4: Hartenstraat 37, tel. 020/626-9212, www.hestervaneeghen.com; 1pm-6pm Mon., 11am-6pm Tues.-Sat., noon-5pm Sun.

Socks We Love

This shop is stuffed with every type of sock, from knee-high to slouchy varieties and an array of colors and patterns. It's difficult to only buy one pair here with so much stock to choose from. The storefront window shows off funky seasonal styles, like lace in summer and wool in winter, while the inside features an endless sea of options. Antique decorations are mixed with dressers, racks, and tables of socks on display.

MAP 4: Gasthuismolensteeg 5, tel. 020/622-8523, www.sockswelove.com; 11am-6pm Mon.-Fri., 10am-5pm Sat.

GIFTS AND SOUVENIRS

Nieuws

This offbeat gift shop across the street from Westerkerk takes the cake for quirky Amsterdam gifts. Find something for everyone: clever tote bags, oddball socks, color-able maps, cocktail-making sets, hipster soaps, and more. This shop gives off a witty, wise guy vibe. The inventory may not be specific to Amsterdam, but it's fun to look through everything. Gift wrapping is included.

MAP 4: Prinsengracht 297, tel. 020/627-9540, www.nieuws.eu; 11am-6:30pm Mon., 10am-6:30pm Tues.-Fri., 10am-7pm Sat., 11am-6pm Sun.

The Otherist

The Otherist truly lives up to its identity as a *wonderkamer,* or cabinet of

framed insect displays at The Otherist

curiosities. Visiting this shop is like walking into an explorer's trophy room, full of old globes and animal skeletons on wooden shelves. The framed exotic butterflies and beetles are fascinatingly odd, as is the collection of glass eyes dating from before World War II. Also here are golden rings that look like twigs, a necklace with a crab claw pendant, and portraits of animal heads on human bodies. Think of it as a gift shop for the peculiar spirit.

MAP 4: Leliegracht 6, tel. 020/320-0420, www.otherist.com; 11am-6pm Wed.-Sat., noon-5pm Sun.

BATH AND BEAUTY

Marie Stella-Maris

This brand, selling cosmetics and mineral water, has a cause: Portions of every sale go directly to increasing access to clean drinking water worldwide. Its flagship store looks something like a cross between a Broadway signage shop and a perfumery, highlighting products and letters that spell out their mission. The staff patiently describe the products and the story behind the business. The line of scented beauty products focuses on lotions, creams, balms, scrubs, soaps, and oils. The products have earthy scents, with a healthy dose of natural ingredients in every clear bottle. Since being founded in 2011, the brand has created access for drinking water to over 12,000 people in need.

MAP 4: Keizersgracht 357, tel. 085/273-2845, www.marie-stella-maris.com; noon-6pm Sun.-Mon., 10am-6pm Tues.-Sat.

BOOKS

Boekie Woekie

The time of zines and one-off books might have passed, but anyone with an appreciation for self-published books and creative writing will have a field day at this somewhat forgotten treasure. Most of the books are from Amsterdam-based authors. The store is run by a group of artists who stock typewritten essays and poems, pocket-sized books about the letter U, and 100 illustrated pages about illustrations on napkins. The shelves are packed with zany humor.

MAP 4: Berenstraat 16, tel. 020/639-0507, www.boekiewoekie.com; noon-6pm daily

MUSIC

Waxwell Records

This hole-in-the-wall record shop is a pioneer in importing American hip-hop, soul, and R&B vinyl to the city. DJs come here for old-school samples, and collectors know the inventory is an unusual list of recordings, including jazz, funk, and reggae. This shop is laid-back, unpretentious, and brimming with new and used LPs. The place is a great spot for vinyl lovers looking for niche and hard-to-find items.

MAP 4: Gasthuismolensteeg 6, tel. 020/627-1600, www.waxwell.com; noon-7pm Mon.-Sat., noon-6pm Sun.

Waxwell Records sells soul, reggae, and hard-to-find funk on vinyl.

SPECIALTY FOOD AND DRINK

✪ De Reypenaer

This shop sells rich and delicious cheeses, and it's most known for its outstanding daily cheese-tastings. Downstairs, the small tasting room is equipped with desks, worksheets, cutting boards, and cheese wedges to learn about and taste. At the tasting (€15), customers sample six cheeses, focusing on the smell, texture, color, and taste. Each sample is paired with a wine or port designed to bring out the most flavors. Informative, casual, fun, and social, this is one of the best deals around for cheese-tasting. Customers who participated in the tasting also receive a discount at the shop upstairs.

MAP 4: Singel 182, tel. 020/320-6333, www.reypenaercheese.com; noon-6pm Mon., 10am-6pm Tues.-Sat., 11am-6pm Sun.

De Kaaskamer

This family-run cheese shop feels like walking into a basket of gouda. The walls are lined with wheels of cheese—nearly 400 different types on an endless display of shelves, straw hampers, and tables. They also sell a large selection of cheeses from Italy, France, and Belgium. How about a sharp three-year-old gouda, an aged dry cheese with cumin, or an old sheep cheese with sea lavender from the Dutch island of Texel? Go for the variety packs.

MAP 4: Runstraat 7, tel. 020/623-3483, www.kaaskamer.nl; noon-6pm Mon., 9am-6pm Tues.-Fri., 9am-5pm Sat., noon-5pm Sun.

TOYS AND GAMES

Gamekeeper

Let your inner nerd shine at this specialized store for the modern-day gamer. Long cupboards, three shelves high, are stocked with board games, strategy games, puzzles, backgammon, and chessboards. Twister is laid out on the floor next to dice games, dominoes, and Magic: The Gathering sets. The knowledgeable and low-key staff are usually hanging in the back doing inventory.

MAP 4: Hartenstraat 14, tel. 020/638-1579, www.gamekeeper.nl; 10am-6pm Mon. and Sat., 10am-6:30pm Tues.-Wed. and Fri., 10am-8:30pm Thurs., 11am-6pm Sun.

blouses at Laura Dols

VINTAGE AND ANTIQUES

Laura Dols

Captain jackets, sparkling tube tops, even kids' wear and antique lace are just the beginning. There's more glamour than meets the shopper's eye: Up front at this secondhand vintage shop are coats, sweaters, funny hats, and shoes, but what really stands out is its dazzling costume and evening gown collection downstairs. Sequined dresses, feather boas, skinny ties, and top hats from the decades of yore are for sale.

MAP 4: Wolvenstraat 7, tel. 020/624-9066, http://lauradols.nl; 11am-6pm Mon.-Wed. and Fri.-Sat., 11am-7pm Thurs., noon-6pm Sun.

Prinsheerlijk Antiek

Step into Amsterdam's largest antiques warehouse and be swept back to centuries when leather trunks, bone china sets, and elegant imperial furniture were the trends of the day. Pianos of ivory, fireplace mantles in white and gold, mirrors, round oak tables with thick carved legs, and gowns from the 1700s are just part of the endless collection in a space nearly 6,000 square feet in size. Much of the collection comes straight from the original owners, and only European antiques are sold here. They ship overseas.

MAP 4: Prinsengracht 579, tel. 020/638-6623, http://prinsheerlijkantiek.nl; 11am-6pm Mon.-Sat., 2pm-6pm Sun.

Zipper

Zipper was one of the first secondhand shops that brought finds from the United States across the Atlantic to Amsterdam. Nowadays, its two-floor collection is a range of stylish clothing from the 1950s to the 1990s. The shop is loaded with Levi's and Wranglers, knitted sweaters and flannel shirts, and fur coats and bomber jackets. Zipper has a funky, cool, and fun hipster sensibility and restocks its store three times a week. There's a second location near Nieuwmarkt (Nieuwe Hoogstraat 10, tel. 020/627-0353; noon-6:30pm Mon., 11am-6:30pm Tues.-Sat., 1pm-6:30pm Sun.) and they also have a stall on Monday mornings at the Noordermarkt Flea Market.

MAP 4: Huidenstraat 7, tel. 020/623-7302, www.zipperstore.nl; noon-6pm Mon., 11am-6pm Tues.-Wed., 11am-7pm Thurs., 11am-6:30pm Fri.-Sat., 1pm-6pm Sun.

HOUSEWARES AND FURNITURE

Frozen Fountain

This shop sells the latest in modern designs from architects, interior designers, and color specialists. Frozen Fountain is off the usual shopping path, but perusing here is worth it for the quick lesson on how progressive

Frozen Fountain

modern design has become. From many-armed sputnik lamps to radiators that look like sleek ladders, Italian iridescent glass furniture, and oversized brass wall clocks, everything is impressive and state of the art.

MAP 4: Prinsengracht 645, tel. 020/622-9375, www.frozenfountain.nl; 1pm-6pm Mon., 10am-6pm Tues.-Sat., noon-5pm Sun.

J. C. HERMAN Ceramics

Everything sold here is handmade by ceramic artist J. C. Herman. He also runs the store, with a kiln and shelves of half-finished pieces just behind the register. His shop displays a stunning collection of bowls, vases, and other crockery with an art deco feel and contemporary simplicity. Deep blues and earthy reds contrast with sandy hues. Most pieces are oven and dishwasher safe.

MAP 4: Herenstraat 10, tel. 065/794-5494, www.jcherman.org; noon-5pm Tues.-Sat.

Museumplein — Map 5

CLOTHING

't Schooltje

The ultimate European kids' fashions are found in this two-floor retail store off Overtoom. Dozens of racks hold clothing ranging from school clothes and winter jackets to toddler tuxedos. The upstairs room is all about shoes, with stacks of sneakers and slippers on old carousel displays. As one of the first children's boutiques to open in the country in 1974, the shops boasts a customer list that includes professional soccer athletes and the Dutch royal family.

MAP 5: Overtoom 87, tel. 020/683-0444, www.schooltje.nl; 1pm-6pm Mon., 9am-6pm Tues.-Wed. and Fri., 9am-9pm Thurs., 9:30am-5pm Sat., noon-5pm Sun.

Azzurro Due

This family-owned and -operated high-end fashion house stands out with a trendy interior and incredible garments from the United States and Europe. The interior is industrial, with spotlights above and a steel staircase. The pieces come from designers like Mary-Kate and Ashley Olsen's The Row, Stella McCartney, Nina Ricci, and Alexander Wang, to name a few. Another location is just a few stores down at P. C. Hooftstraat 142, while Azzurro Kids offers designer clothes for children at P. C. Hooftstraat 122.

MAP 5: P. C. Hooftstraat 138, tel. 020/671-9708, http://azzurrodue.com; 1pm-6pm Mon., 10am-6pm Tues.-Wed. and Fri.-Sat., 10am-8pm Thurs., noon-5pm Sun.

Four

This multi-brand, three-level store has a lot of sleek garments with an added layer of urban cool. The ground floor favors the latest trends, the basement room is heavy on street style, and the top floor displays a more tailored look. From the pop art on the walls to the flashy Gino B sneakers and Giorgio Brato jackets, the look here is sharp and cool. Saint Laurent, Jil Sander, Rick Owens, and Alexander McQueen are just some of the high-end designer brands here.

MAP 5: P. C. Hooftstraat 127, tel. 020/679-2244, www.f-o-u-r.com; noon-6pm Sun.-Mon., 10am-6pm Tues.-Wed. and Fri.-Sat., 10am-8pm Thurs.

Linhard

This clothing boutique has remained a reliable retail outlet for independent Dutch and Danish brands since 1924. From handmade jewelry and hand-printed scarves to casual jeans and flowy tops, the wide selection spans a sizable space. Linhard's focus is on long-lasting pieces that go with anything. It's not uncommon to stumble upon an in-store fashion show.

MAP 5: Van Baerlestraat 50, tel. 020/679-0755, www.linhard.nl; 11am-6pm Mon., 10am-6pm Tues.-Sat., noon-5pm Sun.

Oger

This is where Dutch men dream of going for a fashionable suit. Pronounced OOH-she-ay, this suit shop is four rooms wide and easily spotted by its stained-wood exterior and brass lighting. Well-known politicians, celebrities, and style-conscious businesspeople are regulars here. The interior is like an old English lounge, but the sharp suits are Italian. The dozen well-dressed employees are welcoming, and deliver the perfect suit with shoes and socks to match. The shop's first room has a price range for everyone, the second room carries more casual pieces, and the last two rooms display upscale and tailored looks.

MAP 5: P. C. Hooftstraat 75-81, tel. 020/676-8695, www.oger.nl; noon-6:30pm Mon., 9:30am-6:30pm Tues.-Wed. and Fri., 9:30am-9pm Thurs., 9am-6pm Sat., noon-6pm Sun.

SHOES

✪ Shoebaloo

The P. C. Hooftstraat location of Shoebaloo is like walking into a space shuttle decked out in the hottest choice in foot fashion. The glass floor and roof panels light up with different colors, while the shoe racks double as illuminated walls and the cushion-style seats look like parts from a Star Trek ship. Prada, Gucci, and Dolce & Gabbana are here, as well as lower-end designer brands. There is a lot to look at for men and women, from studded slippers to boots covered in feathers.

MAP 5: P. C. Hooftstraat 80, tel. 020/671-2210, www.shoebaloo.nl; noon-6pm Sun.-Mon., 10am-6pm Tues.-Wed. and Fri.-Sat., 10am-9pm Thurs.

Meyer

This small shoe shop looks a bit out of place compared to its dazzling neighbors, but it has been selling one-of-a-kind looks from Italy, Spain, and Portugal since 1934. Men's shoes range from two-tone leather to vibrant suede and real alligator from brands like Enrico Piaceri and Calzoleria. Women have an equally stunning selection of pumps, flats, leather boots, and suede stilettos. As one of the first Dutch shoe shops to import Italian footwear, the look and vibe is fashionably timeless.

MAP 5: P. C. Hooftstraat 45, tel. 020/664-3355, www.meijersschoenen.com; 10am-6pm Mon.-Wed. and Fri., 10am-9pm Thurs., 10am-5:30pm Sat., 1pm-5pm Sun.

BOOKS

✪ Pied a Terre

This bright bookstore is an ocean of travel guides, maps, and atlases. Bookshelves that line the large store are chock-full of guidebooks grouped by continent, country, or activity. Covering everything from the Congo to Calgary, maps are stacked in drawers, shelves, and cubbyholes. Above the shelves are globes galore, some of which glow or are inflatable. The mezzanine houses large atlases, as well as a custom-map printing room. Travel bugs come here to drink a latte in the shop's café and plan their next quest—with over 40,000 guides and 100,000 maps to help them.

MAP 5: Overtoom 135-137, tel. 020/627-4455, www.jvw.nl; 1pm-6pm Mon., 10am-6pm Tues.-Wed. and Fri., 10am-9pm Thurs., 10am-5pm Sat.

Boekhandel Robert Premsela

Feeling inspired by Museumplein? Boekhandel Robert Premsela is just across from the Stedelijk Museum and specializes in art books from baroque to Dalí. As an alternative to the gift shops at nearby museums, this small bookstore has a few hundred coffee table books covering all types of art, from Old Masters to street art.

MAP 5: Van Baerlestraat 78, tel. 020/662-4266, www.premsela.nl; noon-6pm Mon., 10am-6pm Tues.-Fri., 10am-5:30pm Sat., 11am-5pm Sun.

MUSIC

Broekmans & Van Poppel

This CD and sheet music store specializes in selling classical music from acts who have performed at the Royal Concertgebouw next door. The ground floor is stocked wall to wall with new and used sheet music and theory and music books for all levels. Some shelves venture over to jazz and pop, but the focus is mostly on music from composers like Bach, Mozart, and Beethoven. Upstairs is a large collection of classical piano, orchestra, and vocal recordings on CD, many of which are live recordings from performances at the Concertgebouw. Even in the digital age, Broekmans & Van Poppel survives by offering a sea of classical music in some classic ways.

MAP 5: Van Baerlestraat 92, tel. 020/679-6575, www.broekmans.com; 9am-6pm Mon.-Fri., 9am-5pm Sat.

HOUSEWARES AND FURNITURE

Coco-mat

This au naturel bedding and furniture brand is known for its sustainable, top-notch linens. Scents of lavender float around this airy store full of sunlight, surrounded by mattresses made with eco-conscious comfort in mind. Clients favor their clean and fashionable styles made from natural and renewable sources like coconut fibers, sea grass, horsehair, and goose down. The main floor is a haven of excellent beds, cushions, and hammocks, and the downstairs displays linens, towels, blankets, and rugs. In summer, the back terrace is an oasis of greenery, where clients are encouraged to lounge over a cup of herbal tea.

MAP 5: Overtoom 91, tel. 020/489-2927, www.coco-met.com; noon-6pm Mon., 10am-6pm Tues.-Sat., noon-5pm Sun.

Friday Next

This is a spacious concept store full of modern furnishings that also functions as a trendy café and studio for custom orders. The store sells minimalist pieces from established modern brands and new designers. Raw wood tables and chairs are on display alongside Scandinavian dishware, flooring samples, clocks, and decorative vases. Passersby venture inside to have a look and enjoy an espresso and croissant on the colorful terrace.

MAP 5: Overtoom 31, tel. 020/612-3292, www.fridaynext.com; noon-6pm Mon., 9am-6pm Tues.-Fri., 10am-6pm Sat., noon-5pm Sun.

De Pijp **Map 6**

MARKETS AND SHOPPING CENTERS

✪ Albert Cuypmarkt

Albert Cuypmarkt is the top outdoor street market in Amsterdam, offering everything from fresh flowers to Chinese tea cups. Vendors have been selling goods on this pedestrian street since 1904. Until the 1930s, one-third of the vendors were Jewish; after this point, many of the Jewish sellers did not return. Today, the market is about 500 meters long with over 250 stands, the longest and most well-known market in the country. It gets its name from 17th-century Dutch landscape artist Albert Cuyp.

Vendors shout deals at passersby from their tables of fresh fruits and vegetables, farm eggs, and stacks of

olive oil for sale at Albert Cuypmarkt

cheese wheels. In addition to the fresh produce, there are deals to be had on goods like shoes, purses, suitcases, and apparel. A few stands sell spices from Asia, South America, and the Caribbean. Snacks for sale include freshly made *stroopwafels* (caramel cookies), a variety of nuts, chocolates, dried fruits, olives, fresh-pressed fruit juices, pickled herring, and savory kebabs.

On the corner where the market meets Eerste van der Helststraat, there is a bronze sculpture of Dutch folk singer André Hazes holding a microphone. The statue marks the spot where Hazes first began his career, busking for money and beers in 1957. The cafés that dot the market area are prime people-watching spots and summer evening hangouts.

Enter from either the west entrance at Ferdinand Bolstraat or Van Woustraat in the east. Sunny weekends are the busiest times.

MAP 6: Albert Cuypstraat, no phone, www.albertcuypmarkt.nl; 9am-5pm Mon.-Sat.

✪ Hutspot

This indoor pop-up market is a platform for new brands and concepts taking a stab at the trendy, eco-conscious consumer world. Businesses apply for a space to shelve and display their products for a period of 3-6 months. The owner of Hutspot decides who shows, and his taste is both edgy and artistic. Products sold include light bulb terrariums, photography prints lacquered on wood, and handmade clothes, bags, and jewelry. The large space is minimally designed with exposed concrete floors and columns. Upstairs, there is a large workspace where freelancers come to grab a coffee and work on laptops.

MAP 6: Van Woustraat 4, tel. 020/223-1331, www.hutspotamsterdam.com; 10am-7pm Mon.-Sat., noon-6pm Sun.

CLOTHING

The Girl Can't Help It...

Tucked away on a small street of concept boutiques and gift shops is this retro, classy dress shop with pin-up looks and rock 'n' roll chic styles. The inside is a throwback to Miami art deco with pink decor and flamingo wallpaper. Forget petticoats and frilly lace: Fashion here celebrates the feminine silhouette with high-waisted skirts, lipstick red cocktail dresses, and 1950s Grace Kelly looks. The owner is a tailoring school graduate with her own line of simple black dresses and leopard print couture.

MAP 6: Gerard Doustraat 87, tel. 020/233-3399, http://www.thegirlcanthelpit.nl; 11am-6pm Tues.-Sat.

SHOES

✪ Baskèts

This store's name is the French word for sneakers, and entering it is like walking into a white shoebox adorned with colorful options from Converse to lesser-known niche brands and the latest series of Vans. Bright, minimal, and blasting hip-hop, this shop offers inventory that is for everyday wear, rather than athletics. With quirky choices like polka dot Nikes and limited edition Chucks, this high-end sneaker shop is for serious shoe fans.

MAP 6: Gerard Doustraat 96, tel. 020/470-1010, www.baskets.com; noon-6pm Mon., 10am-6pm Tues.-Sat., 1pm-5pm Sun.

CHILDREN

Big & Belg

The name of this kids' clothes and toys store, which translates to Big and

Belgian, has a stylish reputation with city moms searching for cool outfits and toys. The walls are bright with puffer fish cartoon wallpaper and a dozen racks of new and independent Belgian labels for the little ones. A hopscotch game marks the kids' play area in the back. Toys range from fun monster masks to stuffed animals. The stock is modern, fashionable, and of good quality.

MAP 6: Ferdinand Bolstraat 168, tel. 020/752-2339, www.bigenbelg.nl; 10am-6pm Mon.-Fri., 10am-5pm Sat.

MUSIC

Opus 391

This former bike storage became a sheet music store in 1978 and has since become one of the largest collections of secondhand sheet music in the world. While the catalog is online, numbered and structured like a library, the store is a jaw-dropping chamber of old sheet music stacked wall to ceiling. Some sheets date back to the mid-1800s. Genres include salon orchestras, silent movie scores, musicals, operas, and tango. Sheets are for piano, bass, flute, oboe, clarinet, and more. The store itself is hard to spot, but look for the antique trumpet and French horn hanging behind the store windows.

MAP 6: Govert Flinckstraat 249, tel. 020/676-6415, www.opus391.nl; hours vary Tues.-Sat.

RebelRelic

Stuck between two secondhand guitar shops is this rustic hidden basement space that recreates custom vintage guitars from new parts. RebelRelic is run by an American who specializes in making custom guitars. RebelRelic can create a Fender from scratch and add authentic-looking knobs and pickups finished by hand to look like a precise model, down to the year. Customers can pick the bodies, neck, and other details, or describe their vision to the maker. You can see the owner's work station behind the shop counter. Billy Gibbons of ZZ Top has even bought one of the shop's pieces.

MAP 6: Gerard Doustraat 20, tel. 020/672-2008, www.rebelrelic.com; 11am-6pm Tues.-Fri., noon-6pm Sat.

The Plug

At first glance, The Plug looks like a pawn shop cluttered with dusty amplifiers and electric guitars. But looks can be deceiving: This legendary music shop has a celebrity clientele, like Oasis and Joe Walsh, who come for the vintage guitars. The Plug is something of a guitar hall of fame with Stratocasters owned by rock gods in the 1960s, unique Gibson series from the 1950s, and Ibanez electrics from the 1970s. The owner, Peter, a former truck driver and member of local 1980s rock band Ladyshavers, stocks a 200-plus guitar collection with amps, pedals, and rare instruments that don't really have a name. If you're lucky, he'll sit down with you on the red chairs outside and tell you all about it over a can of Heineken.

MAP 6: Ruysdaelkade 105, tel. 020/662-4889, www.deplug.nl; 1pm-6pm Mon., 11am-6pm Tues.-Fri., 11am-5pm Sat.

SPECIALTY FOOD AND DRINK

Wijnhandel van Krimpen

This shop began as a liquor store before World War II, and has since turned into a wine shop with about 800 different wines from across the globe. The modern and bright space has a fresh and sophisticated look, with an old decorative fountain in the back. The wines are displayed by region, each earning their own space on cupboards organized by country. From Old World Italy and France to New World Chile and South Africa, some labels are familiar to wine connoisseurs, but others are more obscure. Whether it's pinot grigio from Spain, riesling from Austria, malbec from the Andes, or rosso piceno from Italy, this shop offers the widest selection of varietals in the neighborhood. The cellar downstairs is where the shop offers private storage to customers who buy in large volumes.

MAP 6: Frans Halsstraat 67, tel. 020/671-6130, www.vkwijn.nl; 10am-7pm Tues.-Fri., 10am-6pm Sat.

antiques from around the globe at Buitengewoon

VINTAGE AND ANTIQUES

Buitengewoon

Buitengewoon (Something Special, in Dutch) feels like entering a forgotten warehouse of anthropological relics. The antiques are mainly from Mongolia, India, and Southeast Asia, and some are over 200 years old. The shop is full of decorative chandeliers, mosaic lanterns, and statues that sit atop ornate cupboards, tables, dressers, and wardrobes. Merchandise may include such things as a Romanesque bird bath, large Asian flower vases, menorahs, and ceramic jugs. Most of the pieces sold by the friendly owner are authentic.

MAP 6: Gerard Doustraat 200-202, tel. 020/400-4326, http://home.hccnet.nl/buitengewoon; 1pm-6pm Mon., 10am-6pm Tues.-Sat.

HOUSEWARES AND FURNITURE

Duikelman

The royal standard of professional cookware for most restaurants in Amsterdam hails from Duikelman. The shop's four rooms are stocked with a thousand culinary must-haves, from the newest in stainless-steel pots and pans to cast-iron skillets, meat grinders, and stacks of shiny tools. The knife room is intimidating, the cutlery room is seemingly limitless, and the baking shelves have dozens of silicone molds. Top-of-the-line blenders, mixers, and food processors are displayed like timeless artwork. A few doors down is the outlet, carrying industrial kitchen equipment like gas stoves, fridges, and espresso machines. Next door, there are cookbooks, fashionable table settings, and porcelain.

MAP 6: Ferdinand Bolstraat 66-68, tel. 020/671-2230, www.duikelman.nl; 9:30am-6pm Mon.-Fri., 9:30am-5pm Sat.

SPORTS AND OUTDOOR GEAR

Dumpstore Amsterdam

In 1974, this army surplus store opened in De Pijp, selling the staples of rugged camping gear for the Netherlands and European Lowlands. This dark and dusty shop has got it all: rows of Dutch leather mud boots, rubber rain galoshes, fishing vests, and military backpacks from Germany, all in the affordable price range. The racks of army and camouflage clothing come from France, Austria, and Holland. In winter, they sell piles of thick snow sweaters from Nepal.

MAP 6: Ferdinand Bolstraat 156, tel. 020/671-1794, www.dumpstoreamsterdam.nl; 10:30am-6pm Tues.-Thurs., noon-6pm Fri., 10:30am-5pm Sat.

Jordaan — Map 7

MARKETS AND SHOPPING CENTERS

Noordermarkt Flea Market

A handful of small stands hold peculiar antiques, old books, random records, and piles of clothes at the small Noordermarkt Flea Market. Various stands of flowers and plants sit next to locals selling their collections of Dutch kitchenware and decor. Nearly free of cheesy souvenirs and tacky touristy T-shirts, this flea market is great for surprise finds. Lovers of vintage fashions come for the goods. Dig around the boxes of random items, or watch shoppers searching for a score while sipping coffee at a nearby café terrace. Open on Saturdays, the flea market cozies up next to the stalls of the Noordermarkt Organic Farmers Market.

MAP 7: Noordermarkt 48, tel. 020/626-6436, http://www.noordermarkt-amsterdam.nl; 9am-5pm Sat.

Noordermarkt Organic Farmers Market

Amsterdammers know the best fresh local produce and culinary delights are found at the organic farmers market on Noordermarkt. The lively market was started in 1987 by a nearby café that put out a few food stalls to attract Saturday shoppers. Today, the market has grown to a few dozen stalls of local farmers selling an array of produce, dairy, meat, and pastries, including freshly cut Thai basil, buckets of olives, jars of honey, lemon curd, pesto, and woven baskets full of wild mushrooms. Bakers offer assorted pastries, breads, and cakes made with flour from Dutch windmills. Dairy options range from sheep's cheese aged in wooden barrels to soft and hard varieties of gouda. Butchers offer grass-fed and free-range meats, and sauces vary from fresh chutneys to vegetarian pâté. On-the-go eats include cartons of Dutch cherries and apples, Scottish shortbreads, French crepes, and freshly shucked oysters from the North Sea. Cruise around the tables, admire the delightful displays, and snack on scrumptious foods.

MAP 7: Noordermarkt 48, tel. 020/626-6436, http://www.noordermarkt-amsterdam.nl; 9am-5pm Sat.

DELFTWARE

Galleria D'Arte Rinascimento

For anyone on the hunt for Delftware (a style of white ceramic pottery decorated with blue paint that was made in 17th-century Delft, in the Netherlands), this shop will stand out. The shop is overwhelming and impressive. Thousands of figurines and trinkets in display cases stand next to large Delft platters and dishware sets portraying remakes of Vermeer and Rembrandt paintings. Determining the difference between new and old pieces, and those that are printed

BEST SOUVENIRS

CHEESE

The favorite food among locals is fresh farmer's cheese or gouda, which can be soft and young or hard and aged, or many variations in between. Specialty shops and supermarkets sell small wheels sealed with a wax covering, which are safe to bring overseas.

CLOGS

A traditional Dutch fashion, *klompen* (wooden clogs) have been worn as gardening shoes since the 1200s. Authentic clogs are mostly found at traditional dairy farms that double as clog factories, but the easiest way to nab a pair for yourself is by visiting the toy store Knuffels, which has an on-site clog-maker.

DELFTWARE

This style of pottery first emerged in the Dutch Golden Age. Made of white porcelain, the pieces feature landscape scenes and portraits painted in what is known as Delft blue. These depictions were painted onto place settings, kitchen tiles, and vases, among other items. Specialized antique and Delft stores Jorrit Heinen and Galleria D'Arte Rinascimento are good places to find a piece for your home.

SWEETS

A common treat in Amsterdam is the *stroopwafel,* two thin waffle cookies with a lightly sweet syrup sandwiched between them. A favorite during the holidays, *speculoos,* a cinnamon-flavored gingersnap, goes perfectly with a cup of coffee. The most unusual treat is the classic salty black licorice known as *drop.* All of these can be found in the candy and cookie aisles of any grocery store or specialty shop. *Stroopwafels* are also sold at stands at the city's ubiquitous outdoor markets.

TULIPS

Amsterdam's most famous and most colorful export is the tulip. Tulip bulbs are only available seasonally and must be purchased and planted in the fall. Look for the golden seal on the package that certifies that your bulbs are safe to transport through customs. If you're visiting outside of tulip season, stop by the Tulip Museum for flower-themed trinkets to remember your trip by.

versus hand-painted, can be tricky. Anyone with an inkling of interest in Delftware should come here.

MAP 7: Prinsengracht 170, tel. 020/622-7509, www.delft-art-gallery.com; 9am-6pm daily

CLOTHING

Jutka & Riska

One of Haarlem's best boutiques for used and new clothing has expanded into Amsterdam with the same stylish look and selection. Its own line of clothing is mixed in with finds from the 1970s, 1980s, and 1990s. Upstairs, there are new pieces, and downstairs, you'll find the curated vintage scores. With funky animal decor, this shop stands out from the rest on the block.

MAP 7: Haarlemmerdijk 143, tel. 062/466-8593, www.jutkaenriska.nl; 10:30am-7pm Mon.-Fri., 10am-7pm Sat., noon-6:30pm Sun.

Yosha Fasion

This basement vintage boutique is a hidden gem, run by the daughter of a designer from the 1960s and 1970s who made costumes for Elton John, Led Zeppelin, and the like. The shop's selection is not as flamboyant as a typical rock star outfit, but the stock of women's wear is fashionable and elegant. While the front part of the small one-room shop is all new designer brands, the back has vintage picks, from snakeskin boots to sequined halter tops.

MAP 7: Prinsengracht 300, tel. 020/785-4431, www.yoshafashion.com; 1pm-6pm Mon., noon-6pm Tues.-Sat.

ACCESSORIES

Concrete Matter

This rustic-looking store decorated with taxidermy birds sells old-fashioned accessories to the fashion-conscious guy, like aftershaves and shaving brushes, wilderness survival guides, aviator shades, weather-resistant notepads, and compasses. This is a great stop for those looking for trendy gifts.

MAP 7: Haarlemmerdijk 127, tel. 020/261-0933, http://eng.concrete-matter.com; 1pm-6pm Mon., 10am-6pm Tues.-Sat., noon-5pm Sun.

CHILDREN

Teuntje

Teuntje is the destination for fancy Bugaboo strollers, long racks of sustainable designer clothes, and toys galore. Sailor-striped fleece, star-spangled leggings, winter sports jackets, and trendy summer sandals are part of the regularly rotating stock. Dolls, games, and rattles appease infants and toddlers. It's a bit pricey, but it has a lot of stock in a space larger than most upscale city kids' stores.

MAP 7: Haarlemmerdijk 132, tel. 020/625-3432, www.teuntje.nl; 1pm-6pm Mon., 10am-6pm Tues.-Fri., 10am-5pm Sat.

GIFTS AND SOUVENIRS

&Klevering

Off Haarlemmerstraat, &Klevering is a gift shop that sells sustainable modern products, Scandinavian toys, and its own brand of ceramics and household wares. One corner has a kids' section featuring games and puzzles with a contemporary aesthetic, while another area focuses on housewares from Finland and Denmark, like hand-painted egg holders and place settings. There are soaps, candleholders shaped like Dutch canal houses, and mugs with animal illustrations, and all have something extra special in their shape, color, or design.

MAP 7: Haarlemmerstraat 8, tel. 020/422-2708, www.klevering.nl; noon-7pm Mon., 10am-7pm Tues.-Fri., 10am-6pm Sat., noon-6pm Sun.

't Stomerijtje

With tens of thousands of options, this is the perfect spot to find a unique and creative postcard, from the cute to the disturbingly funny. Postcards with trendy illustrations, Polaroid prints, and adorable animals wearing outfits make it difficult to walk out empty-handed. There are a few notebooks and pens, but the best part is the ability to send international mail right in the store.

MAP 7: Haarlemmerdijk 56, tel. 020/626-9860; 11am-6pm Mon., 10am-6pm Tues.-Fri., 10am-5pm Sat., noon-5pm Sun.

BATH AND BEAUTY

Back Stage

The shop's name is an homage to makeup artists that work on performers before the curtains lift. A lot happens at this shop: Not only is it a studio for professional makeup artists, it's also a supply store for those in the theater industry. The space is large, modern, and buzzing with artists working on models or helping customers. From all colors of eye shadow to every sort of bobby pin, nail polish, and airbrushing tool, Back Stage makes for a fun wander for any stylist or fashionista.

MAP 7: Rozengracht 101-103, tel. 020/622-1267; 11am-6pm Mon., 10am-6pm Tues.-Fri., 10am-5pm Sat.

La Savonnerie

Soaps are the primary attraction inside this adorable toiletry shop. Over 70 fragrant handmade soaps are on display in an array of colors and shapes. There are ceramic liquid-soap dispensers and trays hand-painted from Poland, hand-knitted towels, and toiletry bags hanging from wall hooks. There is also a men's line of shower gels, shaving creams, and soaps.

MAP 7: Prinsengracht 294, tel. 020/428-1139, www.savonnerie.nl; 10am-6pm Mon.-Sat.

MUSIC

Velvet Music

There are quite a few secondhand record shops in the Jordaan, but this one has a good balance of new and used, as well as a healthy stock of CDs. You'll find used records in the back, while newly pressed albums are in the front and center of the shop. Rock, blues, local talent, pop, and soul are the big genres, though there is a bit of everything. There are some new, retro-style record players against the walls; the rest of the wall space is devoted to some of the best vinyl cover art made. The place stays busy with its regulars, and there are occasional live gigs promoting new releases.

MAP 7: Rozengracht 40, tel. 020/422-8777, www.velvetmusic.nl; noon-6pm Sun.-Mon., 10am-6pm Tues.-Sat.

SPECIALTY FOOD AND DRINK

Cheese Museum

Walk into this treat of a shop-cum-museum to sample over a dozen cheeses while learning about the history of cheese in Holland. Inside are stacks of every possible type of cheese, like truffle-infused, beemster, soft gouda, smoked ham and herb, green wasabi, and white goat cheese—and customers can sample them all. The free museum downstairs offers a fun story about Dutch dairy farming, with traditional dairy tools on display. Most of the cheese here can be taken overseas and through customs.

MAP 7: Prinsengracht 112, tel. 020/331-6605, www.cheesemuseumamsterdam.com; 9am-7pm daily

Grape District

There are a couple hoity-toity wine shops on Haarlemmerstraat, but Grape District is a wine shop that's anti-snob and has an expansive selection. This chain has six small stores in Amsterdam, each with a colorful sign and organized by wine descriptions: smooth, mellow, rich, rosy, and so on. This location has color-coded cupboards to indicate the type of wine available, with green meaning light white wines and blue indicating bubbly proseccos. The prices are reasonable, and the selection beats that of supermarkets, with a well-informed staff ready to recommend a bottle for any occasion.

MAP 7: Haarlemmerstraat 112, tel. 020/638-8570, www.grapedistrict.nl; 1pm-7pm Mon., 11am-7pm Tues.-Wed., 11am-8pm Thurs.-Fri., 10am-7pm Sat., noon-5pm Sun.

Ibericus

This is the place to get up close and personal with pig legs and shoulders. Named after the part of Spain that delivers the famous *jamon negra*, Ibericus has cuts of ham on display, hanging from the walls, on the counters, and in deli cases, ready for the next layers to be thinly shaved for an order. These pigs are fed acorns for a nutty, tender flavor, and are traditionally served over melon slices. Order by the gram, and don't be afraid to ask for recommendations (or samples). The meat is cured, so you can ostensibly buy it to bring back home, but you may need special certificates and labels from the butcher to get through customs.

MAP 7: Haarlemmerstraat 93, tel. 020/223-6573; 10am-7:45pm daily

Jordino

Ever seen a chocolate high-heeled shoe before? There are so many of these confections, covered in many colors of sprinkles throughout this shop that it feels like a glamor queen's closet—but all chocolate! Jordino has a counter stocked with handmade chocolates, pralines with delightfully sweet fillings, and 24 flavors of Italian sorbet and gelato. Anyone wanting to eat a painting made out of chocolate can order that, too.

MAP 7: Haarlemmerdijk 25-A, tel. 020/420-3225, www.jordino.nl; 1pm-6:30pm Sun.-Mon., 10am-6:30pm Tues.-Sat.

Papabubble

Who knew hard candy could look like Venetian glass? This quaint candy shop creates sweet treasures with customized designs and edible lettering. There is always someone behind the counter practicing the 400-year-old candy-making method from Scandinavia. Pop in for a look at (and free sample of) Papabubble's wares, from swirled lollipops to small, dime-sized candies in an array of flavors. Downstairs in the shop's kitchen, visitors can watch the colorful candy being made.

MAP 7: Haarlemmerdijk 70, tel. 020/626-2662, www.papabubble.nl; noon-6pm Mon.-Fri.,10am-6pm Sat.

Tea Bar

The most popular shop on the street, Tea Bar specializes in offering up to 100 of its own blends of all types and flavors of tea. The shop is set up to be self-serve, so use the small scales to weigh your preferred amount (the minimum is 50 grams). Flavors change with the seasons, but past varieties have included Old Dutch apple pie, cranberry fields forever, and icy mojito. Buyers are encouraged to smell the chai, green teas, grey teas, and rooibos that peak their interest. Teas stay fresh for a year. Only credit cards are accepted.

MAP 7: Haarlemmerdijk 71, tel. 020/623-3211, www.teabar.nl; 11am-6pm Mon., 10am-6pm Tues.-Fri., 10am-5pm Sat.

TOYS AND GAMES

A Space Oddity

Ask the owner how many action figures he has in this shop, and he will guess between 4,000 to 5,000 (not including what's in storage). The tiny store has a small room and smaller loft packed to the max with toys related to film and television. The specialty is Star Wars and Transformers, but all the big stars play a part: Disney, Super Mario Brothers, rock bands like KISS, G.I. Joe, and even *Breaking Bad*. Not into action figures? Check out the mugs, shirts, and other knickknacks.

MAP 7: Prinsengracht 204, tel. 020/427-4036, www.spaceoddity.nl; 11am-5:30pm Tues.-Fri., 10:15am-5pm Sat.

Het Paard

This game and puzzle store is all about tests and brain teasers. Het Paard (The Horse) refers to the knight piece in a chess game. There are books on strategy in playing card games, as well as backgammon and the latest

3-D puzzles that make the Rubik's cube look like child's play (although they have those too). The variety of chess sets and pieces is dizzying, from metal, wood, and glass to pieces styled like superheroes. It's a whiz kid's paradise.

MAP 7: Haarlemmerdijk 173, tel. 020/624-1171, www.schaakengo.nl; 1pm-6pm Mon., 10am-6pm. Tues.-Wed. and Fri.-Sat., 10am-8pm Thurs.

VINTAGE AND ANTIQUES

Timeless Interiors

Inside this large maze of a shop are aisles of display cases holding antiques from a dozen different eras with an English theme. Every single piece on display is numbered, from the teaspoons to the cuckoo clocks. Write the number down, press a button on the wall, and someone will come help you. China sets, sterling silver place settings, Dutch dollhouses, porcelain, cameras from the 1920s—think of something antique and it's probably here. Many pieces are reasonably priced. Connected to the shop is The Blazer Brasserie, a café where patrons can admire their purchases.

MAP 7: Lijnbaansgracht 193, tel. 020/422-2656, www.deveson.nl; 1pm-5pm Mon., 11am-5pm Wed. and Sat.-Sun., 11am-4pm Fri.

Wini

This secondhand boutique throws fashion back to the 1960s and is one of the long-surviving vintage shops on the Haarlemmerstraat. The owner is often working at the counter repairing clothing that she'll eventually sell. The collection is ample, but not piled high like other stores. The clothing racks are tasteful and carefully curated for men and women.

MAP 7: Haarlemmerstraat 29, tel. 020/427-9393, http://winivintage.nl; 10:30am-6pm Mon.-Wed. and Fri.-Sat., 10:30am-6:30pm Thurs., noon-6pm Sun.

HOUSEWARES AND FURNITURE

Kitsch Kitchen

This shop is known for exactly what its name says: all things kitschy and fun for the kitchen. Two floors of aprons, baskets, party favors, and wrapping paper in bright tones are on display. Grab a cheerful umbrella or funky piñata and peruse the flamingo shower curtains, tropical toilet roll holders, toddler toys, and stationery.

MAP 7: Rozengracht 12, tel. 020/462-0050, www.kitschkitchen.nl; 10am-6pm Mon.-Sat., noon-5pm Sun.

Moooi

Anyone searching for inspiration in modern home design and artistic decor will be amazed with everything in this showroom. One floor feels like a 7,500-square-foot exhibition of modern design in the form of colorful furniture, creative lighting, rare rugs, and modern fixtures with unique shapes. Moooi has even turned an electric three-wheel car into a portable espresso café.

MAP 7: Westerstraat 187, tel. 020/528-7760, www.moooi.com; 10am-6pm Tues.-Sat.

SPORTS AND OUTDOOR GEAR

Fjällräven

Fjällräven has been a top-notch wilderness backpacking brand since it started in the 1960s. This location, their Dutch flagship store, is huge (three levels and over 5,000 square feet) and colored with bright hiking packs, specialized tents, sleeping bags, and seasonal outdoor clothing. You can get your outerwear waxed and even test out hiking boots by standing on a bridge made of rough tree trunks.

MAP 7: Rozengracht 219-225, tel. 020/428-1760, www.fjallraven.nl; noon-7pm Mon., 10am-7pm Tues.-Wed. and Fri., 10am-8pm Thurs., 10am-6pm Sat., noon-6pm Sun.

Plantage

Map 8

MARKETS AND SHOPPING CENTERS

✪ Waterlooplein Market

Landing somewhere between traditional and quirky, Waterlooplein Market offers up colorful trinkets, Dutch knickknacks, secondhand clothing, and a spread of antiques. The overall feel is junky at first, with piles of clothes strewn over tarps and penny-pinchers arguing over discounts. But, under the clutter, you can uncover vinyl albums, costumes, fixed-up bikes, and old postcards. Dutch wooden clogs sit beside unique brass sculptures and porcelain figurines. Shoppers will appreciate the variety of apparel, from the fur coats to the surplus of army fatigues, winter jackets, and leather goods.

MAP 8: Waterlooplein 2, tel. 020/552-4074, www.waterlooplein.nl; 9:30am-6pm Mon.-Sat.

BOOKS

Het Fort van Sjakoo

In the 1600s, Amsterdam had its version of Robin Hood: A man who went by the name of Sjakoo stole from the rich and gave to the poor. This independent bookstore echoes the philosophy of that left-wing libertarian. Run by volunteers since 1977, this shop offers literature on topics ranging from international politics to unconventional philosophy. Coming here feels like walking into a den owned by a smart anarchist pirate.

MAP 8: Jodenbreestraat 24, tel. 020/625-8979, www.sjakoo.nl; 11am-6pm Mon.-Fri., 11am-5pm Sat.

VINTAGE AND ANTIQUES

✪ Episode

The trendiest spot for recycled threads in Amsterdam, Episode is a used clothing shop that repairs old items of clothing and sells them as like-new creations. Miniskirts made out of sweatshirts are next to mounds of trendy secondhand sneakers and long rows of faux fur coats. This shop (and its four other locations) draws a young and trendy clientele. The prices are moderate, but the attention paid to each piece makes it worth the cost.

MAP 8: Waterlooplein 1, tel. 020/320-3000, www.episode.eu; 10am-6pm Mon.-Sat., 1pm-6pm Sun.

HOUSEWARES AND FURNITURE

Zalio Atelier

This shop is filled to the brim with floral ornaments and homey decor, as if a queen had emptied her closet of jewels and crafts. A sign at the entrance announces a maximum capacity of two people. It would be easy to miss if not for the woven baskets, pottery, and potted plants that extend to the sidewalk. Once down the steps, you'll find everything from bamboo root to jade stones, decorative birds, and seashells.

MAP 8: Amstel 33, tel. 020/420-3342, www.zalio.nl; 11am-6pm Tues.-Sat.

SPORTS AND OUTDOOR GEAR

De Fietsfabriek

If Willy Wonka had a bicycle factory, De Fietsfabriek would be his wonderland. Handcrafted in the Netherlands by passionate cycle fanatics, these are the Mercedes of the bike world. The storefront is a showcase of impressive craftwork with sturdy frames, customized colors, and gleaming metal chains. The box bikes carry kids around in polished wooden box seats, while city cruisers shine and sparkle. Though priced for the serious buyer, it's fun just to marvel at these top-of-the-line masterpieces.

MAP 8: Sarphatistraat 141-A, tel. 020/737-0899, www.defietsfabriek.nl; 9am-6pm Mon.-Fri., 9am-5pm Sat.

IJ River

Map 9

HOUSEWARES AND FURNITURE

Pols Potten

This is where all the trendy bars, cafés, and hotels have come to find inspiration for the latest in Dutch design since 1986. In a large warehouse space on KNSM Island, the store is divided by vivid color schemes, integrating the latest design innovations. The inventory, which includes gold pineapple statues, candlesticks made from mechanical tools, wooden hanging lamps, and watering cans shaped like dogs, may sound tacky, but the designs are sleek and simple. Rows of pillows, lamps, furniture, and Scandinavian tables are available to tie together any interior.

MAP 9: KNSM-Laan 39, tel. 020/419-3541, www.polspotten.nl; 10am-6pm Tues.-Sat., noon-5pm Sun.

WHERE TO STAY

The first thing to know about hotel rooms in Amsterdam is that they are small compared to other cities. Many hotels lack elevators, and stairways are steep and narrow. Amsterdam has strict regulations about renovating historic buildings, with the aim to preserve as many as possible as historic monuments. This can present challenges for visitors with limited mobility; call your hotel ahead to ask about accessibility.

Grand Hotel Amrâth Amsterdam

High season in Amsterdam is generally mid-April to mid-October, when hotels are known to double their rates—and then triple them during holidays like Easter, King's Day, Gay Pride, and Christmas. Low season, mid-October to mid-April, sees much lower rates. The lowest prices can be found during the frigid and rainy months of November, January, and February.

Solo backpackers, bachelor parties, and other party types usually stay in the **Red Light District,** which itself is part of the **Old Center.** Because this neighborhood is the oldest part of the city, the area isn't always sparkling clean, but it's the heart of Amsterdam's nighttime pleasures. Accommodation options around buzzing **Nieuwmarkt** are a mix of boutiques, hostels, and apartment rentals.

Quaint hotels with romantic canal views are common along the **Canal Belt.** These hotels are usually pricey, but budget-friendly options are scattered throughout. Stay in one of the hotels or hostels around Rembrandtplein or Leidseplein to hook into the area's entertainment scene.

HIGHLIGHTS

- **MOST HOMEY:** The **Hotel Brouwer** radiates charm thanks in part to its bright rooms filled with Dutch antiques (page 217).
- **BEST AMENITIES: Misc Eatdrinksleep** offers luxury-level extras, like a rainfall showerhead, white noise machine, and complimentary snacks (page 217).
- **BEST WAY TO FEEL LIKE A LOCAL: Hotel Weber** offers rooms that emulate modern apartments, down to the kitchenette and Scandinavian furniture (page 219).
- **BEST ANTIQUES:** The rooms at **Seven Bridges Hotel** are stuffed with furnishings and accent pieces—all of which were collected by the hotel's owners—dating as far back as the 18th century (page 219).
- **BEST OVERALL: The Toren** is the city's top hotel, thanks to its lavish decor, warm hospitality, and canalside location (page 222).
- **TRENDIEST HOTEL: The Hoxton, Amsterdam** is the cool hipster kid in town, with a modern, rustic sensibility and a brown-bag breakfast left at your door each morning (page 223).
- **BEST FOR BACKPACKERS:** Amsterdam is home to its fair share of hippie-ish hostels, but the **Flying Pig Uptown** is the cleanest and most friendly (page 228).
- **FRIENDLIEST B&B:** At the quirkily named **Frederic Rent-a-Bike,** you can expect smiles and warm conversation from the owner (page 231).
- **BEST CHANCE TO FEEL LIKE (OR SEE) A CELEBRITY:** The luxurious **InterContinental Amstel Amsterdam** is a haven for visiting A-listers. With its stunning canal views, upscale decor, and impeccable service, it's easy to see why (page 232).
- **MOST CREATIVE:** Funky **Ecomama** caters to artistic, social types with its communal spaces and imaginative design elements (page 233).

PRICE KEY

$	Less than €150 per night
$$	€150-300 per night
$$$	More than €300 per night

Hotels around **Museumplein** come in one of two general types: elegant and historic or decent and slightly neglected. Either way, the area is perfect for museumgoers, and many hotels border the pretty Vondelpark.

De Pijp is experiencing a growth in tourism, and the most common accommodation choices are small budget hotels and B&Bs. It's a sought-after neighborhood among the city's residents thanks to its community feel and buzzing restaurant and nightlife scene.

The **Jordaan** is a quaint residential neighborhood with limited accommodation options beyond B&Bs. If you want to stay here, book early and you'll be rewarded with hospitable proprietors and rooms with personal touches.

The handful of accommodation options in the **Plantage** are a healthy mix of budget stays, hostels, and boutique hotels. The Plantage is close to the city center, yet the quietness and greenery make it feel farther from the center.

The area along the **IJ River** offers a few budget-friendly options, including a campground. Staying in this area means you're away from the bustle of the city center, but still close enough to easily travel to the major attractions.

ALTERNATIVE LODGING OPTIONS

Consider staying in one of the residential neighborhoods just beyond the Canal Belt, like Westerpark, Oude West, Oost, and Zeeburg. Hotels and hostels here can be more modern, spacious, and budget-friendly than the options in the city center. AirBnB, where residents rent out rooms (or entire apartments), has taken off in these neighborhoods, leading to competitive prices.

The Dutch love camping, and there are a handful of campgrounds just outside Amsterdam, like Amsterdamse Bos, Amsterdam Nood, and Zeeburg parks, perfect for a summer visit. If you don't have a tent (or don't want to pack one), these parks offer options ranging from a glamping tent to cabins and small caravans. **Camping Zeeburg** (Zuider IJdijk 20, tel. 020/694-4430, www.camping-zeeburg.nl), nestled over a 10-acre island on a lake, offers tent and RV campsites, double rooms made from renovated trailers, and four-person eco-cabins. The campground has everything from showers to Internet access and barbecue grills, along with an open kitchen and indoor restaurant serving a full dinner menu. Canoes, kayaks, stand-up paddleboards, and bikes are available to rent.

Areas like Amsterdam Sloterdijk, Amsterdam Zuid, and Amsterdam Schiphol Airport are home to large hotel buildings with all the modern amenities that are sometimes hard to find in downtown Amsterdam. Amsterdam Sloterdijk and Amsterdam Zuid are a 10- to 15-minute train or subway ride from the center; they cater to business travelers and conference guests.

Old Center

Map 1

Art'otel $$$

This designer hotel lives up to its name, with functional art installations that double as furniture and red reception desks carved into oversized faces. This five-star lodging shines with perks like a 24-hour cigar room, an indoor pool, and a gym with a protein shake bar, as well as Mediterranean restaurant and cocktail bar 5&33. The 107 rooms are a blend of art and comfort, each exhibiting its own unique artwork above clean and soft double beds. The modern bathrooms are sectioned off by frosted glass, and views range from Amsterdam Centraal Station to a quiet courtyard. Art'otel outshines the surrounding five-star hotels with the edgiest take on luxury. Light sleepers should avoid the first-floor rooms, into which echoes of DJ turn tables seep through at night.

MAP 1: Prins Hendrikkade 33, tel. 020/719-7200, www.artotelamsterdam.com

Hotel Estherea $$$

It's hard to believe the dazzling and colorful Hotel Estherea began as a boardinghouse during World War II. The place has flourished into 93 rooms across eight 17th-century canal houses. The lavish interior resembles an endless tea party, from the extravagant chandeliers to the floral arrangements, mismatched antique furniture, decorative wood paneling, and ornate grandfather clock. Rooms are of a similar style. Choose between a canal or courtyard view. The staff is extremely friendly, and the reception area has a coffee and pastry corner with refreshments always available.

MAP 1: Singel 303-309, tel. 020/624-5146, www.estherea.nl

Hotel V Nesplein $$$

This retro chic hotel behind Dam Square offers a level of contemporary cool that's setting the bar for other four-star hotels in the city. The style leans toward shaggy rugs, mustard wallpaper, tweed curtains, and wood-tiled floors. Leather chairs and headboards enhance the 43 spacious rooms, and service is attentive. The popular restaurant The Lobby is downstairs.

MAP 1: Nes 49, tel. 020/662-3233, http://hotelvnesplein.nl

INK Hotel Amsterdam $$$

This contemporary hotel is high tech and fashionable, with a finger on the pulse of the industry's latest trends. The 149 rooms are new and sparkling, and personal touches are everywhere. Murals on the walls look like hand-drawn notes and street maps, and the bathrooms have homey accessories. Shots of fresh juices are offered at reception. The central location is ideal for stylish couples and solo travelers.

MAP 1: Nieuwezijds Voorburgwal 67, tel. 020/627-5900, www.accorhotels.com

NH Collection Amsterdam Grand Hotel Krasnapolsky $$$

With Dam Square at its doorstep, five-star Krasnapolsky is impossible to ignore. The only hotel that can offer a view of the Royal Palace facade, this 468-room lodging was one of the first grand hotels to open in Amsterdam, circa 1855. Some rooms are on the small side, but the top floor houses luxury suites. The Winter Garden, the hotel's dining area, has been named a national monument due to its impressive glass ceiling and ornate iron decor.

MAP 1: Dam 9, tel. 020/554-9111, www.nh-collection.com

Sofitel Legend the Grand $$$

This is a glamorous see-and-be-seen five-star hotel, with Lamborghinis parked at the entrance and a dazzling white marble lobby. The large building stands atop grounds that housed a convent in the 1400s. Rooms are modern and spotless, with designer furniture, flawless bathrooms, rainfall showerheads, and new amenities. The two courtyards, indoor pool, and spa are peaceful.

MAP 1: Oudezijds Voorburgwal 197, tel. 020/555-3111, www.sofitel.com

Die Port van Cleve $$

This charming four-star hotel is hidden in the shadow of the Royal Palace. It was the original Heineken brewery and now holds 122 modern rooms. They have a thing for Delft prints, from the linens to the bathroom soaps and the art on the walls. The location can't get more central than this. Some rooms in the rear feel forgotten and unattended, and there are no extras like a spa or fitness center. But the staff is friendly and outgoing. Request a room in the front and don't forget to check out the downstairs bar for a beer and trip back in time.

MAP 1: Nieuwezijds Voorburgwal 176-180, tel. 020/714-2000, www.dieportvancleve.com

Hotel de Gerstekorrel $$

This is a no-frills but good-value budget hotel next to Dam Square. The 31 rooms are typical Amsterdam small, with a narrow staircase and no elevator. The beds are soft and the bathrooms are clean and up to date. Quads and triple rooms are available, albeit a squeeze. Come here for the central canalside location and budget-friendly price, not the luxury.

MAP 1: Damstraat 22, tel. 020/624-9771, www.gerstekorrel.com

Résidence Le Coin $$

The quaint three-star Résidence Le Coin has 42 rooms, each with its own kitchenette space. The location is a combination of historic houses, just across from the Amstel River and University of Amsterdam, down a quiet street where Rembrandt once lived. The simple rooms get a boost with natural light and more space than comparable hotels. Bathrooms can be small, but are spotless. The kitchenettes include a sink, minifridge, stove top, and coffeemaker. Breakfast is included.

MAP 1: Nieuwe Doelenstraat 5, tel. 020/524-6800, www.lecoin.nl

Swissôtel $$

Swissôtel's 110 rooms deliver cleanliness and comfort next to Dam Square. The employees are known for friendly and attentive service, and prices are fair despite its central location. The basic rooms are complemented with comfortable beds, fresh linens, and modern bathrooms. The fitness and business centers are nothing special, but the place is perfect for those who are out by day and recharging at night.

MAP 1: Damrak 96, tel. 020/522-3000, www.swissotel.com

Westcord City Centre Hotel Amsterdam $$

This Dutch chain hotel is a three-star experience at a fair price in the city center. This central location has 116 simple, small rooms. Everything is clean and current, from the white sheets to the sleek showers and toilets. What the rooms lack in luxury is made up for in the friendly staff.

MAP 1: Nieuwezijds Voorburgwal 50, tel. 020/422-0011, www.westcordhotels.nl

✪ Hotel Brouwer $

Welcome to a dreamy boutique hotel with 10 adorable, antique rooms named after famous Dutch artists. The canal house setting is from the 1600s, and authentic Dutch Delft tiles still line the staircase. Single-paned French windows overlook a canal, and old paintings of the city hang on the walls. Rooms are bright and airy, with wooden floors and modern bathrooms. Hotel Brouwer is cute as a button and as cozy as grandma's house. Breakfast is included. Only cash payments are accepted.

MAP 1: Singel 83, tel. 020/624-6358, www.hotelbrouwer.nl

Stayokay Amsterdam Stadsdoelen $

This Stayokay location is a mellow hostel that focuses on being a refuge rather than a party place. The dorm rooms are basic, with bunk beds and cubby lockers. Breakfast is served at tables that double as a cozy lounge, complete with a foosball table, orange couches, and a bar. The shared bathrooms are pristine and simple. It's not the cheapest hostel around, nor does it have the most attentive staff, but the location and clean facilities are a big plus. Try to get a bed with a canal view.

MAP 1: Kloveniersburgwal 97, tel. 020/624-6832, www.stayokay.com

Red Light District and Nieuwmarkt

Map 2

Grand Hotel Amrâth Amsterdam $$$

Entering this hotel is like walking onto the set of a Wes Anderson movie, where art nouveau meets maritime classicism in a 19th-century building. Stained-glass windows are checkered blue and green with nautical iron features, while burgundy wallpaper and engraved wooden furnishings carry an antique charm. The hotel's 165 rooms have high ceilings, long drapes, and a Nespresso machine. The clientele includes business travelers, well-to-do adventurers, and retirees. Try to get a room with a waterfront view.

MAP 2: Prins Hendrikkade 108, tel. 020/552-0000, www.amrathamsterdam.com

✪ Misc Eatdrinksleep $$

A boutique hotel just off Nieuwmarkt, Misc Eatdrinksleep has six double rooms in a 17th-century canal house with canal and garden views. Room themes include baroque, African tribal art, and classic Rembrandt. Little touches like a white noise machine and rainfall showerheads add extra charm. The cozy lobby, personable staff, and complimentary drinks and snacks make this a modern gem. Breakfast is included.

MAP 2: Kloveniersburgwal 20, tel. 020/330-6241, http://misceatdrinksleep.com

Hotel Luxer $$

Hotel Luxer is a modern three-star spot with a modest bar and lobby. The 47 rooms are typically small, but clean and contemporary with updated bathrooms. The overall feel is surprisingly quiet for the party street location, and the condition of the rooms is light-years ahead of neighboring competitors.

MAP 2: Warmoesstraat 11, tel. 020/330-3205, http://hotelluxer.nl

Greenhouse Effect $

Greenhouse Effect is a good-time Red Light District hotel with a friendly staff. The clean rooms have a bohemian look with themes like Turkish Delight or The Sailor's Cabin, and sizes vary between a spacious single studio to tight-fit triple bedrooms, but everything is tidy and cared for. On weekends, DJs spin at the dive bar downstairs. The smoking lounge behind the lobby adds to the social, festive scene. Breakfast is included.

MAP 2: Warmoesstraat 55, tel. 020/624-4974, www.greenhouse-effect.nl

Shelter City $

Despite its Red Light District location, this 180-bed Christian hostel is a drug-free zone, with family or same-sex dorms with 4-20 beds per room. Hot breakfasts, DIY laundry, cheap bike rentals, and affordable boat tours are just some of the ways the hostel creates a hospitable atmosphere. The volunteer employees are great with offering tips and promoting a safe environment. Morning church services and Bible studies are an optional daily activity. Breakfast is included.

MAP 2: Barndesteeg 21, tel. 020/625-3230, www.shelterhostelamsterdam.nl

St Christopher's Inn at The Winston $

Situated above Belushi's sports bar and The Winston nightclub, St Christopher's holds 67 rooms with doubles, twins, and 6- to 8-bed dorms. Quentin Tarantino resided at this hostel-hotel for three months while he wrote the script for *Pulp Fiction*. Rock-and-roll-themed mural art splashes across the walls, while the rooms themselves are basic. Social couples and solo travelers will feel right at home. Breakfast is included.

MAP 2: Warmoesstraat 129, tel. 020/623-1380, www.winston.nl

Banks Mansion $$$

Personal touches, hospitable staff, and complimentary perks make Banks Mansion the type of hotel where you'll feel truly on vacation. Walk through the revolving door and you'll be greeted by a lobby stocked with an open bar that also serves *bitterballen,* cheese, and sweets. Inspired by Frank Lloyd Wright, the hotel's design blends the past with the modern. Every room boasts crisp linens, a rainfall shower, and art deco decor. Pay a little extra for the Executive Room and enjoy a canal view.

MAP 3: Herengracht 519-525, tel. 020/420-0055, www.carlton.nl

Hotel V Frederiksplein $$$

It's hard to miss stylish Hotel V, with its oversized illuminated "V" and golden bulldog statue in the lobby. The 48 clean rooms are cool looking, despite some being tiny, and bathrooms are modern. Prices can get high, but the hotel tries to make up for it with a retro and rustic decor of chesterfield couches, black hallways, metallic lamps, and animal hide throws. Go for the large double room with a balcony, and watch out for the noise coming from busy Frederiksplein out front.

MAP 3: Weteringschans 136, tel. 020/662-3233, www.hotelvfrederiksplein.nl

✪ Hotel Weber $$

Hotel Weber is more like seven large studio apartments, where breakfast is waiting at your door every morning, but otherwise you're on your own. Since 2005, the hotel has been run by a friendly expat couple who live downstairs and are ready to answer questions and offer recommendations. Each bright and modern room is a sizable 250 square feet, with a kitchenette, Scandinavian furniture, and minimal decorations. Bathrooms are clean and modern. The price is a great deal considering the spacious rooms and the hotel's location next to Leidseplein.

MAP 3: Marnixstraat 397, tel. 020/627-2327, www.hotelweber.nl

✪ Seven Bridges Hotel $$

This is one of the most impressive and artistic secrets of Amsterdam accommodations. Seven Bridges is a cozy, eight-room boutique hotel in a canal house from 1720. The owners have been collecting antiques for decades, enough to dress the entire hotel in pieces from the 18th-20th centuries, including a Napoleon clock, a French empire table from 1760, and a 1920s Tiffany stained-glass lamp. The hotel has steep stairs and very large rooms, each with special touches like a stucco ceiling, brass mirrors, Italian-tiled bathrooms, and signed Karel Appel prints. Rooms have either a garden or canal view, and all have air-conditioning, minifridges, and free Wi-Fi.

MAP 3: Reguliersgracht 31, tel. 020/623-1329, www.sevenbridgeshotel.nl

Amstelzicht $$

One of the most severely leaning houses in the city, dating from 1659, is the Amstelzicht hotel, known as one of the city's three "dancing houses." This basic but pleasing hotel offers 14 rooms and romantic Amstel River views. The lobby is stunning, with white marble flooring and an exposed brick wall. Up the narrow staircase, the standard doubles are small and carpeted, with a retro 1970s look. Showers are clean, and rooms are small, with windows overlooking houseboats on the river. The staff is helpful and the location is convenient.

MAP 3: Amstel 104, tel. 020/623-6693, www.hotelamstelzicht.com

Asterisk $$

Asterisk gets props for being a no-frills budget hotel that's clean, modern, and well-located. Room sizes vary; some are small, so be sure to ask for a spacious double. Decor is bare bones, furniture is basic, but the beds are soft with clean white linens and the location is quiet. There are 44 rooms across four historic Dutch houses, so the stairs are narrow. Breakfast is included in the bright and fresh dining area. Book on the website for a 10 percent discount.

MAP 3: Den Texstraat 16, tel. 020/626-2396, www.asteriskhotel.nl

Backstage $$

Music lovers and bands that play at nearby concert halls Paradiso and Melkweg usually end up in one of Backstage's 22 cozy rooms. Throughout the years, bands like Future Islands, Tune-Yards, and Kensington have left behind trinkets, which are now on display in the lobby, and have signed their names on pieces of furniture. Sometimes musicians have jam sessions in the downstairs bar. The black-and-white rooms give off a 1970s rock vibe and feature music-themed accessories like instruments, drum stools, and stage lighting.

MAP 3: Leidsegracht 114, tel. 020/624-4044, www.backstagehotel.com

the steep stairway at Cocomama

Hampshire Hotel–Amsterdam American $$

This historic hotel is famous in the city for its original art deco grand café, unique outdoor fountain, and stunning exterior design. Big with business travelers and summer tourists, the hotel was built at the turn of the 20th century and features art deco elements like ornate stained glass. A 2016 renovation of the 175 rooms saw the addition of large comfortable beds and balconies. All rooms have bathtubs and are clean and cozy. Ask for a room with a balcony or a canal view to add a little more space.

MAP 3: Leidsekade 97, tel. 020/556-3000, www.hampshire-hotels.com

Hotel Nicolaas Witsen $$

Hotel Nicolaas Witsen is named after a former mayor, maritime writer, and cartographer of the Dutch East India Company. Its 28 rooms, spread across three buildings, are clean and simple doubles. The hotel's look is a bit outdated, though the red carpet and large photos of tulips and windmills can be charming and kitschy. The owner and staff are friendly, and breakfast is included. Book a room on the opposite side of the busy street where trams run. The prices, location, and easygoing feel make this hotel an attractive place to stay.

MAP 3: Nicolaas Witsenstraat 4, tel. 020/626-6546, www.hotelnicolaaswitsen.nl

Cocomama $

Cocomama combines the look and price of a hostel with the intimate atmosphere of a boutique hotel, making it perfect for mellow backpackers. Set in a former brothel, the hotel has held onto remnants of its sultry past, such as the stripper pole at reception. Rooms are playfully themed, and include a cheese room, a farm room, and a forest room. The largest of the three dorm rooms contains two sets of triple bunks. There are also five private rooms. Bathrooms are private and clean. The large living room and ample communal kitchen downstairs are great settings for DIY meals. The young staff are helpful and organize nightly activities like comedy shows, tours, and local bar crawls.

MAP 3: Westeinde 18, tel. 020/627-2454, www.cocomamahostel.nl

Hans Brinker $

At this hostel, a whopping 520 beds are in rooms fitting up to eight bunks per room. All rooms have en suite bathrooms. The hostel was built in a former school, and has been a family-owned and -operated place since 1981. There's a sense of backpacker camaraderie here. Whether it's the happy hour specials at the on-site bar or the gritty basement disco, at Hans Brinker, nothing matters beyond fun.

MAP 3: Kerkstraat 136-138, tel. 020/622-0687, http://hansbrinker.com

the bar at Hans Brinker

Canal Belt West

Map 4

✪ The Toren $$$

The Toren is easily the best hotel in Amsterdam. Its 38 rooms spread across two historic canal houses on the Keizersgracht; each room is unique in size, and the decor varies from traditional to trendy. The interior looks like a lush boutique, with elegant French wallpaper, stained wood, fresco ceilings, and lavish chandeliers. The bedrooms and en suite bathrooms, some of which have hot tubs, are spotless. The hotel prioritizes establishing relationships with their guests.

MAP 4: Keizersgracht 164, tel. 020/622-6352, www.thetoren.nl

Ambassade Hotel $$$

Ambassade Hotel opened in 1953. Its 57 rooms occupy 11 historic canal houses from the 17th century. Rooms have either a canal or courtyard garden view, with colorful and patterned decor and comfortable beds. Bathrooms are modern, and all rooms have air-conditioning. The most stunning feature is the large amount of contemporary art. Works here could just as easily be featured in the Stedelijk Museum. The library bar holds over 4,000 signed books from publishing houses across the country. Service is kind and attentive, catering to a clientele of business travelers and tourists.

MAP 4: Herengracht 341, tel. 020/555-0222, http://ambassade-hotel.nl

The Toren's lounge and bar

Andaz Amsterdam $$$

Inspired by *Alice in Wonderland*, the lobby of the Andaz greets guests with oversized lampshades, lipstick-red emperor chairs, and pop art video installations. The building was once the city library and has since been revamped as a 122-room upscale hotel with a gorgeous courtyard garden. Room decor is eccentric, with retro lamps, vanity mirrors, bowl sinks, and unique wallpaper designs. Complimentary perks include bike rentals and wine and snacks in the evening.

MAP 4: Prinsengracht 587, tel. 020/523-1234, www.hyatt.com

Canal House $$$

For visitors who want to feel pampered, Canal House is worthy of a splurge. This deluxe boutique hotel with 23 glamorous rooms occupies two 17th-century canal houses. A basic, modern room includes a king-size bed, rainfall shower, leather headboard, silk wallpaper, and plush velvet curtains. Service is excellent. The sophisticated lobby and classy bar are surrounded by old Dutch art above white marble floors. Breakfast is included.

MAP 4: Keizersgracht 148, tel. 020/622-5182, www.canalhouse.nl

Pulitzer Hotel $$$

The Pulitzer Hotel is more like an urban resort, connecting 25 historic canal houses into a 225-room spread that was designed by Herbert Pulitzer. The wooden floors, camel leather decor, crisp linens, exposed ceiling beams, and heated bathroom mirrors come together for a remarkable look. The interior of the hotel has an immaculate feel, from the white marble floors to the winding staircases and glass-encased hallways. Scan the QR code at the door for the history of your room.

MAP 4: Prinsengracht 315-331, tel. 020/523-5235, www.pulitzeramsterdam.com

Sebastian's $$$

What started as a hostel has evolved into a top-rated, 35-room hotel occupying two 17th-century canal houses. The location is just on the cusp of the Jordaan and Canal Belt, the staff is helpful, and rates are reasonable. Each room has either a courtyard or canal view. The ruby red and violet velvet decor lend a bit of character.

MAP 4: Keizersgracht 15, tel. 020/423-2342, www.hotelsebastians.nl

The Dylan Amsterdam $$$

The Dylan feels like a castle hidden in the city, with a dazzling marble lobby and rustic chic dining lounge. There are just 40 rooms in this two-building hotel. Wooden floorboards, black leather lounge chairs, and golden walls enhance the 18th-century feel. The two-story rooms are contemporary, albeit small, with cozy beds and sparkling bathrooms. The peaceful courtyard is leafy and intimate. The staff is friendly and helpful. The clientele leans toward couples and newlyweds—The Dylan is a popular location for wedding receptions.

MAP 4: Keizersgracht 384, tel. 020/530-2010, www.dylanamsterdam.com

✪ The Hoxton, Amsterdam $$

The Hoxton, a hotel brand that originated in East London's Shoreditch district, is a hipster hotel with reasonable prices and luxury style. The 111 rooms come in three size-based categories, and most rooms boast a canal view. The look is modern rustic, with rainfall showerheads, copper towel warmers, and original exposed ceiling beams. Rooms include a minibar with a few freebies, and the hotel offers a snack and drink menu with beer and champagne. A light breakfast is included, packaged in a brown bag and left at your door each morning. The hotel's lounge and restaurant is a see-and-be-seen spot for locals.

MAP 4: Herengracht 255, tel. 020/888-5555, https://thehoxton.com

Hotel Clemens $$

Don't let the narrow stairway turn you away: This small, bright, and airy budget hotel is just down the street from the Westerkerk and the Anne Frank Huis Museum. Its warm lobby has views of Westerkerk Tower down to the Royal Palace dome. The 14 rooms are small and basic, but clean and modern. Go for a double deluxe room with a brick-covered balcony. Those with cat allergies should look elsewhere—the hotel has two sweet felines who greet you at reception. Breakfast is included.

MAP 4: Raadhuisstraat 39, tel. 020/624-6089, www.clemenshotel.nl

Max Brown Hotel $$

With its copper ceiling, black-painted brick walls, and trendy espresso bar, Max Brown doesn't look like an average hotel. The 34 cozy rooms are mostly doubles with plaid or wood-paneled walls, patchwork blankets, hanging bulbs, and a cabin-chic decor. Try to get a superior with a canal view, and watch out for the steep stairs. The bathrooms are dated but clean. Breakfast is included.

MAP 4: Herengracht 13-19, tel. 020/522-2345, www.maxbrownhotels.com

Hotel Hegra $

Started by two friends in 1994, Hotel Hegra is located in a 1656 canal house

modern luxury on a budget at The Hoxton, Amsterdam

maximum comfort at Maes B&B

a short distance away from Dam Square. Marked by a red awning and split door, this charming, plain spot boasts fair prices and is accordingly popular. A typical Dutch house, Hegra is equipped with steep stairs, exposed ceiling beams, and bright rooms with canal views. The nine simple rooms are small but not cramped, with checkered linens. The modern bathrooms are a squeeze.

MAP 4: Herengracht 269, tel. 020/623-7877, www.hotelhegra.nl

Maes B&B $

Back in the 1990s, the owners of Maes vacationed in San Francisco and were inspired by their visit to create one of the first bed-and-breakfasts in Amsterdam. Two large and lovely rooms, both with a private bath, offer luxury with a homey feel. The building is a historic former merchant's house, with a large living room, comfortable dining area, and kitchen that's open for communal use. Breakfast includes fresh fruit, yogurt, and bread from a local bakery. The rates in this country-style hideaway stay the same regardless of whether it's high or low season, although there is a minimum two-night stay.

MAP 4: Herenstraat 26, tel. 020/427-5165, www.bedandbreakfastamsterdam.com

Museumplein

Map 5

The Conservatorium $$$

The Conservatorium is the crème de la crème of luxury in a charming and remarkable setting. The massive, well-preserved building next to the Stedelijk Museum was built as a bank during the turn of the 19th century. Its original brick hallways are lined with painted tiles. The exceptional chandelier is made of violins, a nod to the building's former tenant, a music conservatory. The 129 rooms are huge for Amsterdam standards and feature sparkling modern decor, chic furnishings, and pristine bathtubs. The penthouse suite is over 1,800 square feet, with floor-to-ceiling windows on all sides. The dining area has a glass roof, open layout, and Italian designer furniture. A number of luxury shops wrap around the entrance, selling everything from Cuban cigars to jewelry.

MAP 5: Van Baerlestraat 27, tel. 020/570-0000, www.conservatoriumhotel.com

Apple Inn Hotel $$

This modern hotel occupies a renovated 19th-century manor house just next to Vondelpark and offers 29 chic and contemporary rooms. Room sizes vary from singles to quads, all equipped with light wooden furniture and flooring. The look is fresh, with crisp gold-colored pillows and chairs. The spotless bathrooms are up-to-date, with a rainfall shower. Try to book a room with a balcony that overlooks the garden. The hotel's back

The Conservatorium

patio is a quaint slice of serenity. The chic bar and coffee lounge is a bonus.
MAP 5: Koninginneweg 93, tel. 020/662-7894, www.apple-inn.nl

Bilderberg Hotel Jan Luyken $$
This contemporary hotel, set in a historic house, has 62 modern rooms with a simple, polished style. Situated on a quiet street, the building has French balconies and white bay windows that blend in with the classy neighborhood. A polished reception area with white marble flooring and wooden paneling welcomes visitors. The taupe-colored rooms are soothing, and bathrooms have modern rainfall showers with bathtubs. The small lobby bar serves cocktails and snacks. The separate breakfast room adds an extra touch of class with white tablecloths.
MAP 5: Jan Luijkenstraat 58, tel. 020/573-0730, www.bilderberg.nl

Conscious Hotel Vondelpark $$
This large and ecofriendly hotel offers quality rooms that are shockingly modern and sleek. The café and lobby demonstrates up-cycling at its best, from the plant wall to the pillows made of rugs and tables made from yogurt cartons. The 81 rooms throughout the six floors are designed to limit water and energy usage and give the hotel a clean and simple look at a low price. Its sister property, **Conscious Hotel Museumplein** (De Lairessestraat 7, tel. 020/671-9596), while smaller in size, is just as green-minded.
MAP 5: Overtoom 519, tel. 020/820-3333, www.conscioushotels.com

Flynt $$
This small B&B has three spacious and spotless rooms in a house close to Vondelpark. The couple who run Flynt welcome guests with coffee and sightseeing advice. Breakfast is included, along with 24-hour kitchen access, a quiet backyard patio, and a grill. Choose a room based on theme: bicycles, the post office, or cats. The furnishings are old-fashioned with a minimalist antique look, with tiled bathrooms and spotless showers. The rooms are spacious and comfortable for two or three guests.
MAP 5: Eerste Helmersstraat 34, tel. 020/618-4614, www.flyntbedandbreakfast.nl

Hotel Aalders $$
The 32 rooms of this family-run hotel are a stone's throw from Museumplein. People love its convenient location, friendly atmosphere, and historic interior. The singles and some doubles are small, but the triple and family rooms are spacious. The furnishings are a bit outdated, which adds to the hotel's charm. Beds are comfortable, pillows are fluffy, and some rooms have a balcony. The bathrooms are simple but sparkling clean. The charming breakfast room has a white marble fireplace, wood trim, and large windows that overlook the neighborhood. There is also a separate bar and café. Breakfast is included and bicycle rentals are available. Aalders is a great value during weekdays and the off-season.
MAP 5: Jan Luijkenstraat 13-15, tel. 020/662-0116, https://hotelaalders.nl

Hotel Fita $$
The 20-room Hotel Fita, just behind the Van Gogh Museum, is run by a friendly Dutch family. The rooms are simple and tidy, ranging from small to spacious. The bathrooms are clean, and some rooms have balconies and patios. Breakfast is included. In the lobby is a minibar that relies on the honor system.

MAP 5: Jan Luijkenstraat 37, tel. 020/679-0976, www.fita.nl

Hotel Piet Hein $$

This contemporary gem sits on the outskirts of Vondelpark, a stylish boutique hotel worthy of a splurge for its location and modernity. The downstairs lobby and bar have spotless white marble floors, and room sizes vary from snug to lavish. The rooms are modern and sleek, and most bathrooms have a whirlpool tub or bathtub as well as modern fixtures. The backyard garden and patio is an ideal place to unwind in summer.

MAP 5: Vossiusstraat 52-53, tel. 020/662-7205, www.hotelpiethein.com

Hotel Roemer $$

Of the properties owned by the Vondel Hotels brand, Hotel Roemer stands out for its spacious suites and contemporary edge. The stylish lavender lobby doubles as the breakfast room. White leather couches populate the reading room, and the backyard patio is bright and green. Art hangs in the 23 rooms, which range from small to luxurious. There are an additional 15 rooms in their second building across the street. The staff is friendly and attentive to its corporate clients and visiting couples. Close to Vondelpark and Leidseplein, but on a small street, Hotel Roemer is a peaceful choice in a convenient location.

MAP 5: Roemer Visscherstraat 10, tel. 020/589-0800, www.hotelroemer.com

Hotel Vondel $$

Hotel Vondel is an ideal lodging with 86 rooms across a row of historic houses dating from the 1700s. Each room is unique in design but similar in comfort. Air-conditioning and an elevator are great perks, as is the tranquil patio garden and attached restaurant. Part of the Vondel Hotels chain, this classic choice is a stone's throw from Vondelpark. The friendly staff are welcoming to the typical clientele of couples of all ages.

MAP 5: Vondelstraat 18-26, tel. 020/612-0120, www.hotelvondel.com

The Neighbor's Magnolia $$

This 21-room, family-run boutique hotel combines friendly atmosphere with a homey experience. Situated off a street just next to Vondelpark, the pastel green rooms are snug, simple, and feature modern furniture from Scandinavian designer HAY. Hanging lamps and the plum and red tones give a chic dormitory look, and bathrooms are private. Try for a room with an added balcony, patio, or rooftop terrace. Breakfast is included.

MAP 5: Willemsparkweg 205, tel. 020/676-9321, www.magnoliahotelamsterdam.com

✪ Flying Pig Uptown $

The hippie look and feel at Flying Pig Uptown give off a friendly and laidback vibe to its backpacker clientele. This first location of the Flying Pig chain has 200 beds in 30 rooms, from 12-person dorms to private twins and doubles. Most bathrooms are shared, and the building is much cleaner than the average backpacker hostel. It's more easygoing and less of a party here than at its downtown location. Breakfast is included.

MAP 5: Vossiusstraat 46/47, tel. 020/400-4187, www.flyingpig.nl

Stayokay Vondelpark $

Families on a budget and large groups love this hostel for its spacious modern look and affordable extras, from bike rentals to free breakfast and an in-house café/bar. Over 500 beds occupy rooms ranging from 12-bed mixed dorms to private doubles. The large communal room has a computer station, tour booking desk, and is home to the bar, which offers daily specials. Clean, large, and efficient, Stayokay also benefits from a location on the doorstep of Vondelpark.

MAP 5: Zandpad 5, tel. 020/589-8996, www.stayokay.com

The Collector $

The name of this bed-and-breakfast, on the second floor of a historic house, is an allusion to its owner Karel. His collection of clogs decorates the stairs that lead to two spacious rooms equipped with a double bed, breezy balcony, and spic-and-span bathroom. The music-themed room has a collection of antique instruments above the wardrobe, while the clock-themed room features timepieces. Breakfast is served in the kitchen, a throwback to the 1950s, with lipstick-red cookware. The service is personal, the rooms are ideal, and the location is quiet and convenient.

MAP 5: De Lairessestraat 46, tel. 020/673-6779, www.the-collector.nl

De Pijp — Map 6

Okura Hotel $$$

While it might not look like much from the outside, this concrete tower on the outskirts of the city is a 23-story luxury hotel offering breathtaking views. Business travelers and honeymooners are treated like royalty, from the soft and silky beds to the caring and attentive staff. While the hotel is a bit far from the city center, the modern building makes up for it with larger rooms. The queen and superior rooms are a similar price to downtown hotels with small rooms.

MAP 6: Ferdinand Bolstraat 333, tel. 020/678-7111, www.okura.nl

Sir Albert Hotel $$$

This hotel takes its name from its location on Albert Cuypstraat. Sir Albert has 90 rooms that vary from small rooms to suites big enough to fit a whirlpool tub. The rooms are contemporary and sleek, with black trim and white bathrooms. Take a look at the art installation of hippo heads near reception—it's the most photographed part of the hotel.

MAP 6: Albert Cuypstraat 2-6, tel. 020/305-3020, www.siralberthotel.com

Cake Under My Pillow

Cake Under My Pillow $$

Cake Under My Pillow is homey, if a bit out of date. Each of the three rooms is decorated with a color and theme. Artwork made of old cross-stitch patterns is framed on yellow walls and the hallway is full of throw rugs. The bathrooms are clean, and the linens are fresh. The best perk is the vouchers for free cake at the downstairs bakery Taart van m'n Tante.

MAP 6: Eerste Jacob van Campenstraat 66, tel. 020/751-0936, www.cakeundermypillow.com

BBbyServio $

Guests at this bed-and-breakfast get a deluxe example of ordinary life. Wake up to a private breakfast with coffee, fruit, and a fridge full of fresh cheese and ready-to-bake bread from nearby Albert Cuypmarkt. The Green Room is spacious, with a double bed and grassy hues from walls to pillows. The Delft Blue Room features a loft with a double bed and a lounge area. The shared bathroom is modern and sparkling. The owner comes from Texel, a small Dutch island. Other residents include a cat named Boris and a dog named Bink.

MAP 6: Govert Flinckstraat 109, tel. 062/171-3772, www.bbbyservio.nl

Between Art & Kitsch $

Owner Irene has an eye for classic antiques with a twist. Her two-bedroom bed-and-breakfast is adorned with odds and ends picked up from flea markets, antique shops, and former churches. The Baroque Room is a spacious rustic cabin with a chandelier, antique table, and gold-plated mirror, and the Art Deco Room has a uniquely tiled bathroom and a view of the Rijksmuseum. Breakfasts are an assortment of breads and spreads. Beware the steep staircase.

MAP 6: Ruysdaelkade 75, tel. 020/679-0485, www.between-art-and-kitsch.com

Bicycle Hotel $

The Bicycle Hotel was the first place in Amsterdam to offer bike rentals with a room back in 1991. Now the budget-friendly hotel with a hostel feel has 16 beds, a small back garden, and a breakfast room. The dorm-like rooms have worn furnishings, but are colorful, bright, and clean. Some bathrooms are shared. The rooftop has solar panels for electricity.

MAP 6: Van Ostadestraat 123, tel. 020/679-3452, www.bicyclehotel.com

Ollies Bed and Breakfast $

Three big, bright, and contemporary Nordic rooms await couples who book this friendly B&B on a quiet corner in a residential area. The owners are a welcoming couple who run their own café downstairs, which doubles as the breakfast room. Rooms have high ceilings, furry rugs, lounge chairs, big beds, and en suite bathrooms. The place is a roomy, private paradise.

MAP 6: Saenredamstraat 26-I, tel. 065/327-0607, www.olliesbedandbreakfast.com

The Bank Hotel $$

This hotel has 24 bright, soundproof rooms with air-conditioning, marble bathrooms, and crisp white linens. The decor is funky contemporary—even the bathtubs are painted with vivid colors. Try to get a double or grand double with a French balcony, or splurge on the panorama penthouse, which offers top views of the city. The rates are on the high side, but the location is hard to beat, with the nicest part of town at your doorstep.

MAP 7: Haarlemmerstraat 120, tel. 020/366-78086, www.thebankhotelamsterdam.nl

Hotel Wiechmann $$

Darling Hotel Wiechmann is known for its antique charm and warm family welcome. The hotel is made up of three historic canal houses, offering a touch of quaintness in each of the 37 rooms, from wooden furnishings to stained-glass sliding doors. Favorite elements include the living room feel of the lobby, the teapot collection, and the breakfast café overlooking the canal. Rooms are clean, with an antique vibe thanks to Old World features like ornate rugs, oak china cabinets, and nautical knickknacks. Go for the double with the canal view. Anyone with dog allergies should know about the elderly but sweet in-house pooch. Breakfast is included.

MAP 7: Prinsengracht 328-332, tel. 020/626-3321, www.hotelwiechmann.nl

Linden Hotel $$

Linden Hotel is on the cusp of the Jordaan in a 19th-century historic triangle building with small but clean rooms and a friendly staff. The 25 modern rooms are newer than most Amsterdam flats, with spic-and-span bathrooms and new linens. Sizes range from a shoebox single to a spacious quad. Couples who want wiggle room should consider the superior double.

MAP 7: Lindengracht 251, tel. 020/622-1460, www.lindenhotel.nl

✪ Frederic Rent-a-Bike $

In addition to serving as a bike rental shop, as its name suggests, Frederic Rent-a-Bike is a B&B with seven guest rooms, as well as 10 apartments and five houseboats off-site. The guest rooms and apartments are clean and come equipped with fresh sheets and free Wi-Fi. Guests staying on-site can enjoy a breakfast of fresh breads from Petit Gateau, one of the best bakeries in town. The owner is personable, with a genuine interest in his guests.

MAP 7: Brouwersgracht 78, tel. 020/624-5509, www.frederic.nl

B&B Eelhouse $

The elegant Eelhouse has three large rooms with queen-size double beds and space that is a cross between an apartment and a bed-and-breakfast. There are wooden floors and long plum curtains, and the space is bright even in winter. While the top floor offers scenic views, all rooms have large windows. Bathrooms are simple and spotless, and the minifridge, microwave, and complimentary wine, fruit, and chocolates are great perks. An in-room breakfast is served every morning, featuring fresh produce and pastries.

MAP 7: Tweede Lindendwarsstraat 21, tel. 020/330-0544, http://eelhouse.eu

Jordan's B&B $

Two boutique double rooms make up this bed-and-breakfast nestled in the narrow streets of the Jordaan. The look here is rustic romantic, with country-chic decor, like ladders in the corners and cacti on the desks. The rooms are sunlit, with cozy beds and clean bathrooms. Artwork from a local Amsterdam illustrator hangs on the walls. Breakfast, included in the price, is served at nearby Bar Brandstof.

MAP 7: Akoleienstraat 2, no phone, www.jordansbnb.com

Sjudoransj B&B $

This two-room B&B offers luxury-size rooms in a central location at a competitive price. Both rooms have a king-size bed, a Nespresso machine, fresh and modern decor, and all the expected amenities. Breakfast each morning comes from a local bakery and deli, with an array of treats served the traditional way—on a table that rolls over the bed. One room has a garden view and the other a view of the quiet street.

MAP 7: Goudsbloemstraat 91-1, tel. 064/267-4809, www.sjudoransj.nl

Plantage

Map 8

✪ InterContinental Amstel Amsterdam $$$

This is the best of the luxury hotels in Amsterdam, and has won the hearts of a long list of celebrities, from Brad Pitt and Madonna to the Rolling Stones. The elegant 19th-century building sits along the Amstel River, with breathtaking views of the waterfront and city center available from nearly every one of the 55 rooms and 24 suites. The Amstel boasts turndown service, French designer furnishings, and marble bathrooms. In addition to the indoor heated pool, there's also a formal restaurant, brasserie, and a riverside terrace bar on-site. The lobby dazzles with chandeliers and Persian carpets.

MAP 8: Professor Tulpplein 1, tel. 020/622-6060, www.amsterdam.intercontinental.com

The Bridge Hotel $$

This family-run hotel wins points for its friendliness and rooms with views of the Amstel River and Magere Brug. The sizes of the hotel's 53 rooms vary; those with canal views are a bit larger. The comfortable double rooms have combined twin beds, with simple decor and clean, private bathrooms. There is a private courtyard. Breakfast is included, and the breakfast room is decorated with photos of the city's soccer team, the AFC Ajax. The marble-clad lobby harkens back to when the building was a marble factory. Watch out for the narrow stairs.

MAP 8: Amstel 107-111, tel. 020/623-7068, www.thebridgehotel.nl

Hampshire Hotel—Lancaster $$

This 19th-century building is a no-frills arrangement in a classic European style, just across from Artis Zoo. Some of the modern, tidy bedrooms overlook a tiny park. The snug rooms (a usual size for Amsterdam) are ideal for couples but a tight squeeze for families. Zoo noises are not an issue for light sleepers. Bike rentals are available.

MAP 8: Plantage Middenlaan 48, tel. 020/535-6888, www.hampshire-hotels.com

Hotel Hermitage Amsterdam $$

This quaint 22-room hotel offers basic accommodations. Features include the backyard garden and breakfast nook. Though it has thin walls, steep stairs, and small rooms typical of old Amsterdam hotels, the Hermitage stands apart thanks to its convenient and quiet location next to Carré Theater and the Skinny Bridge.

MAP 8: Nieuwe Keizersgracht 16, tel. 020/623-8259, www.hotelhermitageamsterdam.com

Ibis Amsterdam Centre Stopera $$

An extra-large hotel, Ibis Amsterdam Centre Stopera has 207 rooms and is in walking distance of Waterlooplein. This chain hotel is known for its modern atmosphere and reliable service. The property is small on decor but big on extras like flat-screen TVs and air-conditioning. Rooms are more spacious than average Amsterdam hotels, and some offer canal views.

MAP 8: Valkenburgerstraat 68, tel. 020/721-9173, www.ibis.com

Stout & Co. $$

A prime example of modern Dutch design, Stout & Co. is an old brewery that's been transformed into a contemporary guesthouse. Each of the five modern studios is named after a color scheme, from coral red to pale blue. All are equipped with a kitchenette, private bath, minibar, and seating area. Bathrooms are stocked with organic toiletry products. Bonus features are the earthy rooftop terrace and the included organic breakfast, served on wooden cheese boards.

MAP 8: Hoogte Kadijk 71, tel. 020/220-9071, www.stout-co.com

TownHouse Inn $$

This compact and bright four-room canal house is in walking distance from Amsterdam Centraal Station, the city center, and the waterfront. Steep stairs lead the way to modern double rooms, each with a view of Kadijksplein or a quiet courtyard garden. Rooms are clean and bathrooms are spotless. The details, like rolled-up towels, and the warm, hospitable owner make staying at this hotel a personable experience. The included continental breakfast has a great reputation.

MAP 8: Schippersgracht 12-A, tel. 061/350-0859

✪ Ecomama $

Ecomama is a massive space that blends the social vibe of a hostel with the perks of a hotel. The lobby features fun design elements like a check-in desk made of stacked books and a giant communal teepee, which guests are welcome to lounge in. The rooms are bare and bright, with giant maps and aerial photos functioning as wallpaper. Room sizes vary from eight-bed mixed dorms to deluxe private doubles. Some rooms don't have windows or en suite bathrooms. There is a two-night minimum.

MAP 8: Valkenburgerstraat 124, tel. 020/770-9529, www.ecomamahotel.com

Budget Hotel Hortus $

Next door to the Botanical Gardens, Budget Hotel Hortus offers 21 modest rooms at hostel prices. Renovated in 2012, rooms are plain but fresh. The staff is friendly and easygoing.

Hortus is smoker-friendly—all rooms are marijuana and cigarette puff zones, except for the lobby. A lounge space, beer vending machine, and small courtyard keep the setting fun. Cheaper rooms have shared bathrooms, but private bathrooms are also available.

MAP 8: Plantage Parklaan 8, tel. 20/625-9996, www.hotelhortus.com

IJ River

Map 9

DoubleTree Hilton $$$

This modern and central hotel is a stone's throw from Amsterdam Centraal Station, boasting fantastic city views in a luxury environment. Perks include the SkyLounge bar and an attached Starbucks location downstairs. The hotel has a whopping 553 rooms, all equipped with soundproof windows, soft beds, fresh sheets, and modern furnishings. The multilingual staff is welcoming and inviting. For the best views, ask for a "city" room.

MAP 9: Oosterdoksstraat 4, tel. 020/530-0800, http://doubletree3.hilton.com

Studio INN B&B $$

Bright, white, and airy, the Studio INN is a two-room bed-and-breakfast with a waterfront view of the Westerdok area. The secluded location and privacy of the B&B make it a luxury experience. Guido, the owner, makes breakfast daily with eggs, fruit, bread, and jam. This is an ideal spot for couples and families who want a bit of breathing room from the compact city center.

MAP 9: Barentszplein 3, tel. 061/477-6865, www.studio-inn.nl

Lloyd Hotel $

Lloyd Hotel has a rich history—it was originally a luxury hotel built for emigrants boarding vessels bound for South America at the nearby shipping yards. Today, this 117-room hotel is off the beaten path, with views of the waterfront and a grand multilevel café. The rooms are modern and unique, with fresh white sheets, wood flooring, and thick-paned windows that keep out the cold and street noise. Bathrooms are clean yet small, and some are shared.

MAP 9: Oostelijke Handelskade 34, tel. 020/561-3636, www.lloydhotel.com

Pension Homeland $

This budget hotel is situated in old Dutch army barracks, the former sleeping quarters of sergeants and lieutenants. The 31 rooms are divided between 12 singles and 17 doubles with private bathrooms and large windows with a view of the Eastern Docklands. Each room has a nautical mural, a comfortable bed, and clean white sheets. The attached café and restaurant offer waterfront views. Although the area is essentially a peninsula surrounded by water, the location is central.

MAP 9: Kattenburgerstraat 5, tel. 020/723-2550, www.pensionhomeland.com

BACKGROUND

The Landscape

Amsterdam is located in the Dutch province of North Holland, and is the capital of the Netherlands. The city is about 130 square miles. The Netherlands is about the size of Connecticut and, with 17 million residents, the most densely populated country in Europe.

Netherlands translates to lowlands in English, so it should come as no surprise that nearly a third of the country is below sea level. Most of Amsterdam is between 6 and 10 feet below the waterline. As the city was being built, its cobblestone alleys and brick houses were constructed upon a labyrinth of dikes made of mud, logs, and sand.

A few traditional windmills are still standing in Amsterdam.

The low-lying country is susceptible to flooding. The last major flooding was the North Sea Flood of 1953, when a tide surge killed nearly 2,000 people and destroyed several seaside villages.

With nearly 60 miles of canals and 1,000 bridges, Amsterdam has earned the nickname the Venice of the North. Much of the city center is a UNESCO World Heritage Site. Amsterdam boasts an impressive amount of greenery, from leafy parks to courtyards hidden behind canal houses.

CLIMATE

While a city made from sand and surrounded by waterways may sound like a seaside resort, Amsterdam is anything but tropical. Winters are cool and mild, and always see a light dusting of snow. Every few years it gets cold enough that the canals freeze over. Summers, too, are temperate—enough so that most homes and hotels lack air-conditioning. On any given day, the weather in the city may be sunny, cloudy, windy, rainy, or all of the above.

Drizzling rain is a constant from October to March. When the spring sun finally reveals itself, you'll find Amsterdammers bundled up on restaurant terraces taking in the first afternoon rays of the year.

PLANTS AND ANIMALS

Amsterdam's waterside location has made this part of the Netherlands a haven for over 400 species of birds. Great blue herons can be seen all around the city, and the Jordaan neighborhood is even a bird preservation zone. The most common avian residents are storks, geese, swans, gulls, coots, and an array of ducks. Some of the rarer birds native to the city are rose-ringed parakeets. Nearly 5,000 of these swift green parrots live within the city limits throughout the year and can be heard at dusk, singing from tree branches.

History

ORIGINS OF THE CITY

Beginning in the early 1200s, settlers arrived at what was then a boggy wilderness and began to build. First came the dikes, then, in 1270, the dam. By 1306, Amsterdam obtained city rights, elevating its power and status within the Netherlands. The city expanded to accommodate a booming medieval maritime village of fishing and commerce. The Miracle of Amsterdam (see *Religion*, page 244) in 1345 drew the attention of Catholic pilgrims who soon came to settle in what they saw as a holy land.

Fishing was an important industry to the growing city. Improvements in ship technology meant fishermen could sail farther out to sea, whereupon they discovered an abundance of shoal herring. By the early 1400s, a new form of long-term fishing was developed: Sailors could catch and prepare cured herring in barrels at larger quantities than previously possible—about 200 million a year. Business was booming, and by the late 1400s, Amsterdam had joined and dominated the Hanseatic League, a confederation of maritime merchants along the North and Baltic Seas. The self-governing city had become an essential trading port in Europe, distributing grain to major cities in Belgium, France, and England.

While churches and abbeys were commonplace throughout Amsterdam, the streets were also lively with merchants, artisans, and buccaneers who recognized no church taxes nor manorial serfdoms, unlike other prosperous European towns. With a booming trade industry and a budding banking system, Amsterdam had become a locus of liberalism and opportunity that would define its history for centuries to come.

DUTCH INDEPENDENCE

During the 1500s, the Netherlands was ruled by the Spanish (and Catholic)

Habsburg family. Amsterdam's prosperity and wealth, gained on its own terms, made it difficult for the city to accept being controlled by the Holy Roman Empire. The Protestant Reformation had simultaneously been gaining momentum in Europe. Local authorities tolerated Dutch Protestants, but King Phillip II of Spain was an extreme Catholic, bent on eliminating Protestantism entirely. He punished liberal Amsterdam by levying extra taxes, imposing a centralized government, and initiating the Spanish Inquisition. Provinces fought against this stifling new way of life and warred with the Spanish from 1568 to 1648 in what would be known as the Eighty Years' War (also called the Dutch War of Independence). When the dust cleared, it was the tiny Dutch country that defeated mighty Spain. The Netherlands had originally declared independence in 1581; by 1648, it was officially recognized as an independent nation.

THE GOLDEN AGE

The Golden Age spanned the 1600s, and was a time when Amsterdam was at its wealthiest, dominating trade around the world. The city was brimming with exotic spices, textiles, and other luxury goods. Rembrandt, Johannes Vermeer, and their contemporaries were churning out paintings at an unstoppable pace. The world's first stock exchange was dealing ferociously in the tulip trade. The first newspaper in Europe was printed in Amsterdam and devoted to trade reports.

The demographic makeup of Amsterdam in the 1600s was a melting pot of cultures unlike anywhere else in Europe. Jews escaping persecution from Portugal and Spain arrived, as did Huguenots from France, sailors from Germany, and more Jews from Eastern Europe. When Spain reconquered the busy port of Antwerp, its population fled to Amsterdam, subsequently boosting trade in luxury goods and printing.

Aside from a brief four-year crisis due to the Black Plague (when 10 percent of the population perished), Amsterdam was an unstoppable force. The Golden Age would eventually end from a loss of power at sea after jockeying for position with the French, English, and German, but it would take almost 200 years to do so.

RISE OF THE DUTCH EAST INDIA COMPANY

Amsterdam created what is considered the first multinational corporation in the world: the Dutch East India Company (Vereenigde Oost-Indische Compagnie, or VOC for short). The VOC strategy was simple. Though one merchant sailing around the seas could earn a good living, dangers like storms, pirates, and aggressive competitors (like the British) meant merchants risked more the farther they ventured. But if a group of merchants sailed together, and spread their goods equally across a fleet, these risks lowered considerably. Not only would a fleet of ships intimidate pirates and competitors, but there would be a better chance of their goods surviving storms at sea. The plan was open to anyone interested in investing: Any merchant could put their own money into this concept, which opened new territory to Dutch traders and began the country's rise to power.

The VOC established trade routes eastward, sailing to South Africa around the Cape of Good Hope and beyond. Merchant captains represented the Dutch Republic and were granted the ability to make trade agreements and set up outposts where they saw fit. Trading with Indonesia brought new spices, woods, and coffee to Europe, while China and India introduced silk, cotton, and porcelain. The VOC also created inter-trading, supplying China with goods from India, for instance. As more ships sailed safely around the world, more goods were brought into Amsterdam and the city continued to prosper. By the mid-1600s, the Dutch were leaders in maritime innovation, with more vessels asea than the English and French combined.

Next came the Dutch West Indies Company, the arm of the VOC that sailed westward to the Caribbean and South America. They set up posts and colonies on Caribbean islands known as the Dutch Antilles (Aruba, Curacao, and St. Martin), Suriname, and Brazil, and on American soil at New Amsterdam (New York) and Dutch Island (Rhode Island) for trade in slaves, furs, sugar, and tobacco.

Amsterdam's strong hold on world trade was always being challenged, as evidenced during the Anglo-Dutch Wars, a series of battles at sea between the British and Dutch for control over a colony or post. The British began to take over locations in the West, then eventually in the East. But the Dutch kept control over Indonesia, Suriname, and South Africa, which would all become long-standing colonies of the Netherlands.

DECLINE OF THE GOLDEN AGE

The Netherlands didn't have enough men to support an army and global trade. To buy themselves out of war and invasion, the Dutch made sure VOC money made its way into the pockets of the French and English as a sort of peace payment, which led to a quiet period in Amsterdam. Nearby port towns like London and Hamburg became more prominent and prosperous, while Amsterdam's economy stagnated.

Winters in the 1700s were rough; 1740 and 1763 saw cold temperatures so severe that people were freezing to death. Dutch fortunes continued to wane. In the late 1770s, John Adams came to Amsterdam as an American ambassador to the Dutch Republic. He was given a 30-million guilder loan to help the United States in their War of Independence. Word got back to the British, who retaliated by closing down the rest of the Netherlands' trading posts, effectively ending the Dutch East India Company.

France invaded the Netherlands in 1794. The Dutch republic was overthrown and the Netherlands became a monarchy. In 1806, during his reign as emperor, Napoleon placed his brother Louis Napoleon on the Dutch throne, and Amsterdam's city hall became his royal palace.

The Dutch took an instant dislike to the king. In addition to instituting new laws replacing traditional gable stones (wall engravings that indicated a family's trade) with house numbers and requiring every Dutch citizen to create a last name, Louis was also not entirely fluent in Dutch—during one of his proclamations, he told Amsterdammers, *"Ik ben uw konijn"* ("I am your rabbit") instead of *"Ik ben uw koning"* ("I am your king"). Napoleon's defeat in 1813 led to the French retreat from the country. The Netherlands then crowned its first king, William VI of Orange. The

House of Orange has been the royal family ever since.

THE INDUSTRIAL REVOLUTION

King William VI had his work cut out for him. Amsterdam was in a slump, its harbor abandoned, with sandbanks making it impassable to ships. The city set its sights on being the first to bring the railway to the Netherlands. In 1839, the first railroad from Amsterdam to Haarlem was built, which would later increase Holland's involvement and profit during Europe's Industrial Revolution.

A new wave of immigration from the Dutch countryside came in the later part of the 19th century, and business boomed again in the trade and farming industries. As the city grew more prosperous, Amsterdam Centraal Station was built as a transit hub. Karl Marx had instigated stirrings of socialism, and Amsterdam had its fair share of socialist riots and street fights. Catholicism was allowed to be practiced publicly again.

THE WORLD WARS

During World War I, the Netherlands was able to stay neutral. While tradesmen sold arms (to both sides), the country's poor faced food shortages, which led to riots and revolts in 1917 and 1935.

Amsterdam remained an industrial center in the years between the World Wars, with the Dutch Shipbuilding Company pumping up the economy by way of the steel and motor-making industries. Continuous trade with the East Indies brought in tobacco and cocoa, and KLM Airlines was the world's first to offer regular flights from Amsterdam to London. The Heineken Brewery was enjoying a healthy profit, and the Olympic Games in 1928 came at a perfect time for Amsterdam to boast of its success.

But the Wall Street Crash of 1929 came soon after, and in 1930, Amsterdam fell into the global depression. Germany was hit harder. With the collapse of the German economy, many German families moved to Amsterdam in hopes of a better future. Adolf Hitler was appointed chancellor in 1933, World War II began in 1939, and on May 10, 1940, German forces invaded the Netherlands. The war had arrived in Amsterdam.

The Dutch initially resisted and Rotterdam was destroyed almost immediately by Nazi bombing. Yet, Hitler had big plans for Amsterdam. He saw the Dutch as cousins to the Germans, with a similar language, look, and rich history. The German occupiers set up headquarters for the Gestapo and Security Police in Amsterdam.

Although Amsterdam remained for the most part physically undamaged, and many residents of the city didn't see much change in the city, the situation for Jewish Amsterdammers was an entirely different story. Jewish teachers were dismissed, Jewish city council members were forced to resign, and Jews were subjected to routine violence from local Nazi thugs. Witnessing this widescale Nazi persecution, Amsterdammers attempted a revolt. In February of 1941, a large meeting was held in the Noorderkerk, and the Communist Party led the call for a general strike. The following day, Amsterdam came to a halt, catching the Germans completely off guard. Fliers were distributed to trade unions throughout the city and surrounding towns encouraging the strike. Trams and ferries stopped running and the city's workforce came to a standstill.

The February Strike of 1941 only lasted a day, but it was a major act by a Nazi-occupied city standing up for its Jewish residents and against German oppression.

In the aftermath of the strike, Jews were compelled to wear the yellow Star of David on their clothes to be identified, an 8pm curfew was instituted, and Jews were banned from public spaces, including restaurants, libraries, public buses, and city parks. Random raids on Jewish homes were carried out as intimidation tactics. Deportations to work, concentration, and extermination camps began that July. (By the end of the war, more Jews per capita from the Netherlands were murdered in the Nazi Holocaust than from any other country in Europe.) Just 1 in 16 Amsterdam Jews survived the war.

Meanwhile, the Dutch Resistance attempted to offer some relief for Jews, offering hiding locations and forged identity documents. By the time the Canadian Allies came and liberated the country on May 5, 1945, Amsterdam was in a dismal state. The Jewish Quarter was in ruins, thousands of Dutch had died from hunger, and Amsterdam had been cut off from public utilities. With the help of American aid under the Marshall Plan, the country began to rebuild.

POSTWAR RECOVERY

After World War II, economic recovery was the city's primary goal. New residential blocks were built across the city over the next few decades. Political parties worked as a coalition to renew social programs that could protect and promote its citizens. Schiphol Airport and the Port of Amsterdam were the main sources of income during this time. Indonesia and New Guinea (and soon Suriname) were granted independence from the Netherlands; many citizens of these newly independent nations then came to Amsterdam for work. The Netherlands, needing a larger work force for faster results, also invited guest workers from Turkey and Morocco. Amsterdam's population swelled.

PROVO MOVEMENT

The liberal 1960s arrived in the form of the Provo movement, formed on the basis of provoking police and other authorities. The Provos were anti-monarchy, anti-authority, and led feminist movements for women's abortion rights.

The Provos also supported squatters' rights. The influx of immigrants led to Amsterdam's highest population levels yet, resulting in a housing shortage in the 1970s. Riots and protests commonly occurred between squatters and police. The police eventually took extreme measures, such as using tanks to evict squatters in the 1980s. Squatting was common in Amsterdam until it was officially banned in 2010.

CONTEMPORARY TIMES

Since the 1980s, Amsterdam has cleaned up its act. The hippie movement dissolved, and the city is no longer a haven for drug users as it was during the height of the pro-squatting movement. Coffeeshops (cafés where cannabis is sold and smoked) and prostitution are remnants of the city's liberal past, although both industries are now regulated. Tourism in Amsterdam is at an all-time high, encouraging business owners to upgrade their restaurants, cafés, nightlife venues, and theaters.

Government and Economy

GOVERNMENT

The Netherlands has had a monarchy since 1815, with the House of Orange as the royal family ever since. William VI was the country's first king. The current monarch, King Willem-Alexander, has reigned since 2013.

Amsterdam is the capital of the Netherlands, but the legislative and judicial branches do most of their work in the city of Den Haag (The Hague), about 40 miles away. Mark Rutte, a leader of the center-right People's Party for Freedom and Democracy (VVD), has been the prime minister since 2010.

The Dutch Parliament (equivalent to the United States' Congress) has two parts: the 150-seat House of Representatives (also called the Second Chamber) and the 75-member Senate (also known as the First Chamber). Both houses are responsible for legislation, but only the Senate can propose or change bills.

From the 20 or so political parties in the country, the two majority parties that make up over half of parliament are the center-right VVD (conservative liberal) and the center-left Labor Party, PvdA (social democrat).

In Amsterdam, Mayor Eberhard van der Laan (PvdA) was elected by the 45-member city council in 2010. Below the city council are district committees for each of Amsterdam's eight boroughs, which handle neighborhood-level actions like increasing bike racks, planting trees, or considering renovation suggestions.

REGULATION OF PROSTITUTION AND DRUGS

The Netherlands is most known for its lenient policies on drugs and prostitution. Amsterdam is seen around the world as a liberal free-for-all, but this comes with heavy government regulation. The government's stance is one of tolerance for illegal activities.

Amsterdam's Red Light District is infamous. Here, sex workers occupy some 400 windows, advertising their wares. Annually, over 5.5 million people visit the Red Light District. The government regulates the market by making prostitution as transparent an industry as possible. Women who are sex workers in the Netherlands must register at the chamber of commerce and pay taxes. Sex workers have their own union, access to free legal advice and medical care, and specialized help for STD testing, psychological support, self-defense classes, Dutch language classes, and tax advice. Other sex businesses must submit a business plan, and can only receive a license to operate when standards of safety and cleanliness are met. There are security cameras around much of the Red Light District, along with police surveillance, and every red light window is equipped with a panic button.

In the 1970s, Amsterdam's Red Light District was beleaguered by drug addicts and dealers. The government decided to focus on eradicating hard drugs. The Narcotics Act was passed in 1976, banning the use of hard drugs (cocaine, heroin, ecstasy, and amphetamines). Not long after, the drugs and associated violence lessened substantially. That isn't to say that the use of hard drugs has stopped completely. The city takes a harm-reduction approach to illegal narcotics, offering drug verification services, where users can receive immediate results to make sure their drugs are not fake. There are also health centers in the city where addicts can receive minimal doses of drugs to prevent withdrawal symptoms. During the AIDS pandemic, Amsterdam was one of the first cities to offer a needle-exchange program.

The Narcotics Act decriminalized cannabis, hash, psychedelic mushrooms, and herbal drugs. The country's policy of tolerance means that despite the illegality of these soft drugs, prosecution for drug use is rare. Rather than shutting down an industry that brings in millions of tourists yearly, the government instead levies high taxes and enforces strict regulation for drug-related businesses, like coffeeshops and smartshops.

At a coffeeshop (cannabis dispensary and café), employees sell cannabis products, and customers consume their purchases within the confines of the shop. Coffeeshops must get business licenses and adhere to strict rules that regulate everything from the amount a shop can stock and sell to the age limits of customers. The same regulations apply for smartshops—dispensaries selling psychedelic mushrooms. Thanks to these laws, the government can track the amount of soft drugs sold throughout the country.

Conservative criticism has led to tighter laws in recent years. In 2008, coffeeshops were banned from selling and serving alcoholic beverages. The same year, a law passed forcing the closure of coffeeshops within a 270-yard radius of any school. Also in 2008, 200 types of mushrooms were banned from being sold; however, smartshops found a loophole and were able to keep selling psychedelic truffles. In 2012, a law was passed that banned tourists from purchasing cannabis due to a drug-trafficking complaint in the southern part of the Netherlands. This proof of residency requirment drew international attention and scorn from tourists, until Amsterdam's mayor proclaimed that the city was exempt from the new law.

TULIP TOURISM

Spring (mid-March to mid-May) is tulip season. The famous flowers draw visitors the world over to visit the region's botanical gardens and tulip farms. Tulip farming is a big industry, and the Netherlands is the largest exporter of tulips and flowers in the world. The world's largest flower auction house is in Aalsmeer, just south of the capital, where about 20 million flowers and €6 million are exchanged daily. The Keukenhof gardens outside of Amsterdam are one of the most photographed places on earth. Cycling trips along the Dutch countryside during tulip season are some of the most popular routes in Europe.

Local Culture

DEMOGRAPHICS

The Netherlands has a population of about 17 million people, the most densely populated country in Europe. About 800,000 people live within Amsterdam's city limits. The city's population, inclusive of its outer suburbs, is 1.3 million.

A little over half of Amsterdam's residents have a Dutch background; many Dutch come to the "big city" as students and never leave. Other residents come from a long line of Amsterdammers who haven't strayed far from the canal houses present since the city's founding days.

Today, Amsterdam is home to 180 different nationalities, one of the widest ranges in the world. Though many Amsterdammers have foreign roots or have recently migrated to the city, about 88 percent of the city's residents are Dutch citizens. One-third of non-Dutch Amsterdammers come from North America and the United Kingdom. Another third come from former Dutch colonies like Aruba, Suriname, South Africa, and Indonesia. A small minority of non-Dutch residents hail from Middle Eastern countries, most notably Turkey.

LANGUAGE

People in the Netherlands speak Dutch, a Germanic language that sounds like a mix between German, English, and Scandinavian. Words are pronounced with a soft "j" and a guttural "g," with Amsterdammers adding a rolled "r." There are about 35 Dutch dialects spoken in the Netherlands and the Flemish part of Belgium, a surprisingly large amount for an area so small.

Most Dutch are fluent English speakers with an accent that can sound strangely American.

GAY RIGHTS

The Netherlands has long led the charge for gay rights. The Equal Rights Law in 1993 banned prejudice on the basis of sexual orientation in employment, housing, and more. Five years later, a law passed allowing domestic partnership benefits for same-sex couples. The Netherlands was the first country to legalize same-sex marriage on April 1, 2001. Amsterdam's then-mayor, Job Cohen, officiated that day, marrying four same-sex couples in one sweeping ceremony.

Amsterdam is consistently voted one of the most LGBT-friendly cities in the world. In both 1993 and 2016 Amsterdam was home to Europride, a two-week long celebration of LGBT pride. The city's annual Gay Pride weekend is a massive celebration.

GENDER EQUALITY

Dutch women have been fighting for equal rights for several hundred years. In 1841, Barbera van Meerten-Schilperoort founded the Netherlands' first women's organization, Hulpbetoon aan Eerlijke en Vlijtige Armoede, which aimed to help Dutch women find employment in fields like nursing, teaching, and retail. Van Meerten-Schilperoort's work ignited the suffrage movement in the country. (She would go on to become Europe's first woman physician and open Amsterdam's first women's birth control clinic.) The country granted women the right to vote in 1912, the third country in Europe to do so after Finland and Sweden.

In the late 1970s, feminist groups fought for access to abortion, rape crisis centers, and women's shelters. About 160 feminist groups were active in the country by the end of the 1970s. The movement won many legal battles, and in the 1980s, the government funded 30 rape crisis centers, the Abortion Bill was passed, and married women were granted full legal equality in family law issues.

Today's Dutch workforce has fewer women in full-time positions and a lower proportion of women in executive positions as compared to other Western countries. In 2001, about 60 percent of Dutch working women were employed part-time (compared to 15 percent in the United States), with only 4 percent saying they wanted to work full-time. A study in 2004 found that women earned 22 percent less than men in the business sector and 14 percent less than men in the public sector.

The country is also troubled by violence and discrimination against minority women. Minority women are disproportionately affected by domestic violence and human trafficking. Although the Netherlands isn't considered a hotbed for human trafficking, it's still relatively common for women, especially those from Eastern Europe, to be forced into prostitution. A study in 2014 found that the Netherlands had the fourth highest rate of physical and sexual violence against women in Europe.

Religion

THE MIRACLE OF AMSTERDAM

In 1345, a dying Catholic man lay in his bed with nuns caring for him. A priest entered his home and gave him his last rites, which partially consisted of feeding him a small piece of bread and a sip of wine (considered to represent the body and blood of Christ). The man regurgitated the bread (known as the host) due to his illness, after which a nun cleaned up the mess and threw it into the fire.

Somehow, the host was not burned and was retrieved intact from the ashes of the fire the next day. Later, after the man died, his home was rebuilt as a shrine to house the miraculous host. One night a fire ignited a large part of Amsterdam, resulting in much of the city burning to ashes, including the shrine—but again, the host remain unburned.

This was the Miracle of Amsterdam that made the city famous to Catholics around the world. The miracle caused a massive influx of Catholic pilgrims to settle within the walls of Amsterdam. To this day, an annual silent procession honors the Miracle of Amsterdam.

CATHOLIC VERSUS PROTESTANT

Following the Miracle of Amsterdam in 1345, Amsterdam became a hub of Catholicism. Nearly 20 monasteries and convents were built within a decade, as immigrants from around Europe came in waves to resettle in this newly religious city. Many of today's hotels and restaurants are built on the grounds of former abbeys, convents, and monasteries. In the Red Light District, some streets still hold onto their pious names: Heiligeweg (Holy Way), Monnikstraat (Monk Street), and Bloedstraat (Blood Street, referring to the blood of Jesus Christ) are just a few examples.

By the 1500s, however, figures like Martin Luther began to chafe against the stifling rule of Catholicism, fomenting the Protestant Reformation. A power shift occurred in Amsterdam as a result, and soon Calvinism (a Protestant denomination) was the official religion of the city. Other forms of worship were tacitly permitted, if done in private homes. Today, Amsterdam still houses two "secret" Catholic churches: **Our Lord in the Attic (Ons' Lieve Heer Op Solder),** set in the attic of a merchant's house in the Red Light District, and the **Begijnhof Kapel,** which is located within the Old Center's peaceful Begijnhof.

In 1853, Catholics were granted the right to worship in public. Large, dramatic churches, like **Basilica of Saint Nicholas (Sint Nicolaasbasiliek)** and **Krijtberg Church,** were built, giving Catholics much more spacious venues in which to attend mass. As time wore on, the city embraced the Age of Enlightenment. Science and philosophy caught people's interest, and the city began to associate less with its previous religious identity.

As of 2013, Amsterdam's population was about 11 percent Roman Catholic, 6 percent Protestant, 11 percent Muslim, and less than 1 percent Jewish, with about 63 percent of residents expressing no religious affiliation.

JEWISH IDENTITY

During the 16th and 17th centuries, Amsterdam was a haven for Sephardic Jews fleeing the Spanish Inquisition and Ashkenazi Jews escaping persecution in Eastern Europe. Most refugees settled in a neighborhood that would become known as the Jewish Quarter (today's Plantage). Though Jewish people (and those of other religious affiliations) weren't allowed to publicly practice their religion, they were accepted into the city's trades, in fields like printing, retail, and medicine. Amsterdam Jews eventually became renowned for their expertise in the diamond industry.

It was the appointment of Adolf Hitler as chancellor in Germany that brought the final large wave of Jewish immigrants to Amsterdam. Before the Nazi occupation of 1940, 80,000 Jews lived in Amsterdam. By the end of World War II, in 1945, only 5,500 of Amsterdam's Jews had survived the Holocaust and remained in the city. Today, there are about 15,000 Jews living in Amsterdam, over half of whom are non-practicing.

Art and Architecture

ART

The Netherlands' most significant contribution to the art world was the **Dutch School,** a term encompassing painters working from the 16th century through the 18th century. One of the periods within the Dutch School is the famed Golden Age, which was active for about 100 years, beginning in the early 1600s.

During the earliest years of the Dutch School, many artists drew inspiration from religion and Italian Renaissance art. Jacob Cornelisz van Oostsanen (1470-1533) was one of the first notable wood carvers and painters in Amsterdam. Other notable Amsterdam artists were Jan van Scorel (1495-1562) and his altarpieces, Lucas van Leyden (1495-1533) and his engravings, and Jan Mostaert (1475-1555), who painted portraits and foreign landscapes as described by the city's merchants. Later, Pieter Bruegel the Elder (1525-1569) created lively peasant scenes and landscapes. Many works by these early Dutch School artists (as well as the later Dutch masters) are on display at the **Rijksmuseum.**

17TH CENTURY: THE GOLDEN AGE

By the end of the Eighty Years' War, the Netherlands was a wealthy and independent nation. No longer reliant on their former Catholic rulers (and patrons), Dutch artists moved away from depicting biblical and religious scenes in their artwork. Instead, they produced more still lifes, landscapes, and everyday scenes of Dutch life—these are the works known as **Golden Age paintings,** many of which were created by the famed Dutch masters. From 1600 to 1680, more than four million paintings were made in the Netherlands. Numerous artist guilds and art schools were established across the nation, with Dutch masters requiring hard work and devotion from their pupils.

Frans Hals (1580-1666) had a rougher style than his contemporaries. His brushstrokes are more noticeable and he commonly employed the chiaroscuro technique (a contrast between light and dark), yet his works are still classified as realism. Hals lived just next to Amsterdam, in Haarlem, and became known for his portraits of wealthy civil guard groups called *schutterstuk*. Famous examples are *The Banquet of the Officers of the St George Militia Company in 1616* and *Regentesses of the Old Men's Almshouse*. One of Hals's most well-known portraits is that of the philosopher René Descartes, which he painted in 1649.

Jan Steen (1626-1679) was born into a wealthy Catholic family of brewers from Leiden. His paintings reflected scenes of cheerful debauchery and daily life. Many of his most famous works are imbued with humor, such as *The Feast of Saint Nicholas*.

Rembrandt (1606-1669)

Rembrandt van Rijn is undoubtedly the most famous of the Dutch masters. In his mid-20s he began a successful career commissioning portraits. Rembrandt's clients included a number of wealthy and influential bourgeoisie Amsterdammers as well as fellow artists.

Rembrandt was most well-known for his paintings. His earlier works were composed with fine, exacting brushstrokes and using the technique of chiaroscuro, which focused on the contrast between light and dark. Some of his most famous works, such as *The Night Watch, The Jewish Bride,* and *The Anatomy Lesson of Dr. Nicolaes Tulp,* are examples of this detailed style. Rembrandt also created etchings and engravings, some of which can be seen at **Rembrandt House (Rembrandthuis),** his former residence in the Plantage.

Rembrandt was himself an avid art collector and a commercially successful painter, but he could not sustain his good fortunes. Rembrandt and his wife, Saskia, suffered the deaths of three of their four children. Not much later, when she was just 30 years old, Saskia died; the couple had been married for only eight years. Thanks in part to several love affairs gone wrong and a tendency to live beyond his means, Rembrandt died a poor man, in debt to the government. His remains were buried in an unmarked grave.

Johannes Vermeer (1632-1675)

Johannes Vermeer created relatively few paintings during his career—just 34 paintings are attributed to him—but he is considered one of the most prominent Dutch masters. He mostly painted portraits and interior scenes, set in his house in Delft (a small town just east of The Hague). He is known for his expert eye for detail and his ability to capture and use light in his work. He also famously used very expensive and vivid pigments in his paintings, a rarity among his peers. These colors can be seen in some of his most famous works, *Girl with a Pearl Earring, The Milkmaid,* and *The Love Letter.* The latter two can be seen at the Rijksmuseum.

18TH CENTURY: DECLINE OF THE GOLDEN AGE

The end of the 1600s saw the decline of the Dutch Golden Age. Demand for art slowed and the popular style of paintings transitioned to a heavy French style.

Cornelis Troost (1696-1750) was an Amsterdam actor-turned-painter whose performing past could be seen in the stage and theater backgrounds of his portraits. One such painting, *Portrait of Joan Jacob Mauricius,* depicts Troost's friend, Mauricius, sitting in front of a bookshelf stuffed with famous plays. This painting can be seen at the Rijksmuseum.

Jacob de Wit (1695-1754) specialized in painting religious scenes on the ceilings and doors of mansions all over Amsterdam's Canal Belt. These large-scale scenes were of a dreamy yet detailed style, and often featured god, cherubs, and other religious figures. Some of his work can still be seen in many canalside mansions that double as musems, like **Huis De Pinto, Willet-Holthuysen Museum,** and **Huis Marseille Museum for Photography.**

19TH CENTURY: IMPRESSIONISM TO VAN GOGH

The dawn of the Industrial Revolution revived the creativity of 19th-century Dutch artists. **Johan Barthold Jongkind** (1819-1891) depicted the ever-changing skies of the Dutch landscape. He is seen as one of the first to bring French impressionism to the Netherlands.

George Hendrik Breitner

(1857-1923) became fixated on painting Amsterdam street scenes. Breitner painted with the impressionist style of visible brushstrokes and focused on the depiction of light. His focus was on the gritty side of Amsterdam, seeing himself as "the people's painter." *Girl in a Red Kimono* and *The Singel Bridge at the Paleisstraat in Amsterdam* are notable examples of his work.

Isaac Israëls (1865-1934) was an Amsterdam impressionist who devoted much of his life to traveling and painting. In Amsterdam, he spent a lot of time with Breitner, trying to capture the thrills of city life, albeit with an eye for the wealthy class. His travels presented him with new subjects, from ballerinas in London to musicians in Bali. His painting technique employed wide brushstrokes, giving a fast-paced, rushed feeling to his works. Some good examples of his style can be seen in *Amsterdam Household Maids* and *Shop Window.*

Vincent van Gogh (1853-1890)

Unlike the Dutch masters, who worked at a time when art commissions could comprise most of an artist's career, Van Gogh was never rich or successful during his lifetime, and was even considered a failed artist. He famously suffered from mental illness and committed suicide when he was 37 years old. Today, Van Gogh is regarded as the greatest post-impressionist painter of the 19th century. Post-impressionism pushed up against the boundaries of realism, with a focus on accentuating color and contour, leading to exaggerated and distorted subjects.

Van Gogh didn't seriously pursue painting until his late 20s. At 33, after moving to Arles in southern France, he produced some of his most famous paintings, including the *Sunflowers* series, the *Wheat Fields* series, and *The Yellow House.* During his career, which lasted just over a decade, he created over 2,000 artworks. Many of his pieces can be seen at the **Van Gogh Museum.**

20TH CENTURY: MODERN AND CONTEMPORARY ART

At the beinning of the 20th century, art moved into abstraction and Amsterdam was the source of the abstract movement known as **De Stijl** (also called neoplasticism), which employed thick black lines, random squares, and a limited palate of primary colors. De Stijl showed up in fashion and interior design as well as on canvases. The movement was cofounded by Piet Mondrian and Theo van Doesburg.

Maurits Cornelis Escher (1898-1972) was a famous Dutch graphic artist with a fascination for mathematical themes. His work experimented with perspective and visual illusions, receiving international attention and awe. A remarkable collection of his work is at Het Paleis in The Hague.

World War II and the Nazi occupation had a near-devastating effect on Amsterdam and the surrounding region, but the art world slowly crept back thanks to the contemporary art movement known as **CoBrA,** named after Copenhagen, Brussels, and Amsterdam. The tri-city collective founded this avant-garde style that employed bold, intense color and seemingly simplistic techniques. Karel Appel (1921-2006), Constant Nieuwenhuys (1920-2005), and Corneille Guillaume Beverloo (1922-2010) were the most notable artists of CoBrA. Their first major exhibition was held at the **Stedelijk Museum** in 1949, which still holds a small collection of CoBrA works on permanent display.

21ST CENTURY: URBAN ART AND DESIGN

Today's art scene in Amsterdam has evolved to focus on street art and sustainable interior design. Some of the city's art galleries, like **Go Gallery** and **Lionel Gallery,** boast fine collections of urban and street artworks. Home design shops like **Moooi** and **Frozen Fountain** are devoted to clever modern designs.

ARCHITECTURE

Amsterdam is a city of layers, holding many types of structures, dating from as far back as the Middle Ages. Early settlers used oak timber for building frames; as a result, not many original structures survived over the years (which saw two major fires, among other large-scale disasters). Only two houses with wooden facades from the 15th century remain in the city center: **Café In 't Aepjen** and **Houten Huys,** inside the Begijnhof.

Amsterdam's next iteration was constructed with sandstone and brick, two fireproof materials that would become inextricably linked with the city's identity for centuries to come. The city's famed canal houses were built on a foundation of long wooden pillars hammered deep into the ground, through multiple layers of sand that preserved the pillars' structural integrity. Over time, the city's water levels changed, and the upper parts of the pillars were exposed to water and oxygen. This led to small amounts of corrosion and, eventually, the structures themselves began to list to one side.

THE WALLED CITY

Medieval Amsterdam originally was protected by fortified walls. Today, street names like Oude Waal (Old Wall) and Kromme Waal (Curved Wall) hint at the city's former structure. The wall was torn down to expand the city during the prosperous Golden Age. At periodic points along the walls were gates, towers, and other structures that functioned as throughways into the city. Some of these, like **Mint Tower (Munttoren), The Scales (De Waag),** and **Schreierstoren,** can still be seen in the Old Center and the Red Light District, the oldest parts of the city.

CANAL HOUSES

The city levied high taxes on canalside houses based on their width, so many of Amsterdam's homes were designed to be narrow but deep. Canal houses had a simple blueprint, starting with servants' quarters and a kitchen in the basement. The ground floor was usually an office or storefront, and the top two levels were the family's home. A courtyard garden out back was ideal. Many canal houses today appear to lean forward. This is partially due to a design that maximized floor space, with each level gradually widening. This slanted facade also made it easier for merchants to transport their goods (with a hook and pulley connected to a wooden beam) from street level up to the attic, which acted as a storage space. Many buildings in Amsterdam had such narrow staircases that this was the best method for moving unwieldy objects. This is still a fairly common method employed today for moving into or out of a canal house.

Many of the city's canal houses feature subtle ornamentation, sometimes seen in the form of red, yellow, or gray brick set against bands of white sandstone, as well as pilasters (ornamental columns). Gables were an especially popular feature, and often appeared in either a stepped style or a bell shape. Most gables were adorned with ornate sandstone statues, cornices, scrollwork, and—most importantly—a **gable stone,** a type of plaque that depicted the family's trade.

PROMINENT STYLES AND ARCHITECTS

The city's most famous architect was **Hendrick de Keyser** (1565-1621). A master stonemason and sculptor from Utrecht, De Keyser ushered in a style that would come to be known as Amsterdam Renaissance. De Keyser took inspiration from the Italian Renaissance and adapted it. Where Italian styles employed features like columns, arches, and domes, De Keyser's designs used these elements in decorative, rather than structural, ways. Some of his work can still be seen today, such as **North Church (Noorderkerk), Westerkerk,** and the **East India House (Oost Indisch Huis).**

Dutch architects employed more austere designs than their Italian brethren, who were veering into a baroque period. Using brick and sandstone as their main materials, they favored Greek and Roman classicism, but with fewer decorative elements, such as unembellished gables and flatter roofs. The most impressive example of this style, referred to as **Dutch classicism,** can be seen in the **Royal Palace (Koninklijk Paleis),** which was built in 1648 by Jacob van Campen (1596-1657) to function as Amsterdam's city hall.

As the Golden Age dawned, Dutch classicism evolved to become even more restrained. This movement was led by mathematician and architect **Adriaan Dortsman** (1635-1682), known for his sober designs, which came largely as a response to the increasingly extravagant interior designs of Amsterdam's wealthy residents. The best example of Dortsman's work can be seen at the **Van Loon House,** with its relatively plain facade and symmetrical appearance.

Construction declined in lockstep with the ebbing of the Golden Age, and it wasn't until the end of the 19th century, when the Industrial Revolution came to Amsterdam, that the city began another expansion. Architects of this era were nostalgic for the Golden Age, creating **neoclassical** and **neo-Gothic** churches and other structures. The sandstone facade of the **Royal Concertgebouw** is a good example of the neoclassical trend—look for the Corinthian columns and Renaissance-inspired brickwork.

Pierre Cuypers (1827-1921) was an architect commissioned to create two of the most prominent buildings in Amsterdam: **Amsterdam Centraal Station** and the **Rijksmuseum.** Both buildings are grand: tall, wide, and with brickwork reminiscent of the Renaissance.

Several different architectural styles blossomed during the 1900s. **Art nouveau** drew inspiration from nature, specifically the fluidity of plants. The facade of the 1921 **Pathé Tuschinski** movie theater is a prime illustration of art nouveau, with its curving, elegant lines. **Art deco** was sleeker than art nouveau, employing geometric shapes and patterns and bold colors. **Sauna Deco,** which still features its original 1920s fixtures, is an example of art deco. Perhaps the most important style of this time was introduced by **Hendrik Petrus Berlage** (1856-1934), who is considered the father of modern Dutch architecture. He created large brick buildings with minimal flare, which were the origins of the **Amsterdam School** style. Berlage's most famous work in the city is the **Beurs van Berlage,** the stock exchange building.

Michel de Klerk (1884-1923) and **Piet Kramer** (1881-1961) were the leaders of the Amsterdam School movement and promoted their vision that social housing should embrace modern design. One such building is the **Grand Hotel Amrâth Amsterdam.**

ESSENTIALS

Transportation

Bicycling is a popular mode of transportation for the Dutch.

GETTING THERE

AIR

Amsterdam Schiphol International Airport (AMS, Evert van de Beekstraat 202, tel. 020/794-0800, www.schiphol.nl) is the main hub for international flights in and out of the Netherlands. The airport lies nearly 20 kilometers south of Amsterdam's city center. The entire airport, including the landing strip and airfield, sits at 11 feet below sea level. It's one of the oldest international airports in the world, founded in 1916. Direct flights from the United States are available; KLM and Delta are a joint venture.

Airport Transportation

From the airport, it's a 20-minute direct train ride to Amsterdam Centraal Station, the city's main train station. Trains leave every 10 minutes, and travelers can buy one-way tickets (€3.70) at the yellow kiosks in the main airport plaza. The kiosks accept coins, EU debit cards, and credit cards. Night trains run hourly between the airport and train station.

To get to central Amsterdam by bus, take the Amsterdam Airport Express (bus 197), which leaves every 10 minutes from platform B9, just outside the main entrance to the airport. (Between 1am and 4am, the bus leaves hourly.) The bus drops passengers off at hotel-dense locations like Museumplein and Leidseplein. The Airport Express costs €5 for a one-way trip.

A cab from the airport to Amsterdam Centraal Station costs about €50. The airport offers a private cab service, called **Schiphol Travel Taxi.** This blue van can either be booked privately (€50) or shared (€20), with multiple drop-offs.

All the major car rental companies, including Hertz, Avis, Sixt, and Europcar, have counters at Amsterdam Schiphol. Rates here are cheaper than at rental locations elsewhere in the city. To rent a car, you must be 23 years old or older and show a valid driver's license and a major credit card.

TRAIN

Amsterdam Centraal Station (Stationsplein 9, tel. 020/344-5074) is the city's main national and international train station, with train destinations all over the Netherlands and fast trains to London, Paris, Brussels, and many German cities. **NS** (Nederlandse Spoorwegen, www.ns.nl) is the country's main rail operator, running its yellow and blue trains throughout all of Europe. There are many public transit connections from the train station to other parts of the city.

BUS

There are a few European bus companies that bring backpackers and budget travelers in and out of Amsterdam. The most popular is **Eurolines** (www.eurolines.com), which offers a great web of routes that take travelers from the south of Italy all the way to London or Latvia and beyond. Their ticket office and departure/arrival point is at **Amsterdam Amstel Station** (Julianaplein 1), which is a 10-minute train ride southeast of Amsterdam Centraal Station.

Megabus (www.megabus.com) offers similar coverage as Eurolines, with routes to Spain, France, Italy, Germany, Belgium, Ireland, and the United Kingdom, as well as throughout the Netherlands. Prices are usually cheaper than Eurolines. Buses arrive at Amsterdam Sloterdijk Station (off Hatostraat), a five-minute train ride northwest of Amsterdam Centraal Station. **Flixbus** (www.flixbus.com) is another low-cost coach company serving most locations in Germany. It also arrives at Amsterdam Sloterdijk Station.

GETTING AROUND

Amsterdam is a compact city that is extremely walkable. The landscape is flat, with seemingly endless sidewalks and bicycle lanes.

BICYCLE

The best way to get around the city is on bicycle. Locals prefer it to any other mode of transport, rain or shine. Bikes here are so easy to ride they're called *omafiets* (grandma bikes) and *opafiets* (grandpa bikes), featuring a simple frame, pedal brakes, front and rear lights, and a cheerful bell.

There are a few dozen bicycle rental shops around the city, offering rates by the hour or day. Because bike theft is prevalent in the city, rentals come with a back wheel lock and a snake lock. Insurance is always offered as an add-on. Test the lights before you leave the shop.

Helmets are neither required nor common—even for children. However, biking in Amsterdam is very safe, thanks to the maroon-colored designated bike lanes and the generally slow pace of bikers.

PUBLIC TRANSPORTATION

GVB (www.gvb.nl) is the city's public transit authority, running buses,

ESSENTIALS

TRANSPORTATION

ferries, metro trains, and trams throughout Amsterdam. Most of the transit options in the city center consist of electric trams. The **GVB Tickets & Info kiosk** (Stationsplein 10; 7am-9pm Mon.-Fri., 10am-6pm Sat.-Sun.) is across from Amsterdam Centraal Station. Here, you can pick up maps and tickets. Buses and trams run regularly from about 5am to just after midnight, with night buses running throughout the night.

As of 2017, GVB implemented a cashless system for buses, meaning riders can no longer use cash to buy their tickets on board. Eventually, trams will also be cashless. One option for traveling on public transit is to use the **OV-chipkaart** (€7.50), which users load money onto, then check in and out of trams, buses, and other GVB vehicles. The card comes in two varieties, personal and anonymous. The anonymous option is easiest for travelers and can be bought at the GVB Tickets & Info kiosk or at any metro station.

The most convenient way to use public transportation in Amsterdam is with a disposable **1-hour card** (€2.90) or **24-hour card** (€7.50). One-hour tickets can be bought on board from tram conductors and bus drivers. The 24-hour tickets aren't always available on board, so try to purchase one at a train station in advance. Tickets are valid across the network of buses, metro, and trams, from the time of purchase within your chosen time frame. Don't forget to check in and out by placing your ticket on the readers upon entering and exiting vehicles.

TAXI

Taking a cab is a popular choice after a night out. Most of the city's cabs are luxury cars, often new models with leather interiors. Taxi rates vary, but in 2017 the starting price was €2.95 with a per-minute rate of €0.36 and a per-kilometer rate of €2.17. There are official taxi stands at Amsterdam Schiphol Airport, Amsterdam Centraal Station, and Leidseplein, among other locations.

It's possible to hail a cab here, but beware of unofficial taxis. An official cab will always have a meter on, accept any trip destination, and bring passengers to their exact destination. **Taxicentrale Amsterdam** (TCA, tel. 020/777-7777, www.tcataxi.nl) has the best reputation in the city.

DRIVING

Because Amsterdam is so compact and crowded, driving isn't necessary to get around. If you do decide to rent a car, it's important to note that parking in central Amsterdam is about €5 per hour (though Sundays are free).

Seatbelts are required at all times, and children under 12 years old must ride in the backseat. Cars share the road with trams, which always have the right of way. Look out for cyclists, who have the right of way when cars are turning right. Amsterdam also has many roundabouts, in which oncoming traffic has the right of way.

Travel Tips

VISAS AND OFFICIALDOM

Most visitors to Amsterdam need just a valid passport. U.S. citizens traveling in the European Union can do so with a passport for up to 90 days. No extra permit or visa is required. Citizens of European Union countries only need their national identity card.

Be sure that there are at least six months of validity left on your passport before your departure date. If you're traveling in Europe beyond Amsterdam and the Netherlands, getting a **Schengen visa** may make your travels easier, as it allows the possessor to travel freely across the borders of the Schengen area (European Union countries, plus a few others). Refer to the U.S. Department of State website (http://travel.state.gov) for more information.

The **American embassy** in Amsterdam is located at Museumplein 19 (tel. 070/310-2209, http://amsterdam.usconsulate.gov; 8:30am-5pm Mon.-Fri.). Visiting the embassy is allowed by appointment only. American citizens in need of **emergency assistance** outside working hours should call tel. 020/575-5309. Lost passports need to be reported to the police. Take the police report to the U.S. embassy to be issued a temporary emergency passport (usually good for three months).

Some of the most common souvenirs to bring home from Amsterdam include tulip bulbs and cheese. Make sure all bulbs come with a certificate that allows them to pass through customs. Any cheese with a wax shell around it can be brought overseas.

ACCESS FOR TRAVELERS WITH DISABILITIES

Travelers who use a wheelchair should make sure in advance that their hotels can accommodate wheelchairs and that they have elevator access. All of the city's top attractions and museums are wheelchair-friendly, as is public transportation like buses, trams, and trains.

MONEY

CURRENCY

The euro has been the Dutch form of currency since 2002 (replacing the guilder). Bills come in denominations of 5, 10, 20, 50, 100, 200, and 500. Coins come in 5-, 10-, 20-, and 50-cent denominations, as well as €1 and €2 coins.

EXCHANGE RATES

As of 2017, the exchange rate was $1 U.S. to €0.94. **Travelex** (www.gwk-travelex.nl), providing foreign currency exchange, has several locations in Amsterdam, including at the airport (tel. 020/653-5121; 6am-10pm daily), Amsterdam Centraal Station (tel. 020/627-2731; 8am-8pm Mon.-Sat., 10am-5pm Sun.), and in the city center.

ATMS

Cash machines are common in banks and grocery stores and in popular shopping areas around Amsterdam. Dutch banks run on the European PIN card, a type of debit card with a chip inside. Most shopping outlets, bars, and cafés will have a PIN machine at the counter; many Amsterdammers prefer to pay even the smallest amounts with their PIN card. It's easy to confuse PIN machines with credit/debit card machines, so double check before you pay. Most supermarkets do not accept credit cards (only PIN cards and cash).

Because PIN cards are not the same as American credit cards with chips, you'll need to contact your bank in advance of your trip to receive the card's PIN number.

COSTS

Amsterdam is the seventh most expensive European capital, but visiting on a budget is possible. Most spending will go towards accommodations, food, and museum admissions. Book online for discounts on hotels, or look at AirBnB options in Amsterdam.

TIPPING

Tipping in the Netherlands, like much of Europe, is not commonplace outside of restaurants. Employees in the hospitality industry are paid a living wage and do not depend on tips.

In restaurants, tipping anywhere from 5 to 10 percent is acceptable, and if the service was poor, no tip is expected. At bars or when ordering drinks at a café, it's not standard to add a tip; if you do so, just round up to the nearest euro. Taxi drivers and hotel employees don't expect tips.

COMMUNICATIONS AND MEDIA

INTERNET ACCESS

Wireless Internet is usually available for free in hotels, restaurants, bars, and cafés, though you'll often have to ask for the network password. There's free Wi-Fi on trains and at the Schiphol Airport. All Starbucks locations have free Internet as well.

CELL PHONES

The Netherlands' major wireless carrier is **KPN** (www.kpn.com). While there are a few phone booths around the city, mobile phones have become the norm.

Those staying in Amsterdam for a longer period of time should invest in a phone with a SIM card. Euro-friendly SIM cards can be bought at kiosks and electronics stores and include information on how to load credit onto the phone via the Internet. This allows visitors to possess a local cell phone number, and it's a common strategy for long-term visitors who do not want to commit to monthly or yearly plans.

Make sure your cell phone is compatible with a temporary SIM card. If not, there are many small electronic shops selling disposable phones starting at €20.

TOURIST INFORMATION

VISITORS CENTERS

Amsterdam's main tourist information office, the **I amsterdam Visitor Centre Stationsplein** (Stationsplein 10, tel. 020/702-6000, www.iamsterdam.com; 9am-6pm daily) is just outside Amsterdam Centraal Station.

POSTAL SERVICE

TNT Post (www.tntpost.nl) is the national mail service, with many outlets at Primera kiosks that mail both letters and packages. These outlets are usually open 8am-6pm, and some locations include: Waterlooplein 169 (Old Center), Rapenburg 91A (Old Center), Haarlemmerdijk 168 (Jordaan), Westerstraat 114 (Jordaan), and Singel 250 (Canal Belt West). Look for the orange sign that reads "Post" in white.

WEIGHTS AND MEASURES

The Netherlands uses the metric system for weight and measurements. Electrical outlets in Amsterdam are the same as the rest of the European continent, with two pins and 220-240 voltage.

Amsterdam is on Central European Time (CET), nine hours ahead of Pacific Standard Time, six hours ahead of Eastern Standard Time, and two hours behind Greenwich Mean Time. Daylight saving time in Amsterdam runs from the end of March to the end of October.

Health and Safety

Amsterdam is an extremely safe city; the main safety or health issues that arise revolve around intoxicated tourists and theft via pickpockets.

EMERGENCIES AND MEDICAL SERVICES

The emergency hotline for police, fire, and ambulance is 112. The non-emergency police phone number is tel. 090/08844.

There are two hospitals open 24 hours daily: **Onze Lieve Vrouwe Gasthuis** (Oosterpark 9, tel. 020/599-9111, www.olvg.nl) and **VU University Medical Center** (De Boelelaan 1117, tel. 020/444-4444, www.vumc.com). **Etos** and **Kruidvaat** are two common pharmacies in the city.

DRUGS AND ALCOHOL

Possession of soft drugs like cannabis is technically illegal, but it's decriminalized, meaning authorities will not detain or arrest people for possessing less than five grams of hash or marijuana. It's neither legal nor acceptable to smoke marijuana anywhere except in the city's coffeeshops.

Possession of hard drugs is considered a serious crime; most nightclubs will search your belongings upon entrance looking for illegal narcotics.

You must be 18 years old or older to purchase beer, wine, liquor, or soft drugs in the Netherlands.

THEFT

Pickpocketing does happen in Amsterdam. Most pickpockets are looking for smartphones and cash. If you realize something of yours has been stolen, report it to the closest police office from where the incident occurred.

RESOURCES

Glossary

appletaart: apple pie (try it with *slagroom*—whipped cream)

balti: a thin wok used in Bangladeshi, Indian, and Pakistani cooking

biertje: literally, "small beer"; the most popular way to order beer

bitterballen: fried meatballs; commonly served in brown bars

drop: salty black licorice; a Dutch classic

frites: French fries; commonly served in paper cones and eaten with sauce like the Amsterdam favorite *oorlog* (half mayonnaise and half peanut satay)

genever: Dutch gin

hemelse modder: chocolate pudding; literally, "heavenly mud"

klompen: wooden clogs

koffie: coffee

koffie verkeerd: latte

omafiet: popular woman's style bicycle ("grandma bike"); features a step-through frame so the rider can comfortably wear a skirt or dress

opafiet: popular men's style bicycle ("grandpa bike")

rijsttafel: Indonesian sample platter; literally, "rice table"

speculoos: cinnamon-flavored gingersnap

stamppot: mashed potatoes mixed with meat, gravy, and root vegetables; the Dutch national dish

stroopwafel: two thin waffle cookies with a lightly sweet syrup sandwiched between them

traiteur: delicatessen

wijn: wine

Dutch Phrasebook

English-speaking tourists should find themselves feeling relieved when traveling to Amsterdam: just about everyone in the city speaks English. In fact, English is so widely used that many Dutch people, particularly younger folks, find it insulting when a tourist asks, "Do you speak English?" Most Dutch people are proud of their bi- (and often poly-) lingual skills and are more than happy to speak English.

That being said, a basic understanding of Dutch pronunciation can come in handy, especially when asking for directions or menu items.

PRONUNCIATION

VOWELS

e (at the end of a word) like uh, as in "alive." Unlike the silent "e" in English, this vowel is pronounced and does not make preceding vowels long.

ei and ij like aye, as in "time"

oe like oo, as in "pool"

ui like ow, as in "town" or "out"

CONSONANTS

g and ch a guttural sound, a bit like ghhh, and one of the sounds that makes Dutch often incomprehensible to English speakers

r slightly rolled, almost like an English d

BASIC EXPRESSIONS

Good day *Goededag*

Good evening *Goedenavond*

Good morning *Goedemorgen*

Good afternoon *Goedemiddag*

Welcome *Welkom*

Excuse me *Pardon*

Sir *Meneer*

Madam *Mevrouw*

Do you speak English? *Spreekt u Engels?*

I don't speak Dutch *Ik spreek geen Nederlands*

How are you? *Hoe gaat het?*

Very well, thank you *Heel goed, dank u wel*

My name is... *Mijn naam is...*

What's your name? *Hoe heet u?*

Please *Alstublieft*

Thank you *Dank u*

I'm sorry *Het spijt me*

Goodbye *Tot ziens*

yes *Ja*

no *Nee*

cozy, quaint *gezellig* (generally used to describe a setting, mood, or feeling of utter bliss; one of the most popular Dutch adjectives)

TRANSPORTATION

How do I get to...? *Hoe ga ik naar...?*

Where is...? *Waar is...?*

the airport *schiphol*

the subway *de metro*

the train station *het station*

the train *de trein*

the bus stop *de bus halte*

the bus *de bus*

the exit *uitgang*

the street *de straat*

the garden *de tuin*

canal *gracht* (singular)/*grachten* (plural)

a taxicab *een taxi*

a hotel *een hotel*

a toilet *een WC*

a pharmacy *een apotheek*

a bank *een bank*

the tourist office *de VVV*

a telephone *een telefoon*

HEALTH AND SAFETY

Help! *Help!*

I am sick *Ik ben ziek*

I am hurt *Ik heb pijn*

I need... *Ik heb.... nodig*

a hospital *een ziekenhuis*

a doctor *een huisarts*

an ambulance *een ambulance*

the police *de politie*

medicine *medicijn*

FOOD

I would like... *Ik wil graag...*

a table for two *een tafel voor twee*

to see the menu *een menukaart even zien*

breakfast *ontbijt*

lunch *lunch*

dinner *diner*

to eat (a meal) *eten*

the bill *de rekening*

nonsmoking *rook-vrij*

a drink *een drankje*

water *water*

beer *bier*

white wine *wittewijn*

red wine *rodewijn*

I am... *Ik ben...*

vegetarian *vegetarisch*

diabetic *diabetisch*

allergic *allergisch*

kosher *kosher*

delicious *lekker* (also used to describe nonfood things that are good, exciting)

SHOPPING

Do you have...? *Heeft u...?*
Where can I buy...? *Waar koop ik...?*
May I try this? *Mag ik dit even proefen?*
How much is this? *Hoeveel kost dit?*
cash *contant*
credit card *credit card*
too... *te...*
small *klein*
large *groot*
expensive *uur*

TIME

What time is it? *Hoe laat is het?*
It is... *Het is...*
eight o'clock *acht uur*
half past ten *half elf*
quarter to five *kwart voor vijf*
midnight *middernacht*
during the day *overdag*
in the morning *s'morgens*
in the afternoon *s'middags*
in the evening *s'avonds*
at night *s'nachts*

DAYS OF THE WEEK

Monday *maandag*
Tuesday *dinsdag*
Wednesday *woensdag*
Thursday *donderdag*
Friday *vrijdag*
Saturday *zaterdag*
Sunday *zondag*
this week *deze week*
this weekend *dit weekend*
today *vandaag*
tomorrow *morgen*
yesterday *gisteren*

MONTHS

January *januari*
February *februari*
March *maart*
April *april*
May *mei*
June *juni*
July *juli*
August *augustus*
September *september*
October *oktober*
November *november*
December *december*
this month *deze maand*
this year *dit jaar*
winter *winter*
spring *lente*
summer *zomer*
fall *herfst*

NUMBERS

zero *nul*
one *een*
two *twee*
three *drie*
four *vier*
five *vijf*
six *zes*
seven *zeven*
eight *acht*
nine *negen*
ten *tien*
eleven *elf*
twelve *twaalf*
thirteen *dertien*
fourteen *viertien*
fifteen *vijftien*
sixteen *zestien*
seventeen *zeventien*
eighteen *achttien*
nineteen *negentien*
twenty *twintig*
one hundred *honderd*
one thousand *duizend*

STREET NAMES

inner *binnen*
outer *buiten*
bridge *brug*
embankment *dijk*
cross-street/side street *dwarsstraat*
canal, quay *gracht*
court *hof*
quay *kade*
canal, channel *kanaal*

little, short *kleine*
court, short street *korte*
avenue *laan*
market, marketplace *markt*
new *nieuwe*
old *oude*
plaza *plein*
lane, alley *steeg*
street *straat*
canal *vaart*

Index

C

D

E

KL

M

N

INDEX

O

PQ

R

S

T

UV

WXYZ

Restaurants Index

Nightlife Index

Shops Index

Hotels Index

Photo Credits

Title page photo: © Caro Bonink

Photos © Audrey Sykes except page 4 (top) © Van Gogh Museum, (bottom) © Red Light Secrets; page 6 © Digikhmer | Dreamstime; page 8 (top) © John Lewis Marshall, (bottom) © Cbomers | Dreamstime.com; page 9 (top) © Dutch Cities / Alamy Stock Photo, (middle) © Anne Frank House, photographer Cris Toala Olivares, (bottom) © Lornet | Dreamstime.com; page 12 © Richard de Bruijn; page 21 (top) © Corepics Vof | Dreamstime.com, (middle) © The Seafood Bar, (bottom) © W. H. Boegem; page 23 (top) © Jaroslav Moravcik | Dreamstime.com, (middle) © Artmakush | Dreamstime.com, (bottom) © Anibal Trejo | Dreamstime.com; page 25 (top) © Tassenmuseum Hendrijke, (bottom) © Digi Daan; page 27 (top) © Alex Prior, (middle) © Randall Runtsch | Dreamstime.com, (bottom) © Ahavelaar | Dreamstime.com; page 29 © John Lewis Marshall; page 31 (top) © Joyfull | Dreamstime.com, (bottom) © Tonyv3112 | Dreamstime.com; page 33 (top) © Luciano Mortula | Dreamstime.com, (middle) © Dutchscenery | Dreamstime.com, (bottom) © Anibaltrejo | Dreamstime.com; page 35 © Lornet | Dreamstime.com; page 37 (top) © Mario Savoia | Dreamstime.com, (bottom) © Tonyv3112 | Dreamstime.com; page 52 © Anne Frank House, photographer Cris Toala Olivares; page 55 © Jarino47 | Dreamstime.com; page 57 © Jan-Kees Steenman; page 58 © KLM Carto; page 70 © De Taart van m'n Tante; page 72 © Restaurant Haesje Claes; page 86 © Restaurant Blauw; page 96 © Restaurant Moeders; page 103 © House of Bols; page 112 © De Bekeerde Suster; page 143 © Richard de Bruijn; page 147 © Tassenmuseum Hendrijke; page 159 © Kim Krijnen; page 162 © Erik van Gurp; page 172 © Ronald van Weeren; page 175 © Joao M B Costa; page 182 © HAY Amsterdam; page 193 © Nicole, Socks We Love; page 194 © Steven Stoddart; page 195 © Taco, Waxwell Records; page 196 © Coco Duivenvoorde; page 197 © The Frozen Fountain; page 212 © Grand Hotel Amrâth Amsterdam; page 220 © Cocomama; page 221 © Hans Brinker; page 222 © The Toren; page 224 © Alex Prior; page 225 © Maes B&B; page 226 © Conservatorium Hotel; page 229 © Cake Under My Pillow

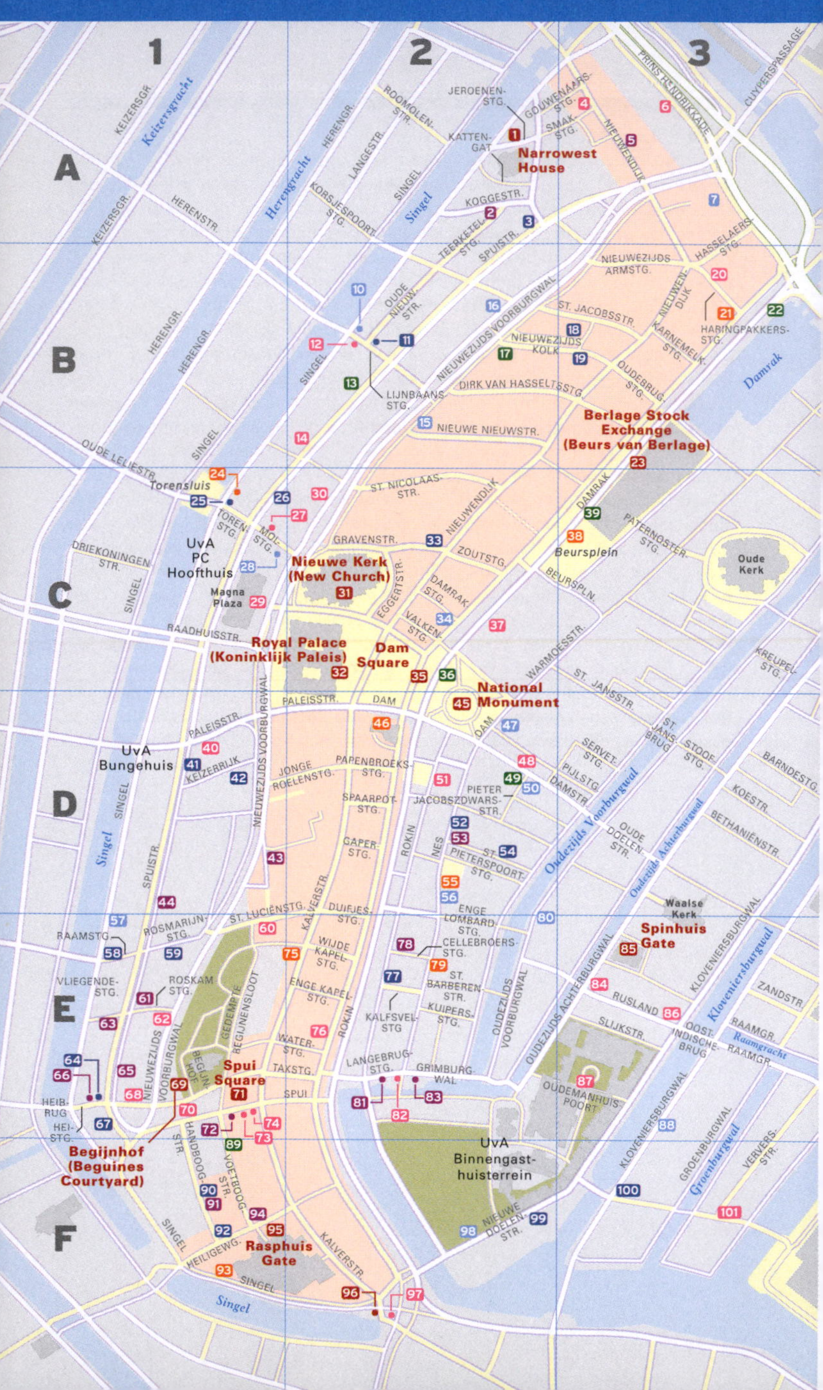

Narrowest House
Berlage Stock Exchange (Beurs van Berlage)
Nieuwe Kerk (New Church)
Royal Palace (Koninklijk Paleis)
Dam Square
National Monument
Spinhuis Gate
Spui Square
Begijnhof (Beguines Courtyard)
Rasphuis Gate
Torensluis
UvA PC Hoofthuis
Magna Plaza
UvA Bungehuis
Beursplein
Oude Kerk
Waalse Kerk
UvA Binnengasthuisterrein
Oudemanhuis Poort
Damrak
Singel
Herengracht
Keizersgracht
Oudezijds Voorburgwal
Oudezijds Achterburgwal
Kloveniersburgwal
Groenburgwal
Raamgracht

SIGHTS

1	A2	Narrowest House	35	C2	Dam Square
8	A4	Amsterdam Centraal Station	45	D2	National Monument
23	B3	Berlage Stock Exchange (Beurs van Berlage)	69	E1	Begijnhof (Beguines Courtyard)
31	C2	Nieuwe Kerk (New Church)	71	E1	Spui Square
32	C2	Royal Palace (Koninklijk Paleis)	85	E3	Spinhuis Gate
			95	F1	Rasphuis Gate
			96	F2	Mint Tower (Munttoren)

RESTAURANTS

2	A2	Hoppy Days	66	E1	Van Stapele
5	A3	Gebroeders Niemeijer	72	E1	The Seafood Bar
43	D1	Stadspaleis	78	E2	Bierfabriek
44	D1	Lucius	81	E2	De Laatste Kruimel
53	D2	Van Kerkwijk	83	E2	Upstairs Pannenkoeken
61	E1	Haese Claes	91	F1	Cannibale Royale
63	E1	D'Vijff Vlieghen	94	F1	Vlaams Friteshuis Vleminck
65	E1	Kantjil & De Tijger			

NIGHTLIFE

3	A2	Bitterzoet	54	D2	De Buurvrouw
9	A4	1e Klas	58	E1	Café Gollem
11	B2	Tales & Spirits	59	E1	Kadinsky
18	B3	The Cuckoo's Nest	64	E1	De Tweede Kamer
19	B3	In de Wildeman	67	E1	Café Hoppe
25	C1	Café Van Zuylen	77	E2	The Tara
26	C1	PRIK	90	F1	Bloemen Bar
33	C2	Belgique	92	F1	De Dampkring
41	D1	Café het Schuim	99	F2	Café de Jaren
42	D1	Beer Temple	100	F3	De Doelen
52	D2	Bubbles & Wines			

ARTS AND CULTURE

21	B3	Sex Museum	55	D2	De Brakke Grond
24	C1	Oode	75	E2	Amsterdam Museum
38	C3	Body Worlds: The Happiness Project	79	E2	Frascati Theater
46	D2	Madame Tussauds Amsterdam	93	F1	Torture Museum

SPORTS AND ACTIVITIES

13	B2	Limo Bike	39	C3	Holland Rent-A-Bike
17	B2	Yellow Bike	49	D2	Damstraat Rent-a-Bike
22	B3	Open Boat Tours	89	F1	The Poolbar
36	C2	We Bike Amsterdam			

SHOPS

4	A3	Dille & Kamille	68	E1	Athenaeum Nieuwscentrum & Bookstore
6	A3	COPA	70	E1	Artplein-Spui
12	B2	Totalitarian Art Gallery	73	E1	Spui Book Market (De Boek Markt op het Spui)
14	B2	Rush Hour Records	74	E1	The American Book Center
20	B3	Amsterdam Kaashuis	76	E2	P. G. C. Hajenius
27	C1	United Nude	82	E2	Lyppens Jewelier
29	C1	Magna Plaza	84	E3	Wonderwood
30	C2	Bij Ons	86	E3	The Book Exchange
37	C2	De Bijenkorf	87	E3	Boekenmarkt Oudemanhuispoort
40	D1	De Bierkoning	97	F2	Heinen Delfts Blauw
48	D2	Chimera Fantasy Shop	101	F3	Puccini Bomboni
51	D2	Betsy Palmer			
60	E1	De Posthumus Winkel			
62	E1	HAY			

HOTELS

7	A3	Art'otel	50	D2	Hotel de Gerstekorrel
10	B2	Hotel Brouwer	56	D2	Hotel V Nesplein
15	B2	INK Hotel Amsterdam	57	E1	Hotel Estherea
16	B2	Westcord City Centre Hotel Amsterdam	80	E2	Sofitel Legend the Grand
28	C1	Die Port van Cleve	88	E3	Stayokay Amsterdam Stadsdoelen
34	C2	Swissôtel	98	F2	Résidence Le Coin
47	D2	NH Collection Amsterdam Grand Hotel Krasnapolsky			

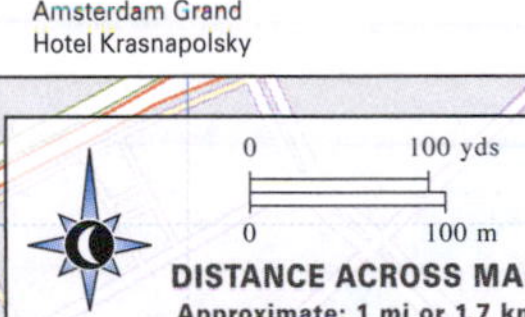

Waterlooplein
JODENBREESTR.
Meester Visserplein
Wertheimpark

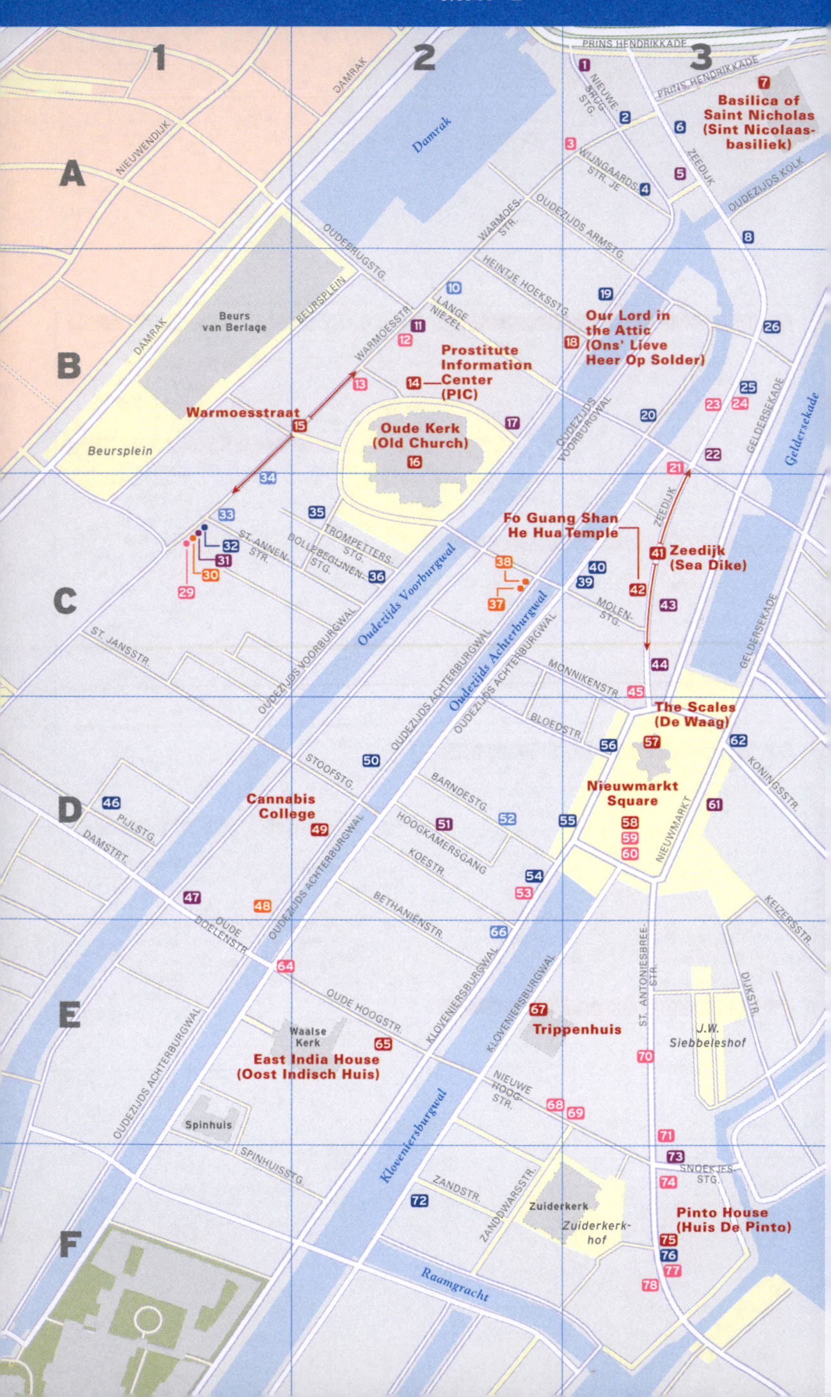

1
2
3
A
B
C
D
E
F
PRINS HENDRIKKADE
Basilica of Saint Nicholas (Sint Nicolaas-basiliek)
Damrak
DAMRAK
NIEUWENDIJK
NIEUWE BRUG STG.
WIJNGAARDS STR. JE
ZEEDIJK
OUDEZIJDS KOLK
WARMOES-STR.
OUDEZIJDS ARMSTG.
OUDEBRUGSTG.
BEURSPLEIN
Beurs van Berlage
HEINTJE HOEKSSTG.
LANGE NIEZEL
Our Lord in the Attic (Ons' Lieve Heer Op Solder)
Prostitute Information Center (PIC)
WARMOESSTR.
Warmoesstraat
Beursplein
Oude Kerk (Old Church)
OUDEZIJDS VOORBURGWAL
GELDERSEKADE
Geldersekade
Fo Guang Shan He Hua Temple
Zeedijk (Sea Dike)
ST. ANNEN-STR.
TROMPETTERS-STG.
DOLLEBEGIJNEN-STG.
Oudezijds Voorburgwal
Oudezijds Achterburgwal
MOLEN-STG.
ST. JANSSTR.
OUDEZIJDS ACHTERBURGWAL
MONNIKENSTR.
BLOEDSTR.
The Scales (De Waag)
STOOFSTG.
BARNDESTG.
Nieuwmarkt Square
NIEUWMARKT
KONINGSSTR.
Cannabis College
PIJLSTG.
DAMSTRT.
HOOGKAMERSGANG
KOESTR.
BETHANIENSTR.
KEIZERSSTR.
OUDE DOELENSTR.
OUDE HOOGSTR.
KLOVENIERSBURGWAL
ST. ANTONIESBREE-STR.
DIJKSTR.
J.W. Siebbeleshof
Trippenhuis
Waalse Kerk
East India House (Oost Indisch Huis)
NIEUWE HOOG-STR.
Spinhuis
SPINHUISSTG.
Kloveniersburgwal
SNOEKJES-STG.
ZANDSTR.
ZANDDWARSSTR.
Zuiderkerk
Zuiderkerk-hof
Pinto House (Huis De Pinto)
Raamgracht

4
5
6
9 Schreierstoren
ODEBRUG
27
KROMME WAAL
28
PRINS HENDRIKKADE
Scheepvaarthuis
WAALSTG.
BINNEN BANTAMMER STR.
NIEUWE JONKER STR.
WAALSEILAND BRUG
BINNENKANT
Waalseilandgracht
63
OUDE WAAL
RECHT BOOMSSLOOT
MONTELBAANSTR.
Recht Boomssloot
Waag speeltuin
Krom Boomssloot
KORTE KEIZERSDWARSSTR.
Oudeschans
OUDESCHANS
OUDESCHANS
0 100 yds
0 100 m
DISTANCE ACROSS MAP
Approximate: 0.65 mi or 1 km
© AVALON TRAVEL
SIGHTS
7 A3 Basilica of Saint Nicholas (Sint Nicolaasbasiliek)
9 A4 Schreierstoren
14 B2 Prostitute Information Center (PIC)
15 B2 Warmoesstraat
16 B2 Oude Kerk (Old Church)
18 B3 Our Lord in the Attic (Ons' Lieve Heer Op Solder)
41 C3 Zeedijk (Sea Dike)
42 C3 Fo Guang Shan He Hua Temple
49 D2 Cannabis College
57 D3 The Scales (De Waag)
58 D3 Nieuwmarkt Square
65 E2 East India House (Oost Indisch Huis)
67 E2 Trippenhuis
75 F3 Pinto House (Huis De Pinto)
RESTAURANTS
1 A3 Dwaze Zaken
5 A3 Skek
11 B2 De Bakkerswinkel
17 B2 Quartier Putain
22 B3 Bird Thais
27 B4 Lastage
31 C1 Metropolitan
43 C3 New King
44 C3 Latei
47 D1 Oriental City
51 D2 Blauw aan de Wal
61 D3 Cafe Bern
63 D4 Hemelse Modder
73 F3 Betty Blue
NIGHTLIFE
2 A3 In de Olofspoort
4 A3 The End
6 A3 Café In 't Aepjen
8 A3 Queen's Head
19 B3 De Prael
20 B3 Mata Hari
25 B3 Café 't Mandje
26 B3 Café Zilt
32 C1 The Winston
35 C2 Ton Ton Club
36 C2 The Bulldog
39 C3 The Old Sailor
40 C3 Bananenbar Amsterdam
46 D1 Wynand Fockink
50 D2 Casa Rosso
54 D2 De Bekeerde Suster
55 D3 Lokaal 't Loosje
56 D3 Greenhouse Effect
62 D3 Café Stevens
72 F2 Café de Engelbewaarder
76 F3 Coffeeshop Bluebird
ARTS AND CULTURE
30 C1 W139
37 C2 Red Light Secrets Museum of Prostitution
38 C2 Erotic Museum
48 D1 Hash Marihuana & Hemp Museum
SHOPS
3 A3 Kokopelli
12 B2 RoB
13 B2 Jemi
21 B3 Madchique by Chimera
23 B3 DeMask
24 B3 Patta
29 C1 Condomerie
45 C3 Henk Comics
53 D2 Jacob Hooy & Co
59 D3 Nieuwmarkt Farmers Market
60 D3 Nieuwmarkt Antiques Market
64 E1 Capsicum
68 E2 De Hoed van Tijn
69 E3 Joe's Vliegerwinkel
70 E3 RecordFriend Elpees
71 E3 Bis!
74 F3 Knuffels
77 F3 Pantheon Books
78 F3 Henxs
HOTELS
10 B2 Greenhouse Effect
28 B4 Grand Hotel Amrâth Amsterdam
33 C1 St Christopher's Inn at The Winston
34 C1 Hotel Luxer
52 D2 Shelter City
66 E2 Misc Eatdrinksleep

SIGHTS

- 7 A3 Metz & Co Building
- 8 A3 Krijtberg Church
- 37 B2 Leidse Square (Leidseplein)
- 55 B4 Golden Bend (Gouden Bocht)
- 57 B5 Rembrandt Square (Rembrandtplein)
- 70 B6 Gijsbert Dommer Huis
- 87 C5 Amstelkerk
- 97 D5 De Duif
- 103 D6 Fredericks Square (Frederiksplein)

RESTAURANTS

- 6 A3 Greenwoods
- 43 B2 De Sneeker Pan
- 44 B2 Café de Klos
- 45 B3 Bocca Coffee
- 49 B3 RED
- 58 B5 Coco's Outback
- 62 B5 Ponte Arcari
- 64 B5 Zuivere Koffie
- 65 B5 Loekie
- 68 B6 Breitner
- 81 C3 Lavinia
- 86 C5 Tempo Doeloe
- 88 C5 Brasserie Nel
- 89 C5 Segugio
- 98 D5 Uliveto
- 99 D5 Van Vlaanderen
- 100 D5 Pata Negra
- 105 D6 Café Kale

NIGHTLIFE

- 2 A1 De Zotte
- 3 A2 De Pieper
- 4 A2 The Dolphins
- 11 A4 Club NYX
- 12 A4 Exit Après Chique
- 14 A4 De Duivel
- 15 B4 Door 74
- 17 A5 Café Montmartre
- 19 A5 Club Escape
- 20 A5 Mulligans
- 22 B1 Bar Weber
- 24 B1 Lux
- 26 B1 Melkweg
- 28 B1 Café Americain
- 30 B2 Sugar Factory
- 31 B2 Jimmy Woo
- 32 B2 Café Eijlders
- 33 B2 The Waterhole
- 34 B2 Chicago Social
- 38 B2 Club Up
- 39 B2 Jazz Café Alto
- 40 B2 Bourbon Street
- 41 B2 The Cave
- 42 B2 Café Genootschap der Geneugten
- 59 B5 Coco's Outback
- 60 B5 Lellebel
- 63 B5 Boerejongens Centre
- 66 B6 AIR
- 67 B6 Café Langereis
- 71 C2 Café in De Balie
- 73 C2 Paradiso
- 74 C2 L&B Whiskeycafe
- 75 C2 Café de Spuyt
- 92 D3 Café de Wetering
- 93 D3 Café Brecht
- 101 D5 Café Slijterij Oosterling

ARTS AND CULTURE

- 16 A5 Pathé Tuschinski
- 18 A5 De Kleine Komedie
- 25 B1 Theater Bellevue
- 27 B1 De La Mar
- 35 B2 Stadsschouwburg
- 47 B3 Jaski Art Gallery
- 48 B3 Peter Pappot Art Gallery
- 53 B4 Amsterdam City Archives (Stadsarchief Amsterdam)
- 56 B4 Foam
- 61 B5 Museum of Bags and Purses (Tassenmuseum Hendrikje)
- 69 B6 Willet-Holthuysen Museum
- 72 C2 De Balie
- 76 C3 The Public House of Art
- 77 C3 Lionel Gallery
- 82 C4 Okker Art Gallery
- 83 C4 Van Loon House
- 90 D3 Reflex Gallery

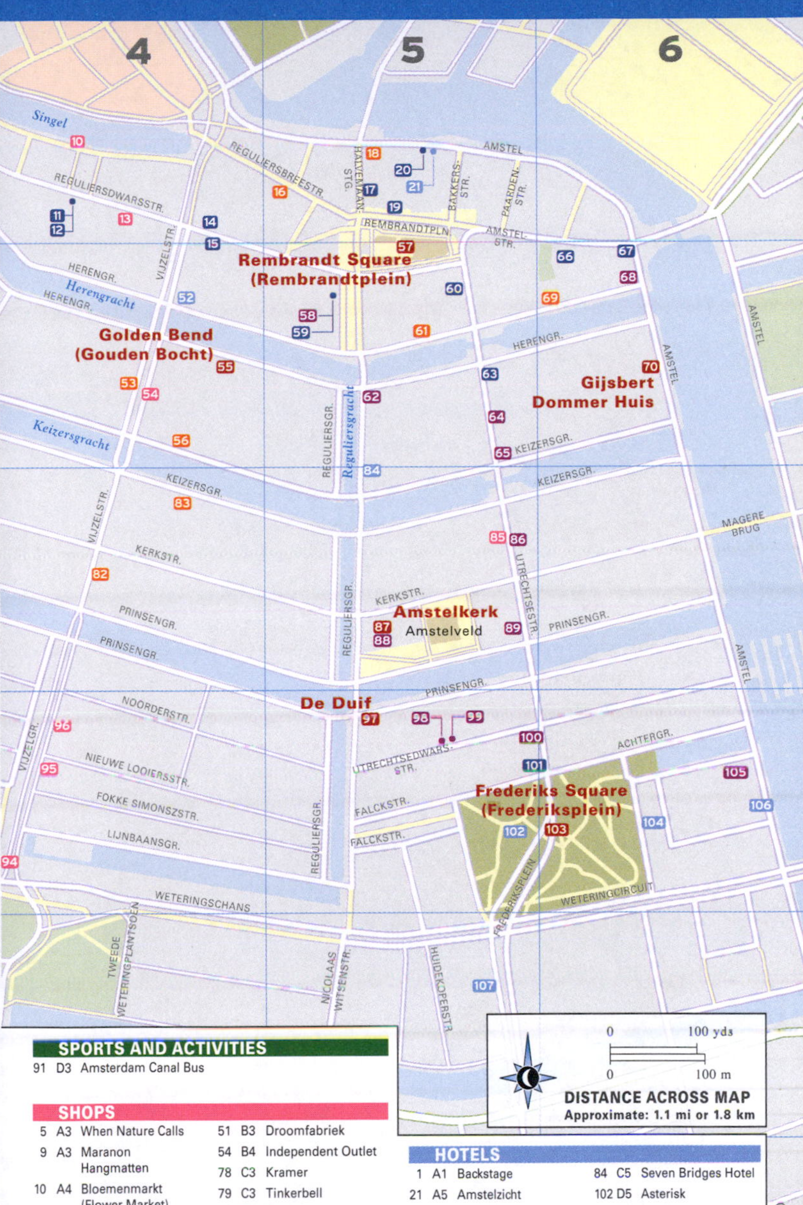

SPORTS AND ACTIVITIES

91 D3 Amsterdam Canal Bus

SHOPS

5 A3 When Nature Calls
9 A3 Maranon Hangmatten
10 A4 Bloemenmarkt (Flower Market)
13 A4 Shirt Shop
36 B2 International Theater and Film Books
50 B3 Dick Meijer
51 B3 Droomfabriek
54 B4 Independent Outlet
78 C3 Kramer
79 C3 Tinkerbell
80 C3 Tamago
85 C5 Concerto
94 D4 Mail & Female
95 D4 De Badjassenwinkel
96 D4 Hart's Wijnhandel Amsterdam

HOTELS

1 A1 Backstage
21 A5 Amstelzicht
23 B1 Hotel Weber
29 B1 Hampshire Hotel – Amsterdam American
46 B3 Hans Brinker
52 B4 Banks Mansion
84 C5 Seven Bridges Hotel
102 D5 Asterisk
104 D6 Hotel Nicolaas Witsen
106 D6 Hotel V Frederiksplein
107 E5 Cocomama

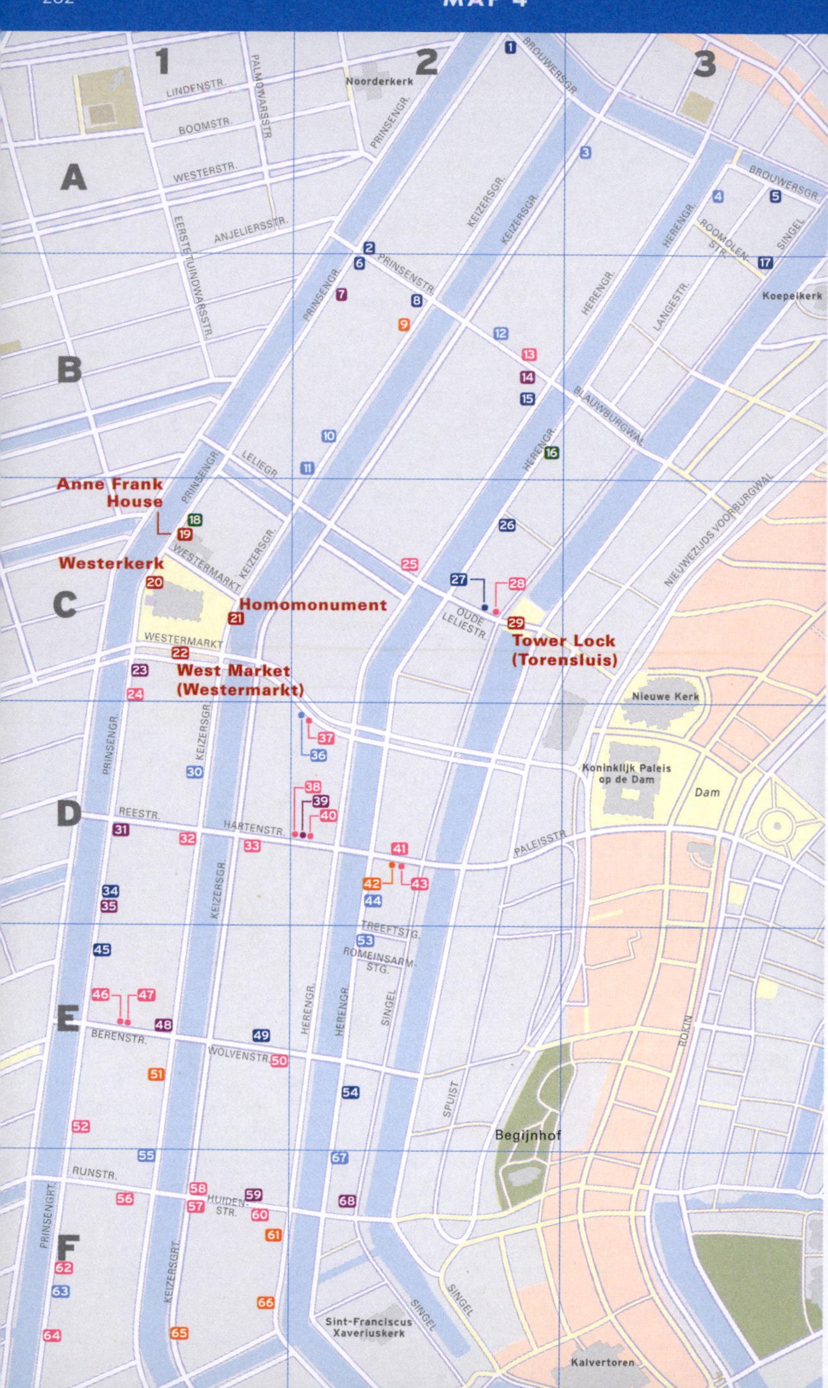

Anne Frank House
Westerkerk
Homomonument
Tower Lock (Torensluis)
West Market (Westermarkt)
Noorderkerk
Koepelkerk
Nieuwe Kerk
Koninklijk Paleis op de Dam
Dam
Begijnhof
Sint-Franciscus Xaveriuskerk
Kalvertoren
LINDENSTR.
BOOMSTR.
WESTERSTR.
ANJELIERSSTR.
PALMDWARSSTR.
EERSTE TUINDWARSSTR.
PRINSENGR.
KEIZERSGR.
HERENGR.
BROUWERSGR.
PRINSENSTR.
ROOMOLENSTR.
LANGESTR.
SINGEL
BLAUWBURGWAL
LELIEGR.
OUDE LELIESTR.
NIEUWEZIJDS VOORBURGWAL
WESTERMARKT
REESTR.
HARTENSTR.
PALEISSTR.
TREEFTSTG.
ROMEINSARMSTG.
BERENSTR.
WOLVENSTR.
RUNSTR.
HUIDENSTR.
SPUIST
ROKIN
PRINSENGRT.
KEIZERSGRT.

SIGHTS

19	C1	Anne Frank House	22	C1	West Market (Westermarkt)
20	C1	Westerkerk	29	C2	Tower Lock (Torensluis)
21	C1	Homomonument			

RESTAURANTS

7	B2	The Pancake Bakery	39	D2	Screaming Beans
14	B2	Chez Georges	48	E1	Struisvogel
23	C1	Bistro Bij Ons	59	F1	Chocolaterie Pompadour
31	D1	Koffiehuis De Hoek	68	F2	Singel 404
35	D1	Envy			

NIGHTLIFE

1	A2	Tabac	17	B3	Café Louis
2	A2	De Vergulde Gaper	26	C2	Amnesia
5	A3	Siberië	27	C2	Grey Area
6	B2	Café de II Prinsen	34	D1	Van Puffelen
8	B2	J. D. William's Whiskey Bar	45	E1	Vyne
15	B2	Arendsnest	49	E1	Brix
			54	E2	De Admiraal

ARTS AND CULTURE

9	B2	De Rode Hoed	66	F1	House of the Canals Museum (Grachtenhuis Museum)
42	D2	Brilmuseum			
51	E1	Felix Meritis			
61	F1	Bible Museum and Cromhouthuizen			
65	F1	Huis Marseille Museum for Photography			

SPORTS AND ACTIVITIES

16	B2	Sauna Deco	18	C1	Canal Bikes

SHOPS

13	B2	J. C. HERMAN Ceramics	43	D2	Socks We Love
24	C1	Nieuws	46	E1	Marlies Dekkers
25	C2	The Otherist	47	E1	Boekie Woekie
28	C2	De Reypenaer	50	E1	Laura Dols
32	D1	Amsterdam Watch Company	52	E1	Denham Concept Store
33	D1	Hester van Eeghen	56	F1	De Kaaskamer
37	D2	The Pelican Studio	57	F1	Van Ravenstein
38	D2	Gamekeeper	58	F1	Marie Stella-Maris
40	D2	Exota	60	F1	Zipper
41	D2	Waxwell Records	62	F1	Prinsheerlijk Antiek
			64	F1	Frozen Fountain

HOTELS

3	A3	Sebastian's	44	D2	The Hoxton, Amsterdam
4	A3	Max Brown Hotel	53	E2	Hotel Hegra
10	B2	Canal House	55	F1	The Dylan Amsterdam
11	B2	The Toren	63	F1	Andaz Amsterdam
12	B2	Maes B&B	67	F2	Ambassade Hotel
30	D1	Pulitzer Hotel			
36	D2	Hotel Clemens			

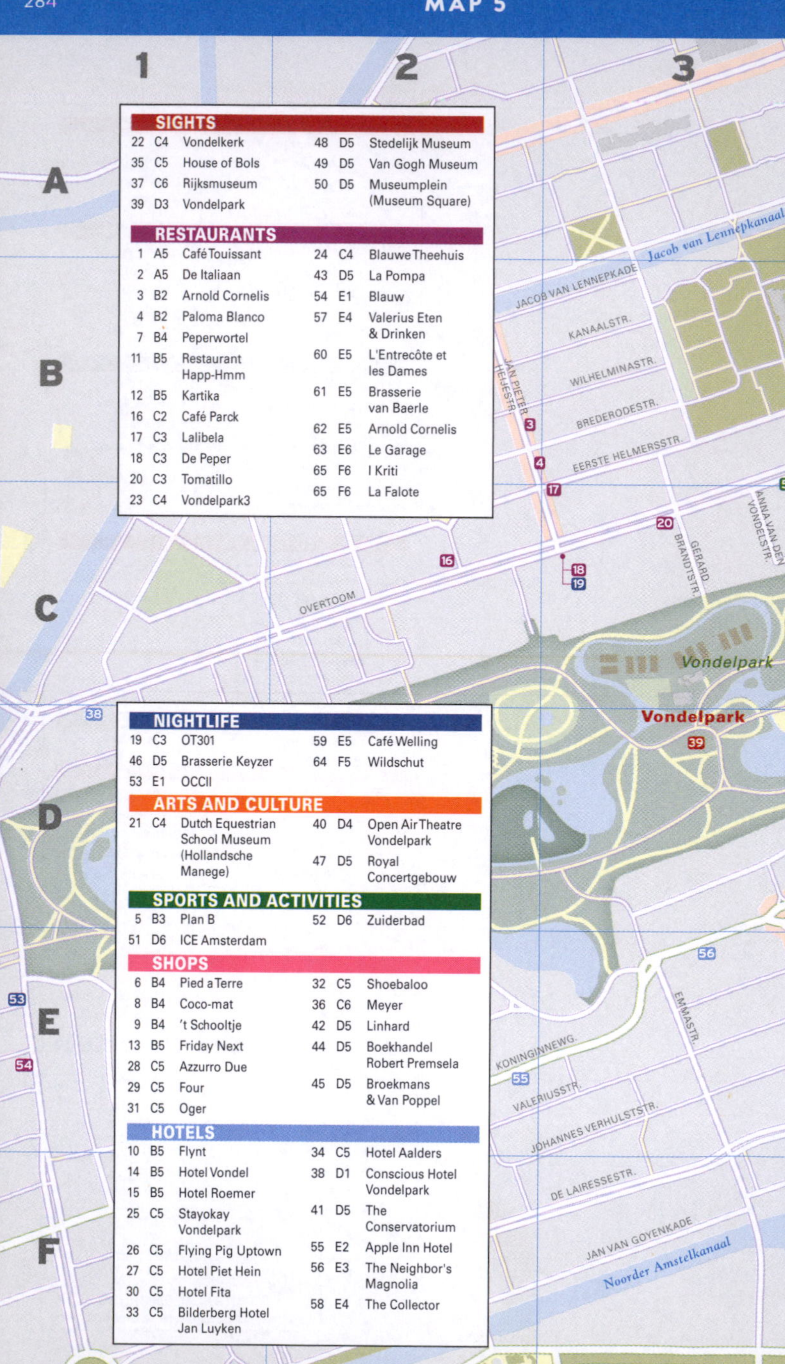
1
2
3
A
B
C
D
E
F
SIGHTS
22 C4 Vondelkerk
35 C5 House of Bols
37 C6 Rijksmuseum
39 D3 Vondelpark
48 D5 Stedelijk Museum
49 D5 Van Gogh Museum
50 D5 Museumplein (Museum Square)
RESTAURANTS
1 A5 Café Touissant
2 A5 De Italiaan
3 B2 Arnold Cornelis
4 B2 Paloma Blanco
7 B4 Peperwortel
11 B5 Restaurant Happ-Hmm
12 B5 Kartika
16 C2 Café Parck
17 C3 Lalibela
18 C3 De Peper
20 C3 Tomatillo
23 C4 Vondelpark3
24 C4 Blauwe Theehuis
43 D5 La Pompa
54 E1 Blauw
57 E4 Valerius Eten & Drinken
60 E5 L'Entrecôte et les Dames
61 E5 Brasserie van Baerle
62 E5 Arnold Cornelis
63 E6 Le Garage
65 F6 I Kriti
65 F6 La Falote
NIGHTLIFE
19 C3 OT301
46 D5 Brasserie Keyzer
53 E1 OCCII
59 E5 Café Welling
64 F5 Wildschut
ARTS AND CULTURE
21 C4 Dutch Equestrian School Museum (Hollandsche Manege)
40 D4 Open Air Theatre Vondelpark
47 D5 Royal Concertgebouw
SPORTS AND ACTIVITIES
5 B3 Plan B
51 D6 ICE Amsterdam
52 D6 Zuiderbad
SHOPS
6 B4 Pied a Terre
8 B4 Coco-mat
9 B4 't Schooltje
13 B5 Friday Next
28 C5 Azzurro Due
29 C5 Four
31 C5 Oger
32 C5 Shoebaloo
36 C6 Meyer
42 D5 Linhard
44 D5 Boekhandel Robert Premsela
45 D5 Broekmans & Van Poppel
HOTELS
10 B5 Flynt
14 B5 Hotel Vondel
15 B5 Hotel Roemer
25 C5 Stayokay Vondelpark
26 C5 Flying Pig Uptown
27 C5 Hotel Piet Hein
30 C5 Hotel Fita
33 C5 Bilderberg Hotel Jan Luyken
34 C5 Hotel Aalders
38 D1 Conscious Hotel Vondelpark
41 D5 The Conservatorium
55 E2 Apple Inn Hotel
56 E3 The Neighbor's Magnolia
58 E4 The Collector
Jacob van Lennepkanaal
JACOB VAN LENNEPKADE
KANAALSTR.
WILHELMINASTR.
BREDERODESTR.
EERSTE HELMERSSTR.
JAN PIETER HEIJESTR.
GERARD BRANDTSTR.
ANNA VAN DEN VONDELSTR.
OVERTOOM
Vondelpark
Vondelpark
KONINGINNEWG.
EMMASTR.
VALERIUSSTR.
JOHANNES VERHULSTSTR.
DE LAIRESSESTR.
JAN VAN GOYENKADE
Noorder Amstelkanaal
3
4
5
16
17
18
19
20
38
39
53
54
55
56

4
5
6
Bilderdijkgracht
Singelgracht
Prinsengracht
Vondelkerk
Rijksmuseum
House of Bols
Van Gogh Museum
Stedelijk Museum
Museumplein (Museum Square)
Boerenwetering
OVERTOOM
VONDELSTR.
P.C. HOOFTSTR.
VAN BAERLESTR.
HOBBEMAKADE
STADHOUDERSKADE
0 200 yds
0 200 m
DISTANCE ACROSS MAP
Approximate: 1.4 mi or 2.4 km
© AVALON TRAVEL

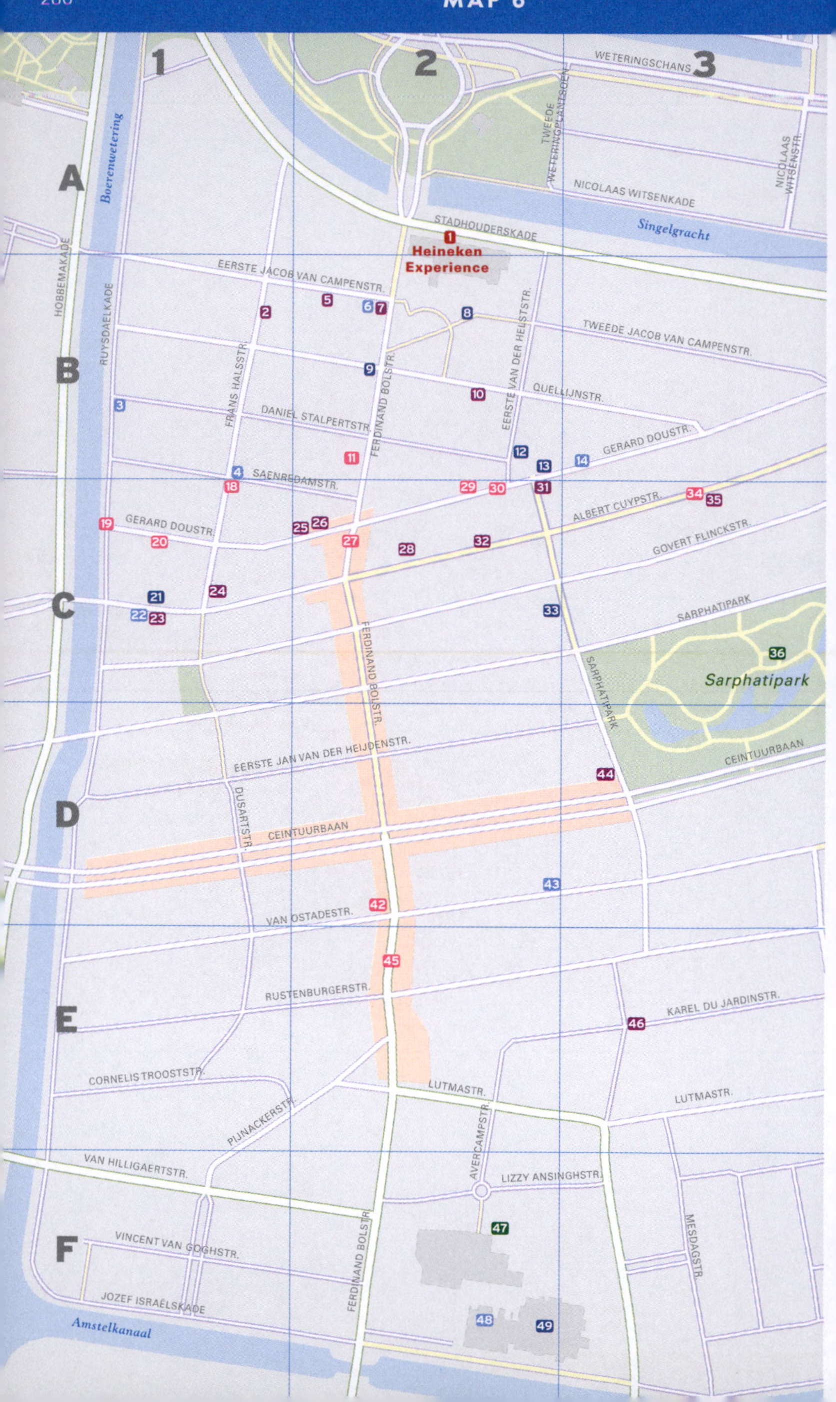
1
2
3
A
B
C
D
E
F
WETERINGSCHANS
TWEEDE WETERINGPLANTSOEN
NICOLAAS WITSENSTR.
NICOLAAS WITSENKADE
Singelgracht
Boerenwetering
STADHOUDERSKADE
1 Heineken Experience
HOBBEMAKADE
RUYSDAELKADE
EERSTE JACOB VAN CAMPENSTR.
TWEEDE JACOB VAN CAMPENSTR.
EERSTE VAN DER HELSTSTR.
FRANS HALSSTR.
FERDINAND BOLSTR.
QUELLIJNSTR.
DANIEL STALPERTSTR.
GERARD DOUSTR.
SAENREDAMSTR.
ALBERT CUYPSTR.
GOVERT FLINCKSTR.
SARPHATIPARK
Sarphatipark
EERSTE JAN VAN DER HEIJDENSTR.
CEINTUURBAAN
DUSARTSTR.
VAN OSTADESTR.
RUSTENBURGERSTR.
KAREL DU JARDINSTR.
CORNELIS TROOSTSTR.
LUTMASTR.
PIJNACKERSTR.
AVERCAMPSTR.
VAN HILLIGAERTSTR.
LIZZY ANSINGHSTR.
MESDAGSTR.
VINCENT VAN GOGHSTR.
JOZEF ISRAËLSKADE
Amstelkanaal
2
3
4
5
6
7
8
9
10
11
12
13
14
18
19
20
21
22
23
24
25
26
27
28
29
30
31
32
33
34
35
36
42
43
44
45
46
47
48
49

SIGHTS

1 A2 Heineken Experience
41 C5 House with the Gnomes (Huis met de Kabouters)

RESTAURANTS

2 B1 De Waaghals
5 B2 Bakers and Roasters
7 B2 De Taart van m'n Tante
10 B2 Mamouche
16 B4 Vamos a Ver
23 C1 Izakaya
24 C1 Balti House
25 C2 Saray
26 C2 Warung Spang Makandra
28 C2 Pho 91
31 C2 Wasserette
32 C2 The Butcher
35 C3 Bazar
37 C4 Little Collins
38 C4 Artiste
44 D3 Scandinavian Embassy
46 E3 District V

NIGHTLIFE

8 B2 De Kleine Valk
9 B2 Kingfisher
12 B2 Het Paardje
13 B2 MASH
21 C1 Braque
33 C2 Katsu
39 C5 Yo-Yo
40 C5 Café Bloemers
49 F2 Twenty Third Bar

SPORTS AND ACTIVITIES

36 C3 Sarphatipark
47 F2 De Pijp Petting Zoo (Kinderboerderij de Pijp)

SHOPS

11 B2 Buitengewoon
15 B4 Opus 391
17 B4 Hutspot
18 C1 Wijnhandel van Krimpen
19 C1 The Plug
20 C1 RebelRelic
27 C2 Duikelman
29 C2 The Girl Can't Help It...
30 C2 Baskèts
34 C3 Albert Cuypmarkt
42 D2 Dumpstore Amsterdam
45 E2 Big & Belg

HOTELS

3 B1 Between Art & Kitsch
4 B1 Ollies Bed and Breakfast
6 B2 Cake Under My Pillow
14 B3 BBbyServio
22 C1 Sir Albert Hotel
43 D2 Bicycle Hotel
48 F2 Okura Hotel

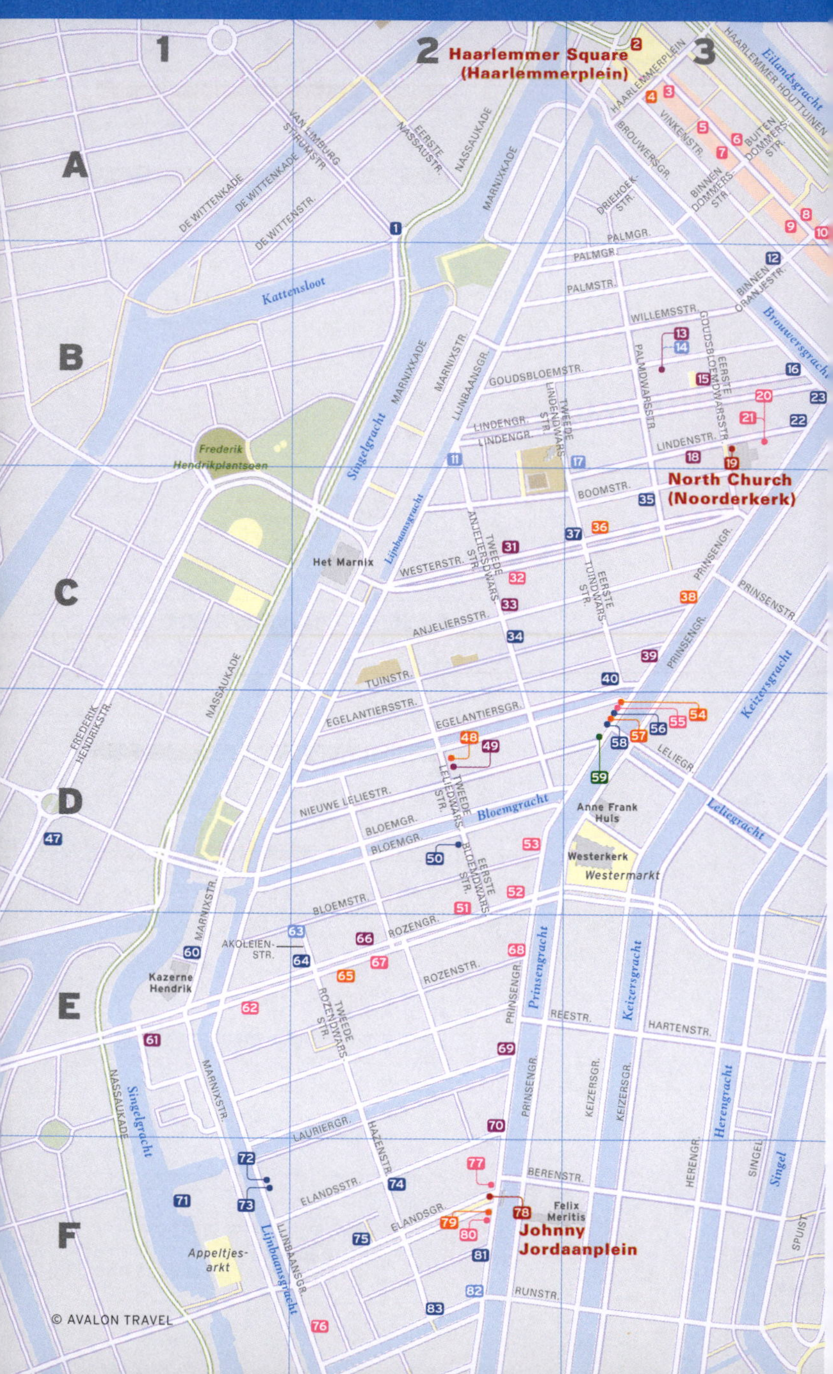
Haarlemmer Square (Haarlemmerplein)
North Church (Noorderkerk)
Johnny Jordaanplein
Het Marnix
Anne Frank Huis
Westerkerk
Westermarkt
Kazerne Hendrik
Frederik Hendrikplantsoen
Appeltjesmarkt
Felix Meritis
Kattensloot
Singelgracht
Lijnbaansgracht
Bloemgracht
Prinsengracht
Keizersgracht
Herengracht
Leliegracht
Brouwersgracht
Eilandsgracht
Singel
HAARLEMMER HOUTTUINEN
HAARLEMMERPLEIN
VINKENSTR.
BUITEN DOMMERSSTR.
BINNEN DOMMERSSTR.
BROUWERSGR.
DRIEHOEKSTR.
PALMGR.
PALMSTR.
WILLEMSSTR.
BINNEN ORANJESTR.
GOUDSBLOEMSTR.
LINDENGR.
LINDENSTR.
BOOMSTR.
WESTERSTR.
ANJELIERSSTR.
TUINSTR.
EGELANTIERSSTR.
EGELANTIERSGR.
NIEUWE LELIESTR.
BLOEMGR.
BLOEMSTR.
ROZENGR.
ROZENSTR.
REESTR.
HARTENSTR.
LAURIERGR.
ELANDSSTR.
ELANDSGR.
BERENSTR.
RUNSTR.
PRINSENSTR.
LELIEGR.
DE WITTENKADE
DE WITTENSTR.
VAN LIMBURG STIRUMSTR.
EERSTE NASSAUSTR.
NASSAUKADE
MARNIXKADE
MARNIXSTR.
LIJNBAANSGR.
FREDERIK HENDRIKSTR.
AKOLEIENSTR.
HAZENSTR.
SPUISTR.
© AVALON TRAVEL

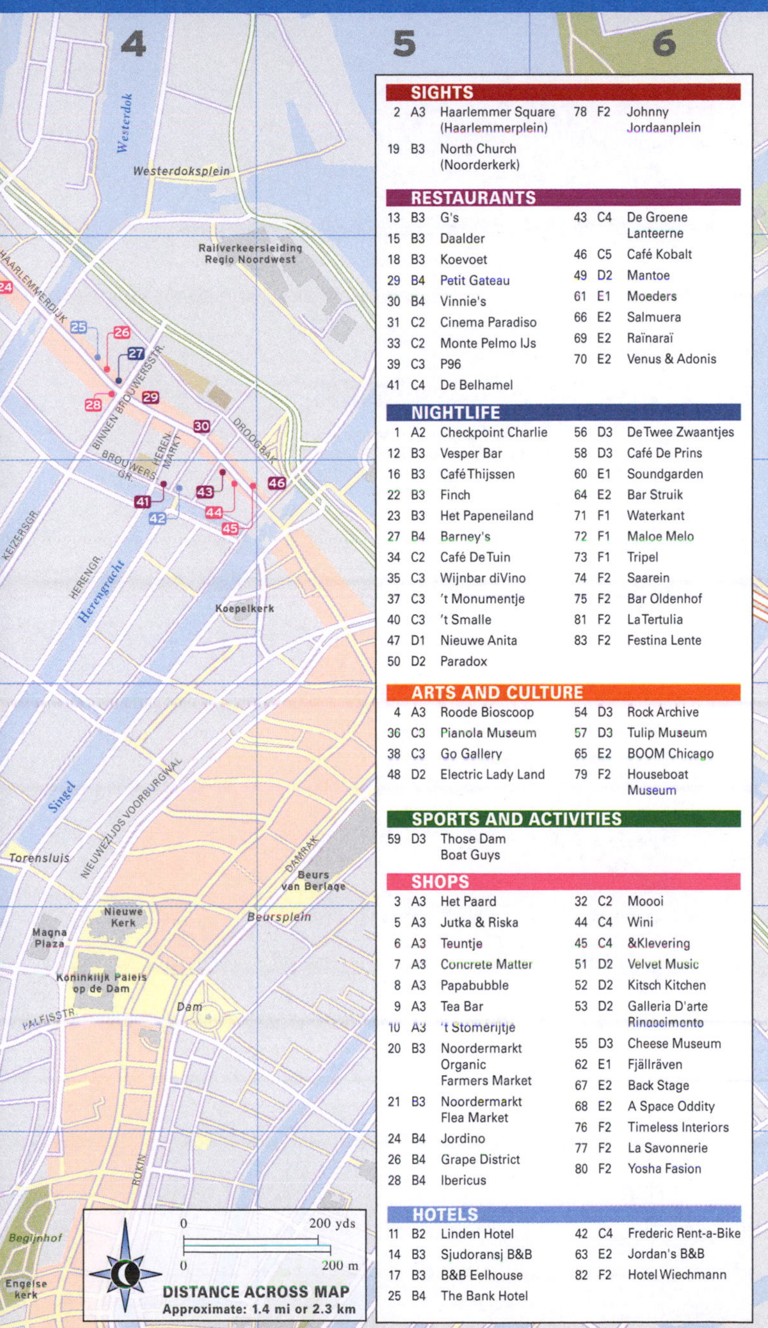
4
5
6
Westerdok
Westerdoksplein
Railverkeersleiding Regio Noordwest
HAARLEMMERDIJK
BINNEN BROUWERSSTR.
BROUWERS GR.
HEREN-MARKT
DROOGBAK
KEIZERSGR.
HERENGR.
Herengracht
Koepelkerk
Singel
NIEUWEZIJDS VOORBURGWAL
Torensluis
DAMRAK
Beurs van Berlage
Nieuwe Kerk
Magna Plaza
Beursplein
Koninklijk Paleis op de Dam
Dam
PALFISSTR
ROKIN
Begijnhof
Engelse kerk
0 200 yds
0 200 m
DISTANCE ACROSS MAP
Approximate: 1.4 mi or 2.3 km
SIGHTS
2 A3 Haarlemmer Square (Haarlemmerplein)
19 B3 North Church (Noorderkerk)
78 F2 Johnny Jordaanplein
RESTAURANTS
13 B3 G's
15 B3 Daalder
18 B3 Koevoet
29 B4 Petit Gateau
30 B4 Vinnie's
31 C2 Cinema Paradiso
33 C2 Monte Pelmo IJs
39 C3 P96
41 C4 De Belhamel
43 C4 De Groene Lanteerne
46 C5 Café Kobalt
49 D2 Mantoe
61 E1 Moeders
66 E2 Salmuera
69 E2 Raïnaraï
70 E2 Venus & Adonis
NIGHTLIFE
1 A2 Checkpoint Charlie
12 B3 Vesper Bar
16 B3 Café Thijssen
22 B3 Finch
23 B3 Het Papeneiland
27 B4 Barney's
34 C2 Café De Tuin
35 C3 Wijnbar diVino
37 C3 't Monumentje
40 C3 't Smalle
47 D1 Nieuwe Anita
50 D2 Paradox
56 D3 De Twee Zwaantjes
58 D3 Café De Prins
60 E1 Soundgarden
64 E2 Bar Struik
71 F1 Waterkant
72 F1 Maloe Melo
73 F1 Tripel
74 F2 Saarein
75 F2 Bar Oldenhof
81 F2 La Tertulia
83 F2 Festina Lente
ARTS AND CULTURE
4 A3 Roode Bioscoop
36 C3 Pianola Museum
38 C3 Go Gallery
48 D2 Electric Lady Land
54 D3 Rock Archive
57 D3 Tulip Museum
65 E2 BOOM Chicago
79 F2 Houseboat Museum
SPORTS AND ACTIVITIES
59 D3 Those Dam Boat Guys
SHOPS
3 A3 Het Paard
5 A3 Jutka & Riska
6 A3 Teuntje
7 A3 Concrete Matter
8 A3 Papabubble
9 A3 Tea Bar
10 A3 't Stomerijtje
20 B3 Noordermarkt Organic Farmers Market
21 B3 Noordermarkt Flea Market
24 B4 Jordino
26 B4 Grape District
28 B4 Ibericus
32 C2 Moooi
44 C4 Wini
45 C4 &Klevering
51 D2 Velvet Music
52 D2 Kitsch Kitchen
53 D2 Galleria D'arte Rinascimento
55 D3 Cheese Museum
62 E1 Fjällräven
67 E2 Back Stage
68 E2 A Space Oddity
76 F2 Timeless Interiors
77 F2 La Savonnerie
80 F2 Yosha Fasion
HOTELS
11 B2 Linden Hotel
14 B3 Sjudoransj B&B
17 B3 B&B Eelhouse
25 B4 The Bank Hotel
42 C4 Frederic Rent-a-Bike
63 E2 Jordan's B&B
82 F2 Hotel Wiechmann

1
2
3
A
B
C
D
E
F
UILENBURG
OUDESCHANS
NIEUWE UILENBURGERSTR.
Rembrandt House (Rembrandthuis)
Gassan Diamonds
VALKENBURGERSTR.
ANNE FRANKSTR.
HOUTKOPERSDWARSSTR.
JODENBREESTR.
Waterlooplein
WATERLOOPLN.
LANGE HOUTGANG
Markenplein
RAPENBURGERSTR.
NIEUWE HERENGR.
Meester Visserplein
MUIDERSTR.
TURFSTEEG
JONAS DANIEL MEIJERPLN.
Portuguese Synagogue
Wertheimpark
PLANTAGE PARKLAAN
NIEUWE AMSTELSTR.
Jewish Historical Museum (Joods Historisch Museum)
Jonas Daniël Meijerplein
WATERLOOPLN.
Blue Bridge (Blauwbrug)
Botanical Gardens (Hortus Botanicus)
WEESPERST
National Holocaust Memorial (Hollandsche Schouwburg)
NIEUWE HERENGR.
Hoftuin
AMSTEL
PLANTAGE MUIDERGR.
NIEUWE KEIZERSGR.
NIEUWE KEIZERSGR.
Wittenberg
DIRK VAN NIMWEGENBRUG
Sarphatihuis
NIEUWE KERKSTR.
Skinny Bridge (Magere Brug)
MAGERE BRUG
NIEUWE PRINSENGR.
NIEUWE PRINSENGR.
AMSTEL
ONBEKENDEGR.
NIEUWE ACHTERGR.
NIEUWE ACHTERGR.
Amstel Locks (Amstelsluizen)
AMSTEL
WEESPERPLN.
VALCKENIERSTR.
SARPHATISTR.
PROFESSOR TULPPLN.
© AVALON TRAVEL

SIGHTS

2	A1	Rembrandt House (Rembrandthuis)
5	A1	Gassan Diamonds
11	A4	Kadijks Square (Kadijksplein)
16	B1	Jewish Historical Museum (Joods Historisch Museum)
17	B2	Portuguese Synagogue
19	B4	Dutch Resistance Museum (Verzetsmuseum)
20	B5	Entrepotdok
22	C1	Blue Bridge (Blauwbrug)
26	C3	Botanical Gardens (Hortus Botanicus)
28	C3	National Holocaust Memorial (Hollandsche Schouwburg)
34	D1	Skinny Bridge (Magere Brug)
37	E1	Amstel Locks (Amstelsluizen)
42	E6	Muiderpoort City Gate

RESTAURANTS

9	A4	Een Vis Twee Vis
12	A4	Café Kadijk
30	C4	Burgermeester
43	F2	Bakhuys Amsterdam

NIGHTLIFE

1	A1	Café Sluyswacht
8	A3	Café De Druif
24	C1	Green House
29	C4	Café Koosje
35	D1	Eetcafé De Magere Brug
40	E3	Het Ballonnetje
44	F2	Bar Lempika

ARTS AND CULTURE

15	B1	Dutch National Opera & Ballet
25	C1	Hermitage Amsterdam
38	E1	Koninklijk Theater Carré

SPORTS AND ACTIVITIES

14	B1	MacBike
18	B3	Wertheimpark
32	C5	Artis Zoo
39	E3	In De Gracht

SHOPS

3	A1	Episode
4	A1	Het Fort van Sjakoo
13	B1	Waterlooplein Market
23	C1	Zalio Atlier
41	E4	De Fietsfabriek

HOTELS

6	A2	Ecomama
7	A3	Ibis Amsterdam Centre Stopera
10	A4	TownHouse Inn
21	B5	Stout & Co.
27	C3	Budget Hotel Hortus
31	C4	Hampshire Hotel—Lancaster
33	D1	Hotel Hermitage Amsterdam
36	E1	The Bridge Hotel
45	F2	InterContinental Amstel Amsterdam

1
2
3
A
B
C
D
E
F
BARENTSZ-PLN.
ZANDHOEK
WESTERDOKSDIJK
CÉRAMIQUELAAN
IJ-PROMENADE
BADHUIS-KADE
TOLHUISWG.
OVERHOEKS-PLN.
BUIKSLOTERWG
Noordhollandsch Kanaal
NIEUWE LEEUWARDERWG
MEEUWENLN.
DE RUYTERKADE
IJ
IJ-TUNNEL
Amsterdam Centraal
DE RUYTERKADE
OOSTERDOKSSTR.
ODEBRUG
OOSTERDOKSKADE
DIJKSGR.
NIEUWEZIJDS VOORBURGWAL
Beurs van Berlage
DAMRAK
Oude Kerk
Nieuwe Kerk
GELDERSEKADE
Oosterdok
PRINS HENDRIKKADE
BINNENKANT
NEMO
PALEISSTR.
Waag
KONINGSSTR.
RECHT BOOMSSLOOT
PEPERSTR.
ROKIN
Waalse Kerk
KLOVENIERSBURGWAL
OUDESCHANS
NIEUWE UILENBURGERSTR.
RAPENBURG
NIEUWE FOELIESTR.
NIEUWEVAART
Zuiderkerk
JODENBREESTR.
HOOGTE KADIJK
LAAGTE KADIJK
ENTREPOTDOK
ZWANENBURGWAL
RAPENBURGERSTR.
NIEUWE HERENGR.
PLANTAGE DOKLAAN
PLANTAGE KERKLAAN
AMSTEL
AMSTELSTR.
Hortus Botanicus
HERENGR.
HERENGR.
AMSTEL
WEESPERST
NIEUWE KEIZERSGR.
PLANTAGE KERKLAAN
PLANTAGE MIDDENLAAN

4
5
6
SIGHTS
14 C4 Eastern Docklands
23 D3 NEMO
39 F5 De Gooyer Windmill
RESTAURANTS
4 B2 The Coffee Virus
6 B3 Al Ponte
8 B5 Hotel de Goudfazant
9 C2 Choux
18 D3 La Place
31 E2 Gebr. Hartering
35 E4 Frank's Smoke House
NIGHTLIFE
5 B2 Tolhuistuin
7 B4 Oedipus Brewery
15 D2 SkyLounge
21 D3 Hanneke's Boom
28 D6 De Kompaszaal
29 D6 Kanis En Meiland
30 E2 Hiding in Plain Sight
36 E5 Roest
37 E6 Koffiehuis KHL
40 F5 Brouwerij 't IJ
ARTS AND CULTURE
3 B2 Eye Film Institute
12 C3 Bimhuis
13 C3 Muziekgebouw aan 't IJ
17 D2 De Appel
19 D3 Conservatorium van Amsterdam
22 D3 MediaMatic
24 D5 Mezrab
27 D6 Rademakers Gallery
32 E3 Amsterdam Center for Architecture (ARCAM)
33 E3 National Maritime Museum (Het Scheepvaartmuse-um)
38 F4 The Kromhout Shipyard (Museum Werf 't Kromhout)
SPORTS AND ACTIVITIES
2 A1 Canal Motorboats
10 C3 Star Bikes
11 C3 Powerzone
20 D3 De Klimmuur
SHOPS
26 D6 Pols Potten
HOTELS
1 A1 Studio INN B&B
16 D2 DoubleTree Hilton
25 D6 Lloyd Hotel
34 E3 Pension Homeland
GEDEMPT HAMERKANAAL
AAMBEELD-STR.
IJ
Eastern Docklands
SUMATRAKADE
IMOGIRITUIN
JAVAKADE
IJhaven
SURINAMEKADE
BOGORTUIN
KNSM-LAAN
LEVANTKADE
VERBINDINGSDAM
VEEMKADE
PIET HEINKADE
Dijksgracht
OOSTELIJKE HANDELSKADE
RIETLANDPARK
RIETLAND-PARK
MARINIERS-KADE
KATTENBURGERSTR.
KATTENBURGERKADE
DIJKSGR.
D.L. HUDIGSTR.
KLEINE WITTENBURGERSTR.
WITTENBURGERKADE
JACOB BONTIUS-PLAATS
ISAAC TITSINGHKADE
VAN REEDESTR.
POOLSTR.
WAAIGAT
WITTENBURGERGR.
OOSTENBURGERGR.
CZAAR PETERSTR.
KEERWAL
KRUITHUIS-STR.
De Gooyer Windmill
CRUQUIUSKADE
FUNENKADE
ZEEBURGER-STR.
0 0.2 mi
0 0.2 km
DISTANCE ACROSS MAP
Approximate: 2.4 mi or 3.6 km
© AVALON TRAVEL

Also Available

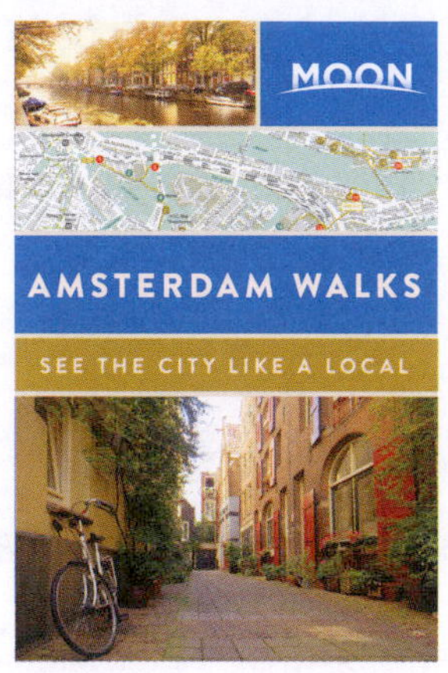

MAP SYMBOLS

Expressway	City/Town	Airport	Golf Course
Primary Road	State Capital	Airfield	Parking Area
Secondary Road	National Capital	Mountain	Archaeological Site
Unpaved Road	Point of Interest	Unique Natural Feature	Church
Trail	Accommodation	Waterfall	Gas Station
Ferry	Restaurant/Bar	Park	Glacier
Railroad	Other Location	Trailhead	Mangrove
Pedestrian Walkway	Campground	Skiing Area	Reef
Stairs			Swamp

CONVERSION TABLES

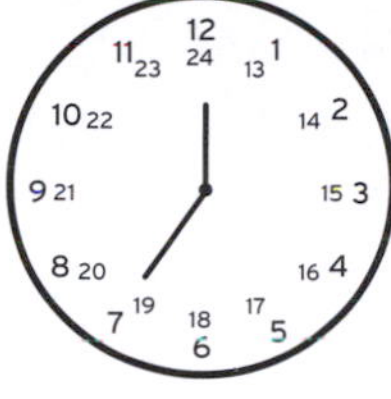

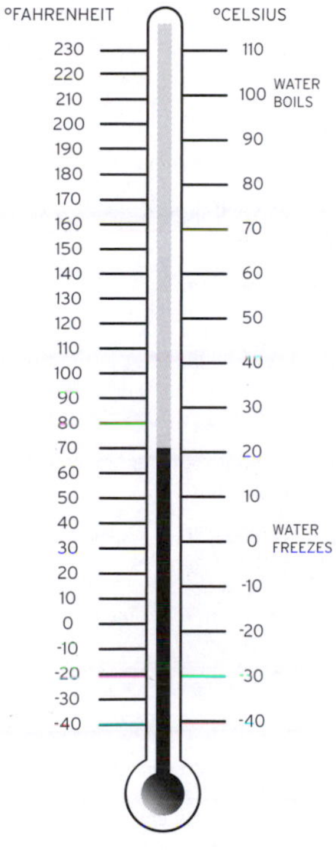

°C = (°F - 32) / 1.8
°F = (°C x 1.8) + 32
1 inch = 2.54 centimeters (cm)
1 foot = 0.304 meters (m)
1 yard = 0.914 meters
1 mile = 1.6093 kilometers (km)
1 km = 0.6214 miles
1 fathom = 1.8288 m
1 chain = 20.1168 m
1 furlong = 201.168 m
1 acre = 0.4047 hectares
1 sq km = 100 hectares
1 sq mile = 2.59 square km
1 ounce = 28.35 grams
1 pound = 0.4536 kilograms
1 short ton = 0.90718 metric ton
1 short ton = 2,000 pounds
1 long ton = 1.016 metric tons
1 long ton = 2,240 pounds
1 metric ton = 1,000 kilograms
1 quart = 0.94635 liters
1 US gallon = 3.7854 liters
1 Imperial gallon = 4.5459 liters
1 nautical mile = 1.852 km

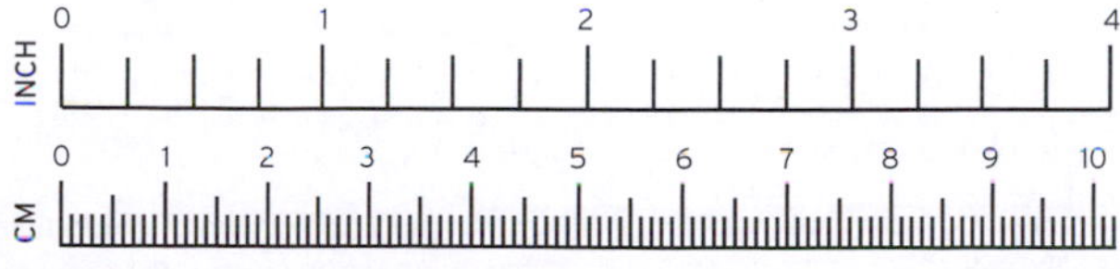

MOON AMSTERDAM
Avalon Travel
Hachette Book Group
1700 Fourth Street
Berkeley, CA 94710, USA
www.moon.com

Editor and Series Manager: Leah Gordon
Copy Editor: Naomi Adler-Dancis
Graphics and Production Coordinator: Darren Alessi
Cover Design: Faceout Studios, Charles Brock
Interior Design: Megan Jones Design
Moon Logo: Tim McGrath
Map Editor: Albert Angulo
Cartographers: Albert Angulo, Brian Shotwell
Fact Checker: Rosemarie Leenerts
Proofreader: Ashley Benning
Indexer: Deana Shields

ISBN-13: 9781631212352

Printing History
1st Edition — March 2018
5 4 3 2 1

Front cover photo: Amsterdam canals at night near Red Light District © Wim Wiskerke/ Alamy Stock Photo

Back cover photo: The canal Oudezijds Achterburgwal in the Red Light District © Yuliya Heikens | Dreamstime

Printed in China by RR Donnelley